ZHUKOV

ZHUKOV

By OTTO PRESTON CHANEY, JR.

Foreword by Malcolm Mackintosh

NORMAN
UNIVERSITY OF OKLAHOMA PRESS

International Standard Book Number: 0–8061–0951–3

Library of Congress Catalog Card Number: 74–145505

Copyright 1971 by the University of Oklahoma Press, Publishing Division of
the University. Composed and printed at Norman, Oklahoma, U.S.A., by the
University of Oklahoma Press. First edition.

For Loyce

FOREWORD

by Malcolm Mackintosh

THE name of Marshal Georgi Zhukov, the distinguished Soviet
military leader of World War II and a controversial postwar minister of defense, conjures up a picture of a severe and ruthless Soviet
commander, one of the few who appeared never to have lost a battle,
and who was allowed by Stalin out of the shadows which normally
surround Soviet personalities briefly, at least, to share some of the
glory of Soviet victories during the war.

No one would deny that a good and accurate biography of a soldier
of Zhukov's status and achievements has been lacking for some time.
After all, lives of most of the outstanding Allied and German commanders have been available for many years. Scholars, historians, and
the general public have long awaited a biography of their most successful Soviet counterpart—a man who, in the closing stages of the war, had
under his direct operational command up to fourteen field armies and
many thousands of tanks and aircraft.

This book has filled the gap, insofar as the evidence available in the
West allows such a book to be produced. In order to assess the measure
of the author's achievement, we must take into account the obstacles
set in the path of a Western scholar who wishes to write an authentic
biography of a Soviet military leader, even one as well known as Marshal Zhukov. Such a scholar has no access to the personal papers of his
subject, no opportunity to talk to family or friends, no chance to read
letters or diaries. The author cannot freely study in centers or private
homes occupied by his subject, or even search for officers and soldiers
who served with him, from his senior staff officers to his personal
servants, pilots, and drivers. In spite of the biographer's best endeavors,
the Soviet military leader remains personally a shadowy figure. We
cannot see him at home, with his wife, children, and grandchildren, nor
can we learn much about his personal likes or dislikes, his family life,
his moments of despair and elation. Although Soviet secrecy plays a
strong part in formulating these restrictions, they are to some extent
also in the tradition of Russian letters, and any biographer of Marshal
Zhukov who rests his case, as Chaney does, on the strictest accuracy in
the utilization of his source material, has to make his book a study of
Zhukov the soldier and relatively little of Zhukov the man.

Chaney brought to his task a wide knowledge of the Soviet military scene, the Russian language, and the country's history and a deep and absorbing interest in his subject. He studied the available literature in English, Russian, and German, including the very large body of Soviet military-historical memoirs published in the Soviet Union since 1956, a number of them by high-ranking military officers who served with or under Marshal Zhukov during the war, such as Marshals Konev and Rokossovsky. Probably the best document available to him was Marshal Zhukov's own, *Recollections and Reminiscences.* Chaney has made skillful use of this tantalizing work, in which the marshal presents himself as an almost unerring and tireless piece of military machinery capable of accepting limitless responsibilities in the prosecution of the war, in close collaboration with Stalin, regardless of his physical well-being or the nervous strain involved. Nevertheless, there are moments, which Chaney has captured in his account, when Zhukov the man clearly breaks through: his hesitation over a quick visit to his mother (and her subsequent rescue) during the Battle of Moscow in late 1941; his burst of anger against Stalin over his recommendation to evacuate Kiev in August, 1941; and his disconcerting discovery that Stalin's hearing was so exceptionally acute that a whispered comment about a Stalin plan to Marshal Vasilevsky was picked up at the other end of a long room by the alert dictator. Chaney has woven these glimpses of the human side of Zhukov into his study but has wisely refrained from trying to build a complete picture of Zhukov the man from such brief flashes of insight.

As a soldier himself, Chaney is in a good position to assess professionally the progress of Marshal Zhukov from a conscript in the Russian Imperial Army in World War I, through the Russian civil war and the long years of intense though sometimes misdirected training, to his ultimate positions as deputy supreme commander in chief in World War II and as postwar minister of defense. Zhukov was dismissed in disgrace from the latter post in 1957 and partly "rehabilitated" after the fall of Khrushchev in 1964.

Although we sometimes tend to think of Zhukov, the Russian soldier's soldier, as a typical Russian infantryman, the whole of his military career until he entered the ranks of the higher command in 1939 was in the cavalry and in the armored mobile forces which developed out of the cavalry of the civil war. Indeed, as Chaney shows, Zhukov probably owed his survival during Stalin's terrible purge of the Red Army in the

1930's to his membership in the civil war "cavalry clique," led by Marshals Voroshilov, Budenny, and Timoshenko, which enjoyed Stalin's special patronage. All through this period, during which Zhukov moved up through the command of a cavalry squadron to that of a cavalry corps (with brief intervals in Moscow for study and staff work), the future marshal is realistically portrayed as a dedicated, ambitious, and ruthless commander, whose restless temperament would not allow him to relax until he had made his unit or formation the best in the corps or indeed in the military district. (In passing I am not sure that the case that Zhukov studied in Berlin in the 1920's or served in Spain is entirely made out. On the whole, the Red Army sent its highest commanders to Germany during the Soviet-German collaboration in military affairs from 1923 to 1933, at a time when Zhukov was only a squadron or regimental commander—though many a German general would willingly claim the credit for educating the future Soviet marshal. It may be significant that the most nearly complete official accounts of Soviet participation in the Spanish Civil War do not mention Zhukov, either by name or by cover name.)

Chaney gives the reader a dramatic description of Zhukov's sudden emergence into prominence through his victory over the Japanese on the Mongolian border in 1939, where his characteristic tactics made their appearance: ruthlessness in decision making, thorough preparation, faultless timing, and the exploitation of every available source of military power from the buildup to the final blow. There followed rapid promotion in the warm glow of Stalin's approval and a controversial and, for Zhukov, unhappy period as chief of the Soviet General Staff, which carried Zhukov into the opening months of the German invasion.

Chaney's analysis of Zhukov's wartime career is carefully analytical and objective. The marshal's part in the defense of Moscow as the responsible commander is vividly portrayed. Apart from two periods of army-group command in early 1944 and from January to May, 1945, Zhukov's assignments during the rest of the war were as a member of Stalin's Supreme Headquarters. In this capacity he traveled from sector to sector, planning, co-ordinating, inspecting—the last often with frightening results for the local commanders and staffs. He spent most time of all in the Kremlin with Stalin, arguing, debating, and developing the leaders' strategic plans for the war—always, apparently, listened to carefully, sometimes having his advice accepted, sometimes overruled. And so he emerged from the war: Stalin's senior deputy supreme commander in chief, an almost mythical hero to the Russian soldier and the scourge of many of the most senior field commanders and their staffs.

After the wartime chapters, Chaney illuminates the brief period before Zhukov's first disgrace in 1946, when the marshal, as commander in chief of the Soviet forces in Germany, was exposed to Western gaze. He describes in detail the views formed of Zhukov by General Eisenhower and other American military and civilian leaders in the Western zones of occupation. This picture of the marshal is an especially interesting one, because we see him against his own Soviet background, authoritarian, rough, and something of a parade-ground martinet,—yet in exchanges with Eisenhower, for example, unsure of himself, eager to please, and, within his limitations, bordering on the emotional.

Suddenly, in the summer of 1946, Zhukov disappears. The Soviet system under Stalin swallows him up, and Chaney's prose conveys the difficulty of trying to sift the rumors and twilight evidence surrounding the fate of a Soviet "unperson."

When he does formally reappear, in 1953, as a first deputy minister, and later as minister of defense, Marshal Zhukov has aged. He gives the impression in these pages of having lost the more sympathetic side to his nature. He was, as minister, heavy-handed, tactless, overbearing, and arrogant. When raised to full voting membership of the Party Presidium in 1957, a few months before his fall, he showed himself to be excessively overconfident, and a meddler as well. With whatever justification in terms of the need to defend the army against the Party and the KGB, or of his tremendous and well-deserved reputation as a soldier, especially the Russian soldiers' image of a *polkovodets*—a "real commander"—Zhukov's last year or two in office do not evoke sympathy.

Happily, however, Chaney manages to convey a more benign picture of Zhukov after his rehabilitation in 1964. We are left with a view of a remarkable old soldier, crippled (perhaps as a result of illness), but enjoying writing his memoirs in retirement and returned, to the applause of the ordinary Russian soldier and citizen, to his rightful place as Russia's most distinguished soldier of the twentieth century. Chaney has written a fine and understanding study of this gifted and controversial soldier. It will remain the best in the field for many years to come.

London, May 1, 1971

PREFACE

ON December 2, 1956, the Central Committee of the Communist Party of the Soviet Union presented Marshal Georgi Konstantinovich Zhukov his fourth Gold Star medal, another award for the most decorated man in Soviet history. "The Communist Party and the Soviet people," declared the committee, "highly value your services in building the armed forces [and] in the defense of the Socialist Fatherland. In the grim years of the Great Patriotic War you skillfully and courageously led the Soviet forces in decisive engagements for the freedom and independence of our land. In the years of peaceful work you unceasingly gave all strength and knowledge to the further building of the Soviet government [and] to the matter of strengthening the defensive capacity of our country."

Exactly eleven months later the Central Committee again brought Zhukov's name to the fore: "Zhukov imagined that he was the sole hero of all the victories achieved by our people and their armed forces under the Communist Party's leadership, and he began flagrantly violating the Leninist Party principles of leadership of the armed forces. . . . He proved to be a politically unsound person, inclining toward adventurism both in his understanding of the primary objective of the Soviet Union's foreign policy and in his leadership of the Ministry of Defense." With this announcement, Marshal Zhukov was stripped of his post in the powerful Party Presidium, from Central Committee membership, and from his position as defense minister.

A decade afterward, in December, 1966, Georgi Zhukov was awarded his nation's highest award, the Order of Lenin, in recognition of "services to the armed forces." No less significant, while Zhukov sat for sculptor Victor Dumanian, a number of articles about him were being published in Soviet journals and newspapers, and his memoirs were being read and discussed by Russian citizens.

Zhukov's known attributes, enhanced and contradicted in turn by the vagaries of Soviet politics, inevitably need clarification. Moreover, material available on the man and his life, seemingly sparse and widely scattered, as is the case with almost all modern Russian notables in various fields, represented a challenge to undertake a study of Zhukov's real contributions to the Soviet scene. It was my sincere belief that the truth could be uncovered somewhere in the collection of biting criticism, timeserving flattery, intentional omissions, and rare objective reporting.

Although Georgi Zhukov achieved fame in his own country and abroad, there are no definitive works dealing with his life and career. The *Bolshaya Sovetskaya Entsiklopediya* (*The Large Soviet Encyclopaedia*), for example, contains only a short paragraph on him (less, incidentally, than the treatment provided in the one-volume *Columbia Encyclopedia* published in the United States). World War II histories written while Zhukov was in disfavor either omit his name entirely or simply include him in a long list of commanders who participated in a particular operation. One recent (disappointing) source, a thick volume on the war, listed several Zhukovs, but not Georgi K. The same book, which treated Nikita S. Khrushchev in a flattering light, proved to be all the more ludicrous when, shortly after its publication, Khrushchev abruptly left the scene and Georgi Zhukov was slowly but unmistakably resurrected.

The most important Soviet history of World War II, the monumental six-volume *Istoriya Velikoy Otechestvennoy Voiny Sovetskogo Soyuza* (*History of the Great Patriotic War of the Soviet Union*), relegated Zhukov's labors in certain campaigns to a brief footnote, while lesser commanders were lauded ad nauseam. In a subsequent one-volume compendium Khrushchev virtually disappeared from its pages and Zhukov reemerged. When one considers that Zhukov was out of favor fifteen years of the twenty-five following the war, the researcher's problem can be more fully appreciated. The curse of being deleted from histories and consigned to the status of an unperson is nowhere as ignominious and damning as it is in Soviet Russia.

This book discusses Georgi Zhukov's early life, his service in World War I and the civil war, and his gradual rise to power under the tutelage of Semyen Budenny and Joseph Stalin. Zhukov's role in Red Army preparations for a war with Germany is described at length, and the surprise attack is examined to determine whether Zhukov bore responsibility for the initial disasters experienced by the Soviet defenders. Zhukov's participation in the planning and conduct of certain decisive wartime operations is emphasized, especially his personal impact on the battles of Leningrad, Smolensk, Moscow, Stalingrad, Kursk, and Berlin. His part in the counteroffensive at Moscow and in the final drive against Germany is evaluated in the light of his own recently published version.

New and important Soviet materials, restoring credit to Zhukov and the Stavka for successful strategic planning throughout the war, have been incorporated.

Little has been written on Marshal Zhukov's postwar career, his role in various power plays, and his involvement in certain significant events in the years since the war. This volume discusses his participation in the German surrender, his membership in the Allied Control Council, his ouster by Stalin, and his reemergence from obscurity on the day of Stalin's funeral. Zhukov's role in the Beria episode, his participation in the Soviet defense debates of 1953–56, his support of Khrushchev in the *borba za vlast* ("struggle for power") with Georgi Malenkov, his role in the de-Stalinization campaign and the Polish October, his crushing of the Hungarian uprising, and his substantial aid to Khrushchev in the Party secretary's struggle with the anti-Party group are dealt with at some length. Also described are Soviet attempts to create in the person of Georgi Zhukov a symbol of East-West rapprochement. Finally, the reasons for Zhukov's dismissal are reviewed, and I have included accounts of Khrushchev's bid for the support of his former defense minister in the spring of 1963 and Zhukov's eventual rehabilitation in 1965 and 1966.

I have already pointed out several problems connected with my research. Zhukov fell into disfavor on not one but two occasions, in 1946 and again in 1957. Twice he was resurrected. Even when he was enjoying Stalin's patronage during the war years, little was published on his life and career. Stalin, as is well known, refused to allow any Soviet personality to eclipse his own image, even temporarily. Despite these obstacles, I believe that I have been able to put Zhukov's unquestionably major contributions to Soviet history, and the criticisms of his military rivals, in reasonably accurate perspective. Whatever his faults, Zhukov demonstrated outstanding virtues as a soldier, leader, and patriot.

Zhukov's memoirs have now been published, and whenever possible I have let him speak for himself from his own writings, particularly recollections of his youthful years, which contain poignant views of life in Tsarist Russia. His later memoirs are limited in scope and reflect only a fraction of the coverage and none of the over-all perspective presented here. To my knowledge this is the only full account of Zhukov that has not been subject to censorship by one regime or another. In compiling it, I have sought to emphasize his key role in practically every major Soviet military effort from Mongolia to Hungary, for he is one of the few men of importance whose influential career spans the entire Soviet period, from the Bolshevik Revolution to the present day. Thus an account of his life is, in effect, the story of Soviet Russia.

Some comments about the style adopted for spellings are appropriate at this point. Methods of designating military divisions vary widely from country to country. For the sake of consistency and ease in reading, it was decided to adopt in the text of the book a uniform system for designating Russian, German, and other armed forces. Military units numbered below 100 have been spelled in ordinal form (Eleventh Cavalry Corps); those numbered above 100 have been given in figures (332d Infantry Division). The maps included in the book—most of them official Soviet war maps—appear exactly as originally published. The variant spellings shown in them should give the reader no trouble.

For the purposes of this book, I have chosen a simplified system of transliteration, also for the reader's convenience. For example, the single and double apostrophes are not used, and in most cases personal and place names are spelled according to their accepted usage in the West, for example, Beria, Budenny, Yeremenko, Moscow, and Warsaw.

Many persons have assisted me in this venture, and I could not possibly acknowledge all of them. First, my teachers in the United States Army Institute for Advanced Russian and East European Studies guided my efforts in the mid-1950's. Encouragement also came from a number of sympathetic professors at Georgetown University, including my friends Roman Debicki and the late Olegerd Sherbowitz-Wetzor. I owe a special debt of gratitude to my distinguished mentors at American University, Samuel L. Sharp, Frederick J. Piotrow, Ralph L. Powell, Eric Willentz; to Leon Herman; and to one of the noblest of men, the late Jan Wszelaki.

I am also especially grateful to my long-term friend Lester J. Holtschlag, of Johns Hopkins University, who not only read the manuscript and offered many helpful suggestions but also inspired and encouraged me throughout my writing; Walter Darnell Jacobs, of the University of Maryland, who generously read the manuscript and gave me the benefit of his experience and knowledge; Roman Kolkowicz, of the Institute for Defense Analyses, who took time from a very busy schedule to read the manuscript and offer words of advice and encouragement; Lieutenant Colonel Ralph C. Little, a friend and coworker, who helped in many ways; Mrs. Ethel Slagle, research librarian, who determined the whereabouts of dozens of volumes essential to my work; Mrs. Mabel Hemphill, who provided considerable background material; Mrs. Donna Traxler and Mrs. Annie L. Seely, of the United States Army Photographic Agency, and Charles A. Thomas, of the National Archives, who helped me find photographs for this book; to Miss Bettie Sprigg, of the Audio Visual Division of the United States Department of Defense, who also assisted with the photographs; William Henheoffer, who gave me the benefit of his knowledge; and a large number of other friends who drew my attention to material or offered wise counsel.

In particular, and above all, to my wife, Loyce, who spent countless hours assisting me, I extend my undying gratitude and devotion.

OTTO PRESTON CHANEY, JR.

Springfield, Virginia
January, 1971

CONTENTS

ILLUSTRATIONS

ILLUSTRATIONS

MAPS

ZHUKOV

The right to command
is no longer a privilege
transmitted by nature, like an inheritance;
it is the fruit of labor,
the price of courage.

VOLTAIRE

I. THE EARLY YEARS

For a soldier I listed, to grow great in fame,
and be shot at for sixpence a day.

Charles Dibdin

GEORGI Konstantinovich Zhukov was born on December 2, 1896, in Strelkovka, a village in Kaluga Province, southwest of Moscow. Georgi's father, Konstantin Andreevich Zhukov, was a poor shoemaker; his mother, Ustinya Artemyevna, worked on a farm.

Zhukov wrote in his memoirs:

The house where I was born stood in the middle of the village. It was very old, and one corner had sunk deeply into the ground. Sometimes the walls and roof were covered with moss and grass. Altogether the house consisted of one room with two windows. My mother and father did not know by whom and when our house had been built. From stories of the old folk it was known that at one time there had lived in it the childless widow Annushka Zhukova. In order to ease her loneliness she took from the orphanage a two-year-old boy, my father. Who his real parents were no one was able to say, and my father did not later on try to find out. It was known only that some girl had left the three-month-old boy on the doorsteps of the orphan home, leaving a note: "Call my son Konstantin." What forced a poor woman to abandon her child on the entranceway of an orphanage it is impossible to say. It is doubtful that she acted out of a lack of maternal feelings; most likely it was for reasons of a hopelessly difficult situation.

After the death of his foster mother, who had just turned eighty, my father became apprenticed to a shoemaker in the village of Ugodsky Zavod. He recounted that his training consisted mainly of household work, caring for the master's children and tending the livestock. Having "studied" in this manner about three years, my father set out to find a new place. On foot he journeyed to Moscow where he finally settled down with the master shoemaker Weisa. Weisa had his own shop of fashionable shoes.

I do not know the details but, according to my father, he and a large number of other workers were discharged after the events of 1905 and sent from Moscow for participation in the demonstrations. From that time until the day of his death in 1921 my father lived the entire time in the village, occupied with shoemaking and peasant tasks.

My mother was born and raised in the neighboring village of Chernaya Gryaz in an extremely poor family. When my father and mother married, mother was thirty-five and father fifty. For both it was their second marriage. After their first marriage both had soon lost their mates. Mother was physically a very strong woman. She could easily lift a five-pood sack of grain and carry it a considerable distance.* It is said that she inherited her physical strength from her father—my grandfather Artem, who could creep under a horse and lift him or take him by the tail and with one jerk pull him down on his haunches.[1]

The poverty of the family forced Zhukov's mother to take a second job. In the spring, summer, and early fall she struggled in the fields, and in late autumn she traveled to the district city of Maloyaroslavets for grocery items which she delivered to the merchants of Ugodsky Zavod.

* One pood equals slightly more than thirty-six pounds.

For each trip she earned from one ruble to one ruble twenty kopecks.* Zhukov protests in his memoirs:

> But what kind of salary was this? If one deducts the expenses of feeding the horses, lodging for the night in the city, food, repair of shoes, and so on, then very little was left. I believe beggars in that time collected more. However, there was nothing that could be done about it; such was the lot of the poor peasant, and my mother worked without a murmur. Many women of our village did the same in order not to starve to death. In the thick, impassable mud and the cold, hard frost they carried their goods from Maloyaroslavets, Serpukhov, and other places, leaving their very young children in the care of grandmothers and grandfathers, who were barely able to get around.
>
> Most of the peasants of our village lived in poverty. Our land was small and produced poor crops. Field work was carried out mainly by women, old people, and children. The men labored in Moscow, St. Petersburg, and other cities doing seasonal work. They received little—it was a rare peasant who arrived back in the village with a good salary in his pockets.
>
> Of course, there were in the villages rich peasants—the "kulaks." They did not live badly: they had large, well-lighted homes with comfortable furnishings; outside were many cattle and fowl, and in the barns were large stores of meal and grain. Their children dressed well, ate plenty, and studied in the best schools. The poor people of our village worked mostly for these people, often for wretched salaries—some for bread, some for feed, some for seed.
>
> We, the children of the poor, saw how our mothers suffered, and we bitterly endured their tears. And what happiness we had when they brought us a biscuit or cake from Maloyaroslavets! If we were able to save a little money before Christmas or Easter for ham turnovers, then our delight had no bounds.
>
> When I was five and my sister already seven years old, my mother gave birth to another boy whom they called Aleksei. He was very thin, and everyone was afraid that he would not survive. Mother cried, saying: "And on what is the child going to grow strong? On water and bread, eh?" Several months after his birth she decided to go again to the city in search of a living. The neighbors pleaded with her, advising her to take care of the child, who was still very weak and needed his mother's milk. But the threat of starvation to the entire family forced mother to leave, and Alyesha†

---

* About twenty-five to thirty cents.
† Diminutive of Aleksei, pronounced "Alyosha."

was left in our care. He did not live long—less than a year. In the fall we buried him in the cemetery in Ugodsky Zavod. My sister and I—as well as our father and mother—deeply mourned Alyesha and often visited his little grave.[2]

In the same year another misfortune overtook the Zhukovs. The dilapidated roof of their house caved in, and the family had to move. "We must leave here," Zhukov's father declared, "but we'll all be together. While it's warm, we'll live in the shed, and then we'll see. Maybe someone will rent us a hothouse or a threshing barn."

Zhukov's father contrived a little stove for cooking, and the family settled down in the shed. Mrs. Zhukov proposed selling the cow to buy lumber to repair the house, but her husband protested, saying that it would leave them only with one old horse. After a short time Zhukov's father was able to buy a small amount of timber on installment, and his neighbors helped him transport it. By November the house was rebuilt, and new straw covered the roof. Zhukov recalls:

> From outward appearances the house looked worse than others; the porch was thrown together from old boards, and the windows were cracked. But we were very happy that we would have a warm corner when winter came, and concerning closeness—as is said—the more the merrier.
>
> In the winter of 1902 I was beginning my seventh year. This winter was a very difficult year for our family. It was an unproductive year, and we only had enough grain until mid-December. My father and mother's earnings went for bread, salt, and debts. Thanks to the neighbors, we were sometimes provided with porridge or cabbage soup. Such mutual assistance in the villages was not unusual but rather the tradition of friendship and solidarity among Russian people living in great need.[3]

Young Zhukov studied for seven years in a parish school in the nearby village of Velichkovo, receiving excellent grades and making the honor list. Further study was a luxury his family could not afford, and the eleven-year-old boy was apprenticed to an uncle, a Moscow furrier named Pilikhin. By the age of sixteen Georgi had mastered the craft. In his travels between Moscow and his home in Strelkovka during those years young Georgi became thoroughly familiar with the flat, wooded terrain of the region, knowledge which would prove very useful to him in the critical autumn days of 1941.

Despite exceptionally difficult living conditions and the hard training in Pilikhin's workshop, Zhukov continued his studies, mostly in the

time he decided to join the Red Guards, he fell seriously ill with typhus, and in April he suffered relapsing fever. Not until six months later, in August, 1918, had he recovered sufficiently to join the Red Army. He volunteered for the Fourth Cavalry Regiment of the First Moscow Cavalry Division.

In the fall of 1918, Zhukov joined former Sergeant Semyen Konstantinovich Timoshenko's cavalry brigade, one of two brigades in a division commanded by Semyen Mikhailovich Budenny. Zhukov was to spend much of the civil war with Budenny's cavalry, sharing in its glories and vicissitudes. As a member of this elite group, which was greatly admired by Joseph Stalin, he would be swept along inextricably in its wartime and postwar activities.

Budenny, a professional cavalryman, had served with distinction in the Tsarist army and soon became one of the most popular heroes of the civil war. He met Stalin for the first time in July, 1918, when he handled himself well in response to questions on tactics put to him by General Snesarev. In the same month Budenny and Kliment E. Voroshilov met while planning a cavalry raid that proved to be highly successful.[6] Although Budenny's future service would be less than brilliant, at that time he was regarded as a brave, colorful leader. The fact that Zhukov was a member of Budenny's group served to enhance the young soldier's career.

In the winter of 1918–19, the Reds and the Whites began consolidating their forces for spring and summer campaigns. With the collapse of the Central Powers in November, 1918, the balance of forces shifted to the Bolsheviks. Nevertheless, a significant threat was posed by White forces in southern Russia, where three armies, the Army of the Don, the Volunteer Army, and the Army of the Caucasus, were poised. The Whites' objective in the 1919 campaigns was a joint operation against Moscow and Petrograd, with General Anton I. Denikin's armies clearing the northern Caucasus and, advancing into the Ukraine, joining forces with the Siberian armies of Admiral Aleksandr V. Kolchak which were attacking from the east.[7]

Early in 1919, Kolchak's armies launched a sweeping offensive which pushed the Red armies back toward the Volga. The newly formed Polish army drove into western Russia in April and May, while in the northwest White General Nikolai Yudenich moved toward Petrograd.

Leon Trotsky, then the Red commissar of war, decided to deal with

Kolchak first. He divided the Eastern Front into the Northern Group and the Southern Group, placing the talented Mikhail V. Frunze in command of the Southern Group. This unit, which included the First, Fourth, and Fifth armies, was directed against the important city of Ufa, in the western foothills of the Urals. After bitter fighting, Frunze's troops seized their objective in June.[8]

Zhukov's First Moscow Cavalry Division, which was part of Frunze's unit, waged its first fight on the approaches to the Shipovo Station, near Uralsk. The division was soon moved up to Nikolayevsk to fight the Whites there, and in August the entire Fourth Cavalry Regiment was sent to Vladimirovka Station.

In the meantime, Zhukov had joined a group of Communist sympathizers in his squadron who were preparing for Party membership. "At that time," Zhukov recalls, "there still had not been established a candidate stage for joining the Party."[9] The group numbered only five persons, but the secretary of the Party Bureau and a commissar visited them twice a week to discuss domestic and international issues and the measures taken by the Party to strengthen Red forces. On March 1, 1919, Zhukov was accepted into membership. "Since then I have forgotten many things," he writes, "but the day I was accepted into Party membership will remain in my memory throughout my life."[10]

In September, 1919, fierce fighting broke out around Tsaritsyn (Stalingrad after 1925). During hand-to-hand combat between Zaplavnoye and Akhtube, Zhukov was wounded in the left leg and side by fragments from a hand grenade. Once again he was evacuated to a hospital.

Upon his discharge Zhukov received a month's recuperation leave, and he took the opportunity to visit his parents. When he returned to duty, he appeared before the Military Committee to request assignment to a combat army. Since he was still not completely recovered from his wounds, he was sent instead to a reserve battalion at Tver, and in January, 1920, he was assigned to a cavalry course for future commanders. This school, in Starozhilov in Ryazan Province, was mainly designed for those who had distinguished themselves in combat. Zhukov became a cadet master sergeant of the first squadron.

In July, 1920, after completing the cavalry course, Zhukov was commissioned an officer and sent to Moscow for further training. While there, he learned that his former love, Maria, had married. He never saw her again.*

By then, Zhukov's career had come to the attention of Red leaders who would later assist him in his climb up the military ladder. In the campaigns with Budenny's cavalry his talents had undoubtedly been brought to the attention of Voroshilov and Frunze—and of Stalin, who had served as head of the Military Council of the North Caucasus Military District. Frunze, one of Russia's most distinguished military leaders and an outstanding theoretician, helped shape the military doctrine of the young Soviet state and formulate basic principles for building the Red Army.

About that time a new crisis arose which was to have far-reaching effects on Budenny's cavalrymen. Hostilities with Poland erupted, and the Red Army under Mikhail N. Tukhachevsky launched a spectacular drive on Warsaw. In August, 1920, as the fighting reached the critical stage, Tukhachevsky sent for Budenny's First Cavalry Army, but Budenny questioned the validity of the order, and by the time he received confirmation, his army was deeply committed at Lvov, 185 miles southeast. Before Budenny could extricate himself, the Polish commander Joseph Pilsudski was dealing a severe blow to the Red units in what became known as the "miracle of Warsaw." Both Soviet cavalry forces, Budenny's army and G. D. Gai's corps had to fight their way out of encirclement, and only Budenny was successful. The demoralized Soviets retreated to their frontiers.

Vladimir Lenin was especially critical of the First Cavalry Army, and Tukhachevsky later condemned its actions as a major factor in determining the fate of the Red Army at a decisive stage. Stalin defended Budenny in the debates that followed, placing the blame on Tukhachevsky, with the result that the veterans of the First Cavalry Army—Budenny himself, Timoshenko, and others—"gathered more closely around the Stalin banner."[11]

Later in August, the composite battalion to which Zhukov was assigned was deployed to Krasnodar, in the northern Caucasus. From there it moved against the forces of Petr Wrangel, who had consolidated the Whites in their last redoubt, the Crimea and adjacent Black

* Some years later Zhukov met another girl, Alexandra, whom he married and who bore him two daughters, Era and Ella. Era, who holds a master's degree in juridical sciences, married the flyer son of Marshal A. M. Vasilevsky. Ella married the grandson of Kliment E. Voroshilov. "Marshal Zhukov," USSR Illustrated Monthly, September, 1956, 4.

Sea area. By mid-August, Wrangel had organized three landing groups to strike at the Reds, and Zhukov's unit was sent against the group commanded by General Ulagai. Having taken Timoshevskaya, Ulagai was threatening to join forces with the anti-Soviet partisans at the rear of the Ninth Red Army. The Caucasian command, under V. M. Gittis and G. K. Ordzhonikidze, committed the Ninth Army against Ulagai's forces and by September 10 had succeeded in repelling his attack. The signing of the provisional peace treaty by the Poles and the Russians on October 12 was the beginning of the end of Wrangel's Whites, who, without the Poles' assistance, were now outnumbered four to one. Red forces again attacked Wrangel on October 28 and on November 16 seized Kerch. Wrangel evacuated the remnants of his forces to Constantinople, and warfare in the Crimea drew to a close.[12]

Zhukov's battalion did not participate in the final operations against Wrangel. By then the cadets were needed elsewhere. Some of the better-trained cadets were graduated ahead of time and sent to staff cavalry units which had lost significant numbers from command cadres in battles with Wrangel's forces. Other cadets were sent after bands of Whites who had escaped into the Caucasus Mountains. Later Zhukov learned that they had been ambushed in the mountains and had suffered heavy losses.

Many of the cadets, including Zhukov, were sent to the Fourteenth Separate Cavalry Brigade near Novozherelievskaya Station to continue operations against isolated forces of Ulagai's men and local bands. Zhukov joined the First Cavalry Regiment, commanded by an old soldier, the Don Cossack A. A. Andreyev, who had a reputation as a brave leader and talented swordsman. Given command of a platoon, Zhukov introduced himself to the men: "Well, comrades. They have designated me your commander. Whether I am a good or bad commander, whether you are good or bad soldiers, we'll see in the future. But right now I want to inspect your horses and military equipment and become acquainted with each of you personally."[13]

Zhukov's regimental commander warned him that the troops were making fun of the red trousers which had been issued to some of the officers. Zhukov told his platoon that he was aware of their feelings about the trousers but that they were a gift from Soviet authorities and a symbol of the revolution. A few days later Zhukov led the platoon against bands along the coast. His men killed or captured enemy troops without any losses to themselves. "After the fight," Zhukov recalls, "not one of the soldiers said anything to me about the red trousers."[14]

Zhukov was soon promoted to commander of the Second Squadron of the First Cavalry Regiment. At the end of December, 1920, the entire brigade was transferred to Voronezh Province to put down a kulak uprising and destroy a band led by Kolesnikov. The survivors of the band escaped to Tambov Province and joined kulak and Social Revolutionary bands of guerrillas led by a one-time head of the local militia named Antonov who was disgruntled about Soviet land policies.[15]

In December, 1920, the Soviet government established a headquarters for troops of Tambov Province to deal with Antonov's forces. By March 1, 1921, the Tambov command numbered about 32,500 infantrymen and nearly 8,000 cavalrymen. General Tukhachevsky was placed in command of this impressive force, which in May became locked in bitter combat with Antonov. Despite hard fighting by Zhukov's Fourteenth Separate Cavalry Brigade, the Red forces were not able to destroy him. The remnants of his band escaped toward Penza, and only later were they completely routed. Antonov's final defeat signaled the end of concerted resistance to the Communists, although as late as the summer of 1921, Red units commanded by I. P. Uborevich were still pursuing small groups of rebels.

When hostilities ended, Zhukov decided to remain in the army, though he was aware that in peacetime army promotions would be slow, with few vacancies in command positions. Zhukov's promotions came faster than most. From June, 1922, to March, 1923, he commanded a squadron in the Thirty-eighth Cavalry Regiment, and then was promoted to assistant commander of the Fortieth Samara Cavalry Division. In April, 1923, he was appointed commander of the Thirty-ninth Bazuluksk Cavalry Regiment.

In 1924 the Communist Party began remodeling the Red Army in an effort to increase its fighting efficiency and incorporate new developments in military science. The key figure in this military reform was General Frunze. Appointed chairman of the Revolutionary Military Council and people's commissar for military affairs, Frunze set about replacing some of the conservative officials at the top with young commanders who had seen active service in the civil war. By the end of 1924 reorganization and demobilization had reduced the army from 5.5 million to 562,000 men.

When the program to revamp the army was initiated, many wartime leaders—especially Budenny's men—were resentful about what they felt was a downgrading of their war records. But others, among them Zhukov, understood the need for reform and took advantage of the opportunities it afforded for study and advancement.[16] In the decade or so following the civil war Zhukov completed a number of courses. In 1924-25 he attended a cavalry course for command personnel in Leningrad. His classmates included I. Kh. Bagramyan, A. I. Yeremenko, and K. K. Rokossovsky—all destined to gain fame in World War II. From 1929 to the spring of 1930 he attended an advanced course for senior officers at the famous Frunze Academy in Moscow.[17] In the intervening period he commanded the Thirty-ninth Regiment.

Although Soviet sources deny it, at least one German general says that Georgi Zhukov attended the War Academy in Berlin during the period of German-Soviet rapprochement following the Treaty of Rapallo in 1922. As early as 1919 high-ranking German officers had been considering agreements with the other "bad boy" of Europe, Soviet Russia. As E. H. Carr has written, "In the Germany of 1919 all roads led to Russia, all the roads that mattered, all the roads that were open."[18] Clandestine military collaboration between the Reichswehr and the Soviet government began about 1922 and continued until Hitler's rise to power. During that time German pilots and tank experts circumvented restrictions laid down by the Versailles peace agreements and trained their crews in the broad expanses of Russia. The Soviets, in turn, sent their officers to the War Academy in Berlin, where the Germans trained them in modern tactics and in use of new weapons.[19]

Spurred by the desire for revenge and for revision of the terms of the Versailles Treaty, Germany played a leading role in the development of modern military thought. Old military concepts and principles had been altered by the introduction of two new types of weapons into the armies of the world, tanks and airplanes. For many nations the problem of assimilating and mastering them proved almost overwhelming, but not for Germany. German theories deeply impressed Soviet visitors, who returned home advocating their introduction into the Red Army. They found their patron in Tukhachevsky, the brilliant young deputy war commissar, who admired the Germans' military efficiency and observed German army maneuvers at first hand in the late 1920's.[20]

Georgi Zhukov learned his lessons well in Berlin. German officers recall that he and his Russian friends behaved "uproariously," consuming vast quantities of liquor after dinner. "But," writes General F. W. von Mellenthin,* who fought against him in World War II, "in the military sphere it is clear that Zhukov's time was not wasted."[21] In Germany, Zhukov was exposed to the teachings of General Hans von Seeckt, a foremost theorist of the new German army, who stressed the use of armor in breakthrough operations. Von Seeckt's blitzkrieg tactics, based on a fast-moving mechanized army, made an indelible impression on Zhukov. When he returned to the Soviet Union, he became a leading proponent of mechanization and modernization of the Red Army.†

* Major General F. W. von Mellenthin served as chief of staff of the Forty-eighth Panzer Corps in the Soviet Union. After the Normandy invasion he was sent to Army Group G in the West, where he became chief of staff. Before his capture by American forces on May 3, 1945, he had been appointed chief of staff of Hasso von Manteuffel's Fifth Panzer Army.

† There is conflicting evidence about Zhukov's training in Berlin. He may or may not have studied there, but he certainly was influenced by German military doctrine, as were a host of other Soviet officers.

II. THE "TANKIST"

Zhukov: Outspoken man of action whose qualities are more those of the will than of the intellect. He is highly regarded in Soviet military circles and is considered to be an especially capable officer and good organizer. He was the first to stand up for the massed use of tanks and successfully carried it off in practice.

Captured German military document, May, 1943

GEORGI Zhukov's efforts to improve his skills and leadership techniques contributed much to his rapid rise in the armed forces. Writing of Zhukov's formative years, a Soviet biographer observes that "the outstanding command qualities, the steadfast and painstaking work of G. K. Zhukov in improving his education, and his concern for the combat and political preparation of his units did not go unnoticed."[1]

The "Tankist"

In 1928, Zhukov was commanding the Thirty-ninth Cavalry Regiment in a division led by the talented D. F. Serdich.* Komdiv (Division Commander) Serdich wrote in his efficiency report on Zhukov: "An energetic and decisive commander. Thanks to the work of Comrade Zhukov, directed to education and combat training, the regiment rose to the required level in all respects. . . . He is excellently trained as a regimental commander and one-man chief. He should be promoted to brigade commander ahead of time."[2] The reference to "one-man chief" (*yedinonachalnik*) was significant. The principle of *yedinonachalie* had been introduced into the Soviet armed forces in 1925. It has been defined by the Soviets as follows: "*Yedinonachalie* combines in the person of the commander all the rights and obligations connected with the military, political, administrative and logistical control of a formation, unit and subunit."[3] Until 1925 military commissars and commanders comprised a dual command in military units, and all command and battle orders had to bear the signatures of both the commander and the commissar.[4] Throughout his career Zhukov strongly believed that the civil authorities should trust a commander to run his unit without the interference of a commissar forever at his elbow.†

* Danilo Fedorovich Serdich, born in 1896 in Yugoslavia, was a hero of the civil war. After graduating from the Frunze Academy in 1932, he commanded the Fourth Cavalry Corps and in 1935–37 the Third Cavalry Corps (Belorussian Military District). In 1936 he was appointed a member of the Central Committee of the Communist Party of Belorussia. He was arrested on June 15, 1937, and executed July 28. See I. Ochak, "Komkor D. F. Serdich," *Voyenno-Istorichesky Zhurnal*, August, 1966, pp. 127–28.

† N. Galay writes: "When the Red Army was created in 1918 it contained relatively few Party members. Because of the lack of Communist personnel, politically unreliable officers of the Tsarist Army had to be given positions of command. As a result, military commissars were introduced on April 6, 1918, which meant that henceforth authority would be dual in structure. All command and battle orders had to bear the signatures of both the commander and the commissar. The function of the latter was to be the government's representative, the bearer of revolutionary discipline and organization, who would suppress 'the treacherous activities of individual commanders.' Instructions for regimental commissars on active service, published in 1919 at the height of the Civil War, made it clear that the commissar was the commander's aide in military affairs and should assume primary responsibility for defending the interests of his subordinates. 'The commander is the head, the commissar the father and soul of a unit.'

"The inevitable shortcomings of this system, both during the Civil War and in

While Zhukov was commanding a cavalry regiment, the Soviets organized their first tank regiments, and Zhukov's unit was chosen to experiment with the new weapons. His successes and his subsequent rapid rise through the Soviet chain of command were observed at first hand by P. Ruslanov.* Noting that Zhukov advanced from regimental

---

ensuing years, led in 1925 (at the beginning of the army reforms linked with Frunze's name) to the abolition of dual control and the establishment of *yedinonachalie*. The change which was made by an order of the Revolutionary War Council of the USSR on March 2, 1925 may have been motivated by an increase in Communist personnel in the army, which had incidentally become more proletarianized. For a long time, however, the new principle was applied in a limited way and permitted only in units and formations where the commander was a Party member. In this case, a political assistant was subordinated to him as his deputy. When commanders were not Party members, the former commissar system was retained. The elimination of dual authority was achieved gradually, by continual efforts to communize the army, by the careful selection of men, and in particular of officers, and by accepting only Party members and socially reliable elements—the workers. Consequently the non-Party element in positions of command was reduced in size and the principle of *yedinonachalie* was increasingly developed."

The Soviets introduced the commissar system, or dual command, three times, in 1918, 1937, and 1941. Three times they instituted the principle of *yedinonachalie*, in 1925, 1940, and 1942. "The emergence of the commissars," Galay notes, "has always coincided with a period of political instability, not merely in the army but in the country itself; when outside events (the Civil War and World War II) were revealing internal weaknesses of the regime, or when a bitter Party struggle or a reign of terror throughout the country was in progress. *Yedinonachalie* has always been reintroduced for strictly military reasons. In 1925 it was essential to create a regular army out of the partisan-type forces then in existence." N. Galay, "Principles of Command in the Soviet Armed Forces," *Bulletin of the Institute for the Study of the History and Culture of the USSR*, Vol. II (June, 1955), 12–13.

* P. Ruslanov, an engineer by profession, served in the Soviet Army of Occupation in Germany in World War II and took up residence in West Germany in 1948. The two articles which Ruslanov wrote for the New York Russian-language magazine *Sotsialistichesky Vestnik* in 1955 (and which appeared in abridged form in English in *Russian Review* in 1956) are among the most rewarding sources I found in my research on Zhukov's pre–World War II activities. In fact, they are a unique source of insight into Zhukov as a regimental commander. I therefore chose to use Ruslanov's account almost in its entirety. He states: "I shall limit myself to relating only what I know of Zhukov from personal observations when he served as commander of a tank regiment in the Belorussian Service Command during the thirties; from what was told me by personal, low-ranking acquaintances of mine who were on the staff of the army commanded by

commander to chief of the General Staff of the Red Army, then to deputy commander in chief of all the armed forces of the country in just a few years, Ruslanov comments:

> Such a rise on Zhukov's part can in no way be explained by his abilities alone. Among the generals of the Soviet Army there have been, and there are now, able military leaders; but either they perished in prisons during the years of the great purges under Yezhov or else they hold minor secondary positions. Thus, the reasons for Zhukov's rapid rise have other roots and these must be sought in the historical conditions which favored his career. Such conditions were at hand at that time.[5]

The most important of the "conditions" Ruslanov mentions were the basic organization of the entire Red Army, its mechanization and motorization, and the purging of Tukhachevsky. World War II should also be counted, but by the time it began, Zhukov had already climbed high on the military ladder and his subsequent advancement was assured. Mechanization and motorization of the Red Army had begun even earlier, but after Hitler came to power, the entire program was accelerated. Hitler based his foreign policy on expansion to the east (*Drang nach Osten*), and the Kremlin, well aware of what that meant for the Soviet Union, hastened to modernize the army.

The military philosophy of Germany's General von Seeckt was of great interest to Soviet Army leaders, especially Marshal Tukhachevsky, who at that time still enjoyed Stalin's support. It was only natural to follow the German initiative by mechanizing the cavalry divisions of Budenny's former army. This was begun in the cavalry corps of the Belorussian Service Command. Each division was to have a regiment of high-speed tanks, and inasmuch as the experiment was an important one, the commanders of the two tank regiments had to be outstanding officers. Moscow (that is, Stalin himself) decided to make the final selection. Zhukov and another outstanding regimental commander, Dmitri G. Pavlov, were chosen.

According to Ruslanov, some persons believe that Stalin could not have occupied himself with such minor matters as the appointment of Zhukov to the post of regimental commander. On the contrary, Rusla-

Zhukov during the battles on the Khalkhin-Gol River in Mongolia; and from stories told me by his personal adjutant, Major M., who was in Zhukov's service for twenty years. I know little about Zhukov after his transfer to Moscow before and during the war."

nov believes that "Stalin's distinction and success stemmed from the fact that he himself paid close attention to minor details, frequently very petty ones, which seemed important to him." To corroborate his assertion, Ruslanov cites several examples, including Stalin's close interest in the nonstop Moscow–United States flight of Valery P. Chkalov, G. F. Baydukov, and A. V. Belyakov across the North Pole in 1937; his order to the armaments designer Vasily A. Degtyarev to design a new machine gun; and other matters which the dictator personally supervised:

> For Stalin, the search for necessary capable personnel was something of a sport. He did it systematically, thus constantly injecting new life into his elite. The personal idiosyncrasies of his character also played a certain role in this. If he simply liked someone, that person's success was assured, and this frequently decided the fate of writers, actors, military men, and scholars. Pilot Chkalov chanced to come to his attention, a man who really had nothing to offer but did possess great bravery and boldness in the air. He was discharged from the air force several times for his recklessness, but Stalin took a liking to him, and he too became a famous hero of the Soviet Union, an admiral, and even a doctor of geographical sciences. Zhukov, too, came to Stalin's attention. Chkalov and Papanin did not reveal great capabilities, though they remained show figures. Zhukov, however, did reveal remarkable capabilities, and Stalin's patronage proved to be decisive in Zhukov's appointment to the position of commander of the experimental tank regiment.[6]

Zhukov still had to pass a severe practical test: he must organize his new regiment, run it under the watchful eyes of the Kremlin, and work out the problems which would surely develop. There were many difficulties. Everything was new, and he had to rely more on his own intuition than on service manuals. Tanks were complicated pieces of machinery, and in a unit employing them special consideration had to be given to logistical, maintenance, and operational details. Moreover, staff work, communications, and administration from the rear presented enormous problems. Zhukov "fully realized what was required of him, and he set about his work with unusual zeal and enterprise. His future success was assured by the very fact that he understood his main task only too well."[7]

Noting that Zhukov had to develop a new type of soldier, the tanker, Ruslanov writes:

> A great deal was required of the commander of such a regiment. Zhukov

swiftly became, in the regiment, the center from which everything stemmed: initiative, leadership, and control; he saw everything himself and as a consequence knew everything. He was to be found at headquarters only as often as was necessary for the settlement of staff matters. He spent all the remaining time outside headquarters, personally observing all aspects of regimental life. He observed, learned, and taught others. He did this with a rare patience and self-control and exacted fulfillment of duty in a persistent, methodical, and well-thought-out manner. He never shouted and never upbraided anyone. No one ever saw him lose his temper or burst into a rage. This had tremendous educational value for his subordinates. But if admonitions did not help, then he could, without the slightest hesitation, turn someone over for court-martial, whenever the interests of the service required it.[8]

The principle Zhukov introduced was: "If you don't know how, we'll teach you; if you don't want to, we'll make you."

Zhukov's outstanding leadership, his unrelenting insistence that his subordinates do their best work, and his attention to details—characteristics which would earn him a reputation as a demanding, strict, iron-willed commander—began to manifest themselves early in his career. A few examples may serve to illustrate his successes then and later. Zhukov forbade anyone to appear in fatigue clothes outside the workshops, garages, and tank parks; the prescribed uniform had to be worn at all times. Combat vehicles were to be washed immediately upon returning from field exercises, regardless of the time of day. And Zhukov insisted that the footgear of every member of the regiment be polished.

Special stands were constructed for washing the vehicles as they returned from field exercises, and Zhukov always appeared at the end of each operation. With his hands behind his back and without a word he would observe the progress of the work. He wanted personally to study his men, especially the officers, and if he became convinced that an individual was incapable of performing a good job, he dismissed him from the unit. Ruslanov points out:

> The majority did not want to leave the regiment because it was easier to perform one's duties with Zhukov than with others. One could learn from him, and he had the reputation of being a just commander. He did not require any more of his subordinates than he did of himself. If duty necessitated, he did not take into consideration whether it was night or day. He would frequently conduct inspections at night, and if he found any-

thing out of order, he would have it corrected or would have the badly done work done over, even if it was in the middle of the night.[9]

One night about midnight a company of tanks returned from tactical exercises. The men were exhausted, and the company commander asked the motor-pool officer of the day to permit the lightly washed vehicles to be parked, with the understanding that they would be thoroughly cleaned the following morning. After some hesitation the officer of the day agreed, although he knew full well that this procedure was forbidden by the regimental commander.

About an hour later Zhukov arrived at the motor pool to inspect the vehicles. The officer of the day began to offer excuses for the dirty tanks, saying the tankers had been worn out when they finished their problem. An irate Zhukov said to him:

> Readiness to assist comrades is a very praiseworthy quality, but, you see, you did not help them, but instead, you disobeyed instructions and drove them to a violation of military discipline and order. I know just as well as you do that the men were tired and that it was difficult for them, but, you see, they were called into the army so that they could be trained and prepared for war and its burdens and severe trials. Fatigue during exercises—that's child's play compared with what awaits all of us in wartime. You should be removed from your duty and subjected to military punishment, but by way of exception I shall not do that today. The Party organization will examine your act and will pronounce judgment. That will help you, perhaps, and then we'll see what else should be done with you.

Thereupon Zhukov ordered the company and battalion commanders to see that the washing of the vehicles was completed and to report to him when the task had been carried out. Two hours later the job was finished. Zhukov ordered the company to get some rest, but the company and battalion commanders had to remain behind. Then Zhukov reinspected the tanks. As he left, he turned to the company commander, saying: "I'm getting the impression that you are not mature enough to command a company. Think this over seriously and then tell me your own opinion before it's too late. You won't get off so easily a second time with this sort of thing. I'm warning you!"

Zhukov reminded his subordinates of standing orders by various forceful means. So effective was his manner of reminding his men to polish their shoes and boots that not one of them ever forgot it.

Once at a guard formation Zhukov took the report of the officer of the day and then decided to inspect the guards who were coming on duty. He was satisfied with the appearance of all except one, whose boots were poorly polished. Zhukov asked the new officer of the day what he thought of the guard's footwear. The officer, instead of answering, ordered the soldier to explain why his boots were not shined. Zhukov interrupted: "I'm asking you, not him, and I'm not interested in the response, but in your opinion. The boots won't become clean through explanations!" The embarrassed officer could say nothing, and Zhukov continued more softly:

> In this instance, the only important thing is not that the boots were not cleaned but that you did not pay attention to the matter. He could have neglected to polish them, but you should have required the men to clean their boots all the same before going on their tour of duty. The trouble lies in the fact that there is apparently no one in the regiment except the commander to help him clean his boots.

Zhukov ordered the adjutant to bring a stool and boot-polishing equipment, whereupon he had the soldier put one foot on the stool and watch attentively to see exactly how boots were to be polished. Zhukov then began polishing one boot for the guard; after a few minutes it shone. Handing the soldier the brush, Zhukov told him to shine the other boot and upon completion of the job to report with the officer of the day to headquarters to show the commander the footwear. After the soldier had painstakingly polished the other boot, the officer of the day and the guard commander carefully compared both boots and then went off to headquarters to show them to Zhukov. The incident evoked much laughter and conversation among members of the unit, but afterward the men polished their boots with renewed effort. All expected a severe order with respect to this affair, but none came down.

> Thus [records Ruslanov], gradually Zhukov created in the regiment an orderly atmosphere. The men in the regiment were not afraid of him, but all felt the force of his presence. They depended on him, frequently without realizing it.
>
> The commanders did their best, and the results were rewarding. On maneuvers and inspections Zhukov's regiment rose to the foremost position. All this was noticed at central headquarters. The whole Red Army knew of the regiment. Students from the military academies came to his

regiment to do probationary work [that is, training assignments in varied duties]. The unit participated in training exercises in the presence of representatives of the general staff. It was displayed before foreign military attachés and important foreign guests. At that time Red Army *Pravda*, the newspaper of the Belorussian Service Command, started to give a great deal of attention to Zhukov. It published full-page sketches of his military career, his exploits in the Civil War, and his boundless devotion to the Party of Lenin and Stalin.[10]

Zhukov had passed his test.

In May, 1930, after commanding the Thirty-ninth Regiment for almost seven years, Zhukov was made commander of the Second Cavalry Brigade,* and more praise was heaped upon him. The commander of the Seventh Cavalry Division, Konstantin K. Rokossovsky,† wrote a glowing efficiency report:

> A commander of strong will and decisiveness. He possesses a wealth of initiative and skillfully applies it to his job. He is disciplined. He is exacting and is persistent in his demands. In military respects he is well trained. He loves military matters and constantly improves himself. In the course of a year's period, by his skillful leadership of combat training of the brigade great progress was achieved in the realm of drill and tactical firing, as well as in the total development of the brigade.[11]

In concluding his efficiency report, Rokossovsky recommended Zhukov's promotion to the post of commander of a mechanized formation (*soyedinenie*).[12]

In February, 1931, Zhukov was named assistant to General Budenny, inspector of cavalry of the Red Army (who held that post for thirteen years, from 1924 to 1937). In March, 1933, Zhukov was assigned command of the Fourth Cavalry Division. During the civil war the division had been one of the most distinguished units of Budenny's First Cavalry

---

* Zhukov's brigade, part of the Seventh Samara Cavalry Division, consisted of two cavalry regiments, the Thirty-ninth and the Fortieth. The Seventh Division was part of a corps commanded from February, 1925, until 1929 by S. K. Timoshenko and later by D. F. Serdich.

† Zhukov and Rokossovsky formed a close and lasting friendship. In December, 1966, the two old warriors, both celebrating their seventieth birthdays in that month, were photographed together at celebrations marking the twenty-fifth anniversary of the Battle of Moscow. Interestingly, both were ministers of defense at the same time—Zhukov in Moscow and Rokossovsky in Warsaw.

Army. It was now part of the Belorussian Military District, one of the most responsible districts in the Soviet Union and a training ground for future wartime leaders. In its roster were officers who would prove to be among the most distinguished military leaders of World War II. S. K. Timoshenko commanded a corps; Zhukov, I. S. Konev, and V. D. Sokolovsky commanded divisions; and I. Kh. Bagramyan, Matvei V. Zakharov, R. Ya. Malinovsky, V. V. Kurasov, and A. P. Pokrovsky were also assigned to posts in this important military district.

Zhukov's name appeared more and more frequently in the Soviet press. In 1935 he joined other critics who attacked Tukhachevsky's conduct of Red Army maneuvers, and in the following year he was appointed to the military committee which approved the draft of Stalin's new constitution.[13]

During this period Zhukov and Boris M. Shaposhnikov, chief of staff of the Red Army, sought to convince the army hierarchy that the tank could play an independent role on the modern battlefield—that this new and powerful weapon must not be spread out with slower-moving infantry units, thus dissipating its strength.[14] Writes John Erickson:

> One of the crucial points of the earlier experiments had been the difficult business of synchronising the maneuvers of the fast-moving tank forces and the slower infantry. Zhukov's handling of his mechanized forces contributed most substantially to his success. In addition to the tanks and artillery which worked together, the third indispensable element was motorized infantry, without which there could be no exploitation of the successes of the mechanized forces operating at a distance from the slower-moving infantry.[15]

Zhukov's ideas about the use of armor in contemporary warfare were to prevail only temporarily, for Stalin would later be persuaded that the large tank units had to be disbanded. Only when the Red Army was threatened with disaster in 1941 were Zhukov's views vindicated.

Zhukov distinguished himself in the post of division commander, and his unit made "high showings in combat and political training."[16] N. Svetlishin notes that it was "for his great successes in this matter [that] G. K. Zhukov in 1936 was honored with the high government award—the Order of Lenin."[17] Zhukov has said of this assignment that participation in war games and command and staff training, frequently carried out in the Belorussian Military District under the leadership of two outstanding Soviet military chiefs, A. I. Yegorov and I. P. Uborevich,* contributed much to the broadening of his operational outlook and the formation of theoretical views and command qualities.[18]

While Zhukov was occupying the post, civil war broke out in Spain, and he was soon called to play a role in the conflict. Stalin would have preferred to remain aloof from this struggle a thousand miles from the Soviet Union, involving a government with which the U.S.S.R. had no official representation, but the Fascist powers' insistence on the necessity of intervention convinced Stalin that if he failed to act decisively the insurgents would win an early victory. This would mean the encirclement of France by the Fascists and possibly even the triumph of ever-increasing Fascist tendencies within France herself, with the result that the already tenuous resistance to Hitler in the West would be further weakened. Stalin realized that if this happened the way would then be clear for German aggression toward the East.[19]

After some hesitation the Soviet leaders decided to intervene in the Spanish civil war. "Having made this decision, they pressed the action forward with extraordinary speed and energy," writes the former ambassador to Russia George F. Kennan.[20] General Francisco Franco and his forces would almost certainly have won a resounding victory by the end of 1936 had not the Communist Party rallied the Western liberals to assistance and then supported the entire operation with planes, tanks, and military personnel, which reached the Loyalist government in the early months of the conflict. Soviet intervention also helped Francisco Largo Caballero unite and consolidate the many political parties and trade unions which comprised the Republican government.[21]

Soviet intervention in Spain allowed Zhukov and his military comrades to test Red Army theories of armored warfare in combat and to put Russian tanks through their paces. Thirty years after these events, in 1966, the Soviets discussed this assistance: "In the prewar years the tank troops, along with the entire Soviet Army, were developed, per-

---

* Yegorov became chief of staff of the Red Army in 1931, was first deputy commissar of defense in 1937, and fell victim to the purges. Uborevich (or Uborevich-Gubarevich), who worked closely with Tukhachevsky in reorganizing the Red Army and Soviet defense planning, was commander of the Belorussian Military District before he was arrested and shot without trial in June, 1937. See John Erickson, *The Soviet High Command: A Military-Political History, 1918–1941*, 845–47.

fected, and made more combat ready. In these years, they received considerable combat experience. On battlefields in Spain, around Lake Khasan, at the Khalkhin-Gol River, in the forests of Finland—these were landmarks in the serious tests of our tank troops."[22]

Meanwhile, in the autumn of 1936, Stalin and Voroshilov sent Zhukov to Spain as one of the principal Soviet military observers.[23] He was in distinguished company. The future minister of defense, R. Ya. Malinovsky, was there, as was the capable artilleryman N. N. Voronov, of World War II fame. General Ian Berzin initially headed the Soviet military mission to Spain, and all activities of the Red Army were under his charge.[24] One of the leading tank specialists, General Dmitri G. Pavlov, was also present early in the war, probably from the fall of 1936 to the summer of 1937. As chief of tank operations, Pavlov appeared to one observer to be constantly engaged at his headquarters in writing long reports on the performance of his human and mechanical charges.[25] In spite of his efforts, he drew incorrect conclusions about armor operations. Because of problems which arose in fighting on the Iberian Peninsula, he decided that tanks could not play an independent operational role on the modern battlefield. Later he was able to persuade both Stalin and Voroshilov, over Zhukov's strong objections, that his views were correct.* The Red Army's large tank units, known as "motor-mechanized corps," containing about five hundred vehicles each, were disbanded. Despite all of Zhukov's and Shaposhnikov's work, the tank was relegated to the role of infantry support weapon, with separate tank battalions organized as subdivisions of infantry units.[26]

Available records do not indicate how long Zhukov remained in Spain. He was there at least from the fall of 1936 to the early summer of 1937. One participant in the fighting remembers an unidentified high-ranking officer with General Pavlov's tank headquarters at Alcalá de Henares during May, 1937, who looked very much like Zhukov.[27] Alexander Orlov, the Soviet Union's chief intelligence officer with the Loyalist

---

* Hugh Thomas observes that General Pavlov may have taken this stand before Stalin to escape being branded an admirer of the theories of the disgraced Marshal Tukhachevsky, who had placed great faith in such formations. See Thomas, *The Spanish Civil War*, 615. The hapless Pavlov, who did so much harm to the Soviet army and whose views clashed with those of Zhukov, was ordered shot by Stalin in the early months of World War II as the Red Army defenses crumbled. See Alexander Werth, *Russia at War, 1941–1945*, 154.

forces, recalls that he met Zhukov on several occasions during 1937, and an old Soviet film shows Zhukov addressing a group of volunteers in the International Brigade at Barcelona in 1936. Orlov further notes that Zhukov served as an observer for the High Command.[28]

It was not only in the capacity of observers that the Soviets participated in the struggle in Spain. Organized units manned by regular troops were dispatched to Spain over the objections of Marshal Tukhachevsky, who considered it imprudent to reveal the imperfections of the Red Army.[29] After Soviet tank units arrived on the scene, they did most of the Red Army's fighting.[30] At the very moment Tass was issuing a categorical denial that any Soviet troops were in Spain, saying that "these reports are the fruit of an idle imagination,"[31] foreign observers were encountering Red Army tank units, and a number of them even talked with the crews.[32] Many of these units were not standard order-of-battle organizations, but had been tailored for research and testing. "Thus," recalls a participant, "a first or second lieutenant served as a lowly loader in many instances to test equipment and to get actual combat experience. Practically all the Russians in the tank service were officers or senior N.C.O.'s being groomed as future officers."[33]

Soviet armored units participated in a number of bloody battles, sometimes distinguishing themselves but often suffering defeat and its attendant losses in lives and equipment. The Russians were blamed for several costly Loyalist defeats because of poor tactics or unwise experimentation. At Fuentes de Ebro, for example, against the protests of the non-Russian officers, the Soviet leadership ordered an attack across muddy terrain. Forty new Soviet tanks were sent into the attack, and when the fighting subsided, only twelve made it back to the Loyalist lines.[34]

It is not within the scope of this book to examine the political events which influenced Soviet aid to the Loyalists. Suffice it to say that eventually Stalin could not fail to be convinced that Franco and his insurgents were winning in Spain. German and Italian intervention soon assumed such dimensions that Moscow realized the Republican government could be saved only by a much greater volume of assistance. The Western democracies showed themselves either unwilling or unable to provide even a portion of this assistance. Fearful that it might become involved in a war with the Axis, the Russian government allowed its aid to taper off, having reconciled itself to the eventual defeat of the Republican cause.[35]

The civil war taught Zhukov and his associates many valuable lessons. Spain provided a laboratory experiment in which new weapons were introduced and debatable concepts of modern tactics were studied for their effectiveness. Although it had been hailed as the weapon of the future after its brief workout in World War I, the tank had remained largely untested in fast-moving combat operations. The war in Spain provided this opportunity, and Zhukov, Pavlov, Pavel A. Rotmistrov, Konev, and others were there to take advantage of it.

Zhukov returned home for a new assignment, as commander of the Third Cavalry Corps, where he served for seven months before taking command of the Sixth Kazakh Corps, a post he would occupy for some time. Those who had any doubts about Stalin's personal interest in him would be effectively silenced in the bloody period which was rapidly approaching.

III. STALIN DECAPITATES THE ARMY

Power tends to corrupt, and absolute power corrupts absolutely.

Lord Acton

IN late spring, 1937, General I. E. Yakir, who had commanded the Ukranian and Kiev military districts and served on the Party's Central Committee, wrote to Stalin: "I am an honest soldier, dedicated to the Party, the state and the people, as I have been for many years. All my conscious life has been spent in selfless and honest work before the Party and its leaders. . . . I shall die with words of love for you, the Party and the country, and with a boundless faith in the victory of Communism." Stalin wrote on the letter, "Scoundrel and prostitute." Voroshilov added, "Absolutely precise definition." V. M. Molotov signed his name under Voroshilov's comment, while L. M. Kaganovich wrote in addition: "The death penalty is the only punishment for the traitor, swine, and —— [unprintable]." A few days later Yakir was executed.[1] As he was shot, he exclaimed: "Long live the Party, long live Stalin!" Told of this, Stalin only cursed him.[2]

The tragedy of Yakir was but a page in a thick volume of killings ordered by Stalin. The infamous *chistki*, or purges, had begun. The results were devastating.

In his bid for supreme power Stalin had purged the Party, and now he struck out against all potential opponents and their supporters in a clean sweep of the military apparatus. From 1937 to 1938 about twenty-five thousand commanders of the Red Army fell victim to Stalin. The first to suffer were the commanders of the military districts, who were annihilated almost to a man. Then followed a purge of other command personnel: about 70 per cent of the corps commanders, up to 60 per cent of the division commanders, 50 per cent of the regimental commanders, and 20 to 25 per cent of the remaining command personnel.[3] The number of senior officers purged is shown below:

	Number in May, 1937	Purged	Surviving in November, 1938
Marshals	5	3	2
Army commanders	15	13	2
Corps commanders	85	57	28
Division commanders	195	110	85
Brigade commanders	406	220	186

The two marshals who survived were Voroshilov and Budenny. Tukhachevsky, Yegorov, and Blyukher were shot.[4]

The long arm of Stalin's secret police reached all the way to Spain, and a large number of Soviet officers stationed there were also liquidated. The chief military adviser to the Republican government in the early stages of the fighting, General Ian Berzin, was executed. A number of younger officers were called back to the Soviet Union for trial.[5] Robert Gladnick has recalled that one day in early May, 1937, several Soviet officers were summoned to General Pavlov's headquarters. Some hours later they emerged, "white as ghosts." They had been informed of the arrest of Marshal Tukhachevsky. Gladnick described their reaction to the news:

Then both [Major] Baronov and Lipin told me the story of Tukhachevsky. Later when I was alone with Baronov, he got drunk and cried. He was really afraid to go back to the Soviet Union since he told me that Tukhachevsky had singled him out for special praise for his action at Guadalajara and before that in Russia. He was drunker than a coot that night when I drove him back to Pavlov's headquarters for his return to Russia.[6]

New light on the background of the purges, as well as on the forced confessions, was revealed by Nikita S. Khrushchev in his concluding remarks to the Twenty-second Party Congress in October, 1961:

A rather curious report once cropped up in the foreign press to the effect that Hitler, in preparing the attack on our country, planted through his intelligence service a faked document indicating that Comrades Yakir and Tukhachevsky and others were agents of the German general staff. This "document," allegedly secret, fell into the hands of President Beneš of Czechoslovakia, who, apparently guided by good intentions, forwarded it to Stalin. Yakir, Tukhachevsky and other comrades were arrested and then killed.

Many splendid commanders and political officials of the Red Army were executed. Here among the delegates there are comrades—I do not wish to name them so as not to cause them pain—who spent many years in prison. They were being "persuaded"—persuaded by quite definite techniques—that they were either German or British or some other kind of spy. And several of them "confessed." Even in cases when such people were told that the accusation of espionage had been withdrawn, they themselves insisted on their previous testimony, because they believed it was better to stand on false testimony, in order to put an end as quickly as possible to the torment and to die as quickly as possible.[7]

Fortunately for the Soviet Union, several gifted military commanders survived their prison ordeals, to be salvaged later for World War II service. Corps Commander Konstantin Rokossovsky, for example, was arrested, beaten senseless by the NKVD, and imprisoned. He was reinstated in 1938 and won impressive victories in the war.

During the era of arrests and executions Georgi Zhukov was serving as deputy commander of cavalry forces in the Belorussian Military District. Colonel G. I. Antonov, who had served as regimental commander under Zhukov when he commanded the Fourth Cavalry Division in 1934, later explained how Zhukov escaped the fate of many of his comrades:

Maybe circumstances played a famous role here, since Stalin was especially benevolent toward cavalry leaders, with whom a personal bond had been formed by him already in the past, in that period when he was a member of the military council of the Southwestern Front, the Army of Budenny being a part of this front. Stalin always treated this army and its high command personnel—Budenny, Voroshilov, Timoshenko, Apanasenko, Yeremenko, Gorobikov—with special friendliness. The combat successes of Budenny's "horse" army more often began receiving notice by Stalin himself, particularly the operations in the defense of Tsaritsyn-Stalingrad in 1918–1919.

On the strength of these conclusions the possibility is not excluded that Stalin simply had greater trust in the cavalry chiefs, and that being the case, the higher and senior command personnel of the cavalry units were subjected to repressions in the Yezhov period to a considerably lesser degree, and then only in exceptional cases. Somehow or other Zhukov not only did not suffer or lose his post, but in the summer of 1937 received a promotion and was appointed commander of a cavalry corps in the place of the arrested Serdich.[8]

Another reason for Zhukov's survival is that Stalin had taken a personal interest in him. As I have pointed out, Stalin's patronage was decisive in Zhukov's advancement. Stalin had been impressed with Zhukov's handling of his tank regiment, and Zhukov had not disappointed him in subsequent assignments. Too, Stalin, to keep power firmly in his hands, often played one group against another. In dumping Tukhachevsky, he must have known that he could count on the support of the former members of the First Cavalry Army. It was Tukhachevsky who had heaped condemnation on this army after the disastrous battle for Warsaw in 1920, but Stalin had protected the Budenny men.[9]

The purges virtually decapitated the Red Army. The effects were felt in the critical years which followed. Witness the disasters of the Finnish campaign and the breakdown in the face of the German attack in June, 1941. Says one Soviet history:

> Among the circumstances contributing to the inadequate preparedness of the Red Army for repelling a sudden attack by a strong and crafty enemy was the great loss and damage inflicted on our military cadres, especially the senior echelon, by the criminal gang of Yezhov and Beria [the NKVD]. As a result of the unfounded repressions in the prewar years the Soviet Armed Forces were deprived of a significant number of their experienced commanders and political workers. By the start of [World

War II], many posts in the Army were filled with young cadres who did not possess sufficient knowledge and experience for leading troops in complex conditions. The situation created by the groundless repressions was not conducive to the training of cadres in the spirit of creative initiative.[10]

Thus with the removal of practically the entire stratum of senior officers, much valuable experience was lost to the Red Army. Many of the older officers were veterans of World War I and the civil war. Although a number of them had joined the Communist Party, their views often clashed with Stalin's. Some were critics of collectivization and opposed Stalin's ruthless measures. Stalin considered their ouster a safety measure. Their places were taken by promising young Communist officers, among them Georgi Zhukov. Leonard Schapiro observes that,

> unlike those whom they displaced, these new men owed everything to Stalin. To the Civil War veterans, Stalin was at best an equal. To the new men he was the architect of their careers in a rapidly expanding Army. Again, to a dictator who placed his own security in the forefront, the creation of such a praetorian guard of young officers may have appeared a very desirable end.[11]

Nonetheless, the removal of the senior command personnel, who were thoroughly trained in the military doctrine which had developed from 1933 to 1936, lowered the quality of the Red Army. "With the exception of Shaposhnikov," observes Erickson, "the new high command was stamped either by mediocrity or lack of experience."[12] (The two surviving marshals, Budenny and Voroshilov, would later demonstrate their ineptness.) Although Tukhachevsky's theories had not been faultless, his philosophy was essentially correct. The problems of mass and mobility were being worked out, and much depended on the policy to be adopted toward the armored forces. Tukhachevsky had examined the problems of command resulting from greatly increased technical differentiation in the army, but Stalin's purges succeeded in undoing this work. At the same time the dominance of mediocrity and inexperience coincided with the reorganization of the mechanized forces, brought about in part by incorrect evaluation of the campaigns in Spain. Zhukov and Shaposhnikov were not able to persuade the new leaders that reorganization would have disastrous effects.[13]

The purges had still another effect: they raised serious doubts among

Russia's friends about the Red Army's fighting abilities. In 1936, British and French generals who attended maneuvers in the Soviet Union were favorably impressed by what they saw. The purges served to negate that impression. Isaac Deutscher writes:

> They looked like ominous cracks in the whole edifice of the Soviets. Whether Western statesmen and military men believed the charges levelled against the defendants to be true or not, their conclusions could not but detract from Russia's value as an ally. If so many outstanding politicians, administrators, and military men had in fact formed a monster fifth column, it was asked, then what was the morale of a nation in which this could happen? If the charges were faked, then was not the regime that indulged in such practices rotten from top to bottom?[14]

Winston Churchill wrote: "To Mr. Chamberlain and the British and French General Staffs the purge of 1937 presented itself mainly as a tearing to pieces internally of the Russian Army, and a picture of the Soviet Union as riven asunder by ferocious hatreds and vengeance."[15] One can only speculate on the underlying effects the purges had on France and Britain during their critical discussions with the Soviet Union in the spring and summer of 1939. That the Red Army finally recovered and went on to win impressive victories demonstrated that it contained reserves of military talent, men like Zhukov, A. M. Vasilevsky, and Sokolovsky, who, given time and placed under pressure, could create an effective fighting machine.

Meanwhile, in early 1938, Zhukov was serving as commander of the Sixth Cavalry Corps. Soon he was appointed a deputy commander of the Belorussian Military District. From this post, by order of General Headquarters and with the blessings of Stalin himself, he was sent to China with a Soviet military mission to observe Japanese strategy and tactics. This may not have been his first trip to the Orient. He is said to have gone to China in the early 1920's with "Galin" (the nom de guerre of the shrewd General V. K. Blyukher).[16]

The trip was an outgrowth of Soviet involvement in the Sino-Japanese War. On July 7, 1937, Japan had attacked the Marco Polo Bridge south of Peking, touching off war with China. On August 21, China and the Soviet Union had signed a nonaggression pact, agreeing to refrain "from any aggression against each other individually, or jointly with one or more other powers."[17] By 1938, with the tripartite alliance of Japan,

Germany, and Italy fast taking shape, Moscow had begun to look upon the Sino-Japanese War as a safeguard from attack from the East, and Kremlin officials hoped that the fighting would be prolonged. After the fall of Nanking, when Japanese forces were driving toward Wuhan, the Soviet Union stepped up its material aid to China and adopted closer, friendlier relations.[18]

At the end of 1937 the first group of Soviet pilots arrived in China. They were followed by military instructors, more pilots, aviation technicians, artillery and tank specialists, and engineers. In the summer of 1938 twenty-one high-ranking Soviet officials arrived. This distinguished group included Zhukov, V. I. Chuikov (later the defender of Stalingrad), and P. F. Batitsky (later marshal of the Soviet Union).

Soon the number of Soviet military personnel in China had reached one thousand.[19] Although the pilots saw considerable action in air battles, most of the advisers were attached to field headquarters, where they were available for consultation on technical matters (but not routine staff work) or served at the tank and artillery training centers and at the flying school at Ining (Kuldja). Some Soviet military experts, probably including Georgi Zhukov, occasionally lectured at the staff college, and others held advisory positions on the National Military Council. According to F. F. Liu: "All of them, from the highest to the lowest, were instructed to keep their eyes open at all times and to learn as much as they taught. China was a laboratory into which Russia had sent scientifically trained personnel to make tests and observations."[20]

The influence of Soviet military advisers in the late 1930's never approached the importance it had held between 1924 and 1927. Chiang Kai-shek had made it clear that he looked to them for technical advice rather than formulation of war strategy.[21] In a few instances, however, the Soviets did participate in operational planning. Komdiv A. I. Cherepanov, the chief Soviet adviser in China, helped prepare reserves for one large counteroffensive, and some Soviet planning figured in the successful operation at Changsha in the fall of 1939.[22] But the talents of the higher-ranking Soviet advisers were largely unused, and most of them soon departed.[23] One, however, remained: Vasily Chuikov became the military attaché and chief military adviser to Chiang Kai-shek, a post he held when Germany attacked the Soviet Union in 1941.[24]

Zhukov, who found too little to do in China,[25] was soon given a more urgent assignment. Japan decided to test the seriousness of repeated Soviet declarations that the Red Army would defend Siberian and Outer Mongolian territory. The Soviet armed forces in the Far East—dependent on extended supply lines, weakened by the recent purges and the consequent reorganization—were about to be put to the test, and again Stalin placed the mantle of responsibility on his protégé, Georgi Zhukov.

IV. LAKE KHASAN AND KHALKHIN-GOL

Zhukov is my George B. McClellan. Like McClellan he always wants more
men, more cannon, more guns. Also more planes. He never has enough.
But Zhukov has never lost a battle.

Joseph Stalin

AS war crept ever nearer to Europe and the Japanese grew increasingly bold in the Far East, the Russians became even more deeply
concerned about the security of their frontiers. In a series of steps designed to discourage aggression they fortified regions along the land
frontiers, built firing positions for coastal artillery and automatic
weapons along river and sea lanes, and constructed supply depots, airfields, and roads in the border zones.[1] Particularly worried about its Far

Eastern borders, the Soviet Union had earlier established the Far East-ern *Front** and the Pacific Ocean Fleet.[2] In March, 1936, Moscow had signed a mutual-assistance pact with the Mongolian People's Republic.[3]

The Japanese had been probing the strength of the Red Army for some time, often taking advantage of crises elsewhere on the world scene. Thirty-three border clashes erupted in 1936, and several more occurred during the purges.[4] Now, while the Soviet Union was seem-ingly preoccupied with events in Europe—the Munich crisis and Ger-many's preparations for war—Japan decided to stage a full-scale test of Russia's military might on the Manchurian and Mongolian frontiers.[5] The Japanese aggression was more than a probing action, however. Fighting on two fronts was calculated to enhance the prestige of the Japanese army in the eyes of other nations. Furthermore, Japanese leaders hoped to cut the Soviet Union off from China and thereby stop the flow of aid.

Both sides appear to share some blame for the events of 1938–39. In the summer of 1938 the Red Army occupied two small islands in the Amur River, evoking protests from the Japanese and a demand that they be evacuated. The Kremlin replied that the islands belonged to Russia, substantiating the claim with references to old Russo-Chinese treaties. The incident seemed settled when both sides agreed not to send military forces to the disputed territory, but two days later the Japanese landed military detachments on the islands. In mid-July, in an even more dangerous move, the Soviets dispatched small military detach-ments to the strategically important hills of Zaozernaya and Bezymyan-

---

* The Soviet term *front* is italicized throughout this book (e.g., Eastern *Front*) to distinguish it from the same word meaning an extended battle line in a particular geographic area or between two or more combatants (such as the Russian-German Front). Although the Russian word "front" is also used in the latter context, the same term is often employed to denote a group of armies under a single commander in an even narrower geographical area. Thus a number of *fronts* (the Southwestern, Don, Stalingrad, and so on) comprised the Russian-Ger-man Front. To avoid confusion, when the term is used to describe a group of armies, it will always be italicized.

The Soviet *front* has no exact Western equivalent; it is the highest field head-quarters in the wartime chain of command. It is roughly similar to the Western concept of an army group consisting of several armies. The subordinate Soviet armies are comparatively small, with three to five, and sometimes six, divisions. In the early part of World War II, a "direction" (*napravlenie*) was created, with several *fronts* forming a direction.

naya, situated about 6 miles from the Pacific coast and 93 miles from Vladivostok (see map, page 193). The Red Army command had decided to forestall the Japanese occupation of the hills, which would pose a serious threat to the harbor at Posyet. The governments of Japan and Manchukuo demanded immediate evacuation and hinted at possible dangerous complications, but Moscow refused, claiming the hills were Russian.[6] On July 20 the Japanese ambassador to Moscow, Mamoru Shigemitsu, declared that if the Japanese demands were not met his nation would employ force to see that they were. The Russians did nothing. On July 29 the Japanese-Manchurian forces struck, moving swiftly in the area of Lake Khasan (Hassan). They took full advantage of the terrain, which was extremely unfavorable for the defenders. Lines of communication were vulnerable, and the hills occupied by the defenders were cut off from the rest of Soviet-held territory by Lake Khasan.

As soon as the Japanese made their move, the commander of the Far Eastern *Front*, Marshal of the Soviet Union Blyukher, ordered units of the Fortieth Infantry Division, stationed in the Posyet area, brought to combat readiness and at the same time dispatched two reinforced battalions from this division to Bezymyannaya and Zaozernaya. Fierce fighting soon erupted, the Soviets bringing in an impressive force in the early days of August. Blyukher assigned direct command of the Lake Khasan operation to Corps Commander Georgi Shtern, chief of staff of the Far East Military District, and he immediately began planning his strike. On August 6 the infantry launched its attack following a bombing and brief artillery barrage of the heights. By August 9, after heavy casualties on both sides, the fighting had virtually ceased, and the Japanese relinquished their hold on the disputed territory. The next day Ambassador Shigemitsu arrived at the People's Commissariat of Foreign Affairs in Moscow with a proposal for talks.

The battles around Lake Khasan revealed serious shortcomings in the mobilization status of the troops in the First Far East (Primorsk) Army and in the work of the headquarters and staffs. In November, 1938, after Voroshilov pointed out certain deficiencies, the Main Military Council in the People's Commissariat of Defense took important steps toward improving the combat readiness of forces in the Far East and increasing border security.

The Japanese were not deterred by their reversal. In May, 1939, hostili-

Georgi Zhukov about 1914, working for his uncle, the Moscow furrier Pilikhin.

Ustinya Artemyevna Zhukova, Georgi Zhukov's mother.

For sources of illustrations, see page 491.

Red Army leaders on the Southern Front, 1918. Left to right: Semyen K. Budenny, Mikhail V. Frunze, and Kliment E. Voroshilov.

Joseph Stalin in 1918, when he was a member of the Revolutionary Military Council on the Southern Front.

Right: Zhukov as a young noncommissioned officer, about 1919.

Below: Members of the cavalry course for command personnel held in Leningrad in 1924–25. Second row: far right, Zhukov; fourth from left, K. K. Rokossovsky. First row, seated: far right, I. Kh. Bagramyan; third from right, A. I. Yeremenko.

Above: Zhukov as commander of the Thirty-ninth Cavalry Regiment, about 1923. Zhukov served in this post for almost seven years.

The first five marshals of the Soviet Union, 1935. Seated, left to right: M. N. Tukhachevsky, Kliment E. Voroshilov, A. I. Yegorov. Standing, left to right: S. M. Budenny, V. K. Blyukher. Soon three of them—Tukhachevsky, Yegorov, and Blyukher—would be dead, victims of Stalin's purges.

Opposite: Red Army T-26 tanks, tested in Spain and employed at Khalkhin-Gol.

Above: Zhukov talks with troops at Khalkhin-Gol, 1939. Right: Zhukov confers
with Marshal Khorlogiin Choybalsan, the
commander of the Mongolian forces at
Khalkhin-Gol.

Soviet troops on the attack at Khalkhin-Gol. Above: firing on Japanese positions. Below: moving out under tank cover.

Above: Marshal Semyen K. Timoshenko (left) and Zhukov inspect the model of a new machine gun, 1940. Below: Zhukov observes field exercises, 1940.

ties again broke out. The Japanese claimed a border violation by seven hundred Outer Mongolian horsemen along the Khalkhin-Gol (or Halhin-Gol) River, known to the Japanese as the Halha. Soviet historians consider the campaign a renewed test of Russian strength, coupled with Japanese territorial designs on the Soviet Transbaikal and Far East.[7]

According to Soviet accounts of the struggle the Kwantung army planned to make its move from the area of Bargi, located in Manchuria between the frontiers of the U.S.S.R., the Mongolian People's Republic, and the Great Khingan mountain range. Preparing for a concentration of forces, the Japanese began to increase the capacity of the Harbin–Tsitsihar–Khailar rail line and also started construction of a new railroad from Solun to Ganchzhur, parallel to and one to two miles from the Mongolian border. They decided to seize the Mongolian territory lying on the right bank of the Khalkhin-Gol (see map, page 194). The region east of the river, steppe and unpopulated, was weakly defended. Frontier posts of the Mongolian People's Republic were twelve to eighteen miles from the border, and there were no regular Mongolian forces nearby. Units of the Fifty-seventh Separate Corps of the Red Army, stationed in Mongolia in accordance with the mutual-assistance pact, were about three hundred miles from the threatened area.[8] Japanese troops immediately began extensive training. In the middle of April a special detachment was sent to Khalkhin-Gol to prepare maps of the terrain. In early May, Japanese pilots began reconnaissance flights over Mongolian territory.[9]

On May 11, 1939, Japan struck. Ground forces hit border stations, while the air force bombed an outpost on the mountain frontier. By May 14 about three hundred Japanese cavalrymen had moved up to the Khalkhin-Gol River. Mongolian border troops sent to restore the frontier were scattered by enemy aircraft. The Soviet government, fulfilling its mutual-assistance pact with the Mongolian People's Republic, ordered its troops stationed there to defend the borders of the two countries.

By the end of May the Japanese command had concentrated east of the Khalkhin-Gol with a force of more than sixteen hundred troops and nine hundred cavalrymen, a small number of armored cars, and forty aircraft. The Mongolians moved up their Sixth Cavalry Division, while the Soviets sent in an infantry machine-gun battalion from the Eleventh Tank Brigade, reinforced with an armored-car company, an engineer company, and a battery of artillery. Other Mongolian and Soviet units were on their way to the combat area.

On May 28 the Japanese attacked in an attempt to envelop the Soviet-Mongolian troops from the flanks, strike them from the rear, and cut them off from crossing points on the Khalkhin-Gol. The numerically superior Japanese at first pressed back the Soviet-Mongolian forces, but were soon halted by artillery and one of the infantry companies. That evening troops of the Soviet 149th Infantry Regiment began to arrive in trucks and were immediately committed to battle. Fighting continued through the night. On the morning of May 29 the Soviet-Mongolian units counterattacked and in a day-long battle drove the Japanese back to the border. Four hundred Japanese officers and soldiers were killed in the two-day engagement.[10]

By early June, Zhukov had arrived in the theater to take command of part of the force. In the first days of July the Japanese began concentrating troops for a fresh offensive. Their number had now reached about 38,000 men, supported by 135 tanks, 10 armored cars, and 225 planes. Only 12,541 Soviet and Mongolian troops were available to defend a forty-six-mile front on the east bank of the Khalkhin-Gol. The Soviets had more armor, with 186 tanks and 226 armored cars, which provided Zhukov an excellent opportunity to test the effectiveness of Soviet tanks and tactics.[11]

Their threefold superiority in manpower induced the Japanese to try to surround and destroy the Soviet-Mongolian forces on the right bank of the Khalkhin-Gol. The plan was to move a strong force around the defenders' left flank, cross the Khalkhin-Gol undetected, seize Mount Bain-Tsagan, and strike from the rear. The offensive began on July 2. The infantry and tanks managed to drive a wedge into the Soviet-Mongolian positions, and their advance was halted only at the river. Unnoticed, Japanese troops began crossing to the left bank of the river on the night of July 3, completing their move by morning. The next objective, Mount Bain-Tsagan, was soon occupied, and the advance continued southward, threatening encirclement of the Soviet-Mongolian forces on the right bank.[12]

Zhukov guessed the enemy plan and decided to launch a three-pronged counterattack in which the Eleventh Tank Brigade would strike the Japanese from the north, the Twenty-fourth Motorized Infantry Regiment from the northwest, and the Seventh Armored Car

Brigade from the south. The Soviet strike was so sudden that the Japanese ranks were thrown into disorder. The effectiveness of the counterattack was confirmed by a Nipponese officer, who noted in his diary: "A terrible confusion broke out; horses began running, dragging behind them the gun carriages; automatic weapons were being carried away everywhere."

Surrounded on three sides, the Japanese took up the defense in a desperate effort to keep possession of Mount Bain-Tsagan. Their counterattack on July 4 was frustrated by Red Army air and artillery units. The same evening Soviet-Mongolian units launched a general attack on the mountain; by the next afternoon Japanese resistance had crumbled. Zhukov hurled his tank forces against the enemy, who pulled out and attempted to retreat across the Khalkhin-Gol. The single pontoon bridge laid by the Japanese had been destroyed by the Soviets, and many Japanese soldiers drowned as they tried to swim to safety.

The Japanese, temporarily stymied, began making new plans. After two and a half months of operations the Soviet command saw no solution in sight save a possible prolonged defensive engagement with insufficient troops and the very real possibility of a final Japanese victory. They had managed to hold the line and inflict losses on the enemy, but the command was none too competent and there was some lack of coordination.[13] Erickson observes:

> The only answer seemed to be the release of troops from the interior and a change of command. The answer, it appeared, was G. Zhukov, the corps commander who was assigned to take over the 1st Army Group with the task of defeating the Japanese. Zhukov could have had no illusions about this assignment; failure was out of the question. To win and win decisively, even spectacularly, would alone suffice. With Zhukov came massive reinforcement. Zhukov, with a style for which he was later to become much distinguished, launched his counter-offensive only when he enjoyed a superiority of 1.5 to 1 in infantry, 1.7 to 1 in machine-guns, almost 2 to 1 in artillery and the same in aviation and a fourfold superiority in tanks. Throughout August preparations went ahead with frenzied energy for the counter-stroke against the Japanese, and by the 18th Zhukov was almost ready,* his operations coinciding with the critical stage to which

---

* Zhukov has described the amount of supplies he required for the operation. Carried over a 400-mile stretch of dirt roads, they included 18,000 tons of artillery shells, 6,500 tons of aviation ammunition, 25,000 tons of miscellaneous fuels and

Soviet negotiations with the Western democracies and the simultaneous sounding out of the Germans had advanced in the summer of 1939.[14]

The change of command, by which all Soviet-Mongolian troops came under Komkor (Corps Commander) Zhukov,[15] and the reinforcement of Soviet forces in the Far Eastern theater were highly significant events. Writes former Red Army officer Ruslanov:

> Zhukov's appointment could not have been made without Stalin's knowledge, and it was not accidental. The significance of the Khalkhin-Gol River battles must not be underestimated. The whole world followed their outcome; the matter involved the international prestige of the U.S.S.R., and, primarily, it was a rare opportunity to test new material and tactics under actual combat conditions. For Stalin, the losses were of no importance whatsoever. Zhukov himself knew that this appointment was to test his competence and one which he had to pass.[16]

By the first of August the Japanese had brought in the Seventh and Twenty-third Infantry Divisions (up to full combat strength), an infantry brigade of the puppet Manchurian state, 3 heavy-artillery regiments, and 3 cavalry regiments. Their Fourteenth Infantry Brigade arrived from Manchuria, and they transferred all the antitank batteries of the First Infantry Division to the Khalkhin-Gol area. They also strengthened their air power and sent in a heavy-artillery unit from the Port Arthur stronghold. Total Japanese forces (including those of their Manchurian allies) amounted to 75,000 soldiers, 304 heavy machine guns, more than 500 crew-served guns, 182 tanks, and 300 to 500 planes. On August 10 the assembled units were combined into the Sixth Japanese Army under command of General Ogisu Rippo. They prepared jump-off positions for a general offensive planned for August 24 along the entire forty-three-mile front of the captured bridgehead.

Zhukov began working out an operational plan which consisted of blows to the enemy's flanks, envelopment on the north and south ends of his defenses, and quick annihilation before reinforcements could be brought up. The situation was complicated by the problem of supply, however, since the railhead was 465 miles from the front. Under Zhukov's leadership, the staff of the First Army Group worked out a coordinated plan to employ tanks, artillery, planes, and infantry in

---

lubricants, 4,000 tons of foodstuffs, and 4,000 tons of other materials. Georgi K. Zhukov, *Vospominaniya i Razmyshleniya*, 160.

mutual support. The mission given to the Soviet-Mongolian troops was simple: prepare and carry out a decisive offensive with the objective of annihilating the Japanese who had violated the frontier. But the troops committed to action were insufficient to execute such an operation. Therefore, new forces were brought up to the Khalkhin-Gol from the deep rear: the Eighty-second and Fifty-seventh Infantry Divisions, a regiment of the 152d Infantry Division, the Sixth Tank and 212th Airborne Brigade, artillery regiments, signal units, and others. The number of aircraft was increased to 515. These reinforcements enabled the Soviet-Mongolian command to achieve a numerical superiority over the Japanese.

Interesting—and typical of Zhukov—are the elaborate deceptive measures he employed:

> In order to delude the enemy about their real plans, the Soviet-Mongolian forces made wide use of false information. False reports concerning construction of defensive works and inquiries regarding engineer equipment were transmitted. A powerful sound-effects set brought to the front imitated the sound of pile driving, creating the perfect impression of considerable defensive works under construction. All troop movements were carried out only at night. The noise of tanks massing on departure positions for the attack was drowned out by night bomber raids and by small-arms fire. For ten to twelve days before the attack several tanks with mufflers removed constantly drove back and forth along the front. This was done so that the Japanese, having grown accustomed to the sound of our vehicles as an everyday occurrence, would be absolutely disoriented at the moment of the Soviet-Mongolian attack. With this objective, systematic daylight and night sorties were carried out by our aviation.[17]

Zhukov's efforts even included the unusual and ingenious idea of distributing to his troops the handbook *What the Soviet Soldier Must Know in the Defense*. He kept working parties toiling on defensive positions. Trucks were stripped of their mufflers to mask tank movements. Pilots flew special reconnaissance missions to study the terrain, while night patrols were sent out to spot enemy positions. To help supervise operations and maintain contact, Zhukov attached 12 liaison officers to his staff. By the time he was ready to launch his attack, he had quietly moved in 35 infantry battalions and 20 cavalry squadrons; his 498 tanks included some late models which were forerunners of the T-34.[18]

To implement his plan of envelopment, Zhukov created three groups: Southern, Northern, and Central. The Southern Group included the Fifty-seventh Infantry Division, the Sixth Tank Brigade, the Eighth Mongolian Cavalry Division, the Eighth Motorized Armor Brigade, two tank battalions of the Eleventh Tank Brigade, a battalion of self-propelled weapons, the Thirty-seventh Antitank Battalion, and a company of flame-throwing tanks. The Northern Group consisted of the Eleventh Tank and Seventh Motorized Armor brigades, the 601st Infantry Regiment of the Thirty-sixth Infantry Division, the Sixth Mongolian Cavalry Division, and the Eighty-seventh Antitank Battalion. The Central Group included the Thirty-sixth and Eighty-second Infantry divisions, the Fifth Infantry Machinegun Brigade, and two artillery regiments. His reserve consisted of the Ninth Motorized Armor and 212th Airborne brigades.

Zhukov anticipated the Japanese offensive planned for August 24 by four days, launching his own on August 20. At 5:45 A.M., 150 bombers carried out a massive raid on the forward edge of the Japanese defenses, their close-in reserves, and their artillery positions. Then Zhukov ordered his soldiers into the assault along the entire front. The diary of a Japanese soldier testified to the nightmarish onslaught: "A dark cloud of shells fell in front and behind us. It became terrible. An observation team used everything to find the enemy's artillery, but it was unsuccessful, as bombers were dropping their bombs and fighters were strafing our forces. The enemy was triumphant along the whole front."

It may have been in this push that Zhukov's leadership abilities were witnessed by one observer who later described what he had seen to Ruslanov:

> Zhukov ordered one of his divisions to attack the Japanese fortifications. The outcome of the entire operation depended on the success of this assault. The division was beaten off with heavy losses and found itself pinned to the ground. The commander reported by telephone and requested new orders. Zhukov ordered him to attack again. A short time later, Zhukov himself summoned the division commander to the telephone. Upon finding that he had not yet managed to start the division moving, Zhukov asked: "Will you be able to start the attack?" The division commander cautiously expressed doubt. Then Zhukov said: "I hereby relieve you of command of the division. Hand the receiver over to your Chief of Staff." Zhukov put the same question to the latter. The Chief of Staff answered in the affirmative.

Zhukov: "I hereby appoint you division commander." But the Chief of Staff did not succeed in launching a new attack either. When he reported this fact to Zhukov, he received the same order: "I relieve you of command of the division. Wait for the arrival of a new division commander." Zhukov sent a new commander from his own staff, reinforced the unit with artillery, and gave it air support. At the price of tremendous losses, the attack succeeded. Other phases of the plan for the offensive which he had developed were also successful.[19]

This story was to be told again and again throughout World War II. As Stalin's troubleshooter, Zhukov was sent from one crisis to another, and he soon achieved a reputation as a peremptory commander who had little patience with slow-moving, hesitant, or dull subordinates. In those dangerous times he could not afford the luxury of being a gladhander or backslapper. As will be seen, P. I. Batov, P. A. Belov, and a number of other comrades in arms would later record that Zhukov was severe in his dealings with them.

Another Zhukov trait began to manifest itself. He proved calm under strong pressure, exhibiting at the same time a complete grasp of the situation. War correspondent Richard E. Lauterbach's description of Zhukov's behavior during one phase of the Khalkhin-Gol campaign is typical:

> On the blue-green hill called Khamardaba, nestled among the Mongolian steppes, was a thick-walled blockhouse deeply settled in the ground. Inside a group of Soviet war correspondents were relaxing around an old iron stove. Into this informal gathering strode a thick-set, barrel-chested man with a large round head. The correspondents greeted him respectfully as "Tovarishch General." Tovarishch General had just come from his early morning *banya* [bath] and his full cheeks were pink and glowing. His mood was extraordinarily good. As he dressed he chatted with correspondents. Suddenly two Red Army scouts rushed breathlessly into the room. With heavy apprehension they reported the Japanese massing large units, obviously preparatory to striking a potent counterattack. The correspondents braced themselves, expecting a galvanized Tovarishch General and curt, clear orders. But the general received the news with ironclad calmness. Drawing on his military blouse he coolly informed the scouts that such a counterattack was entirely impossible, that the Japs were in no position to deliver an effective offensive blow.
>
> His words changed the atmosphere in the blockhouse immediately. The scouts wondered how they could have been deceived by their own eyes

and the correspondents wondered how they could have been deceived by their own ears. Everyone felt completely secure. Tovarishch General had spoken and he was never wrong.[20]

On the first day of attack the Southern Group achieved the greatest success. By August 20 the Northern Group had occupied the forward enemy positions, reaching the strongly fortified top of Palets (Fui) Heights, but the Soviet forces were beaten back after a fierce fight.

Exploiting their first-day success, the Soviet-Mongolian forces continued a stubborn battle inside the Japanese defensive lines. In the Southern Group's sector the Sixth Tank and Eighth Motorized Armor brigades enveloped the enemy flank and by August 21 had occupied the area in the rear of the Japanese forces active south of the Khailastyn-Gol River (a branch of the Khalkhin-Gol). Infantry units of the Southern Group drove a deep wedge into the enemy's main defensive zone on August 21, destroyed his close-in tactical reserves, and captured several artillery positions. Every firing point had to be taken by storm, requiring in some cases the use of flame-throwing tanks. Soviet aircraft were particularly active in their support of the ground forces; on one day alone, August 21, the bombers made 256 sorties and dropped more than 90 tons of bombs.

On August 23 the Northern Group, reinforced by the 212th Airborne Brigade, was able to break the enemy's resistance and seize the Palets Heights. In fierce hand-to-hand combat six hundred Japanese soldiers were killed, their bodies scattered about the trenches and dugouts.

Only three days were required to carry out Zhukov's encirclement plan. On August 23 the reduction of the entrapped Japanese forces began. A relief attempt on August 26 was repulsed, primarily by the Sixth Tank Brigade. A breakout attempt on August 27 was also frustrated. Aviation units were successful in interdicting the movement of fresh reserves into the combat area. As many as 218 sorties were made in two days alone (August 24 and 25), resulting in ten encounters and the destruction of 74 Japanese planes.

Simple containment of the encircled Japanese would surely have led to their ultimate surrender. So impetuous was Zhukov's nature, however, that no such passive measures were permitted; a series of attacks would systematically reduce the enemy. The Southern Group was entrusted with the major offensive action. Its attacks on August 27 were successful in capturing Peschanaya Heights and Zelenaya Hill, thus clearing the left bank of the Khailastyn-Gol. Simultaneous assaults were made on Remizov Heights from the rear and both sides, but not until August 31 was that area finally occupied.

In the final stage of the offensive another aspect of Zhukov's resourceful tactical capabilities emerged. The shallow but muddy Khailastyn-Gol had been expected to protect the southern flank of Remizov Heights. To the dismay of the Japanese, however, Zhukov had ordered his engineers to strengthen the riverbed by night, which permitted the Soviet tank forces to attack from this direction also. One night Soviet forces suddenly crossed the river, smashed the Japanese defenses, and methodically began cleaning out pockets of resistance.[21] By the morning of August 31 the territory of the Mongolian People's Republic had been cleared of the Japanese invaders.

Any assessment of the total operations in this area from May to September must acknowledge Zhukov as the prime mover in the striking and decisive Soviet victory. He had shown himself a commander rigid in seeing to the execution of his orders by subordinates but able to temper his rigidity with tactical flexibility when he was convinced it would achieve his goals. This ability is reflected in his tactically superior concentration of forces, his bold and successful encirclement plan, his aggressive but resourceful reduction of the encircled enemy, his coordination of combined-arms forces, correct combination of modern arms, and ad hoc offensive measures—the result of which was a total Soviet victory. Forceful evidence of Zhukov's effectiveness as a commander—if Soviet sources are to be trusted in this respect—can be obtained by comparing casualties. Soviet losses were 10,000 killed and wounded throughout the campaign, while the Japanese lost 52,000 to 55,000 men.[22]

In Moscow on September 15, 1939, the Soviet Union, the Mongolian People's Republic, and Japan signed an agreement calling for all combat actions at the Khalkhin-Gol to cease by September 16. The two sides agreed to exchange prisoners of war, and a commission was created to define the borders of the Mongolian People's Republic and Manchuria in the area of the Khalkhin-Gol. Japanese authorities appeared to have learned a painful lesson, and both sides took steps to preserve the peace. In April, 1941, a Soviet-Japanese nonaggression pact (which Joachim von Ribbentrop tried to undermine) was signed, and the two nations refrained from attacking each other until the Soviet Union broke the agreement in 1945.

With the defeat of the Japanese forces the Soviets began to boast of the emergence of a new type of army which successfully employed the combined actions of infantry, artillery, armor, and aviation. The Japanese were forced to admit that "up to now, we did not know to what extent the Soviet Union had outfitted its motorized units" and that this surprising development had badly shaken them.[23] In particular, the campaign had proved to the Japanese that most of the Soviet ground forces, especially artillery and armor, were far superior to the Japanese army in terms of firepower and mechanization. The logistical aspect was also striking. The Japanese were greatly surprised by the Soviet capability of transporting and storing war matériel at a battlefront about 400 miles from a railway terminal.[24] "Having rid itself of the inflexibility which characterized the old Czarist forces, the Soviet Army proved able to change tactics from battle to battle."[25] Another surprise was the Soviets' facility at improvisation. For example, in the early battles Russian tanks had been easily set afire by gasoline-filled bottles hurled grenade-fashion by Japanese troops. Shortly thereafter the Soviets began using diesel fuel and covering their tanks with wire nets, two measures which made them less vulnerable to incendiaries. Nor had the Russian army lost any of the qualities for which it had been traditionally renowned, particularly as regards its sturdiness: "The Soviet Army was more tenacious than had been expected."[26]

Despite Zhukov's successes with armor, the Soviets discovered that the T-26 BT and T-28 tanks had certain shortcomings and defects. The product of subsequent Soviet research and development was a new family of armored vehicles, including the outstanding tank of World War II, the T-34.

Zhukov had passed the severe test of Khalkhin-Gol, his troops had demonstrated that they were tougher than anticipated, and theories and equipment had been put to hard, practical use in actual combat. Zhukov returned to Moscow to find himself heaped with accolades. He was personally congratulated by a grateful Stalin and awarded the title Hero of the Soviet Union. N. Svetlishin writes:

> In this first great combat operation, carried out by G. K. Zhukov, his leadership capabilities were displayed—his ability to organize and in a

short time to carry out a complete defeat of a powerful enemy. The Soviet government with pride praised the work of Zhukov. In June 1940, by a decree of the Council of the People's Commissars of the U.S.S.R., he was promoted ahead of time to the rank of General of the Army. Soon he was assigned command of the Kiev Special Military District, one of the most powerful in our country.[27]

One great disappointment greeted Zhukov upon his return from the Far East. He had long been convinced that tanks could play an independent role on the battlefield. Operating in conjunction with artillery and motorized infantry, they were capable of deep-thrust actions which could knock an enemy off balance and tear through his defenses. In the Khalkhin-Gol region Zhukov had not allowed his armor to take part in separate battles for isolated strongpoints, but his tanks, supported by air strikes, made comparatively deep penetrations of the Japanese defensive positions. When he returned to Moscow, he found that the Red Army command was disbanding the seven mechanized corps and that the tanks were being distributed to separate rifle battalions as support weapons.

The move was made, over the protests of Zhukov and Shaposhnikov, because armor expert Pavlov, on the basis of the dismal performance of Soviet tanks in Spain, had persuaded Stalin and Defense Commissar Voroshilov that the tank could not play an independent role on the modern battlefield.[28] Only after the German panzer units had given an impressive performance in the west, proving that armor was capable of operating independently, were Zhukov and Shaposhnikov vindicated. But by that time Soviet military planners were under intense pressure, requiring an almost frantic effort to reestablish the large tank groups, with little time for solving training problems and equipping the new formations.[29]

V. BEFORE THE STORM

Virtuous motives, trammelled by inertia and timidity, are no match for armed and resolute wickedness. A sincere love of peace is no excuse for muddling hundreds of millions of humble folk into total war. The cheers of weak, well-meaning assemblies soon cease to echo, and their votes soon cease to count. Doom marches on.

Winston S. Churchill, The Gathering Storm

BY the time Zhukov returned to Moscow from his successful encounters with the Japanese, events in Europe had reached crisis proportions. In February, 1938, Hitler warned Austrian Chancellor Kurt von Schuschnigg: "Don't believe that anyone in the world will hinder me in my decision! . . . England will not lift a finger for Austria.

... And France? ... For France it is too late."[1] A month later Hitler's war machine "lumbered falteringly over the frontier"[2] and, after some embarrassing breakdowns of armor, took possession of Vienna. Hitler declared the Austrian Republic dissolved and its territory part of the German Reich.[3] On March 15, 1939, the Germans, confident that the French and British would not intervene, invaded "post-Munich" Czechoslovakia, completing the dismemberment of that young nation. As Hitler looked menacingly toward the east, the British government on March 31 announced its guarantee to Poland: "In the event of any action which clearly threatened Polish independence and which the Polish Government accordingly considered it vital to resist with their national forces, His Majesty's Government would feel themselves bound at once to lend the Polish Government all support in their power."[4] Events moved rapidly, and in a speech on April 27, Hitler denounced the Anglo-German naval agreement and the nonaggression pact with Poland (at the same time carefully avoiding any attacks on the Soviet Union). A week later Commissar of Foreign Affairs Maxim Litvinov, a Jew who had been verbally abused by the Germans for years, was replaced by V. M. Molotov in a move fully appreciated by the German dictator. Hitler would later declare to his generals: "Litvinov's dismissal was decisive. It came to me like a cannon shot, like a sign that the attitude of Moscow towards the Western Powers had changed."[5]

Germany and the Soviet Union were looking for something to bring the two powers together. German Foreign Minister Joachim von Ribbentrop recorded in his memoirs that an agreement with the Soviet Union was his very own idea, which he urged on Hitler to create a counterweight to the West and to ensure Russian neutrality in the event of a German-Polish conflict. When Stalin made his now-famous statement that the Soviet Union did not intend to "pull the chestnuts out of the fire" for certain Western powers, Ribbentrop showed a copy of it to Hitler and urged the Führer to authorize him to find out whether Stalin was serious about improved relations between the two countries. After some hesitation Hitler allowed Ribbentrop to draft a nonaggression pact between Germany and Russia.

Hitler insisted that Ribbentrop fly to Moscow to represent the German government in the negotiations. Arriving on the afternoon of August 23, the foreign minister was soon brought into the presence of Stalin and Molotov. According to Ribbentrop, in a short speech Stalin said that "although we have poured buckets of watery dung over each other for years, there is no reason why we should not get along." Stalin said that when making his speech last February "he had indeed intended to convey his desire to come to an understanding with Germany."[6] Before midnight the Germans and Soviets had worked out a nonaggression pact which stated that neither signatory would commit aggression against the other, either alone or with other powers. Article 2 provided for neutrality in the event of an attack on either signatory by a third power. The two signatories were obliged not to take part in any grouping of powers which might be aimed, directly or indirectly, at the other signatory.[7] In the "Secret Additional Protocol" the Germans and Soviets divided Eastern Europe into spheres of influence. In Poland these spheres were to be bounded by the line of the Narew, Vistula, and San rivers. The Soviets expressed an interest in laying claim to Bessarabia.[8]

Almost eight days to the hour after the signing of the pact, the German armies attacked Poland. By mid-September they had already swept into large sections of the territory allotted to the Soviet sphere of influence, and the Soviet leaders were obliged to move more hastily than they had anticipated to protect their interests. On September 17, therefore, Soviet troops crossed the Polish border; the action was portrayed as the fulfillment of a "sacred duty" to take under Soviet protection the "kindred Ukrainians and Belorussians" of the region.

These events in Europe occurred almost simultaneously with Zhukov's victory on the Mongolian frontier. Upon his return from the Khalkhin-Gol campaign he became deputy commander of the Ukrainian Military District. The infamous twelve-day operation "liberating" more than twelve million people occupying 190,000 square miles of territory was carried out by the Belorussian *Front* under Army Commander Second Rank M. P. Kovalev and the Ukrainian *Front* under Army Commander First Rank S. K. Timoshenko. It seems almost certain that Zhukov could not have assumed his new duties in time to participate effectively in this brief campaign, the "fourth partition" of Poland.

Zhukov's experiences in the Far East were undoubtedly reflected in the new field regulations prepared by Red Army leaders toward the end of 1939. The regulations were based on the premise that coordination of the actions of all branches of service was the principal condition for success in combat. Only in this way could the enemy be defeated throughout the depth of his defenses. The importance of resupply and rear services was emphasized, as were careful planning of operations, uninterrupted control of troops, and the need for surprise. Since many commanders appeared ignorant of the proper use of reserves, of the principles of echelonment, and of organization for combat, the new regulations covered these topics. The frontages of divisions in the attack were modified slightly, decreasing the average width of a reinforced division in offensive operations to 3,300 yards. The frontage of an attacking infantry battalion in the first echelon was set at about 450 to 650 yards (down from the approximately 650 to 1,100 yards specified in the 1936 regulations). Examining the Far East fighting, the study group emphasized the need for an effective number of artillery pieces per mile of front; excluding long-range weapons, this number was raised from 30–35 to 35–60. Although considerable thought went into the project, the 1939 regulations were never published; military events in Europe overtook them and made completely new studies necessary. Work was resumed after the Russo-Finnish War under the supervision of Marshal Budenny (assisted by N. F. Vatutin, N. N. Voronov, and L. A. Govorov), but the project was again postponed, this time by the outbreak of World War II.

In April, 1938, the Soviet Union had begun pressuring Finland to allow the U.S.S.R. to fortify the Finnish island of Suursaar. In October, 1939, discussions were reopened, the Soviet representatives claiming that war in Europe demanded that no enemy have access to the Gulf of Finland. To protect Leningrad, the border must be moved. Finland rejected the Soviets' demands, and negotiations broke off. At that point Molotov warned: "We civilians can see no further in the matter; now it is the turn of the military to have their say." After a bitter anti-Finnish propaganda campaign and accusations that the Finns had fired several artillery rounds at Soviet forces, the Red Army invaded Finland on November 30.[9]

In the early weeks of the struggle the Finns inflicted heavy casualties, and General K. A. Meretskov's offensive faltered. Soviet histories conveniently omit references to the slaughter which befell the Red invaders. The failure to win a speedy victory in Finland pointed up serious problems in the Soviet military establishment; the cooperation among tanks, artillery, and infantry which had been decisive at Khalkhin-Gol was conspicuously absent.[10] By December 28, however, the Soviet armies had been reorganized and new directives issued. Finally, in early February,

1940, the Russian offensive began to take shape, and on February 11 the Soviets shattered segments of the Mannerheim Line. The Finnish defenses gradually gave way, and on March 12 the gallant but exhausted Finns gave up. Zhukov served briefly as chief of the General Staff in the final stages of the war, temporarily relieving the ailing Shaposhnikov.[11]

After the "Winter War," in which 1,200,000 Red Army troops were involved, steps were taken to correct the many shortcomings which had become evident during the campaign. Following Voroshilov's report to the Party's Central Committee, it was decided that a meeting of the Main Military Council should be convened in the Kremlin. It would include the top military echelons, division commanders and higher-ranking officers who had participated in the war, and representatives from the military districts and academies.

The session, held from April 14 to 17, 1940, produced a number of findings. The infantry had demonstrated that it knew little about war matériel and how to use it properly under cold-weather conditions. More automatic weapons and mortars were needed, and better communication, especially radio equipment, was essential. Troop organization had also been unsatisfactory: rifle divisions were unwieldy, and rear services were difficult to direct. The infantry was at first unable to fight on skis, and only after the war was under way were special ski battalions, engineer units, and horse-drawn-sleigh medical and transportation detachments formed. The Finnish experience had also revealed the need for better winter clothing, vehicle heaters, and bunker stoves. The motor transport service had proved to be poorly organized; spare parts were not available. Road-construction units were in short supply, and traffic-direction services were lacking.

One of the unpardonable errors was the command's failure to find out about the peculiarities of the Karelo-Finnish terrain and weather and the organization, armament, training, and equipment of the Finnish army. Red Army officers had only a very general idea of the location and fortification of the Mannerheim Line, and they lacked experience in assaulting reinforced concrete installations. The lessons learned at Lake Khasan and Khalkhin-Gol and in Poland had not been passed down to the troops. Infantry instruction had been poor. Rifle squads and platoons had not been taught the fundamentals of combat in trenches and forests, the tactics of encirclement, the essentials of reconnaissance and camouflage.

It was concluded that victory in Finland had imposed excessive sacrifices which could have been avoided and that a radical improvement in the armament, organization, training, and instruction of Soviet troops was necessary. Stalin spoke to the gathering on the final day of the meeting and exhorted the participants to study modern warfare and exhibit flexibility and adaptability.

The Main Military Council charged the directorates of the People's Commissariat of Defense with developing new weapons and combat equipment to replace the worn-out matériel. In particular the council asked for better aircraft, tanks, and signal equipment. It also passed a resolution providing for significant changes in training, troop control, and organization. A table of organization and equipment (TO&E) was drawn up for rifle, armor, artillery, and special units.

Another council resolution restored the old ranks of general and admiral, and Zhukov, Meretskov, and I. V. Tyulenev were named full generals. Timoshenko was appointed marshal and given Voroshilov's post as defense commissar. Voroshilov, in turn, was "promoted" to head the Defense Committee within the Council of People's Commissars.

Along with his promotion Zhukov was given command of the heavily manned Kiev Special Military District, one of the most important commands in the Red Army. Khrushchev, who at this time was first secretary of the Ukrainian Communist Party, later commented that "Zhukov was more than satisfactory as Timoshenko's replacement. He was a talented organizer and a strong leader. He was to prove his mettle in the war. Unfortunately, men like Timoshenko and Zhukov were exceptions. After the annihilation of the Old Guard, men like [L. Z.] Mekhlis, [E. A.] Shchadenko and [G. I.] Kulik came in, and the Commissariat of Defense became like a kennel of mad dogs. Mekhlis was one of the worst."[12]

Lauterbach reported that

during his stay in Kiev Zhukov demonstrated a remarkable ability for administrative work. He spent much of his energy drawing up plans for Red Army reform based on the experience gained in the Japanese and Finnish campaigns. Here for the first time he emerged not only as a military executive but as a political leader. His directives were those of a man with complete confidence in himself, and the knowledge that his superiors had given him carte blanche. Ukrainian party leaders looked to him for leadership, and he gave it.[13]

Zhukov became audacious in his speeches. He attacked the system of political commissars in the services, warning that military successes come about as a result of strenuous work by Red Army commanders as well as by political workers. It is only in the light of his enhanced status and demonstrated abilities that Zhukov's increasing boldness can be understood. Certainly he would not have dared attack the system of political commissars in the military if he had held a less secure position. Perhaps Stalin allowed his loyal chieftain to play the role of devil's advocate in this and other matters. At any rate, the *yedinonachalie* theme was resumed, with Zhukov as one of its leading and most outspoken proponents.

Zhukov charged that many of the senior commanders had failed to train the younger officers properly. He urged a closer study of military history and traditions of the Russian army and people. Finally, he warned that the complicated international situation might change at any time and cautioned against a possible "trick" in the complex international scene. His audience knew that he had the Germans in mind. Realizing that the Soviet Union must try to gain time through a non-aggression pact, Zhukov nevertheless always privately anticipated war with the Germans.[14] He favored keeping Red Army troops in western Russia fully mobilized so that they would not be caught unprepared by an enemy.

In June, 1940, Stalin decided to incorporate the Baltic States into the Soviet Union. At the same time he presented an ultimatum to Rumania, forcing her to cede to the U.S.S.R. the province of Bessarabia, as well as northern Bucovina, about which nothing had been said in the agreement with Germany. On June 28, Soviet troops under Zhukov's command moved into Bessarabia and northern Bucovina in two echelons. In the first were mobile units—tank and cavalry troops—and the second was composed of infantry divisions. Although the Rumanian troops had been ordered to make an orderly withdrawal, many threw down their weapons. On June 30, Red Army troops arrived on the banks of the Prut River, and soon Bessarabia and northern Bucovina were in Soviet hands. Zhukov set up his headquarters at Chernovitz. Later in the summer Zhukov, still commanding the Kiev Special Military District, was given his reward: he was elected a delegate to the Supreme Soviet of the U.S.S.R., serving as district representative.

In December, 1940, and early January, 1941, the High Command held an important conference in Moscow, followed by war games executed on maps. According to Marshal Yeremenko, the meeting played "an extremely important role in raising the level of training of the senior command personnel of the Red Army in the field of tactics, operational science, strategy, offensive and defensive actions of all branches of service."[15] The meeting drew the attention of Stalin and the entire defense establishment.

The first order of business was a review of all the military and political preparations of 1940 and the organization of tasks for the current year. At one of the first sessions General K. A. Meretskov, chief of the General Staff, gave a report on a number of problems affecting combat training, noting in particular the maneuvering capability of the infantry. In his discussion of defensive capabilities, he lamented the fact that Soviet command personnel still had not demonstrated an ability to evaluate a combat situation and organize battlefield intelligence. He had special praise for the artillery units of Zhukov's Kiev Special Military District. In the discussions which followed, many valuable proposals for enhancing the training of the Red Army were advanced, with twenty-eight generals offering suggestions.

The second part of the conference was devoted to examining theoretical questions of military art. Five timely reports were delivered, including Zhukov's "Character of the Modern Offensive Operation." Zhukov's report—especially his comments on the massive use of mobile troops—generated much useful discussion. The High Command personnel had no serious differences of opinion with Zhukov's findings; they were concerned about the details of such operations, such as the composition of groups for developing a breakthrough and the formation of their combat order, the width of the zone and times for committing motorized troops in the breach, the organization and coordination of motorized troops with aviation, and their control and logistic support during independent actions by mechanized units in the enemy's operational depth. Thus the conference, having accepted Zhukov's broad theories on mobile warfare, occupied itself with working out the details of such combat.

After the meeting, which ended on January 11, 1941, another two-sided strategic war game was carried out with the defense commissar in charge, and Zhukov was invited to participate. The basic purposes of the exercise were to assist participants in mastering the principles of strategic operations, to determine the probable theaters of military operations, to give the senior command personnel practice in evaluating various situations and making decisions under complicated conditions, and to achieve unity of views on the conduct of modern offensive operations with massive use of artillery, large tank units, and air power.[16]

One of the participants, M. I. Kazakov, recalled in his memoirs that there were actually two games, one played in a western, the other in a southwestern direction. In the first, the Western *Front*, or Eastern side, was led by the commanders of the Western Special Military District, D. G. Pavlov and V. E. Klimovsky. The opposing forces were led by Zhukov and Colonel General F. I. Kuznetsov, commander of the Baltic Special Military District. In the second game the officers changed places, with Zhukov commanding the Southwestern *Front* of the Easterners and Pavlov leading the Western *Front*. Both sides put considerable thought into deep penetrations by the attacking forces in order to defeat large enemy groupings. Several problems were revealed during the course of the exercise, including the failure of both sides to provide for sufficient forces in their second echelons and reserves. An advantage in forces in the direction of the main strike was achieved at the cost of weakening less active sectors of the *front*.

At the conclusion of the games "something unusual" (to use General Kazakov's phrase) occurred: "The critique was carried out for some reason not by the Defense Commissar [Timoshenko] or the General Staff, but by the participants themselves, by G. K. Zhukov and D. G. Pavlov." Immediately afterward the military district commanders prepared to leave Moscow, but suddenly, on January 13, all were summoned to the Kremlin.[17] There a second critique was held, with members of the Central Committee Politburo and the Soviet government in attendance. Among the military representatives were the defense commissar, the chief of the General Staff, deputy defense commissars, commanders of the various branches of service, and commanders of the military districts. Meretskov presented the report.

Much importance was attached to the meeting—its location attested to that fact—and all the participants were extremely interested in the defensive measures which would be adopted as a result of the war games. Unfortunately, Kazakov recalls, Meretskov's report was incoherent and disconnected, one reason being that Stalin had unexpectedly changed the time and place of the session and materials had not been completely worked up. Meretskov attempted to give his report from memory, and on several occasions he strayed from the facts in his conclusions and recommendations. His interpretation of the draft field regulations also evoked criticism. For example, he said that, in preparing the field regulations,

> we proceeded from the fact that our division was considerably stronger than a division of the German-Fascist army and that in a meeting engagement it undoubtedly would defeat the German division. Also in the defense one of our divisions will repel the blow of two to three enemy divisions. In the offensive one and a half of our divisions will overcome the defenses of an enemy division.

Everyone became quite uncomfortable when Meretskov began describing the first of the two war games just concluded, especially when the Eastern side, with sixty to sixty-five divisions, successfully broke the defenses of the Western side and its fifty-five divisions. Stalin asked the obvious question: "How was this achieved with such a small advantage in forces?"

Meretskov's answer was not what Stalin wanted to hear: the commander of the Eastern forces pulled troops from "passive" sectors of the front to give himself a "local" advantage of forces.

Stalin quickly retorted: "In our age of mechanized and motorized armies a 'local' advantage in forces will not ensure success for the attacking side; a defending enemy, having the same means of maneuver at his disposal, in a short time can effect a regrouping of his forces, reinforcing them in the threatened sector, and in such a way negating a 'local' advantage created by the attacker."

When Meretskov began to describe the second war game, he was asked by a sarcastic Stalin: "Well, who won this one? Is it possible the 'Reds' [won] again?"

Meretskov tried to avoid a direct answer, feebly commenting that in war games clear victory does not occur, that the umpires simply evaluate the actions of the sides as correct or in error. "The maneuver," recalls Kazakov, "did not work." He was told that "the members of the Politburo present at the conference still want to know which of the participants of the game was the victor." Meretskov could not give a satisfactory answer.

At the end of the report Stalin spoke. His words were direct and to the point:

Possibly, in the propaganda of the regulations it should be written that our division in a meeting engagement is able to defeat a division of German-Fascist troops, and in the offensive one and a half divisions can penetrate the defense of one of their entire divisions, but in the circle of persons in attendance here, in the company of future *front* and army commanders, it is necessary to speak of realistic capabilities.

Another painfully embarrassing episode followed when G. I. Kulik, a deputy defense commissar, addressed the meeting and pleaded for an eighteen-thousand man division with horse transport. In the question-and-answer session he revealed his ignorance of the weapons and equipment of modern-day warfare. Stalin sharply criticized him and suggested to Timoshenko that, "while there is such confusion in viewpoints on motorization and mechanization, you will have no motorization and mechanization. Modern warfare will be a war of motors: on the land, in the air, on the water and under the water."

Kazakov writes that Stalin's criticism of the leadership of the Defense Commissariat was convincing, but, "like a boomerang, it also inflicted a blow on him." Stalin had participated in the decision of November 21, 1939, to break up the tank corps.[18]

After reports by Zhukov, Pavlov, and others the meeting ended, leaving the participants with mixed emotions: satisfaction about the prospects of further mechanization of the Red Army and embarrassment caused about the report of the General Staff.

On the evening of the day the conference ended, a number of new assignments were made by the Soviet leaders. Zhukov became chief of the General Staff, and Lieutenant General M. P. Kirponos took his place in the Kiev Special Military District. Lieutenant General M. M. Popov became commander of the Leningrad Military District, and Lieutenant General I. S. Konev took charge of the North Caucasus Military District. Meretskov was transferred to the Directorate of Combat Training, obviously as punishment for his poor performance before Stalin and the Politburo. With his appointment as chief of the General Staff, Zhukov received yet another honor. In February, 1941, he was elected an alternate member of the Central Committee of the Communist Party. Meanwhile, the international situation had grown more complex, and Zhukov immediately set about to speed up the reorganization of the army apparatus which had been begun by Stalin and Timoshenko, weeding out incompetent officers, attacking the bureaucracy he found, and generally improving the military system.

By a March 8, 1941, decision of the Central Committee, the distribution of responsibilities in the People's Defense Commissariat was more precisely defined. Leadership of the Red Army was carried out by the people's defense commissar (Timoshenko) through the General Staff (Zhukov) and a system of main and central directorates. Zhukov was named a deputy defense commissar, and he not only headed the General Staff but also supervised the Directorates of Communications, Fuel Supply, and Air Defense, as well as the General Staff Academy. Additionally, the two deputy defense commissars, Zhukov and Budenny, were permitted to go directly to the government with problems concerning the defense establishment.

In the previous month, on February 23, the Red Army's twenty-third anniversary, Zhukov had written the lead article in *Pravda*. There he had discussed the army's progress. "Personnel, armaments, military thought—these are the three cardinal principles of an army," he wrote, adding that the Red Army was now rapidly absorbing these principles. Concerning Khalkhin-Gol, Zhukov claimed that the Soviet forces had undergone "serious and prolonged trial" there. The Finnish campaign, he said, had been an "acid test" and the cracking of the Mannerheim Line "is the only instance to date of a breach being driven through modern permanent fortifications." All was not praise, however, and Zhukov mentioned certain shortcomings:

> But we would not be Bolsheviks if we allowed the glamor of victory to blind us to shortcomings that have been revealed in the training of our men. These shortcomings were the result of conventionalism and routine that have pervaded methods of training. They manifested themselves in the first period of the war and naturally had a negative effect on operations.[19]

Noting that in August, 1940, the officers' "single command" had been restored, Zhukov continued to stress the need for one-man command without constant interference from the political commissar. He sought an extension of rights and authority of commanders and the further strengthening of military discipline. He attached tremendous significance to proper relationships between officers and men, emphasizing that mutual confidence and respect were all-important. And he warned:

"An imperialist war is raging round us. In the reconstruction of our system of military training we have achieved some unquestionable successes. Training is taking place in near-combat conditions, and we have improved the tactical skill of our troops; but it would be a grave error to be smug and complacent about it; much still remains to be done."[20]

In the meantime, Hitler had become increasingly disenchanted with Stalin. Although Molotov had mentioned the Soviet Union's designs on Bessarabia in his August, 1939, arrangement with Ribbentrop, he had not mentioned that they also intended to occupy Bucovina. To the Germans both actions presaged an attempt by the Soviets to crush Rumanian independence. Although the annexations threatened to disrupt ties between Rumania and Germany, Berlin advised the Rumanian government not to resist the Kremlin's demands. But Hitler was unhappy about this turn of events, and relations between Germany and the U.S.S.R. were strained.

In November, 1940, Molotov led a delegation to Berlin, the first visit to Nazi Germany by a Soviet statesman. Stalin, overestimating the strength of his position and misled by the interest Ribbentrop had shown in trying to bind the Soviet Union to the Axis cause, had instructed Molotov to determine how the Germans wanted to divide the world. Additionally, Molotov was to demand from the Germans considerable concessions in Eastern Europe and the Balkans. Although Hitler proposed the area south of the Caspian Sea—Persia, Afghanistan, and India—as a natural field for Soviet expansion, Molotov showed little interest in that territory and made fresh demands, which served only to irk the Germans. Russia, he said, wanted a cessation of all German military activity in Finland, the recognition of Soviet interests in the Balkans and Soviet bases on the Bosporus and Dardanelles, and Soviet military control of Bulgaria and the entire area of the Baltic Straits.[21]

Valentin Berezhkov, one of the two interpreters who accompanied the Soviet delegation to Berlin, described the visit in *Novy Mir*. Molotov, he wrote, asked Hitler why a German military mission had been sent to Rumania and why the Soviet government had not been consulted (the 1939 pact provided for consultation on important questions touching the interests of both parties). And why were German forces in Finland? These remarks, Berezhkov says, fell on the Führer "like a cold shower. He even seemed to shrivel, and, for a moment, confusion could be seen in his face." He recovered and said that the mission had been sent to Rumania, at the request of Ion Antonescu's government, to train Rumanian troops. As for Finland, German forces were not planning to stay there but were on their way to Norway. Molotov retorted that there were too many German units in Rumania for the mission and that the Germans in Finland were moving no farther and were evidently preparing for a long stay.

The next day Molotov continued to pursue the Finnish question, and the talks grew more heated. His insistence on returning to questions which Hitler considered resolved exasperated the Führer, and when the German-Italian guarantees were brought up, Hitler at last lost control and began shouting. Later, when discussions were resumed (in the safety of Ribbentrop's bunker while an air raid was in progress), the Soviet delegate again asked when an explanation might be expected about the purpose behind the presence of German troops in Rumania and Finland. Without hiding his irritation, Ribbentrop replied that if the Soviet Union continued to be interested in these "unessential questions" it should discuss them through the usual diplomatic channels. The next day the Russians left Berlin, and Ribbentrop was the only high-ranking official at the station platform to see them off.[22]

Two weeks later, on November 26, 1940, the Soviet government reiterated its demands in a diplomatic note to Berlin. Hitler considered the demands proof that the Soviets had decided to push their own objectives and resist those of the Germans. The note was not answered. Instead, a few weeks later, on December 18, 1940, an infuriated Hitler issued the order known by the code name "Operation Barbarossa." It began: "The German armed forces must be prepared . . . to crush Soviet Russia in a swift campaign."[23]

Actually, Hitler's decision to attack the Soviet Union had been made months earlier, and Soviet recalcitrance in the fall of 1940 merely served to convince him that he must proceed with his plans. According to Ribbentrop, since 1938, Hitler had feared that Britain and the United States would go to war against Germany and that if Russia joined them in an alliance Germany would have the nightmarish task of fighting on two fronts. The Führer had therefore decided to attack the Soviet Union, firmly believing that he could dispose of the Russian threat in a few months. Nevertheless, he was apprehensive, and his fears were recorded by his foreign minister: "We don't know what strength we shall find once we have really had to push open the door to the East."[24]

Franz Halder, who served as the German army's chief of staff from August 14, 1939, to September 24, 1942, kept a private war journal in which can be found an excellent account of Hitler's decisions concerning war with Russia.[25] On October 18, 1939, the Führer instructed his army that the conquered Polish territory was to be regarded "as an assembly area for future German operations."[26] A few weeks later he prodded his reluctant generals about attacking in the west, declaring that he could oppose Russia only when the Germans were free there (that is, in the west). In July, 1940, Halder noted that Hitler believed Soviet Russia could be attacked in the fall of that year if Britain was not invaded; the Führer instructed the commander in chief of the army, Walter von Brauchitsch, to prepare for the invasion of the Soviet Union.[27]

Hitler announced his decision regarding Russia to his army chiefs for the first time during a conference at the Berghof on July 31. Halder's notes, which contain an almost verbatim record of the Führer's comments, reveal that Hitler, with prospects for an invasion of Britain disappearing, not only had made a definite decision to attack the U.S.S.R. in the spring of 1941 but had already formulated his major strategic aims: "Britain's hope lies in Russia and America. If that hope in Russia is destroyed then it will be destroyed for America too because elimination of Russia will enormously increase Japan's power in the Far East." Convinced that Britain's stubborn determination to continue the war was predicated on eventual involvement of the U.S.S.R., Hitler continued:

> Something strange has happened in Britain! The British were already completely down. Now they are back on their feet. Intercepted conversations. Russia unpleasantly disturbed by the swift developments in Western Europe.
>
> Russia needs only to hint to England that she does not wish to see Germany too strong and the English, like a drowning man, will regain hope that the situation in six to eight months will have completely changed.
>
> *But if Russia is smashed, Britain's last hope will be shattered.* Then Germany will be master of Europe and the Balkans.
>
> *Decision: In view of these considerations, Russia must be liquidated. Spring, 1941.*
>
> *The sooner Russia is smashed, the better.*[28]

Both sides began secret preparations for an armed showdown. German intelligence was active along the frontier; Soviet sources claimed that

German reconnaissance aircraft made more than five hundred over-flights across the Ukraine and Belorussia from October, 1939, to June, 1941. Border troops were categorically forbidden to fire on the intruding aircraft, apparently out of fear that an explosive border incident would result and the Germans would claim provocation.

Soviet plans were executed much too cautiously and too slowly. Who was negligent in failing to prepare the Soviet military establishment for war? Was Zhukov to blame, or was he a convenient scapegoat? Stalin has been presented as the chief culprit since Khrushchev's secret speech in February, 1956. Soviet accounts claim that Stalin believed Hitler would not break the nonaggression pact with the Soviet Union "in the near future" and that he regarded German offensive preparations as a provocation. Should the Soviets respond to German activities along the border, he felt, Hitler would then have an excuse to break the pact and attack Russia. According to the six-volume Soviet history of the war, fear of provoking Hitler was so much on Stalin's mind that "requests of several commanders of the border military districts to authorize them to move troops to defensive positions along the border and increase their combat preparedness were turned down."[29]

Interestingly, the same source also castigates Timoshenko and Zhukov, who "poorly understood the developing military-strategic situation and did not draw the proper conclusions about the necessity of taking urgent measures to bring the armed forces up to combat readiness."[30] It is noteworthy, too, that the first volume of the history assigns blame to secondary individuals: Deputy Commissars G. I. Kulik, L. Z. Mekhlis, and E. A. Shchadenko. Only with the publication of Volume II were the charges against Zhukov and Timoshenko added, suggesting that someone decided at the last moment to include their names.

In fixing blame, however, one must bear in mind Stalin's adamant refusal to believe that Hitler would break the nonaggression pact. Churchill warned Moscow in April, 1941, that Germany would attack, and Count W. von Schulenburg and Gustav Hilger repeated the warning in May, but to no avail.* George F. Kennan found it incredible that

---

* Other individuals warned responsible Soviet officials. Valentin Berezhkov, first secretary of the Soviet Embassy in Berlin in those tense months, recalls that at the end of April he was invited to a cocktail party given by Jefferson Patterson, first secretary of the United States Embassy in Berlin. After greeting Berezhkov, Patterson told him that there was someone at the party he would like him to meet.

Stalin seems, believe it or not, to have conceived something in the nature of confidence in Hitler—of all people, Hitler. How wonderful it is, and yet in a way how logical, that this man Stalin, who was so abnormal, and so helpless in the problem of whom to trust, who mistrusted so many people unjustly and for the wrong reasons, who had so deeply mistrusted the French and British negotiators in the summer of 1939, should now for once, when it came to placing confidence, have made the greatest and wildest and most unbelievable of all possible mistakes.[31]

Stalin's behavior during the last few months before the outbreak of hostilities was certainly consistent; he apparently hoped that by his very insistence on German fidelity he could save the U.S.S.R. from war in 1941.* He took great pains to appease Hitler, continuing deliveries of raw materials and grain even after the Germans had practically ceased their quid pro quo.[32]

After the collapse of Yugoslavia and Greece, Stalin left no stone unturned in the effort to placate Germany. In April, appearing at the railroad station to bid farewell to Japanese Foreign Minister Yosuke Matsuoka, he took the opportunity to pat the German ambassador on the shoulder, asking him to see that Germany and the Soviet Union remained friends. Hilger recalls:

He then introduced Berezhkov to a German air force major. Toward the end of the evening, when the major and Berezhkov were alone for a time and some distance from other guests, the German officer said to him: "There's something Patterson wants me to tell you. The fact is I'm not here on leave. My squadron was recalled from North Africa and yesterday we got orders to transfer to the east, to the region of Lodz. There may be nothing special in that, but I know many other units have also been transferred to your frontiers recently. I don't know what it might mean, but I personally would not like to have something happen between my country and yours. Naturally I am telling you this completely confidentially." Berezhkov, taken aback, thanked him for the information and said that he assumed Germany would observe the nonaggression pact. "At that time," Berezhkov notes, "we feared provocation above all." Nevertheless, the conversation was reported in the regular Soviet Embassy message. See Valentin Berezhkov, "On the Eve of Hitler's Invasion," *Atlas*, Vol. XI (January, 1966), 10–16 (trans. from *Novy Mir*).

* However, according to Alexander Werth, who thoroughly researched this period, Stalin was convinced that war with Nazi Germany would almost inevitably break out in 1942 and that the Soviet government must try by all means at its disposal to stave off a German attack until the autumn of 1941, when it would be too late to launch an invasion that year. See Werth, *op. cit.*, 122–23.

He then turned to a German officer standing close to the ambassador, "made certain he was a German, and virtually insisted that he give confirmation of the lasting friendship between the two countries. The colonel could only say, "Yes, sir!" The demonstration was made in the presence of numerous witnesses, including almost the entire diplomatic corps. During the next week it was followed by further proofs that the Soviet government was trying to keep the German government in a good mood and not to give it any reason for doubting Moscow's loyalty.[33]

As late as June 14, *Pravda* claimed that there was no substance to rumors that Germany intended to break the pact. On the same day *Izvestia* stated: "Rumors that the U.S.S.R. is preparing for war with Germany are lies and provocations."[34]

In view of all this, it is not surprising that Zhukov and his associates in the military establishment were reluctant to argue with Stalin about Hitler's intentions. Reflecting on the situation a quarter of a century later, Zhukov admitted that he should have tried harder to convince Stalin of what was about to happen. He told his biographer, Colonel N. Svetlishin: "I do not disclaim responsibility for the fact that perhaps I did not prove to Stalin in a sufficiently convincing manner the necessity of bringing our Army to combat readiness." But, aware of the futility of such a gesture, Zhukov hastened to add: "Possibly, I did not have enough influence with him for this."[35] Zhukov could only try to persuade; the final decision was, of course, Stalin's.

In fact, those defensive preparations which were made by the Red Army in the spring and summer of 1941 were directed by Zhukov after he became chief of the General Staff. If any criticism of the General Staff is warranted, it would be that its members were preoccupied with the experiences of the recently concluded Finnish campaign and apparently did not pay close enough attention to the course of military operations in Europe in 1939 and 1940. In fact, two tendencies prevailed in the viewpoints of leading military personalities in the six-month period before the outbreak of hostilities. Marshal of the Soviet Union I. Kh. Bagramyan wrote:

One [group] tried to scrutinize future war only through the prism of the civil war and the events in Spain. . . . The other group, having made accurate conclusions from fighting which had taken place in Western Europe, obviously hoped to forestall events. . . . They tried to plan operations using those forces and equipment which the Red Army would have no earlier than 1942. And if the war would begin now?[36]

At the same time Bagramyan* noted that Georgi Zhukov was continually occupied with a realistic examination of the German threat, moving with a sense of urgency. On one occasion Zhukov told Bagramyan: "We are now in great need of troop commanders who are well trained not only in combined-arms but in operational matters as well."[37]

Another problem, almost overwhelming in its extent, was that of defending the territorial acquisitions of 1939 and 1940. It had not been solved by the responsible military authorities. Construction of fortified zones and field positions along the new border was far from complete in the summer of 1941. Erickson writes:

* Bagramyan was summoned by Zhukov to the Kiev Special Military District in September, 1940. Fifteen years had passed since the two men served together at the Higher Cavalry School in Leningrad. Bagramyan describes his reunion with Zhukov and gives an accurate character sketch of the man on whom so much responsibility now rested:

"Georgi Konstantinovich had not changed too much. Actually he was still thickset, his hair was slightly thinner and the lines of his face more deeply etched, which gave him a more serious expression. Yet, in these 15 years he had been much more successful than his classmates. But his successes did not surprise me. Of all the outstanding military commanders who rose with lightning speed in the prewar years, he was, without a doubt, the most brilliant and gifted personality. In the period of our training together in Leningrad, among all of us he was distinguished not only by a truly iron-hard persistence in attaining an established goal, but also by a particular originality of thought. In our exercises he quite frequently amazed us with something unexpected. His decisions always evoked the greatest controversies, and he usually was able with rare logic to defend them. Knowing well his capabilities, I was not surprised by his military career, which was striking, even for those years. In contradistinction to some military leaders of the prewar period, G. K. Zhukov possessed not only military talents, which in the years of military ordeals a military commander could not be without, but also a stern character, having no mercy for unconscientious persons. However, his strictness with respect to his subordinates—thanks to his outstanding mind and highly developed intellect—seldom turned into outspoken rudeness, which characterized a number of military chieftains at that time. He was a terror only for the good-for-nothing.

"And still another character trait of Zhukov hit me in the eyes. If he strove for something, then he absolutely did not like to go toward the objective, as is said, 'by slow step, by timid zig-zags.' In such circumstances, he went directly." Ivan Khristoforovich Bagramyan, "Zapiski Nachalnika Operativnogo Otdela," *Voyenno-Istorichesky Zhurnal*, January, 1967, 55–56.

Some of the blame for the inadequate state of the Soviet defenses has been displaced onto [Zhukov's] shoulders. It is open to question whether this is just or is merely a political convenience. There were high and forbidding barriers standing in the way of establishing a proper solution to military problems, and how much freedom Zhukov possessed is difficult to assess. What is clear is that the Soviet command had embarked on the reorganization of the defenses of the Western frontier, which was now based, from the Barents to the Black Sea, on five military districts—Leningrad, the Baltic Special, the Western Special, the Kiev Special and the Odessa Military Districts. Headquarters of the Special Military Districts were at Riga, Minsk and Kiev.[38]

Other deficiencies were evident. Forward airfields should have been constructed in greater numbers; signal centers should have been established throughout the area. The wide-gauge railway had been extended since the frontier adjustments, but its carrying capacity remained low. In some sectors construction of reinforced concrete pillboxes began only in the spring of 1941.[39]

By April, 1941, the Soviets had realized that German troops were beginning to concentrate their forces along the Russian frontier. Zhukov's May report warned the various Soviet military departments and armies: "Throughout March and April the German Command has been intensely transferring troops from the western front and Germany's central areas to the zone adjacent to the Soviet border." The implications were obvious.

Zhukov and the General Staff had worked out a detailed plan for the defense of the Soviet Union's western borders. It delineated the sectors of responsibility for each army, as well as the defensive lines for each division of the first echelon. With the exception of the northernmost segment of the Finnish border, where troops were to cover only isolated sections, a unified system of defense was organized along the frontier. All the infantry divisions of each army were deployed near the border, in one line as a rule, and assigned the mission of repelling an enemy attack. The second echelon of each army, containing one mechanized corps, had the task of destroying any forces which succeeded in penetrating the border positions.

In May, Zhukov ordered the concentration of part of the Red Army closer to the western frontier. The troop movement was too slow, carried out with insufficient transport. Railroads operated on a peacetime schedule, and the necessary sense of urgency seemed to be lacking in some commanders.

Plans prepared in May by Zhukov and the General Staff called for a rapid reinforcement of the border military districts to take place within several days after declaration of mobilization. It was assumed that there would be some period of time between the beginning of mobilization and the outbreak of hostilities.

The May plans provided that part of the border district forces would act as cover along the frontier. These forces consisted of combined-arms armies of the first echelon of each district, which were to put up a stubborn defense to cover the mobilization and strategic concentration of the nation's main forces. The line along which the main forces were to deploy would be some distance from the border. If the enemy penetrated the defenses, the defenders would shift to delaying actions or to mobile defense. Such actions would serve to delay the enemy as long as possible along each line. Between the defense lines the enemy's advance was to be slowed by obstacles, demolition of bridges, and ambush operations by small detachments. By the eve of the war up to two-thirds of the military districts' strength was included in the covering armies, which were about equally deployed along the entire border to a depth of about 60 to 95 miles. The remaining forces were located approximately 310 miles from the frontier.

According to Zhukov's plan, the 1,240-mile frontier stretching from Palanga to the mouth of the Danube River was to be defended by nine covering armies, with forty infantry and two cavalry divisions forming the first line. Each division was responsible for about 30 miles of the front. In those sectors of the border with natural obstacles (the wooded Carpathians and the Prut and Danube rivers) the width of the defensive front of the infantry divisions was about 60 to 75 miles. (It should be emphasized that these extended frontages were decided on at a time when Soviet military science had determined that the width of a divisions' defense should be 5 to 7.5 miles.) An important part of the General Staff's plan was the advance preparation of border defenses which could be occupied in the event of an enemy threat. Until that time troops designated to serve as covering forces would be stationed in camps at various distances from the border.

With time running out, Stalin continued to ignore warnings from sincere friends, prompting Churchill to record:

Stalin became more conscious of his danger and more earnest to gain time. Nevertheless, it is remarkable . . . what advantages he sacrificed and what risks he ran to keep on friendly terms with Nazi Germany. Even more surprising were the miscalculations and the ignorance which he displayed about what was coming to him. He was indeed from September 1940, to the moment of Hitler's assault in June 1941, at once a callous, a crafty and an ill-informed giant.[40]

Admiral of the Fleet N. G. Kuznetsov, appointed commissar of the navy in 1939, provides an interesting description of the momentous days immediately before the war: " . . . by early 1941 information began to seep through to us on Hitler's far from peaceful intentions. This information was at first very vague, but then became much more definite and varied. Despite its efforts, the German command was unable to conceal its preparations for a major offensive on the far-flung front from the Barents Sea to the Bosporus."[41]

Kuznetsov observes that in February, 1941, he informed the government that the Germans were delaying delivery of components for the partly assembled cruiser *Lützow*, which Germany had sold to Russia after conclusion of the nonaggression pact. Stalin listened to Kuznetsov attentively and asked him to keep the Kremlin informed of developments, commenting that Soviet representatives in Germany were being restricted in their movements.

In mid-June, on the very eve of the war, Kuznetsov reported to Stalin in the latter's office that the number of German merchant ships in Russian ports was rapidly diminishing, further evidence that Germany was preparing to attack the Soviet Union. "Still no instructions were given," says Kuznetsov. He writes of Stalin's actions in the final hours of peace, at the same time showing that Zhukov and the General Staff were not idle:

> Preparation for war is more than a mere accumulation of equipment. If a possible attack is to be beaten back, operational plans must be worked out beforehand and made known to those who will be putting them into action. . . . Did Stalin give this any thought? . . . I believe that he did. I think he was firmly convinced that war was inevitable, and that it was sure to break out either in the west or in the east. Possibly, on both sides at once. It was not for nothing that our troops were being concentrated simultaneously in the west and in the east. The borders were being fortified on both sides. The transfers of senior commanders in late 1940 and early

1941 also indicated that preparations for the war were under way. On the whole, preparations for a possible military conflict began much earlier and were carried on consistently and with good purpose.

. . . At the time, Stalin had developed a morbid suspiciousness and kept to himself his ideas on how the forthcoming war was to be pursued. The men who were to do the fighting were not told. He was also mistaken in respect to the date of a possible conflict and thought there was time to spare. When the pace of events accelerated, there was no longer time to translate ideas into clear-cut strategic schemes and concrete plans. And in 1939–1941 it was precisely such plans that were absolutely essential. Worked out precisely and in full detail, they should have been used to train and prepare the troops and the fleet.[42]

Kuznetsov says that Stalin's authority in military matters had a dual effect:

On the one hand, everyone was firmly convinced that Stalin knew best and would make the necessary decisions when the need arose. On the other hand, this prevented the men immediately around him from thinking for themselves, and stating their opinions frankly and resolutely. In the Navy there was a firm conviction that as there were no instructions there was little possibility of war.[43]

Kuznetsov criticizes leading individuals in the Commissariat of Defense. He complains that Defense Commissar Timoshenko was always too busy to attend fleet conferences dealing with operational matters. He is especially critical of Zhukov:

Our relations with the General Staff, from the moment it was headed by G. K. Zhukov, could not be called good. I believed contact with the General Staff was particularly important also because Stalin relied on its apparatus in dealing with military matters. This meant that the General Staff also received his instructions and directives concerning the Navy. . . . [After Zhukov replaced Meretskov] I went to see him several times, but without success; his demeanor was rather haughty and he made no effort at all to go into naval matters.[44]

Though the admiral had great respect for Zhukov as a field commander, he was not impressed with his performance as chief of the General Staff. "It should have become obvious much earlier that he was temperamentally unsuited for staff work."[45] Kuznetsov was probably too critical; Zhukov's irritability and impatience very likely originated in the endless frustrations and almost unbearable tensions of his job. It must also be borne in mind that Stalin exercised extremely tight control over the Defense Commissariat and the General Staff, which must have irked such energetic and restive commanders as Zhukov. Kuznetsov unwittingly provides an excuse for Zhukov's behavior and that of other leading figures in the military hierarchy when he says that "there was no clear-cut definition of the rights and duties of the military organs and the top leaders of the country." Furthermore, "Stalin, with his grasping for unlimited power, kept full control of the military side."[46] It seems unlikely that any Red Army leader could have been completely effective while laboring under these handicaps.

Several other aspects of the events which were now rapidly unfolding are worth recounting. General M. I. Kazakov, stationed in Tashkent, was summoned to the Kremlin on June 11. As he flew toward Moscow, he saw below him a steady flow of trains filled with military units, all moving northwest. He knew that his own military district was not transferring troops to other regions of the U.S.S.R. and guessed that the forces were from eastern Siberia or Transbaikal.

Arriving at the General Staff building, Kazakov learned from M. F. Lukin, who commanded an army in the Transbaikal Military District, that Lukin's army had moved west by rail. During the next few days Kazakov saw other army commanders in field dress; he was certain that they were not participating in maneuvers because he would have known of such exercises. Kazakov was asked to stay over for several days to resolve some problems connected with his district's operational plan. "In that time," he recalls, "I could not help but notice the ever-growing animation in the General Staff. Lieutenant General Gerasimenko, who was then commander of the Volga Military District, arrived here with his Chief of Staff. Then Lieutenant General F. A. Yershakov, commander of the Ural Military District, appeared." Kazakov sought out General A. M. Vasilevsky, who told him that the Finnish forces were mobilizing and that German units had already massed along the Soviet frontier. Kazakov asked him directly, "When will the war start with Fascist Germany?" Vasilevsky replied, "It will be good if it doesn't begin in the course of the next fifteen to twenty days."[47]

It can be concluded that Stalin and the Soviet High Command knew that war with Germany was only a matter of time. The troops along the western border were not kept fully informed, however, and were even allowed to slip into complacency. Possibly the Soviets were not strategically surprised; at the tactical level the story was quite different.

Several Russians have provided accounts of their experiences on the western border on the eve of the war. One, General Ivan I. Fedyuninsky, then a colonel stationed with one of the frontier units, recalls that on June 18 one of the frontier detachment commanders phoned him: "Comrade Colonel, a German soldier has just come over to our side. He reports very important information. I don't know whether we can believe him, but what he says is very, very significant." "Wait for me," Fedyuninsky ordered, and left at once for the frontier.

Arriving at the headquarters of the detachment commander, Fedyuninsky found a tall young German soldier. The soldier told the interpreter that, while drunk, he had struck an officer and, afraid of being shot, had deserted to the Soviets. "War will soon start," he declared. At 4:00 A.M. on June 22, he told them, German troops would go on the offensive along the entire German-Soviet frontier.

Seeing that his audience had doubts, the young German did his best to convince the Soviet officers that he was telling the truth. "Colonel," he said, "at five o'clock on the morning of June 22 you can shoot me if it appears that I have deceived you." When Fedyuninsky relayed the information to the Fifth Army commander, the general droned in his pipe, "There's no need to believe provocations." Further, there was no need to alert the units, since that "would sound the alarm for no purpose."[48]

General Kazakov arrived at his post in Tashkent on the night of June 21–22. He spent the next few hours reporting on his trip. Then, while he was resting, the duty officer sent for him. An important telephone call was coming through from the General Staff in Moscow. The message was brief: "Nachalos!" ("It has started!").[49]

VI. BARBAROSSA!

Russia is a country easy to enter but hard to leave.

Henri Jomini

WHEN General Heinz Guderian made his terrain reconnaissance on the day before the Germans launched their massive offensive against the Soviet Union, he was convinced that the Red Army "knew nothing of our intentions." The strongpoints along the Soviet side of the Bug River were unoccupied, and during the past few weeks the Soviets had made almost no progress in strengthening their fortified positions. In fact, Guderian believed that the prospects of achieving surprise were so good that he questioned the need for the scheduled artillery preparation.[1]

At ten o'clock on the night of June 21 a Czech Communist serving with a German infantry division made his way across the frontier in the Lvov area to warn the Russians that the Germans were planning to attack at three o'clock the next morning. This information was passed up the chain of command to Moscow, precious hours being wasted along the way. Finally the warning reached Stalin himself, who reacted characteristically: he ordered the informant shot.[2]

"Only on June 21, when irrefutable information arrived concerning the fact that on June 22-23 the German Army would attack our country," comments the *Istoriya*, "did the Soviet government decide to warn the command of the border military districts and the naval fleets about the imminent danger and bring the armed forces to combat readiness."[3] (One cannot help but speculate that the "irrefutable information" may have come from such sources as the hapless Czech deserter.) The *Istoriya* notes that the directive to "bring the armed forces to combat readiness" was issued at 12:30 A.M. on June 22. Because of faulty transmission, however, many officials learned of its contents only after the Germans had attacked.[4] The troops of the Leningrad, Baltic, Western, Kiev, and Odessa military districts were ordered to occupy the fortified regions along the border and to have all aircraft on airstrips by dawn.

The Germans' strategy was brilliantly executed. After concluding operations in western Europe in 1940, they had begun to move troops into East Prussia and Poland, and by May, 1941, almost seventy German divisions were massed along the Russian frontier. The Soviets had also deployed about seventy divisions near their western border, but many of them still lacked essential weapons and equipment.

On May 25, Germany shifted its railroads to a maximum schedule, moving about one hundred troop trains every twenty-four hours. By early June three army groups were poised for an attack on the Soviet Union: Army Group Center, under Field Marshal Fedor von Bock; Army Group North, under Field Marshal Wilhelm von Leeb; and Army Group South, under Field Marshal Gerd von Rundstedt.

Army Group Center, starting from the Lublin–Suwalki line, was given the main objective: to destroy the Soviet forces of Belorussia and then drive against Smolensk and Moscow (see map, page 195). The group consisted of five armies, two of them panzer units. Army Group North's three armies, one of them a panzer, were to start from Suwalki and the Baltic with the aim of crushing the Soviet troops in the Baltic

States and, in conjunction with Finnish forces under Marshal Carl von Mannerheim, secure Leningrad, cutting off communications with Murmansk. Army Group South, between Lublin and the Carpathians, was charged with a drive in the general direction of Kiev. Like Army Group North, it consisted of three armies, including one panzer. Its southern flanks were covered by Rumanian troops under Marshal Ion Antonescu and the German Eleventh Army of General Ritter von Schobert.[5]

Despite the lack of absolutely reliable data, it is expedient to consider here the relative numerical standings of the antagonists to the extent that they can be determined. In all, about 140 Axis divisions, well equipped in general and particularly in tanks (about 3,500), supported by as many as 3,900 aircraft, had been deployed along the Soviet frontier in the three striking groups. On the Soviet side, some 100 divisions were strung out along the frontier from the Barents Sea above Murmansk to the mouth of the Danube on the Black Sea. In addition, about 60 divisions were being moved up from the interior of the border military districts to reinforce the frontier units. Shortly before the attack Zhukov called up five armies from the hinterland to form a Stavka (General Headquarters) reserve, intended for a counteroffensive, but they were still 250 to 310 miles from the imminent scene of action.

Such was the military situation immediately before the attack. The diplomatic measures taken to inform the Soviet government of German intentions were as abrupt as conceivable for such a regime. At three o'clock on the morning of June 22 the German ambassador in Moscow received a telegram ordering him to go to Molotov with the message that Soviet troop concentrations near the German border had reached dimensions which Berlin felt it could not tolerate and that appropriate countermeasures would have to be taken. Visibly shaken, Molotov realized that the Germans were presenting him with a declaration of war and that the matter of Soviet troop concentrations was "sheer nonsense." Furthermore, if the German government had been offended by the presence of Soviet troops, a note to the Soviet government would have sufficed to cause it to withdraw its troops. Instead, Germany was unleashing a war, with all its terrible consequences, Molotov told his visitors, concluding with the pathetic remark: "Surely we have not deserved that." A similar scene was repeated in Berlin, where Ribbentrop informed Berezhkov of the German "defensive measures."[6]

Thus, on June 22, almost to the day of the anniversary of Napoleon's invasion of Russia, Hitler's armies rushed across the frontier, evoking frantic messages by Soviet troops all along the line: "We are being fired upon! What shall we do?" Field Marshal Gunther von Kluge's chief of staff, General Gunther Blumentritt, says that the response from headquarters was: "You must be insane. And why is your signal not in code?"[7]

The chaos resulting from tardy reaction to the German buildup was possibly complicated by Zhukov's last-minute staff directive ordering Soviet forces brought to full combat readiness. Many headquarters received it too late; others had sufficient time only to get their units strung out on the road, easy prey for air attack and piecemeal decimation by the rapidly advancing German armored formations. The Kiev Special Military District, for instance, did not receive notice until four to six o'clock on the morning of June 22—after the war had begun. The Forty-eighth Infantry Division, subordinate to the Baltic Special Military District, was on its way from Riga to the frontier when it was suddenly struck from the air and attacked by German ground forces which had penetrated the border defenses while the division was still about eighteen miles from the border. It was virtually destroyed.

Soviet aircraft failed to disperse to emergency airstrips in time and were swiftly overcome at their permanent bases. In fact, most of the flight personnel of the Western Special Military District were on short leave and were not even available to defend their bases. Soviet sources admit that aircraft losses in the area were especially high, enabling the Germans to gain immediate local air superiority.

A similar situation prevailed in other units assigned to cover the border. Opposite Leeb's group the bulk of the Fifth Division was still in camp 31 miles from the frontier, while the 126th Division was 43 miles away. Moreover, many division and corps artillery units of the Western and Kiev military districts were conducting training at artillery ranges far from the units they were to support. The antiaircraft units of the Kiev District were engaged in training near Minsk, almost 250 miles from their headquarters. Other units with important roles in the operational plan were still laying communications lines.

On the morning of the attack the Germans, with ninety-three divisions on hand, deployed the bulk of their forces north of the Pripyat River. The Soviet divisions were scattered along a much greater line, and some were still not in position. Thus the numerical superiority of the

Axis forces on each of the selected fronts varied from 2.5 to 1 to many times that ratio. For example, the Soviet 125th Infantry Division, which was charged with covering twenty-five miles of the front, was attacked in the Tilsit area by the entire German Panzer Group 4, which, with a first echelon of three tank and two infantry divisions and a second echelon of three motorized divisions, simply overran it. It took several days for the Soviets to bring up four divisions in an attempt to plug the gap. Elsewhere Red Army units were unable to reach the battle area in time to influence operations, and generally they were incapable of fulfilling the missions assigned to them in the 1941 plan for defense of the Soviet Union's frontiers.

Complicating matters for the defenders and adding to the general confusion in the early minutes of the war were air and artillery strikes which knocked out most of the Red Army communications. Staffs were unable to pass orders to their panic-stricken troops, and, conversely, news of the desperate plight of the border-defense units could not be relayed to higher headquarters. As the initial artillery barrage began, German shock and reconnaissance units breached barbed-wire entanglements along the border and destroyed sentry and observation posts which might have provided early information. The surprise was so nearly complete that key bridges essential to the attackers were captured intact all along the front. Sentries assigned to blow them up were overrun before they could set off demolition charges. Subsequent attempts to destroy the bridges often met with disaster; in one sector alone sixty-four attacking Soviet aircraft were destroyed in a single day.[8]

Accounts by participants reflect the ease with which the Germans were able to proceed to their objectives—almost as if they were on maneuvers. Franz Halder's journal entry for June 22 is a masterpiece of understatement: "The enemy was surprised by the German attack. His forces were not in tactical disposition for defense. The troops in the border zone were widely scattered in their quarters. The frontier itself was for the most part weakly guarded."[9]

Soviet historians, considering the reasons for the spectacular German successes in the opening rounds of the war, offer unconvincing excuses. The Red Army, they claim, "did not possess sufficient experience in conducting contemporary warfare." They conveniently forget Spain, China, Khasan, Khalkhin-Gol, Finland, and Poland. However, one of the more candid among them contradicts his colleagues when he states:

"In the prewar years, the tank troops, along with the entire Soviet Army, were developed, perfected and made more combat ready. In these years they received considerable combat experience. On the battlefields in Spain, around Lake Khasan, at the Khalkhin-Gol River, in the forests of Finland—these were landmarks in the serious tests of our tank troops."[10]

Soviet historians blame the Red Army's continuing and subsequent failures on the absence of a second front against Germany in 1941, declaring that, at the moment of attack against the U.S.S.R., combat actions by German ground forces in Europe had been halted and Germany was thus able to concentrate its armies for an invasion of Russia. But one finds wisdom in the words of Churchill, who, in a 1941 letter to Sir Stafford Cripps in Kuybyshev, commented on the second-front arguments. The Russians, he wrote, "have no right to reproach us. They brought their own fate upon themselves when, by their pact with Ribbentrop, they let Hitler loose on Poland and so started the war."[11] Churchill, perhaps recalling Molotov's congratulations to the Germans on the fall of Paris, added: "They cut themselves off from an effective second front when they let the French Army be destroyed." And with obvious resentment, he observed:

> We did not . . . know till Hitler attacked them whether they would fight, or what side they would be on. We were left alone for a whole year while every Communist in England, under orders from Moscow, did his best to hamper our war effort. If we had been invaded and destroyed in July or August 1941, or starved out this year in the Battle of the Atlantic, they would have remained utterly indifferent.[12]

Certainly in a universal sense Churchill was correct in his appraisal. However, another valid reason given for early Red Army reversals was the small quantity of new weapons available in the summer of 1941. Many of the weapons coming off the assembly lines were, in fact, better than those of the Germans, but—and here the Soviet historians are correct—"the new models of equipment and weapons had only begun to reach the troops and still had not been mastered by the personnel." The Soviets, for example, had developed and issued a remarkable new tank which was superior to any German tank. According to Guderian, in the spring of 1941, Hitler had specifically ordered that a Soviet military commission be shown new German tank schools and factories; nothing was to be concealed from this group. The Russian officers refused to believe that the Panzer IV was the heaviest German tank and charged repeatedly that the Germans were hiding their newest models from them, in violation of Hitler's order to show them everything. The Soviets were so insistent that German ordnance officials and manufacturers concluded that the Red Army had already developed better and heavier tanks than the Germans. "It was at the end of July, 1941, that the T-34 tank appeared at the front and the riddle of the new Russian model was solved," Guderian wrote.[13]

Other reasons offered by Russian historians for the initial and subsequent setbacks are also valid: the lingering effects of the purges (including the stifling of the surviving commanders' creative initiative); the reorganization of the armed forces, which was still in progress; and finally, of course, the evacuation of industrial complexes to the east, with the concomitant loss in production.

Primary responsibility for the early disasters has been ascribed to Stalin, who ignored warnings from many sources and was oversensitive about provoking the Germans. Zhukov, too, shared in the blame, but he was partly vindicated in the Soviet history of the war. Though he was not mentioned by name, his concepts about the use of armor, his futile pleas to Stalin for large mechanized groups, and his eventual exculpation were all echoed in the first volume of the *Istoriya*. The Red Army, comments the history, should have put to use the experience gained in Spain, at Lake Khasan and the Khalkhin-Gol River, and in the war with Finland. Furthermore:

> The peculiar and limited nature of the combat actions in Spain was wrongly interpreted. For example, from the experience of this war the conclusion was reached that the creation of large tank groupings was not advisable, although our country had first put them into practice. As a result of this mistaken conclusion, the mechanized corps had been disbanded in 1939 and did not begin to be reconstituted until the very eve of the Patriotic War.[14]

Aware of the exceptional successes of German tank formations in Poland and France in 1939 and 1940, the Soviet High Command was forced to re-create tank divisions on a high-priority basis, but the German attack caught the Red Army in the middle of its hasty reorganization. The long-range plan to set up fifty tank divisions was thus interrupted, and the partly formed units were thrown into battle just as they were. Predictably, they were quickly scattered and demolished, as were most of the separate tank battalions attached to infantry divisions. They were no match for the far-ranging, hard-hitting, though numerically inferior, German tank divisions. By the end of 1941 all large Soviet armored units had been destroyed or disbanded because of heavy losses.[15]

Faced with the stark reality of Germans sweeping over their borders, the Soviets began to take desperate measures to tighten control and eliminate some of the inefficient dualism which had characterized the government's peacetime operations. The entire defense establishment was also hurriedly revitalized in a series of military and political steps. The first was initiated on Monday, June 23, when the Soviet government and the Party Central Committee created the Stavka of the High Command. Defense Commissar Timoshenko was appointed chairman of the Stavka, with Stalin, Zhukov, Molotov, Voroshilov, Budenny, and Kuznetsov as members. The body was entrusted with the leadership of all military activities of the armed forces. Two days later the Stavka established the Group of Armies Reserve, under the command of Marshal of the Soviet Union Budenny. The General Staff, which Zhukov headed, was subordinate to the Stavka and served as a source of planning and information upon which the Stavka could draw.

On July 3, Stalin announced the formation of the State Defense Committee, in which all government authority was vested. (Although the *Istoriya* would conveniently overlook the composition of the committee, the original members were Stalin, chairman; Molotov, deputy chairman; Voroshilov; G. M. Malenkov; and L. P. Beria.) The State Defense Committee became the supreme strategic directorate for the Soviet Union's military, political, and industrial forces, and its initial directives sounded the keynote for the nation's response to the emergency. They included the well-known scorched-earth policy and the removal of industries to the east whenever possible. On the military side the command system was decentralized somewhat by dividing the front into three main sectors, each with its own command. Voroshilov was appointed commander of the Northwest Direction, Timoshenko the Western Direction, and Budenny the Southwestern Direction.[16]

On the political side the *yedinonachalie* principle was abolished. On July 16 the military commissars were reintroduced. L. Z. Mekhlis, head of the Red Army's Political Administration and one of its purgers, was largely responsible for the move. It was extremely unpopular with many of the military leaders—obviously so with Zhukov, who viewed the dual system as implying less than full trust in the commanders. Certainly in the early history of the Red Army, when a number of former Tsarist officers were serving the Soviets, the commissar system had been necessary to ensure political reliability. But now, almost a quarter of a century after the revolution, the continued presence of the watchdogs in each unit was anathema to loyal commanders, many of whom had belonged to the Communist Party most of their adult lives. In addition, when there was an obvious need to press forward with tactical training and to prepare military operations, hours and even days of precious time were consumed with political lectures. Writes Alexander Werth:

> One cannot help suspecting that the reintroduction of commissars was something of a panic measure due to the fear of a latent, if not open, conflict between the Army and the Party, and the doubt whether some of the officers (many of whom had highly unpleasant memories of the purges) would prove reliable. It is difficult to be sure how much hostility to the Party there was among the officers.[17]

There is no doubt about Zhukov's resentment toward Stalin on this account. Alexander Orlov, a former high-ranking NKVD officer and prosecutor in the Soviet Supreme Court, says: "I knew General Zhukov when he came to Spain as an observer during the civil war. I talked to him a number of times and I carried away the impression that Zhukov was no courtier and no stooge of Stalin. The 1937 blot on the honor of the Red Army must have bothered his military conscience ever since."[18] Zhukov was certainly a loyal Party man, but he was probably more army than Party.

Axis forces made deep penetrations into the Russian land mass. According to General Blumentritt, the advance was so swift that German infantry units had a difficult time keeping up with other forces:

> Marches of twenty-five miles in the course of a day were by no means exceptional, and that over the most atrocious roads. A vivid picture which remains of these weeks is the great clouds of yellow dust kicked up by the Russian columns attempting to retreat and by our infantry hastening in pursuit. The heat was tremendous, though interspersed with sudden showers which quickly turned the roads to mud before the sun reappeared and as quickly baked them into crumbling clay once again.[19]

By June 27 the Germans had reached the outskirts of Minsk, completing the encirclement of large Soviet forces in what has become known as the Minsk–Bialystok pocket. The German armor commanders wished to continue the advance toward Moscow, leaving the reduction of the pocket to the trailing infantry armies, and on June 30 the Supreme Command of the German Army (OKH) approved an advance to the Dnieper. But now Hitler intervened, ordering elimination of the pocket by all available forces; the advance eastward was not to be continued until further notice.

The respite gained by fierce breakout attempts of Soviet troops caught in the pocket enabled Timoshenko and Zhukov to concentrate their forces in the general area of Smolensk. On June 27, Defense Commissar Timoshenko issued directives to occupy a line extending from Kraslava in Latvia to Desna, the Polotsk fortified region, through Vitebsk and Orsha, thence down the Dnieper River to Loyev (about 37 miles south of Gomel). A group of armies was formed from the High Command's reserve under Budenny's leadership; it consisted of the Twentieth, Twenty-first, and Twenty-second armies—a total of twenty-eight divisions. Reinforcements were brought up from the second strategic echelon of the interior military districts as Timoshenko and Zhukov took additional steps to strengthen Soviet defenses between Smolensk and Moscow. A secondary defense line was organized about 130 to 150 miles east of the main defensive line, from Nelidovo, Belyy, the upper course of the Dnieper, Elnya, along the Desna River to Zhukovka and Lopush (southwest of Bryansk). Responsibility for defending the two lines was assigned to Marshal Timoshenko, who, as commander of both the Western Direction and the Western *Front*, ensured unified control of the defense. He could expect additional help from the Third, Fourth, Tenth, and Thirteenth armies, retreating from the border. Timoshenko attempted to hold along the Berezina, but the Germans passed the river before an effective defense could be set up. The Stavka allotted at least thirty-seven divisions for Timoshenko's defense of the Western Dvina and the Dnieper, but some units did not arrive, having been committed and destroyed piecemeal elsewhere.

The delay required by the reduction of the Minsk–Bialystok pocket was intolerable to the German armored-group commanders; therefore, despite higher decisions, Guderian convinced his superior, Kluge, of the necessity to continue the advance. Approval was finally obtained, and on July 10–11 the Dnieper was crossed at several points, with very light losses sustained by the Germans. Only locally were the Soviet defensive forces successful in preventing crossings. Near Orsha, for example, the Seventeenth Panzer Division was forced to evacuate its bridgehead and cross at Kopys. But the fact remains that insufficient time had been available to the Soviet command to concentrate effectively on the Dnieper, with the result that no more than twenty-four divisions had been deployed along the long line, and the Germans had no serious difficulty in penetrating it.

By July 20, Panzer Groups 2 and 3 had advanced more than 175 miles, capturing Orsha, Smolensk, Elnya, and Krichev. Counterattacks were beaten off, and in the ensuing struggle the Soviet Sixteenth and Twentieth armies were encircled on the west bank of the Dnieper. Thus ended the first stage of the Smolensk campaign.

Fresh counterattacks were finally successful in halting the German advance, and the Sixteenth and Twentieth armies were able to extricate themselves, withdrawing to the east bank of the Dnieper. Counterstrikes around Elnya on July 23 were particularly fierce, and by July 26 forward Soviet units had broken into the Smolensk bridgehead north of the Dnieper. Savage counterattacks continued into the first week of August. No less than thirteen assaults were launched on Elnya on July 30, though all were repulsed. During the renewed German advance on Roslavl beginning on August 1, the Russian Twenty-eighth Army was surrounded and severely mauled; its commander, Lieutenant General V. Ya. Kachalov, was killed.

The untiring efforts of the Stavka were evident during the Soviets' first successful unified defensive action as it constantly pressed for better control of combat troops at all levels. On July 30 the reserve armies of the Mozhaisk defensive line (excluding the Twenty-ninth and Thirtieth armies, which were already engaged on the Western *Front*) were united to form the Reserve *Front*. Zhukov was allowed to set aside his duties as chief of the General Staff to take command of the new *front*, and the effectiveness of its defense was certainly due in large measure to his solid leadership.*

* Zhukov's memoirs give us a revealing glimpse of the confrontation that led to Zhukov's new command. On July 29, Zhukov told Stalin that Kiev would have to be surrendered, since a counterattack must be mounted in the Elnya salient to prevent the Germans from using that bridgehead for an attack on Moscow. Stalin asked, "What kind of nonsense is this? How could you surrender Kiev to the enemy?" Unable to restrain himself, Zhukov retorted: "If you think that I

Despite Soviet success in slowing the German advance, certain glaring shortcomings were still evident in the organization and conduct of offensive operations. Relatively weak strike groups of only three to four divisions each were being committed on too broad a front without coordination with adjacent units. Long-range reconnaissance was not undertaken, and attacks were not synchronized. The air and artillery support was too weak. No preponderance in forces in the directions of attack was gained. Many commanders lacked the experience necessary to organize offensive operations. A number of those who had headed regiments in 1936 and 1937 were now in command of armies or had become deputy commanders of *fronts*; at the same time, former division commanders were now commanding entire *fronts*.

For the Germans the period following the containment of their advance was filled with uncertainty. The fierceness of the Soviet defense was certainly a revelation to them. Moreover, Hitler seemed to be vacillating about the priority of objectives: Leningrad, Moscow, or the Ukraine. At times all three were considered simultaneously as prime objectives. In vain did the front commanders emphasize the overriding importance of Moscow, the only operation they were convinced would be decisive. Finally, on August 4, the Führer went to Novy Borissov, the headquarters of Army Group Center. There Field Marshal von Bock summarized the opinions of the front commanders regarding continuation toward Moscow. Hitler presented Leningrad as the primary objective, but no decision was made on whether Moscow or the Ukraine was to be the next goal.

The economic resources of the Ukraine were apparently attractive to Hitler; moreover, he felt it essential to neutralize the Crimea, "that Soviet aircraft carrier operating against the Rumanian oilfields." But he also expressed the hope of being in possession of Moscow and Kharkov by the beginning of winter.[20] Certainly these expressions were far from the jubilant expectations of the war's early weeks. The stubborn Soviet defense around Smolensk had seriously upset the timetable and had shaken Hitler's confidence in an early end to the campaign. In fact, it was on this occasion that he made a surprising statement concerning a

---

as the Chief of Staff can only talk nonsense, then I have no business here. I ask to be relieved and sent to the front." Stalin replied that if Zhukov felt that way, "we can do without you." A dejected Zhukov left several hours later to take command of the Reserve *Front*. Zhukov, *Vospominaniya i Razmyshleniya*, 301–302.

book Guderian had written in 1937: "If I had known that the figures for Russian tank strength which you have in your book were in fact the true ones, I would not—I believe—ever have started this war."[21]

On August 23 the die was finally cast: the Ukraine was named the primary objective. In a conference at Army Group Headquarters it was announced that "neither the Leningrad nor the Moscow operations would be carried out, but the immediate objective should be the capture of the Ukraine and the Crimea."[22]

Guderian was selected to present the line commanders' views to Hitler personally at the latter's headquarters in East Prussia, but the Führer's domination of his entourage deprived Guderian of the support he expected. Realizing that further discussion was useless, he resigned himself to carrying out Hitler's orders as well as he could. The Führer's long-awaited directive was issued near the end of August:

> The principal objective that must be achieved yet before the onset of winter is not the capture of Moscow but rather, in the South, the occupation of the Crimea and the industrial and coal region of the Donets, together with the isolation of the Russian oil regions in the Caucasus and, in the North, the encirclement of Leningrad and junction with the Finns.

Only after Leningrad had been "tightly encircled" and the Russian Fifth Army, defending Kiev on the north, destroyed by Army Group Center would forces be allowed to attack Timoshenko's groups. On August 15 one tank and two motorized divisions had been withdrawn from Army Group Center to assist Leeb in Army Group North against strong Soviet counterattacks near Staraya Russa. Thus two and a half weeks of inactivity had completely halted the advance on Moscow. The alert Zhukov was the first to detect the change in strategic objectives, and he wasted no time telling his superiors.

In the first days of August, Guderian had intended to attack toward Moscow but decided instead to turn south to liquidate the threat posed by the Central *Front* to the right wing of Army Group Center. According to two Soviet military historians:

> The turning of part of the forces of Army Group "Center" in a southern direction did not go unnoticed by the Soviet Command. On August 18 the commander of the Reserve *Front*, General of the Army Zhukov, reported to the Stavka the following: "The enemy, convinced of a concentration of strong forces of our troops on the route to Moscow, . . . has temporarily

abandoned the strike against Moscow and, taking up an active defense against the Western and Reserve *Fronts*, is throwing all of his motorized and tank units against the Central, Southwestern, and Southern *Fronts*. The possible concept of the enemy is to defeat the Central *Front* and, advancing to the area of Chernigov, Konotop, and Priluki, to destroy the armies of the Southwestern *Front* after striking from the rear."

To frustrate this plan Zhukov planned to mass a powerful force in the Bryansk area and from there strike the enemy in the flank. Less than twenty-four hours later, he received this message from the Stavka:

> Your considerations concerning the likely advance of the Germans in the direction of Chernigov, Konotop, and Priluki I consider accurate. . . . In expectation of such an undesirable situation and in order to prevent it, the Bryansk *Front* was created under Yeremenko. Other measures were taken which I shall report on in detail. We hope to stop the German advance.[23]

It was signed by Stalin and Shaposhnikov.

In mid-August the troops of the Western *Front* and the Twenty-fourth Army of Zhukov's Reserve *Front* prepared to resume counter-attacks against German forces around Elnya and Dukhovshchina. They jumped off on August 17, achieving limited territorial objectives but pinning down the enemy in the entire sector of the offensive. In combat around Elnya the Germans suffered heavy losses and were soon forced to pull off the line two badly mauled tank divisions, one motorized division, and one motorized brigade. This was also the first recorded instance in which the Russians used a new weapon, a multiple free rocket called Katyusha (Little Kate), which thirty years later in its modern variants is still part of the Red Army's armament.

Meanwhile, Guderian was proposing to OKH "that the Elnya salient, which now had no purpose and was a continual source of casualties, be abandoned." The plan was rejected with the feeble excuse that "it is far more disadvantageous to the enemy than to us." Guderian was heartbroken. "The whole point of my suggestion, that human lives be spared, was brushed aside," he later wrote.[24]

In the final days of August and in early September (the fourth phase of the campaign), bitter battles raged along a wide front from Toropets to Novgorod-Seversk. After the Germans seized Toropets, troops of the Sixteenth, Nineteenth, Twentieth, and Thirtieth armies of the Western

Front went on the offensive, although they soon ran into strong resistance which held their advance to only a few miles. Between September 5 and 8 they finally bogged down, and on September 10, Marshal Shaposhnikov halted the attack and ordered the *front* command to take up defensive positions.

In the meantime, the German Fourth Army was ordered to evacuate the Elnya salient. Guderian commented that "by now the casualties, which I had sought to avoid by a timely withdrawal in August, had been suffered to occur."[25] Zhukov's troops, especially the Twenty-fourth and Forty-third armies, were responsible for Guderian's misery. The Germans knew their troubles were not over, for they detected Soviet rail movements from Moscow to Bryansk and very heavy motorized movement toward Smolensk.

As the campaign passed its second month, the Soviets again went on the defensive. Zhukov and his comrades in arms had accomplished a fantastic feat, and the Germans were well aware of the consequences. The Smolensk campaign had taken much of the shock out of Hitler's blitzkrieg warfare. As Alexander Werth put it:

> The "Smolensk Line" was the shield behind which the Soviet armies were able to regroup and bring up reserves, for the defense of Moscow. But for this, Moscow might well have fallen, as Hitler had originally planned, before winter set in.
>
> From the German point of view the Russian stand in the Smolensk area was the first check to their plans, and the resulting delay faced them with a major strategic problem.[26]

The Stavka had skillfully placed sufficient reserves in the Western Direction and had matched the Germans in manpower, enabling the Red Army to launch a number of counterattacks which halted the German offensive toward Moscow.

Blumentritt described the campaign's effect. "Half a million Russians seemed to be trapped," he said, in discussing the events of late July. "The trap was almost closed—within about six miles—but the Russians once again succeeded in extricating a large part of their forces. The narrow failure brought Hitler right up against the question whether to stop or not. We were now over four hundred miles deep into Russia. Moscow lay two hundred miles farther ahead."[27]

The Smolensk battle forced the Germans into disastrous debates on strategy. Says Blumentritt: "After we reached Smolensk there was a standstill for several weeks on the Desna. This was partly due to the need of bringing up supplies and reinforcements, but even more to a fresh conflict of views within the German command—about the future course of the campaign. There were endless arguments."[28] The battle which was unfolding in the Ukraine would compel Hitler to make a decision.

During the Smolensk campaign Zhukov was brought back to Moscow for a few days to discuss defense plans for the Ukraine. A Soviet staff officer, Captain Ivan Krylov, who observed this Kremlin council of war on August 21, 1941, says that an argument developed between Shaposhnikov and Budenny over defense tactics in the Ukraine. Shaposhnikov, claiming that he was adopting Kutuzov's tactics, suggested a stand on the Kolomak and Samara rivers after wearing the enemy down by constant movements. At this point Zhukov took the floor, asserting: "The point is debatable. The Battle of Borodino was necessary for psychological reasons in order to consolidate the imponderable factor which was operating in favor of the Russian Army. The Battle of Kiev is necessary for the same reason. Comrade Budenny is following entirely in the footsteps of our best captains." After more discussion Budenny's plan to defend the Ukraine was upheld. Krylov claims that the conference was one of Stalin's tricks and that Stalin listened carefully to the generals and then gave the orders. In this way he made certain that he would be credited with all Soviet military successes in the end.[29]

The Battle of Kiev, which Zhukov helped to plan,* was fought in the first half of September and ended in disaster for the Red Army. The mistake was not in deciding to defend this important Ukrainian city but in

---

* Khrushchev comments in his recollections: "I saw Zhukov a number of times early in the war. I was always glad when he flew in to take over the command from [M. P.] Kirponos. People who came to the front from Moscow early in the war were not always as helpful or as welcome as Zhukov." Khrushchev recalls that Budenny was one of those whose visits were unpleasant affairs. Nikita S. Khrushchev, *Khrushchev Remembers* (intro., commentary, and notes by Edward Crankshaw; trans. and ed. by Strobe Talbott), 175. Khrushchev probably is referring to visits by Zhukov to Kirponos' *front* to assist in planning details, not to take over command. Kirponos commanded the Southwestern *Front* in the early weeks of the war. He and many of his staff were killed in September, 1941, during the Battle of Kiev.

failing to pull out of the encirclement on time. Stalin himself was largely at fault. Nikita Khrushchev was at this time a member of the Military Council attached to the staff of the Southwestern Direction commander, Marshal Budenny. When the Red Army reserves in the Kiev salient had been exhausted, Khrushchev and Budenny decided to pull out and salvage what they could. On September 11, Stalin categorically opposed the plan to abandon Kiev for a new defensive line along the Psyol River and ordered Kiev held at any cost. Additionally he instructed his armies to defeat the enemy groupings at Konotop. Stalin then relieved Budenny of his command and assigned Timoshenko to succeed him.

The Germans soon completed their encirclement of Kiev, trapping several hundred thousand Red Army troops and capturing large amounts of matériel. Budenny, Timoshenko, and Khrushchev escaped the fate of their comrades by flying out of Kiev before it fell.

The Kiev move completed, Hitler had to decide whether to be content with his gains for the year or to make another bid for final victory in 1941. Rundstedt felt that the Germans should have stopped on the Dnieper after taking Kiev. Brauchitsch agreed with him, but Hitler, elated by the victory at Kiev, now wanted to push on. Thanks to men like Timoshenko, Zhukov, and thousands of nameless Red Army soldiers, however, the Germans, as Blumentritt recorded, "had been halted during August and September—the best two months of the year. That proved fatal."[30]

VII. LENINGRAD, 1941

The Führer has decided to wipe the City of Petersburg from the face of the earth. After the defeat of Soviet Russia there will be no interest in the further existence of this large population center. . . . It is intended to blockade tightly the city and by artillery and uninterrupted bombings to raze it from the earth. If, as a result of the conditions created in the city, requests for surrender are made, they will be rejected.

German Naval Headquarters Directive, September 22, 1941

IN July, 1941, Hitler decided that Leningrad and Moscow must be leveled and made uninhabitable "so as to relieve us of the necessity of having to feed the population through the winter."[1] This act of genocide was to be carried out by the German air force, the Führer specified, with the result that the "national catastrophe . . . [would] deprive not only Bolshevism but also Muscovite nationalism of their centers."[2]

For two hundred years Leningrad, founded in 1703 by Peter the Great as Russia's "window to the West," had been the capital of the vast Russian Empire. It was in Leningrad (then Petrograd) that the Bolsheviks wrested political power from the Provisional Government in November, 1917. When World War II broke out, Leningrad had more than three million inhabitants and was the second-largest city in the Soviet Union and its most important seaport, as well as a major industrial and cultural center.[3]

The Northwest Direction, which included Leningrad, was entrusted to Stalin's old friend, the inept Voroshilov, in early July, 1941. A. A. Zhdanov became the member of the Military Council, and Major General M. V. Zakharov was appointed Northwest Direction chief of staff.[4] After the surprise attack in June, the Germans made steady progress toward the former Russian capital, and as the summer days ticked off, the city's future became increasingly grim (see map, page 196). By early July the original thirty divisions of the Northwestern *Front* had been reduced to five fully manned and equipped divisions; the remainder had only 10 to 30 per cent of their original complement of men. By August 20 the Germans had bypassed the Luga River defense line and advanced to the area around Krasnogvardeisk (Gatchina). Only a few disorganized Red Army units stood between them and the city. The situation provoked an urgent appeal on that day by Voroshilov and Zhdanov to the troops of the Northwestern *Front*: "A threat hangs over Leningrad," they declared. "The insolent Fascist army pushes toward our glorious city—the cradle of the proletarian revolution. . . . Our sacred duty is to bar the road to the enemy at the gates of Leningrad with our breasts."[5]

The next day German divisions pushed closer to the city. The German First Corps captured the railroad and roadway bridges at Chudovo intact, cutting the October Railroad to Moscow. Eight days later the Germans seized Tosno, advancing on Mga Station, Yam-Izhora, and Ivanovskoe. After bitter fighting they took Mga, an important rail junction, and Leningrad's last railroad connection with the rest of Russia was severed. Now the German Sixteenth Army began to envelop Leningrad from the east, pushing forward along the left bank of the Neva toward Lake Ladoga. Large numbers of planes were committed, even in narrow sectors, in a breakthrough attempt. On September 6, for example, almost three hundred German bombers attacked a small slice of the front defended by the NKVD First Division, inflicting great losses in men and matériel. Following the air strikes the German command threw powerful armored units into the battle for Schlüsselburg (Petrokrepost), and by September 8 the First Division had been split in two. When the Germans reached the southern shores of Lake Ladoga and took Schlüsselburg, the land blockade was complete. They then set about tightening the giant pincers which gripped Leningrad, shelling the city and sending in wave after wave of bombers in an effort to break Russian resistance.[6]

At this critical moment Voroshilov lost his head completely. Some Leningraders reported that he had attempted suicide,[7] while others spread the rumor that he had fled to Moscow or was living at an airfield in order to be able to flee at a moment's notice.[8] Stalin relieved him of his command of the Leningrad *Front** on September 12, kicking him upstairs to the State Defense Committee.[9] General Georgi Zhukov was appointed to replace him, once again becoming "the 'fireman' who in his day was to visit and stabilize practically every dangerous sector of the Eastern Front."[10]

On the morning of September 13 an LI-2 with a fighter escort took off from Moscow's Vnukovo Airport. Aboard were Zhukov and three other hand-picked officers: M. S. Khozin, P. I. Kokopev, and I. I. Fedyuninsky. Initial planning was begun as they made their way north. Fedyuninsky, who had served with Zhukov at Khalkhin-Gol,† was named the commander's deputy. Upon landing at Leningrad, the four left immediately for *front* headquarters at the Smolny.[11]

From his arrival on September 13 until he was transferred to another crisis area on October 7,[12] Zhukov maintained a fantastic work schedule, preparing new defensive works around the besieged city and drafting detailed plans for breaking the German stranglehold. As *front* com-

---

* The Northwestern Direction, which Voroshilov had commanded since July 10, was disbanded on August 30. Voroshilov took over the Leningrad *Front* on September 5, but was relieved exactly a week later. I. P. Barbashin et al., *Bitva za Leningrad* (ed. by S. P. Platonov), 592.

† Fedyuninsky commanded the Twenty-fourth Motorized Regiment under Zhukov at Khalkhin-Gol. Afterward he served as commander of the Eighty-second Division. His memoirs are both informative and entertaining.

mander, he also instilled new confidence in the embattled Red Army men and inspired them to withstand fresh German onslaughts.[13] The vigor of his activity is confirmed by an outstanding and highly articulate observer of the Russian wartime scene, Alexander Werth, who makes it quite clear that Zhukov was indeed the organizer of Leningrad's defenses in the life-and-death struggle:

> . . . Except for a footnote in the official *History* saying that Zhukov was in command of the defense of Leningrad from September 11 till the middle of October, post-war accounts are silent about the changes that took place in the High Command. The dramatic story I heard from several people in Leningrad in 1943 was that about September 10, when there was practically complete chaos at the front, Voroshilov, believing that everything was lost, went into the front line, in the hope of getting killed by the Germans. But on September 11 Stalin dispatched Zhukov to Leningrad, and it was Zhukov who fully organized the defense of the city within three days; in a press interview I attended in Berlin in June 1945, Zhukov proudly referred to this fact, though without going into any details, and Vyshinsky said, "Yes, it was Zhukov who saved Leningrad." It was, undoubtedly, during the short Zhukov reign—after which he was placed in charge of the defense of Moscow—that the front round Leningrad became stabilized.[14]

Years later, speaking to the workers of the Leningrad Bolshevik Plant, Zhukov affirmed that he had commanded the Leningrad *Front* in the "most difficult, critical time when the Germans penetrated to the Pulkovo Hills and individual tanks of the Germans broke through to Myasokombinat."[15]

It is obvious that Stalin had empowered Zhukov to take whatever steps were necessary to restore Leningrad's defenses, regardless of whose toes might be stepped on in the process. Zhukov ruthlessly set about his task, inspiring terror in the hearts of some of his subordinates.

One of the first to experience his abruptness was Voroshilov himself. Zhukov quickly signed the intelligence and operational maps with him, which was one of the formalities in changing command, and then both men went to the telegraph set. The conversation with the Stavka was brief. General A. M. Vasilevsky was on the other end of the line in Moscow. Zhukov transmitted a terse statement: "I have taken command. Report to the Supreme Commander in Chief [Stalin] that I expect to work more actively than my predecessor."[16] Voroshilov did not communicate with the Stavka, but quietly left the room. That night he and most of his staff flew to Moscow. Zhukov had undoubtedly insisted on a replacement of key personnel, preferring to surround himself with individuals whose performance he knew.

The next day Zhukov began sending for those members of the staff who had not returned to Moscow with Voroshilov. One who was to be retained was Boris Vladimirovich Bychevsky. He never forgot his introduction to Zhukov:

> My first acquaintance with the new commander was somewhat strange. Listening to my introduction, which was usual for those circumstances, he looked at me for several seconds with cold, distrusting eyes. Then suddenly he asked sharply [using the familiar form, *ty*]: "Who are you?"
>
> I did not understand the question and reported once again: "Chief of the *Front* Engineer Department, Colonel Bychevsky."
>
> "I asked, 'Who are you?' Where did you come from?" Irritation was evident in his voice. The heavy double chin of Zhukov moved forward. The short, but solid block-like figure was raised up over the table.
>
> "Are you really asking for a biography? Who needs one at this time?" I thought, not considering that the commander expected to see someone else in this post. With uncertainty I began to report that I had served as the chief of the [military] district's engineer administration and later the *front*'s [administration] for almost a year and a half, and during the Soviet-Finnish War I was Chief of Engineers of the Thirteenth Army on the Karelian Isthmus.
>
> "Where's General Nazarov? I sent for him."
>
> "General Nazarov worked in the headquarters of the commander of the Northwestern Direction and coordinated engineer matters of the two *fronts*," I explained. "He flew out last night with the marshal."
>
> "Coordinated . . . flew out," Zhukov repeated. "Well, to hell with him! What do you have with you? Report!"[17]

On his maps Bychevsky showed the new *front* commander what had been done before the German breakthroughs at Krasnoye Selo, Krasnogvardeisk, and Kolpino. He pointed out the work on the Pulkovo positions, the preparations within the city itself, along the Neva and on the Karelian Isthmus. Then he described the tasks currently being carried out by mine-laying teams and pontoon bridge engineers.[18]

> Zhukov listened, not asking any questions. Then—accidentally or intentionally—his arm moved sharply, so that the pages fell from the table

and scattered on the floor. He turned his back and without a word began to examine a large outline of the city's defenses affixed to the wall.

"What are tanks doing in the Petroslavyanka area?" he asked suddenly, again giving me a glance as I stacked the portfolio of maps which had fallen to the floor. "What are you hiding? Come here! There's something wrong here."

"These are tank mockups, Comrade Commander." I pointed on the map to the symbol of a dummy tank formation. . . . "Fifty were made in the workshop of the Mariinsky Theater. The Germans have bombed them twice."

"Twice!" Zhukov remarked sarcastically. "And how long have you been playing these games?"

"Two days."[19]

With bitter humor Zhukov told Bychevsky that the Germans would soon catch on to this trick and start dropping wooden bombs on the mockups. He ordered Bychevsky to have another hundred constructed by the following day and to place them at two locations he indicated on the map. Bychevsky replied that the workshops would not be able to complete that many in one night.

> Zhukov lifted his head and looked at me up and down. "If they can't, you will be tried. Who is your commissar?"
>
> "Regimental Commissar Mukha."
>
> "Mukha?" You tell your Mukha [Russian for "fly"] that you two will go together before a court-martial for failing to carry out an order. I'll check on it tomorrow myself."

Says Bychevsky, "The abrupt, threatening sentences were like blows of a whip." It appeared to him that Zhukov was intentionally testing his endurance. The new *front* commander, obviously disappointed with his predecessor's performance, muttered to himself: "Why did they start fortifying [the Pulkovo Heights] so late?" And then, not expecting an answer, Zhukov told Bychevsky, "You may go."[20]

Other officers were summoned to Zhukov's headquarters, and a number of them fared no better than Bychevsky. Zhukov threatened many of them with courts-martial, removed others from command outright. The latter applied to the chief of the operations section, a Colonel Korkodin. Korkodin had one brief conversation with Zhukov, after which he was sent to Moscow. By the end of the second day after his arrival, Zhukov had changed the command of the Forty-second Army, and a week later he dismissed the Eighth Army commander, Major General V. I. Shcherbakov, and the member of the Military Council, Divisional Commissar I. F. Chukhnov. "As for the purely operational decisions and orders of the new *front* commander," writes Bychevsky, "they were not different in substance from what existed before, and obviously could not be different. The main requirement for 'unceasing counterattacks' remained as before—to take back from the enemy a settlement, station or hill surrendered yesterday."[21]

The problems of morale and discipline were the most immediately pressing ones to be resolved. Indeed, earlier in August, Stalin had been quite concerned about discipline among the troops assigned to defend Leningrad and had announced that those who surrendered to the enemy, regardless of circumstances, would be treated as deserters and shot. There followed a few days later a special order accusing some of "criminal absentmindedness, faintheartedness and cowardice" and reminding them that "such disgraceful individuals cannot be tolerated in the Red Army."[22]

When Zhukov arrived at the front, he found that discipline in the Eighth Army had deteriorated sharply. Division commanders withdrew from the fighting without orders, officers were often drunk, and soldiers were running away at the first shot. Stern measures were necessary. Zhukov and Zhdanov warned that all who failed in their duty would be executed. To put teeth into the warning, a number of arrests and executions of officers, commissars, and soldiers for treasonable actions or unauthorized withdrawals were announced. In some cases entire units were disbanded and the men reassigned.[23]

The battlefield situation Zhukov inherited was indeed critical. The capture of Schlüsselburg had severed all land communications with the rest of the country, and a breach of more than twelve miles along Lake Ladoga now separated the beleaguered Leningrad *Front* from the units east of Mga and along the Volkhov, which were struggling to contain the German armored thrust east of the city. The Soviet Eighth, Forty-second, and Fifty-fifth armies were slowly but inevitably being pushed back within the city's defense perimeter or to the Gulf of Finland. The forces of the Southern Operational Group, the remnants of the Luga battle, which had been bypassed and then surrounded by the advance of Panzer Group 4 to Krasnogvardeisk and Schlüsselburg, had either been liquidated or were fighting their way out of encirclement to the east and northeast. The slower-moving German infantry armies, the Sixteenth and Eighteenth, were gradually succeeding in closing up to the advanced motorized forces. The prerequisites had now been established by the German command for a closer investment of the city.

Intentions for the final attack against Leningrad were apparently threefold. First, flank protection along the Neva and Volkhov would be provided by units of the Sixteenth Army and the Thirty-ninth Motorized Corps of Panzer Group 4, possibly developing into a renewed advance toward a linkup with Finnish forces along the Svir River (east of Lake Ladoga). Second, a two-pronged assault against Leningrad itself from the south and southwest would be made by the other motorized corps of Panzer Group 4, the Eighteenth Army, and support units of the Sixteenth Army (approximately eight divisions from Krasnogvardeisk toward the Pulkovo Heights and Uritsk, against the Forty-second Army, and three divisions in the direction of Kolpino through Pushkin and Slutsk—that is, against the Fifty-fifth Army). Third, the Germans would attempt to liquidate the Eighth Army, defending along the western and southwestern approaches to the city with its back against the Gulf of Finland from Oranienbaum to Kernovo, by a breakthrough to the Gulf of Finland.

After several days' delay entailed by the necessity of regrouping and further preparations, Army Group Center launched its attack on September 9. Despite desperate Soviet resistance, by the end of the first day the forward line of defense had been breached over a six-mile front to a depth of one-half to nearly two miles. The attack was continued on the morning of the tenth, and after fierce fighting the defenders were pushed back beyond the Dudergof Heights. On the west, Krasnoye Selo was penetrated; on the south, Krasnogvardeisk fell. The thrust to the northeast toward Pushkin and Slutsk, with Kolpino the objective, was largely contained, despite some of the most massive air attacks of the battle. The defenders continued their stubborn resistance throughout the next three days but lost ground steadily, and by September 14 the Germans had reached Pulkovo Heights.

Trenches and firing points on the Pulkovo Heights had been prepared for occupation by the Fifth Division of People's Militia. In the meantime, however, the right flank of the Pulkovo positions in the area of Gorelovo Station fell into German hands on September 13, and two regiments of the Fifth Division had to enter the fighting there. The militiamen were able to break through to the station, where they attempted to consolidate. In the afternoon, however, they were attacked by infantry and tank divisions of the German Forty-first Mechanized Corps, and Gorelovo Station fell into enemy hands for the second time. An hour later the Russian division counterattacked and again freed Gorelovo. That night, the commander of the Forty-second Army, Lieutenant General F. S. Ivanov, fearing for the safety of Pulkovo, led one of the regiments from the embattled station to the Pulkovo Heights, leaving only one regiment at Gorelovo. The commander of the remaining regiment, S. I. Krasnovidov, was wounded and was replaced by his commissar, N. A. Smirnov, former secretary of the Vyborg District Committee. On the morning of September 14 the fight for Gorelovo was renewed with increased intensity. The commissar twice led his troops in counterattacks, but by evening German tanks had seized the station for the third time. Zhukov ordered the situation restored by units from an infantry regiment of the Twenty-first NKVD Division.

Most of the fortified belt south of Leningrad had now been breached, and the most advanced German armored units had reached a point less than seven miles from the city. On September 15, despite bitter defensive battles, especially before Uritsk (which had changed hands several times during the day), the German Eighteenth Army penetrated to the Gulf of Finland between Strelna and Uritsk, cutting off the Soviet Eighth Army from Leningrad. It was a critical day, and the Germans felt new intensity in the Russian fighting.

With the idea of halting further attacks by German strike groups in the direction of Uritsk and Leningrad, Zhukov carefully worked out a plan for strengthening the city's defenses. His immediate objectives were to hit the Germans with air and artillery strikes to prevent them from penetrating Soviet defenses, to form five infantry brigades and two infantry divisions by September 18, to man four lines in a close-in defense of Leningrad, to employ the Eighth Army to strike the Germans in their flanks and rear, and to free Mga and Schlüsselburg. The plan called for building up reserves and increasing the depth of the defense by mobilizing all resources in the area, including troops of his *front*, the inhabitants of Leningrad, and the Soviet Navy. In the Forty-second Army's zone Zhukov planned to create a defense which would prevent the Germans from taking Leningrad by storm. He relied heavily on the firepower capabilities of coastal artillery and naval vessels in the

Baltic, both of which would become more effective as the front contracted and approached the sea.

As German units renewed their assaults on the Forty-second Army, Zhukov sent his deputy, General Fedyuninsky, to its headquarters. The front line was so close that bullets were whistling overhead. Entering the headquarters bunker, Fedyuninsky found an exhausted, confused commander, his head propped up with both arms. He asked General Ivanov where his troops were deployed. "I don't know," the general replied. "I don't know anything."

"And do you have communications with your units?" Fedyuninsky asked.

"There are no communications. The fighting today has been hard. Here and there it's been necessary to retreat. Communications were destroyed," Ivanov answered, almost without interest.

Fedyuninsky informed Zhukov of the situation and was ordered to take personal command of the battered Forty-second Army.

On September 16, Zhukov, attempting to avoid a penetration by the Germans through Uritsk to Leningrad, reinforced the Forty-second with a newly formed NKVD infantry division, a People's Militia division, and two rifle brigades of sailors and personnel from various Leningrad air-defense units. These forces took up the defense of the outer ring of the city's fortified line, which stretched from the banks of the Gulf of Finland through Ligovo, Myasokombinat, and Rybatskoye to the Neva River. Zhukov gave orders that troops were not to be pulled off the line without express permission from the *front* command. In this manner he created a strong second echelon and secured an operational defense in depth.

Bychevsky describes the frenzied activities at *front* headquarters while Zhukov was issuing these orders. Since the danger of breakthrough was very real, the commander and his staff were working under intense pressure. In this strained atmosphere Zhukov revealed his irritation as he spoke to his chief engineer, who had not been readily available when the commander sent for him. Bychevsky recalls:

> When, damp and covered with mud, I entered the office, G. K. Zhukov and A. A. Zhdanov were standing, leaning over a map. The commander made a wry face in my direction.
>
> "You finally showed up. Where were you hanging around, that we had to look for you all night long? I guess you were sound asleep. . . ."

The start foreboded nothing good.

"I was carrying out your order, checking the line and antitank defenses along the Circle Road," I replied.

"Well, what about it? Is it ready?"

"Seventy firing positions for antitank artillery are ready. The ditches are dug. The emplacing of obstacles and mine fields has been completed."

"Does the commander of the Forty-second Army know about this line?"

"This afternoon I issued an overlay of the line to the Army Chief of Staff, General Berezinsky. General Fedyuninsky himself had gone to visit the troops."

A blow on the table with his fist was the answer to what seemed to me a clear report.

"You were not asked about which clerks you gave the overlay. I am interested in something else: do you know if the Army commander knows about this line? Can you understand the Russian language?"

When he informed Zhukov that General Fedyuninsky was waiting outside in the reception room, the *front* commander exploded in a rage:

"Do you think out what you say? . . . I know without your telling me that he is here. . . . Do you realize that if Antonov's division does not occupy the defenses on the Circle Road during the night, the Germans will break into the city? I shall then shoot you in front of the Smolny like a traitor."

A. A. Zhdanov made a wry face. He obviously did not approve of such a tone by the commander. Andrei Aleksandrovich did not know how to curse and did not know how to take it; now, wishing somehow to soften Zhukov's coarseness, Zhdanov talked with me:

"Comrade Bychevsky, you could not have suspected where to find Fedyuninsky. He just took over the Army. And Antonov's division, which is supposed to occupy the new line, actually was only recently formed. They will bomb the division if they find it there at daylight. Now do you understand the problem?"

Obviously, I was actually in a state of stupefaction and only now grasped why they had summoned me. It was necessary to ensure quickly, before morning came, the arrival of the Sixth Division of the People's Militia to the new line prepared by us. I did not dare report that until then that day's order of the *front* commander was unknown to me. . . . Instead, I said:

"Permit me, Comrade Commander, to leave now with the [Army] commander, and we shall lead the division to the prepared line."

"You finally hit upon an idea. . . ." Zhukov again cursed. "Quickly direct

German Foreign Minister Joachim von Ribbentrop, Hitler's foil in diplomatic skirmishes. Above, left: with Adolph Hitler. Above, right: conferring with Benito Mussolini (left) in Florence, Italy, October, 1940. Below: welcoming Soviet Commissar of Foreign Affairs Vyacheslav M. Molotov on his state visit to Berlin in November, 1940. Front row, left to right: German Field Marshal Wilhelm Keitel, Ribbentrop, Molotov.

Barbarossa! A German Stuka attacks a Soviet tank-assembly area.

Above: A German machine-gun crew fires into a Russian cornfield on the first day of the German invasion, June 22, 1941. Below: An assault gun moves up to support German infantry.

German soldiers cross the Neman River on June 23, 1941, the second day of the war and one day before the anniversary of Napoleon's invasion of Russia—across the Neman River.

Above: A destroyed Soviet column near Slonim, June 29, 1941. Below: A German motor column passes along the muddy roads of Minsk, summer, 1941.

Above: A long German truck column moves across the broad expanses of the Soviet Union, July 29, 1941. Below: Horse-drawn German artillery passes a burning Soviet tank, summer, 1941.

General Heinz Guderian (second from left), the brilliant young German panzer leader, holds a strategy session beside the road at Roslavl, U.S.S.R., which has just been captured by his tank divisions, August, 1941.

A tragic scene repeated untold times. Leading their livestock, Russian peasants flee from the advancing Germans.

A photograph of Stalin which appeared on the first page of Pravda on July 3, 1941, with a report of his radio appeal for defeat of the Germans—the famous "Comrades! Citizens! Brothers and Sisters! Warriors of Our Army and Navy!"

During the Siege of Leningrad, Red Army tanks move out to defend the city.

The women of Leningrad digging antitank ditches, fall, 1941.

General of the Army Zhukov, with his chief of staff, V. D. Sokolovsky (left), and N. A. Bulganin, reading ticker-tape messages in command headquarters near Moscow, November, 1941.

Muscovites working on the city's defenses. Above: digging antitank ditches. Below: emplacing hedgehogs—rails welded together to form tank obstacles.

The Red Army begins the Moscow counteroffensive, December, 1941. Above, left to right: Brigade Commissar P. F. Ivanov, Commander of the Fifth Army Colonel General L. A. Govorov, and the general's adjutant plan strategy. Below: Soldiers move up to offensive positions.

German leaders confer as the tide of war turns, 1942. Left to right: Field Marshal Wilhelm Keitel, Hitler, Field Marshal Gerd von Rundstedt.

Red Army infantry on the attack. Above: advancing along a bomb-twisted railway. Below: moving toward the front.

On toward Berlin. Above: Zhukov (center), plans the final push of the war with (from left) General V. I. Kazakov, General G. N. Orel, and Military Council member K. F. Telegin, April 21, 1945. Below: Commander of the First Belorussian Front K. K. Rokossovsky.

Soviet artillery firing on German positions.

them [there] and remember that if the division is not in place by nine o'clock I shall shoot you."

When Bychevsky left Zhukov's office, he met Fedyuninsky in the reception room. Bychevsky's countenance reflected his recent ordeal at the hands of the *front* commander. Fedyuninsky could not resist a little banter and asked: "Did you catch it, Engineer?" At that time Bychevsky was not closely acquainted with the good-natured Fedyuninsky, and he considered the latter's remark out of place, even malicious. The colonel could not hold back his sharp retort:

"Somewhat, Comrade General. The commander promised to execute me if the Sixth Division is not on the Circle Road by morning. Let's go. Obviously no one in your headquarters concerned himself with such a small matter as the arrival of a division on the line. And actually the map overlay was located at [your] Army!"

"Don't get mad, Engineer!" The Army Commander, who, it seems, knew Zhukov's character, broke into a broad smile. "You're still in luck. The very same Georgi Konstantinovich promised to hang us with the member of the Military Council. We had already made up our minds to go when you arrived. We decided to wait for a while, as we knew you would not be detained by the commander."

Bychevsky was reassured by Fedyuninsky's smile. They left the Smolny together and plunged into the late-summer night. By morning the Sixth Division had occupied the line without incident.[24]

Having penetrated to the Gulf of Finland, the Germans were dangerously close to Leningrad: less than four miles from the outskirts of the city and no more than three miles from the huge Kirov Plant. Bitter fighting continued on September 16, with Slutsk and Pushkin falling into German hands. Alexandrovka, the terminus of one of Leningrad's streetcar lines, was taken on the seventeenth. On the same day German armored and motorized forces began transferring to Army Group Center. The fruits of victory seemed almost within their grasp.[25]

While the Germans were approaching Volodarsk and Uritsk, Zhukov detected that their left flanks were overextended. He decided to counterattack with units of the Eighth Army and quickly assembled the Tenth, Eleventh, 125th, and 168th infantry divisions and the Third Division of the People's Militia. By means of internal regrouping he created a strike force and at the same time reconstituted its reserve.

On September 17 six German divisions, supported by the air wing of Army Group North, attempted to break through to Leningrad from the south. Zhukov ordered continuation of counterattacks, directing the Eighth Army commander to recover the Volodarsk settlement and strike in the direction of Krasnoye Selo. The Fifty-fifth Army was ordered to throw the Germans back from Slutsk and Pushkin Park. The Forty-second Army was to develop its success in the region of Uritsk and at the same time hold the center of the Pulkovo position near the observatory.

The Forty-second Army was unable to hold Uritsk, however, and by the evening of September 18 the town was again occupied by the Germans. Exceptionally bitter fighting continued, and by September 23 it was obvious that German striking power on the Pulkovo axis had significantly diminished: only twenty tanks took part in the attack. The Forty-second Army successfully repelled continued attacks, and in the latter part of September the German plan for reaching Leningrad through Uritsk or the Pulkovo Heights finally collapsed. The Forty-second Army consolidated on the line of Ligovo, Nizhnyee Koirovo, and Pulkovo.

The strength of the German attack had now been spent or weakened by withdrawals throughout the Leningrad sector, and although relatively heavy fighting continued until September 25, with strong Soviet counterattacks the Germans were able to achieve only minor success. In fact, Army Group North was no longer able to continue its advance with the forces at hand and therefore went on the defensive along the entire front. Efforts were concentrated on establishing a siege in the hope of eventually starving out the defenders.

When the German offensive began to lose steam, Zhukov committed new divisions, brigades, and battalions—which had been quickly put together with sailors, antiaircraft defense troops, the home guard, and reservists—for use in the Krasnogvardeisk and Slutsk–Kolpino fortified regions. He also pulled units from the less active segments of the front and threw them into the threatened zones to reinforce the first-echelon troops and create a defense in depth.

The Red Banner Baltic Fleet rendered significant aid to the Leningrad *Front* in its fight to hold the coastal bridgehead and also in repelling the German onslaught in the Krasnoye Selo, Uritsk, Pulkovo Heights, and Kolpino areas. Fleet aviation, in coordination with the air

power of the Leningrad *Front*, bombed German forces on the battlefield and in their assembly areas and protected Soviet units from German air strikes. Those sectors of the front near the Gulf of Finland
were supported by coastal and naval artillery, which conducted counterbattery operations, participated in artillery counterpreparations, and
otherwise assisted the operations of the Eighth and Forty-second armies.
The use of fleet artillery in the Krasnogvardeisk fortified region and the
coastal bridgehead compensated for the shortage of mobile artillery.

The German command was unrelenting in its pressure on Leningrad,
however, and in certain sectors around the city the Red Army suffered
setbacks. Offensive operations from September 10 to 26 by the Soviet
Fifty-fourth Army and the Neva Operational Group were unsuccessful.

Defensive operations by Soviet troops on the southwest approaches
to Leningrad during August and September lasted for fifty days. Their
resistance upset German plans to capture the city by frontal assaults
from the south and north. By the end of September the front had been
stabilized on the southern approaches to Leningrad, thanks to Georgi
Zhukov and his troops, and remained significantly unchanged until
January, 1943 (when Zhukov returned to break the blockade). By then
the front had been stabilized on the Karelian Isthmus and the Svir River.

Although the Red Army had stopped the Germans at the outskirts of
Leningrad, the fate of the city and its defenders was still uncertain. Failing to win by force, the German command decided to starve the population by blockade and then destroy the city. On September 18, Halder
noted in his journal that "the ring around Leningrad has not yet been
drawn as tightly as might be desired. . . . Considering the drain on our
forces before Leningrad, where the enemy has concentrated large forces
and great quantities of matériel, the situation will remain tight until
such time when hunger takes effect as our ally."[26]

While Zhukov was in charge of Leningrad's defenses, Hitler decided
that capitulation would not be accepted, an amplification of his earlier
decision that the city must be "wiped from the face of the earth." On
September 22, German Naval Headquarters issued its secret directive
"Number 1a 1601/4: Concerning the Future of the City of Petersburg."
It said that the Führer had decided to level Leningrad by blockade and
continuous air and artillery strikes and that requests for surrender were
to be rejected.

The Germans methodically put the plan into effect, blockading the city by land and subjecting it to systematic artillery fire, reinforced by aerial bombardment. In September the Germans conducted twenty-three large air raids, most of them during daylight hours. The first was carried out on September 8. More intensive bombings were recorded on September 19 and 27, with 180 and 200 planes, respectively, participating. From September 21 to 23 the German command carried out a massive air operation with 400 bombers. Their mission was to destroy Kronstadt and wipe out the main forces of the Red Banner Baltic Fleet based there.

The raids failed to accomplish their mission, but the defenders of Leningrad were facing a desperate situation. The sole artery supplying the city—the water route on Lake Ladoga, which was under continual German artillery fire and air bombardment—was only partly able to satisfy the needs of the besieged troops and civilian population.

Zhukov devoted much of his energy to planning and overseeing engineering details of the defensive preparations on the outer edges of Leningrad. The troops of his *front* and residents of the city and surrounding areas managed to create an elaborate defensive zone on the southern, southeastern, and northern approaches to the city. It included main and secondary defensive belts and a number of trench positions and fortified areas. The large amount of work in the sectors assigned to the Twenty-third, Forty-second, and Fifty-fifth armies and the Neva Operational Group, as well as in the immediate proximity of the city, was extremely significant in the defense of Leningrad.

In characteristic fashion, the Russians kept detailed statistics, and their military historians seem to delight in enumerating them. Around Leningrad and in the city itself 93 miles of antitank ditches, escarpments, and counterescarpments were dug; 125 miles of wire entanglements were emplaced; 7,179 trenches for infantry squads and 389 miles of communications trenches were dug; 140 steel and cement-and-stone emplacements were constructed; 487 armor fire points were established; 176 tanks were placed in prepared firing points; 1,500 antitank obstacles and "hedgehogs" (made of rails welded together), plus 1,395 wood-and-earth fire points, were constructed; 809 fire points were set up in buildings; and 1,089 command and observation points and dugouts, together with many other defensive installations, were prepared.

On the average about forty-five thousand persons worked on the defenses each day. Much of the labor was performed by women, who, like their children and parents, were on near-starvation diets. On October 1 workers began receiving fourteen ounces of bread a day; children, invalids, and civil servants received only seven ounces. The sacrifices these women made cannot be fully appreciated by anyone except, perhaps, the participants themselves.

Fedyuninsky cites a touching yet amusing incident which occurred one day while he was inspecting the work of the Russian women. Arriving at a line of new trenches, he wrote, "I got out of my car and, desiring to cheer up these workers, I said, 'You dig well, girls, very well!'

"One of the women, no longer young, in a threadbare coat and dark kerchief tied under her chin, as is done in the rural areas, straightened her tired back and, leaning on her shovel, answered without a smile: 'We dig well, but you fight poorly. You allowed the Germans to get right up to Leningrad.' "

The old woman was right, Fedyuninsky admitted. "How could I answer her?" Trying to change the subject, he asked, "Where is your husband?"

She replied, "Somewhere with you . . . running!" She caught her breath and then went back to work with her shovel.[27]

Zhukov divided the city into six defensive sectors. Several strong positions were created in each sector, with battalion defensive areas forming their bases. Within the sectors ninety-nine battalion areas were set up. Zhukov also stressed the need for barricades throughout the city, ordering antitank ditches dug in front of them.

Antitank positions were distributed throughout the depth of the defense. By November, 1941, forty-one such areas had been laid out in the Forty-second Army's zone. To ensure their effectiveness, Zhukov distributed antitank guns to cover the tank traps with an average density of seventeen guns for each half mile of front.

Air defense of Leningrad was also strengthened. The National Air Defense Organization relinquished central control of its antiaircraft units in the area to the *front* command. Antiaircraft weapons were distributed along the near approaches to the city; some batteries were even deployed on barges in the Gulf of Finland. To complicate matters for German bombers, barrage balloons were positioned over the besieged city.

Hitler had ordered paratroops to Leningrad. To defend the city from airborne assault, Zhukov organized an effective antiairborne defense consisting of teams from the workers' militia, the militarized fire guard, and Komsomol detachments.

The Leningraders were also prepared to destroy German forces inside the city. Factories, bridges, and public buildings were mined; in the event of a German breakthrough, the structures were to be destroyed to trap men and tanks. The civilian populace was prepared to fight in the streets and from the houses and buildings. Thus, as a result of the enormous organizational work carried out by Zhukov and his staff and by the residents themselves, the city was converted into a virtually impregnable fortress. For years afterward, its heroic defense would stir the imagination of men everywhere.

A tribute to the Leningrad defenders was contained in a *Voyenno-Istorichesky Zhurnal* (*Military-Historical Journal*) article written by Zhukov in 1966:

> For all of us who participated in the September battles for Leningrad, we had to live through many difficult days. However, our troops were able to frustrate the plans of the enemy. Thanks to the unprecedented steadfastness and massive heroism of the Soviet soldiers, sailors, sergeants and master sergeants, the endurance and firmness of the commanders and political workers, the enemy on his way to Leningrad met an insurmountable defense. By the end of September the combat tension along all sectors of our *front* had noticeably abated and the line of the front had been stabilized.[28]

Zhukov was no doubt countering past efforts by the Soviet regime to play down Leningrad's great feat and its sacrificial struggles during the long siege. Dmitri Pavlov, whose study of the battle from the logistics standpoint received only limited distribution, writes that the Leningrad Defense Museum, a rich storehouse of materials depicting the heroic struggle of the Leningraders, was "unjustifiably" closed in 1949. When it was finally reopened in 1957, only a few rooms were allotted to the exhibition of materials connected with the battle.[29]

While commanding the Leningrad *Front*, Zhukov, as a member of the Stavka, received continuous reports from the General Staff about the combat situation in other areas, and there was much to cause grave anxiety. His own sector, of course, had become essentially stabilized by the third week in September. German offensive strength had been sapped by the stubborn defense, and the Axis forces had been compelled to dig in for a siege. To what extent the withdrawal of the German motorized and armored units on September 17 had contributed to the salvation of the city can only be conjectured. In any event, their withdrawal was the preliminary to what was hoped would be the final massive assault on Moscow, scheduled to begin at the end of September, in which Panzer Group 4 of the Army Group North was to participate. And it was to this sector, in a desperate situation, that Zhukov was to be called.

From his vantage point in Leningrad, Zhukov received news of frenzied preparations by both sides on the approaches to the Russian capital. Three Soviet *fronts* were defending Moscow: Western, Reserve, and Bryansk.

The Western *Front*, consisting of six reinforced armies and *front* reserves, defended from Lake Seliger to Elnya and had the mission of preventing a German breakthrough along this main axis to Moscow.

The Reserve *Front*, with its Thirty-first, Thirty-second, Thirty-third, and Forty-ninth armies, occupied the defense behind the Western *Front* along the line through Ostashkov, Selizharovo, Olenino, Spas-Demensk, and Kirov. The four armies were held in reserve to repel any penetration of the defensive formations of the Western *Front* and therefore formed a second operational echelon of the Soviet defense. Two additional armies of this *front*, the Twenty-fourth and Forty-third, were deployed in the Western *Front* zone on a line from Elnya and Frolovka.

The Bryansk *Front*, consisting of three armies and an operational group, defended along the eastern bank of the Desna from Frolovka to Putivl. Its mission was to prevent a breakthrough in the Bryansk–Orel direction.

Altogether, at the end of September, these three *fronts* were composed of approximately 800,000 men, 770 tanks, and 9,150 crew-served guns, not counting the replacement units and rear services. The strongest in men and equipment was the Western *Front*.

German Army Group Center numbered more than 1,000,000 men, 1,700 tanks and assault guns, and 19,000 guns and mortars. The powerful Second Air Fleet, commanded by Field Marshal Albert Kesselring, supported the German ground forces.

The German offensive, code-named "Taifun," made good progress in early October. The Nineteenth and Thirtieth armies of the Western *Front* and the Forty-third Army of the Reserve *Front* were hard hit by enemy strikes originating north of Kukhovshchina and east of Roslavl, and the Germans succeeded in breaking through the Red Army defenses. Moving swiftly, they encircled all the Vyazma formations of the Western and Reserve *fronts* from the north and south.

An extremely difficult situation also developed for the defenders of the Bryansk *Front*, where the Third and Thirteenth armies appeared to be threatened with encirclement. Not encountering any real resistance, Guderian's forces rushed to Orel, capturing the city on October 3. The Soviets were taken so completely by surprise that the electric trams were still running when German tanks broke into the rail hub and industrial center. The evacuation of industrial installations was frustrated by the suddenness of the attack, and along the streets the Germans found dismantled machines and crates filled with tools and raw materials. The Bryansk *Front* did not have sufficient forces at Orel to repel the attack; it was now split and its forces badly mauled, forcing a withdrawal to the east and southeast and simultaneously creating a serious situation in the direction of Tula.

Colonel General Ivan Konev, now commanding the Western *Front* (having relieved Timoshenko on September 12 when the latter was assigned to the Southwestern Direction), decided to counterattack the Germans who had penetrated his defenses. For this task he used the operational group of Lieutenant General I. V. Boldin, but the operation was unsuccessful. Toward the end of the day on October 6, a considerable portion of the Western *Front* and the Reserve *Front* had been surrounded west of Vyazma.

Despite their impressive victories the Germans began to entertain serious doubts about the outcome of the campaign. During the night of October 6–7, the winter's first snow fell. "It did not lie for long," Guderian remembers, "and, as usual, the roads rapidly became nothing but canals of bottomless mud, along which our vehicles could only advance at a snail's pace and with great wear to the engines."[30] To complicate matters, winter clothing had not arrived, nor would it reach the half-frozen troops during the remainder of 1941.

Another ominous sign was the ferocity of the Russian defense; Guderian was startled to see how deeply his best officers had been affected by the bitter fighting. One could observe the fatigue of the officers in the front-line units, he noted, although headquarters personnel at OKH and Group were in high spirits. "Here was a radical difference in attitude which as time went on grew wider until it could scarcely be bridged," Guderian observed, adding that the combat units were unaware that their superiors were drunk with the scent of victory.[31]

By October 6, German tank units, having penetrated the Rzhev–Vyazma defense line, were advancing toward the Mozhaisk fortified line some fifty miles west of Moscow. Improved during the summer of 1941, the line consisted of a number of fortified positions extending from Kalinin to Kaluga, Maloyaroslavets, and Tula, but the few troops manning it could not be expected to halt the bulk of the German forces which were making their way eastward. Desperately needed reinforcements were on their way from the Soviet Far East and central Asia.

The Germans, meanwhile, were pulling divisions out of the Leningrad sector and sending them to the Moscow fighting. The First Panzer Division went straight to Army Group Center without a pause for rest and refitting. The Nineteenth and Twentieth Panzer divisions were on their way. A Spanish division was dispatched to Leningrad in the early days of October, but its arrival was briefly delayed when Soviet partisans disrupted rail traffic.

At this critical juncture Stalin once again turned to Georgi Zhukov. The details of his summons to the Kremlin remained untold until August, 1966, when Zhukov began publishing his memoirs of the battle for Moscow in *Voyenno-Istorichesky Zhurnal* as the twenty-fifth anniversary of the event approached. Although it contains a few surprises, the article confirms, for the most part, earlier accounts of the battle.

On the evening of October 6, Stalin telephoned Zhukov and asked how things were going at Leningrad. Zhukov reported that the Germans had stopped their attacks. Prisoners of war said that the Germans had suffered great losses and were now on the defensive. The city was still being bombarded by artillery fire and from the air, however. Soviet aerial reconnaissance had detected a large movement of mechanized and tank columns from Leningrad to the south, Zhukov reported, commenting that the German command was apparently transferring these troops toward Moscow.[32] The day before Halder had recorded in his journal that the attack against the Ladoga sector planned for October 6 had been called off by OKH, and an order had been issued to take out the armored divisions. The attack would be launched with infantry as soon as sufficient strength had been built up.[33]

After listening to Zhukov's report, Stalin remained silent for a moment and then said that a serious situation was developing in the direction of Moscow, especially on the Western *Front*. He told Zhukov, "Turn over your responsibility for acting commander of the Leningrad *Front* to the Chief-of-Staff, General Khozin, and fly to Moscow."[34]

Although Zhukov does not mention it in his memoirs, his first act was to phone Fedyuninsky, who was commanding the Forty-second Army. "You have not forgotten that you are my deputy?" Zhukov asked his friend. "Come right away." Fedyuninsky left quickly for the Smolny, where he learned the reason for the call. Zhukov told him: "Take command of the *front*. You don't need to be familiarized with the situation, since it is known to you. They have sent for me to go immediately to the Stavka."[35]

The records show that Fedyuninsky remained in charge at Leningrad until October 26, when he replaced M. S. Khozin as commander of the Fifty-fourth Army and Khozin came up to lead the *front*. In his memoirs Zhukov skips over these details, simply noting that he transmitted Stalin's instructions to General Khozin, said good-by to the members of the Military Council, and left for Moscow. The battle for that city was already under way, and Zhukov was to play a very significant role in it.

After Zhukov was removed from office by Khrushchev in 1957, military historians often appeared reluctant to identify him by name. In volume after volume he was mentioned almost in passing, or his assignments were merely given in brief footnotes. In the history of the Battle of Leningrad, *Bitva za Leningrad* (the source of much of the material in this chapter), Zhukov is mentioned only once by name, while there are two references to Khrushchev, who was not present. Voroshilov is mentioned five times, and a flattering photograph is included. The authors got around the problem of praising Zhukov for his organization of Leningrad's defenses by referring to him as "*front* commander" or simply "command." The following comment is an example:

> In appraising the disposition and operational formation of the Leningrad *front*, it is necessary to note that the command, creatively assimilating the experience received in the previous battles, refused to divide equally the forces and equipment along the *front* and concentrated the main forces on the decisive axis—the southwestern and southern approaches to Leningrad. This decision was completely timely and correct.[36]

The decision was Zhukov's.

VIII. THE VIEW FROM ISTRA

Russia is big, but there is nowhere to retreat because Moscow is behind us.

Politruk Klochkov to Panfilov's soldiers, November, 1941

AT dusk on October 7, 1941, General Georgi Zhukov's plane touched down at Moscow's Central Airport. He left immediately for the Kremlin, where he found Stalin alone in his office. The Russian dictator had suffered an attack of influenza and was obviously not well. Greeting Zhukov with a nod of the head, he pointed to a map and said: "Look at this! A very difficult situation has developed, but I can't get a detailed report on the true state of affairs on the Western *Front*." Stalin told Zhukov to leave immediately for *front* headquarters, assess the situation, and then telephone back, regardless of the hour. "I'll wait," Stalin said, terminating the conversation.[1]

Fifteen minutes later Zhukov was with the chief of the General Staff, Marshal Shaposhnikov, who had reassumed that post when Zhukov left in the last days of July to take charge of the Reserve *Front* at Smolensk. Shaposhnikov, whose ill health would soon force him to retire, appeared extremely tired. He greeted Zhukov and told him that Stalin had already telephoned instructions to provide Zhukov with a map of the approaches to Moscow, where bitter fighting was in progress (see map, page 197). Said Shaposhnikov: "The map will be here in a minute. The command of the Western *Front* is located at the very same spot where the headquarters of the Reserve *Front* was in August, at the time we were conducting operations against the Elnya salient." (It was there that Zhukov's Reserve *Front* had struck the German forces a powerful blow in early September, throwing them back from the Elnya area.)

After describing the critical situation on the *fronts*, Shaposhnikov added that the work of constructing positions on the Mozhaisk defensive line and on the near approaches to Moscow was still not complete and that almost no troops were stationed there. He believed it necessary for troops to occupy the defensive lines—and the Mozhaisk line first of all. That very night units from the Stavka Reserve and from adjacent *fronts* had begun moving toward the lines.

As soon as Zhukov had familiarized himself with the situation, he left for the headquarters of the Western *Front*, taking his map with him. On the way, with the illumination of a pocket flashlight, he continued to study the locations and operations of both combatants. When he became drowsy, he would stop the car, step out into the crisp autumn air, and run two or three hundred yards.

At *front* headquarters the duty officer reported that the entire staff was with the *front* commander, Colonel General Ivan S. Konev. When Zhukov entered the room, Konev, members of the Military Council, the chief of staff, and the chief of operations were talking in semidarkness relieved by only a few stearin candles. Even in such poor light Zhukov could see the strain in every man's face.

He announced his mission from Stalin. Lieutenant General G. K. Malandin, the chief of staff, answered Zhukov's questions and told him what had happened between October 2 and 7. The Germans had regrouped their forces on the Moscow approaches and now outnumbered the Russians in infantry on the Western, Reserve, and Bryansk *fronts*. The Soviets were most concerned about the possibilities of concentrated strikes on the three fronts; there were gaping holes in the defense, and no reserves were left to plug them.

Zhukov listened to Malandin's summary. Then, at 2:30 A.M., he telephoned Stalin, who was still working at his desk. Zhukov reported that the principal danger at the moment was lack of troops. The weak units deployed on the Mozhaisk line could not prevent a breakthrough toward Moscow by German armored forces, he said. Troops must be moved to Mozhaisk as soon as possible.

According to Zhukov's memoirs, Stalin then asked, "Where are the Sixteenth, Nineteenth, and Twentieth armies and Boldin's group of the Western *Front* and the Twenty-fourth and Thirty-second armies of the Reserve *Front* at this moment?"

"Encircled west and northwest of Vyazma," Zhukov replied.

"What do you intend to do?" Stalin asked him.

"I'm going in to see Budenny. . . ." (Marshal Budenny was at this time commanding the Reserve *Front*.)

"But," asked Stalin, "do you know where his headquarters are now?"

"No, I don't know. I'll look somewhere in the vicinity of Maloyaroslavets."

"All right, see Budenny and call me from there," Stalin said.

It was drizzling as Georgi Zhukov set out to find Budenny. A dense fog hung over the countryside, making visibility poor. By dawn the next day (October 8) Zhukov had reached the Obninskoye siding, about sixty-five miles from Moscow. He noticed two signalmen pulling a cable alongside the bridge over the Protva River. Asking them where they were laying the communications line, Zhukov received an abrupt answer. "Where it was ordered, that's where we'll take it," replied one of the men in a chilling tone. Zhukov told the soldiers that they knew their duty and did right not to answer the questions of someone they did not know. He then identified himself and told them that he was searching for the Reserve *Front* headquarters and Marshal Budenny. One of the signalmen said that Zhukov had already passed the *front* headquarters and gave him instructions on how to reach it.

Ten minutes later Zhukov was in the office of Army Commissar First Rank L. Z. Mekhlis, where the chief of staff, Major General A. F. Anisov, was also headquartered. Zhukov disliked Mekhlis intensely. The latter had actively participated in the purges and had supported the re-introduction of the political-commissar system into the Red Army, a move Zhukov had strongly opposed.[2] Mekhlis was giving someone a tongue-lashing over the telephone when Zhukov walked in. He put the phone down, and Zhukov explained that he had come as a member of the Stavka on orders from Stalin to find Budenny. Mekhlis told him that the commander had been with the Forty-third Army the day before but that headquarters had lost contact with him. His staff was concerned that something might have happened to him, and liaison officers who had been sent to find him had not returned. Neither Mekhlis nor Anisov was able to tell Zhukov anything specific about the enemy position or about the condition of the *front* troops.

"Just look at the situation we've got ourselves into," Mekhlis said. "Right now I'm collecting the men who are retreating. We'll rearm them and form them into new units at the assembly points."

Zhukov headed through Maloyaroslavets and Medyn toward Yukhnov, where he hoped to assess the situation at first hand. Passing Protva and Obninskoye, he found himself recalling his childhood and youth. At the Obninskoye siding, he remembered, his mother had put him on a train when he was twelve years old, sending him to relatives in Moscow to learn the fur business. The countryside was very familiar to him; he had been over it many times in his youth. Now, as he passed through Obninskoye, he began to wonder how the coming conflict would affect his mother, his sister, and her four children, who still lived in Strelkovka, his birthplace. "I didn't want to, but I thought what would happen to them if the Fascists came there. Would they find out about the mother, sister, and nephews and nieces of General Zhukov? And then . . . ? Three days later my adjutant was sent to get them and bring them from the village to my apartment in Moscow."

When Zhukov arrived in Maloyaroslavets, he did not meet a single human being as he made his way to the center of town. When he reached the District Executive Committee Building (Raiispolkom), he noticed two vehicles. A driver was asleep behind the wheel of one. Zhukov recalled: "We had to wake him up, and he said that this was Semyen Mikhailovich's [Budenny's] car and that he had been inside for about three hours. Going into the Executive Committee Building, I saw S. M. Budenny. We greeted each other warmly. It was obvious that he had lived through much in those tragic days."

After hearing about Zhukov's trip to the headquarters of the Western *Front*, Budenny explained that he had not communicated with Konev for more than two days and that while he was visiting the Forty-third Army his headquarters had moved to a new location unknown to him. Zhukov told him where it was and impressed on Budenny the gravity of the situation on the Western *Front*—a large part of its forces had been surrounded.

"It's no better here," Budenny replied. "The Twenty-fourth and Thirty-second armies are cut off, and a defensive front doesn't exist. Yesterday I myself just about fell into the enemy's hands between Yukhnov and Vyazma. Large tank and motorized columns were moving near Vyazma, evidently with the aim of enveloping the city from the east."

"Who's holding Yukhnov?" Zhukov asked his former chief.

"I don't know now. A small detachment and about two infantry regiments were located on the Ugra River, but there was no artillery. I think Yukhnov is in enemy hands."

"Well," Zhukov asked, "who is covering the road from Yukhnov to Maloyaroslavets?"

"When I went there," Budenny said, "I didn't meet anybody except three policemen in Medyn."

With masterful politeness and tact Zhukov writes: "We agreed that Semyen Mikhailovich should go immediately to the *front* headquarters and from there report to the Stavka about the state of affairs, and I would travel to the Yukhnov area and then to Kaluga."

West of Maloyaroslavets, Zhukov met the commandant of the fortified region, who reported on the progress of engineering preparations, the availability of workers' battalions, and the means by which the combat units could defend the approaches to the city. The two talked about how to organize reconnaissance and how to get the fortified area ready for combat. Zhukov then went on to Medyn.

The town was abandoned, except for an elderly woman who was searching for something in the ruins of a bombed-out house.

"Grandma, what are you looking for?" Zhukov asked her. She stood with her eyes open wide, staring, her gray hair disheveled, but did not reply.

"What's wrong with you, old lady?" he asked.

The woman began to dig silently, ignoring Zhukov's questions.

From somewhere out of the ruins another woman emerged, carrying a sack partly filled with belongings. "Don't ask her questions," she said to Zhukov. "She won't answer you, because she's gone crazy with grief." Then she told Zhukov that two days earlier German aircraft had bombed and strafed the town. Many people had been killed or wounded. The survivors had moved on to Maloyaroslavets. The old woman had lived with her small grandson, and the air raid had caught her at the well while she was drawing water. She saw the bombs fall on her house, where she had left the child. The second woman had lost her house too, and she was now digging in the ruins for shoes and clothing. Tears rolled down her cheeks as she spoke to the general. To the question whether Red Army troops had arrived in the town she answered that several vehicles had passed through Maloyaroslavets during the night and trucks had come through with the wounded, but no one else had been there. Saying farewell, Zhukov proceeded toward Yukhnov, "very sorry that I couldn't say anything to comfort this woman, or the other Soviet people to whom the war had brought suffering and grief."

As Zhukov's car moved toward Yukhnov, Red Army troops in coveralls and tank helmets blocked the road where it passed through a forest. One of the men approached Zhukov and told him that he could go no farther. Zhukov identified himself and asked the soldier where his unit was stationed. Told that the tank brigade's headquarters was a little more than one hundred yards away, in the forest, Zhukov asked the soldier to lead him there. Entering the woods, Zhukov saw a tank officer, also in helmet and blue coveralls, sitting on a stump. The officer snapped to and said, "The tank brigade commander of the Stavka Reserve, Colonel Troitsky, reports!"

Zhukov was happy to see an old friend. He had served with I. I. Troitsky at Khalkhin-Gol in 1939. The colonel had been chief of staff of the Eleventh Tank Brigade, which had defeated the Japanese Twenty-third Infantry Division, part of the Imperial Guard, at Mount Bain-Tsagan.

Troitsky reported that the Germans now occupied Yukhnov and that their advance units had seized the bridge over the Ugra River. Patrols sent to Kaluga had learned that the Germans were not there at the moment but that fighting was already under way not far from the city, where the Fifth Guards Infantry Division and several units of the Forty-third Army, which had been withdrawing, were in action. Although it had been in the area for two days, Troitsky's brigade, part of the Stavka Reserve, had not received any orders.

Zhukov told Troitsky to send liaison officers to Reserve *Front* Head-quarters to report to Budenny on the situation. Part of the brigade was to deploy forward and organize a defense to cover the approach to Medyn. Zhukov also instructed the colonel to report the orders he had been given to the General Staff by way of the Reserve *Front* and also to report that he, Zhukov, was going to Kaluga to the Fifth Guards Infantry Division. With that, Zhukov said farewell.

Meanwhile, the need to combine the Western and Reserve *fronts* into a single command became clear. Molotov, Voroshilov, Vasilevsky, N. A. Bulganin, and Konev, meeting at the Western *Front* command post in Krasnovidovo to discuss the situation, concluded that the two forces should be reconstituted immediately as the Western *Front* and pro-posed to Stalin that Zhukov be appointed commander. The Stavka agreed. Zhukov was handed a telegram which read: "The Supreme Commander in Chief orders you to go to the headquarters of the West-ern *Front*. You are assigned as commander of the Western *Front*."

Early on the morning of October 10, Zhukov arrived at the head-quarters, now situated about two miles northwest of Mozhaisk. The members of the State Defense Committee were still there, and he ob-served that, "from the very fact of their hasty arrival at such a tense time on the Western *Front* and from conversations with the members of this commission, it was easy to see that the Supreme Commander in Chief was extremely worried about the difficult and very dangerous situation which had developed near Moscow."

In his memoirs of the campaign Zhukov summarized the problems which had plagued the High Command in the early days of October. The commands of the Western, Reserve, and Bryansk *fronts*, he pointed out, had made serious miscalculations. While the German offensive was being planned, the Western and Reserve *fronts* had not carried out the necessary defensive preparations. Ignoring reconnaissance, they had not distributed their forces along the most seriously threatened axes, al-though the Stavka had warned about the strong concentration of Ger-man forces against them. No defense in depth had been organized, and no antitank units or *front* reserves had been brought up in time. No artillery and air preparations had been made to strike the main enemy concentrations while they were still in their departure areas. After the

Germans had broken through the Russian defenses in the Vyazma area, the command had made no arrangements to withdraw the forces threatened with encirclement. As a result the Sixteenth, Nineteenth, Twentieth, Twenty-fourth, and Thirty-second armies were surrounded.

While Zhukov was conferring with members of the State Defense Committee at *front* headquarters, he received orders to telephone Stalin. The people's commissar of defense (a title Stalin had assumed in July) confirmed his assignment as commander of the Western *Front* and asked him whether he had any objections. Zhukov replied that he had no reason to object. In further conversation it became evident that Stalin intended a thorough overhaul in the leadership of the Western *Front*, now that the commander had been replaced. Zhukov protested that that was not the solution to the problem, and Stalin finally agreed to retain Konev as deputy commander and also concurred with Zhukov's proposal to give Konev the additional duty of commanding the forces around Kalinin, since these troops were far removed from headquarters and needed auxiliary control. Stalin told Zhukov that the remnants of the Reserve *Front* were being transferred to his command, along with those units located on the Mozhaisk line and the Stavka reserves now moving toward that area. "Hurry up and form the Western *Front* and fight!" Stalin ordered, ending the conversation.

John Erickson observes: "With Zhukov, one of the ablest heads in the Red Army had taken up the all-important front. That the *Stavka* did consider it all-important may be gauged from the fact that of all Red Army troops engaged from the Baltic to the Black Sea, 40 per cent were concentrated at the western approaches to Moscow."[3] One of Zhukov's close associates, Konstantin K. Rokossovsky, writes of this episode:

> I had known Georgi Konstantinovich many years before this. The fortunes of the military had thrown us together many times and again separated us for a long time, [and] our official relationship to each other had changed. . . . To my way of thinking, G. K. Zhukov has always remained a person of strong will and resoluteness, brilliant, gifted, exacting, persistent and clear of purpose. All of these qualities undoubtedly are necessary for a strong military chief, and they are characteristic of G. K. Zhukov. True, sometimes his severity exceeded permissible limits. . . . I shall remark that at the height of combat actions at Moscow our *front* commander sometimes, in my view, was guilty of unwarranted abruptness.[4]

One must bear in mind that these traits made it possible for Zhukov to organize Soviet defenses without concern for the personal feelings of subordinates. Under immense pressure to save Moscow and Mother Russia, he often stepped on toes, thereby gaining a reputation as a strict, unyielding, resolute, and even brutal commander.

With characteristic energy Zhukov set about his new tasks. He met with Konev and Sokolovsky (the latter now his chief of staff), and several matters were decided on the spot. First, it was agreed that *front* headquarters should be moved to Alabino. Next, Konev was to be sent with a group of officers to Kalinin to coordinate the actions of the various units on that critical axis. Zhukov was to take Bulganin, a member of the Military Council, to Mozhaisk and examine the defenses on the spot.

Konev left for Kalinin early on October 12. The situation there was extremely complicated, requiring the reorganization and regrouping of troops. He himself took command of the Twenty-second, Twenty-ninth, Thirtieth, and Thirty-first armies. The Germans had seized Kalinin but were not able to move farther. A few days later, on October 17, the Kalinin *Front* was formed, and Konev became its commander.

When Zhukov and Bulganin arrived at the headquarters of the Mozhaisk fortified region, they were greeted by the commandant, Lieutenant Colonel S. I. Bogdanov. Artillery fire and bomb explosions could be heard distinctly as the men began their conference. Colonel Bogdanov reported that the Thirty-second Infantry Division, reinforced by artillery and a tank brigade, was locked in combat with German advance mechanized and armor units on the approaches to Borodino. Zhukov ordered him to hold his defensive sector at all costs. With that, he returned to *front* headquarters at Alabino.

In the meantime, Zhukov's staff had completed many of the organizational and operational tasks he had assigned them. They had also been ordered to work out the details of a strong defense along the line through Volokolamsk, Mozhaisk, Maloyaroslavets, and Kaluga. They were to develop it in depth and form *front* reserves.

The Mozhaisk defensive line possessed a number of advantages for the Red Army troops who would try to hold it. It was protected in front by the Lama, Moscow, Kolocha, Luzha, and Sukhodrev rivers, all of which had steep banks offering natural obstacles to tank movements. The line was served by a system of road and rail communications that would permit extensive troop maneuvers in all directions. The only problem plaguing the Soviet command was the lack of troops to occupy the 136-mile-wide line. Until October 10 only four infantry divisions, the Moscow Artillery and Military-Political schools, the Academy of the Supreme Soviet of the R.S.F.S.R.,* the Podolsk Machinegun-Artillery School, three reserve infantry regiments, and five machine-gun battalions were deployed there. Although it had been anticipated that 150 battalions would man the line, only 45 had been scraped together, which yielded an average density of one battalion to each three miles of front.

The Stavka continued to take urgent steps to defend the capital. On October 9 the command of the Mozhaisk defensive line, redesignated the Moscow Reserve *Front*, received five newly reorganized machine-gun battalions, ten antitank artillery regiments, and five tank brigades. By October 11 the troops on the Mozhaisk line had been combined into the Fifth Army under the command of D. D. Lelyushenko. As units from the various *fronts* withdrew, they began to concentrate on this defensive line.

Zhukov's mission was clear, and time was precious. He and his staff worked long hours, and he later recalled that some of his people literally collapsed on their feet.

In accordance with the Stavka's directive, all combat units and installations of the Moscow Reserve *Front* were transferred to Zhukov's reorganized Western *Front* as of 11:00 P.M. on October 12. Meanwhile, the Stavka had been sending Zhukov much-needed reserves. Beginning on October 7 a number of troops had been transferred from other *fronts* and from the Stavka Reserve to Mozhaisk: fourteen infantry divisions, sixteen reconstituted tank brigades, more than forty artillery regiments, ten mine and flame-thrower companies, and other combat units. At the same time Zhukov was faced with another problem: extricating the encircled Russian armies at Vyazma. In this effort he was only partly successful.[5]

On the south, around Bryansk, the Red Army was engaged in bitter fighting, trying to break out of an encirclement there. Only a small number of troops succeeded in escaping in the Sevsk area on October 9, but, wrote Guderian, "those who did unfortunately seem to have included the staff of the Russian 13th Army."[6] Two days later, while much of the German mechanized force was bogged down in mud, the

* Russian Soviet Federated Socialist Republic, the largest of the Soviet republics.

Soviets attempted to break out of the Trubchevsk encirclement along either bank of the Navlia. Guderian wrote of this battle:

> Between the 29th and 25th [Motorized] Infantry Divisions there was severe fighting and the enemy succeeded in creating a gap in our defenses which was only sealed by the timely arrival of the 5th Machine-gun Battalion. At the same time heavy street fighting took place in XXIV Panzer Corps' area in Mzensk [Mtsensk], to the northeast of Orel, into which town the 4th Panzer Division had fought its way; the division could not receive support quickly enough on account of the mud. Numerous T-34's went into action and inflicted heavy losses on the German tanks. Up to this time we had enjoyed tank superiority, but from now on the situation was reversed. The prospect of rapid, decisive victories was fading in consequence.[7]

Two days later the Russians continued their efforts to break out between the Navlia and Borchevko, and about five thousand men succeeded in fighting their way through the German lines. On October 17, however, the Germans were able to destroy the bulk of the Fiftieth Army, which had been encircled north of Bryansk.[8]

Nevertheless, the stubbornness of the Soviet defense in those critical October days temporarily halted the German offensive. It won precious time to organize the defense on the Mozhaisk line from the flank and prevent the capture of Moscow. Zhukov ordered a number of antitank and artillery strongpoints set up on the most seriously threatened routes of approach, with particular attention to likely ambush positions. When the Kalinin *Front* was organized on October 17, Zhukov's area of responsibility was cut in half, enabling him to concentrate on the defense of the most direct approaches to the capital.

In mid-October the newly reformed Fifth, Sixteenth, Forty-third, and Forty-ninth armies still numbered only ninety thousand men, far below what was needed for a continuous defensive line. Zhukov therefore decided to protect the more important approaches first—the Volokolamsk, Istra, Mozhaisk, Maloyaroslavets, Podolsk–Kaluga axes—reinforcing them with available artillery and antitank weapons. Skilled, experienced commanders were placed in charge: Rokossovsky, the Sixteenth Army and the Volokolamsk fortified region; L. A. Govorov, Fifth Army, the Mozhaisk fortified region; K. D. Golubev, the Forty-third Army, which included the Maloyaroslavets fortified region; and I. G. Zakharkin, the Forty-ninth Army, with responsibility for the Kaluga fortified region.

"All these commanders," Zhukov later wrote, "were experienced and skilled in their jobs as military leaders. One could rely completely on them and on their trusted troops to do everything possible to keep the enemy from getting through to Moscow."[9]

Behind the first-echelon troops Red Army engineers constructed obstacles and antitank defenses along the most likely tank approaches. Reserves were moved forward along the main axes. The *front* headquarters was moved again—from Alabino to Perkhushkovo. "Thus," Zhukov recorded, "a new Western *Front* was created, which was going to repel the strike of the German Fascist troops against Moscow."[10]

On October 13, Zhukov's defenders were forced to abandon Kaluga, and bloody battles were waged on all the main approaches to Moscow. According to *front* intelligence, on October 15 up to fifty German tanks advanced to the area of Turginovo, about one hundred to Lotoshino, up to one hundred to Makarovo and Karagatovo, about fifty in the region of Borovsk, and forty to Borodino. The German Thirteenth Army Corps attacked along the Tarusa axis, seizing the towns of Tarusa and Aleksin and creating a deep envelopment from north of Tula.

The danger to Moscow increased hourly as the Western *Front* was forced to yield to mounting enemy pressure. The command was not able to stabilize the defense on the Mozhaisk line. The deep German penetration in the center of the Western *Front*'s defense along the Naro Fominsk and Podolsk axes and the abandoning of the main line of the Mozhaisk defensive belt by the Fifth, Forty-third, and Forty-ninth armies created an extremely difficult situation on Moscow's near approaches.[11]

At this point tension in the capital became almost unbearable. Pedestrians swarmed the streets, for buses and taxis had been commandeered to carry troops to the front. From the chimneys of public buildings throughout the city "black snow"—charred bits of hurriedly burned documents—was falling. On Wednesday, October 15, Molotov summoned the members of the diplomatic community to inform them that they were to leave Moscow that evening to accompany the government to Kuybyshev. Stalin, however, had decided to stay in Moscow.[12] A witness to these events, journalist Henry C. Cassidy, recalls:

> We had our tickets for Kuybyshev.
> I trudged wearily back to the foreign commissariat to pick up my type-

writer. But first, there was a message to be sent. The A.P. had requested
an article on Lenin's tomb. "Tomb closed," I typed. Then I shut my
machine. With it, I thought, I was closing an epoch.

My last view of the battle of Moscow was a cavalryman on a tawny little
horse, drawing up before a policeman at the corner of Gorky Street and
Kuznetsky Most, and leaning over to speak. My fevered mind conjured
up the picture of him asking the way to the front. "Right up the Mojhaisk
chaussee," I felt like crying, "and not very far."[13]

There was panic as rumors spread that the German tanks might break
into the city at any moment. Shops were stormed, trucks with tinned
food ransacked and overturned, Party cards destroyed, and pictures of
Stalin removed. In his history of the Moscow battle A. M. Samsonov
writes:

> Directly within the city itself an alarming situation arose; this was
> especially evident on October 16, 17 and 18. These were critical days which
> also were days of a serious test of the steadfastness and courage of the
> Soviet people.
>
> ... At the time when the patriotism of the Muscovites and their readiness
> to participate in the courageous struggle were demonstrated with excep-
> tional vigor, manifestations of confusion among a small number of the
> inhabitants were observed. In the capital were found people who spread
> panic, who abandoned their work, and who hurried to desert the city.
> There were also outright traitors who tried to use the situation which
> had arisen to plunder Socialist property and undermine the power of the
> Soviet state.[14]

Zhukov confirms Samsonov's account and describes the steps taken by
the government to cope with the situation:

> The evacuation began on the night of October 16. All these measures
> the Muskovites accepted with full understanding. But, as it is said, it is a
> small flock that has not a black sheep; cowards, panic mongers and self-
> seekers were found who rushed from Moscow in all directions, spreading
> dirty rumors about the inevitability of its surrender. With the aim of mo-
> bilizing to repel the enemy, and also to suppress the cases of panic which
> arose through the fault of provocateur elements in Moscow on October
> 16, the State Defense Committee on October 19 reached the decision to
> declare Moscow and its environs in a state of siege.[15]

The decree, announced in the Soviet newspapers, provided that all
enemies of public order were to be handed over at once to courts-martial

and that all provocateurs, spies, and other enemies inciting riot were to be shot out of hand. It was added that the defense of the capital, to be undertaken on lines sixty-two to seventy-four miles west of the city, had been entrusted to Zhukov.

Now under the most intense pressure of his career, Zhukov worked with even greater energy to save the Russian capital. The defensive line from Volokolamsk through Mozhaisk and Maloyaroslavets to Serpukhov was still manned by weak Soviet forces, and the Germans were occupying points along it. To prevent an enemy breakthrough to Moscow, the Military Council of the *front* selected a new main line of defense extending through Novo Zavidovsky, Klin, the Istra Reservoir, the suburb of Istra, Zhavoronki, Krasnaya Pakhra, Serpukhov, and Aleksin. Zhukov believed it expedient to withdraw all Western *Front* armies from the Mozhaisk line and redeploy them on the new one.

Zhukov's plan allowed for the possibility that the Soviets might not be able to contain the enemy at the Mozhaisk line, in which case they would withdraw to prepared positions along the new one. Rear guards, reinforced with antitank weapons, would launch limited counterattacks to delay the enemy as long as possible. To ensure the free movement of military traffic, no vehicles were to be directed toward or permitted through Moscow or the Moscow hub.

The proposal, dated October 19, was signed by Zhukov, Bulganin (a member of the Military Council of the Western *Front*), and Zhukov's chief of staff, Lieutenant General Sokolovsky. It was sent in secret to the various army commanders, who worked out details pertinent to them. It was submitted to the Supreme High Command and approved on the same day.

Also on October 19, after the radio announcement that Moscow was under siege, those inhabitants who had not left the city met to help organize its defense. In three days' time workers, engineers, scientists, writers, civil servants, and students were mobilized into 25 battalions of home guards, totaling 12,000 men. By the end of October these battalions had grown to 4 divisions numbering 40,000 people. In addition, 169 street-fighting squads and several hundred tank-destroyer squads numbering 10,000 men were organized. Moscow factories began turning out materials needed for defense—hedgehogs, rails, cement, bricks, and other items. Soon 450,000 people, three-fourths of them women, were constructing defense lines around the capital. By the end of November the entire defense system on the far and near approaches to Moscow was virtually complete.

In his description of the battle for Moscow, Zhukov debunks the stories of "General Mud," who, he claims, played no favorites in the campaign:

> In the postwar years much has been said in connection with frequent complaints by Hitlerite generals and bourgeois historians concerning the Russian *rasputitsa* [seasonal impassability of roads] and mud and the freezing Russian weather. . . . I want to draw the readers' attention once again to the reason given by the writer K. Tippelskirch why the German Fascist troops were kept from seizing Moscow. "Movement along the roads became impossible," he writes. "Mud stuck to the feet, to the hoofs of the animals, wheels of the wagons and vehicles. . . . The offensive came to a halt."
>
> Does it turn out that the Hitlerite generals, in planning a campaign in the East, counted on getting to Moscow and farther on smooth, well-built roads? Well, in such a case it was worse for us than for the German troops, which were halted on the approaches to Moscow, as Tippelskirch maintains, because of mud. In those days I saw with my own eyes in the very same *rasputitsa* and mud thousands upon thousands of Moscow's inhabitants, unaccustomed, generally speaking, to hard engineer work, leaving their urban apartments, lightly dressed, digging antitank ditches, trenches, setting up obstacles, constructing barricades, barriers, carrying sandbags. Mud stuck to their feet and to the wheels of the wheelbarrows in which they carried earth, unbelievably increasing the weight of the shovel which, even without the mud, was not very handy for women. I think that it is not necessary to continue this comparison further. For those who are inclined to let mud mask the real reasons of their defeat at Moscow I might also add that in October 1941 the *rasputitsa* was relatively short. It turned colder in the first days of November, snow fell, and the terrain and roads everywhere became passable. In the November days of the "general offensive" of the Hitlerite troops, the temperature in the combat area of the Moscow region was found to be between 7 and 10 degrees of frost [Fahrenheit], and, as we know, mud does not exist in such a case.[16]

Laboring in the cold weather, the people of Moscow were able to create an impressive defense perimeter. On the lines near Moscow and in the city itself 201 miles of antitank obstacles (not counting minefields) were constructed; 158 miles of anti-infantry obstacles were emplaced; 3,800 fire points were prepared, 1,500 of them made of iron and concrete; and 37,500 metal hedgehogs were manufactured and positioned. The defense lines near Moscow were strengthened with explosives and wooden obstructions. Wooden tank obstacles extended from northwest of Aleksandrovsk, in the Ivanovsk Region, to the southeast through an area making up eighteen regions of the Moscow Region and six regions of the Ryazansk Region along a front of 860 miles and to a depth of 54 yards to half a mile. The obstacles encompassed a total area of more than 130,963 acres, or nearly 205 square miles.

As fighting raged on Moscow's western approaches, its inhabitants worked and lived under increasingly difficult conditions. The Germans sent more and more bombers against the capital in October and November. In the midst of these raids the Muscovites continued mass evacuation of the large industrial enterprises in and around the city. More than 88,000 rail cars loaded with equipment, metal, and semimanufactured goods, as well as workers and their families, departed for the Middle and Lower Volga, the Urals, Siberia, central Asia, and Kazakhstan, where new factories were being set up. Before the evacuation to the east, there were 75,000 metal machine tools in Moscow; after the transfer, only 21,000 remained. Before the war Moscow's electric power system had considerably exceeded 1.4 million kilowatts; in the fall of 1941 it did not supply even half that amount. Those factories which were not evacuated stepped up their production of war materials; one Moscow enterprise, for example, was able to turn out 1,500 Pistolet-Pulemet Shpagin (PPSh) machine pistols a day.

Despite the gravity of the situation Stalin decided to maintain the semblance of order—and perhaps show a bold front—by holding the traditional October Revolution parade. On November 1, Zhukov was summoned to the Stavka. Stalin told him: "Besides the ceremonial gathering on the occasion of the October anniversary we want to hold a military parade in Moscow. Do you think that the situation at the front will permit us to carry out these celebrations?" Zhukov replied that the Germans were in no condition to start a large push within the next few days; they had suffered considerable losses in the October battles and were now engaged in reinforcing and regrouping their units. But the German air force was able, and almost certainly would try, to intervene. It was decided that the parade would be held anyway. To prevent air attacks during the ceremonies the capital's air defense was strengthened with additional fighter aircraft from neighboring fronts.

The traditional celebration of the Moscow Party and workers' organizations, held on the eve of the anniversary of the October Revolution, took place in an unusual setting, deep underground in the Mayakovskaya subway station. The next morning, November 7, in a snowy, early-winter haze, Soviet citizens witnessed a unique military parade. Troops equipped for battle marched past Lenin's tomb and then headed for the front. "The domestic, political, and international significance of this November parade undoubtedly was great," Zhukov wrote.[17]

In his speech in Red Square, Stalin sought to inspire his listeners by reminding them that they had survived darker days. He reminded his audience of the year 1918, when three-quarters of the country was in the hands of foreigners. At that time, he said, Russia had no allies and the Red Army was just being created. But in 1941 the story was different: Soviet Russia now had allies who had joined with her to form a united front against the Germans. Soon, possibly within a year, Germany must collapse under the weight "of its own crimes." Invoking the names of Russia's great ancestors and national heroes, Stalin concluded by saying that the Soviets were fighting a war of liberation, that the memories of Alexander Nevsky, Dmitri Donskoi, Kozma Minin, Dmitri Pozharsky, Alexander Suvorov, and Mikhail Kutuzov must inspire them in this war.

In the first half of November the Soviet Supreme High Command took steps to frustrate an expected German offensive against Moscow. Zhukov continued to strengthen the defensive lines near the city and carried out a regrouping of the Western *Front*. A detailed and useful account of his role has been provided by Pavel Alekseevich Belov. In addition to recording operations in his own sector, Belov describes a strategic planning session which he and Zhukov attended. Of special interest is his account of relations between Zhukov and Stalin:

> At 1545 hours [on November 9] I arrived at the rendezvous point on Frunze Street. The sullen, cold day was nearing its end [and] an early fall dusk was setting in. Soon Zhukov's vehicle appeared, and I got in it.
>
> We arrived at the Kremlin through the Borovitskiye Gate. A short part of the journey was on foot. We walked quietly and quickly. Only at one spot did the commander halt a bit and point with his hand to a round pit. "Aerial bomb."
>
> Not far from the bomb crater was an entrance to an underground room. We went down the steps and found ourselves in a long corridor.[18]

Belov describes a number of well-guarded compartments in the underground structure. At the end of the corridor was an open door leading into a spacious, brightly lighted room. In the far-left corner stood a large desk with several telephones.

> Zhukov presented me to Stalin, who stood in the center of the office.
>
> Now, calling to mind the past, I automatically remember the small, insignificant details, the first impression which surprised and puzzled me.
>
> In those years much was written about Stalin in the papers, calling him strong, wise, a genius—in a word, they did not spare epithets.
>
> I had not seen him since 1933. Since that time he had changed greatly; before me stood a man of short height with a tired, sunken face. In eight years he had aged, it seemed, about twenty years. In his eyes there was not the former strength, [and] in his voice confidence was not felt. But the behavior of Zhukov surprised me even more. He spoke sharply, in an imperious tone. The impression was such that the senior chief here might have been Zhukov. And Stalin perceived it properly. At times he even had a somewhat perplexed look on his face.[19]

It is difficult to accept without reservation Belov's description of Zhukov's "imperious tone." He may have been misreading Zhukov's characteristic self-confidence and his awareness of the heavy responsibilities weighing upon him. Moreover, after nearly a year of close work with the general, Stalin could not fail to have been impressed by his undeniable talents. Zhukov's prophetic warning of the impending German attack must have enhanced his standing with the commander in chief. It had been left to Zhukov to salvage the situation after Stalin's cronies Voroshilov and Budenny had failed to stem the German advance. No less, it was Zhukov who had reassured Stalin about the feasibility of the November celebrations in Red Square. In those critical days there seems no reason to doubt that Stalin viewed Zhukov as a man of the hour. Zhukov, in turn, could see his chief as someone more human than the infallible genius portrayed by the Soviet press. Zhukov would later carry over this attitude of equality—perhaps, in a military sense, even of superiority—to his dealings with subsequent Soviet leaders, an attitude which may have produced some of the problems he faced later.*

---

* General Shtemenko has provided an interesting description of Zhukov at about this time: "Much has been said in all the preceding chapters about Marshal Zhukov. But to what has been told already must be added the fact that he was a man with a great gift for generalship, daring and original in his thinking and very firm in the practical execution of his decisions, who would stop at no

According to Belov's account, after listening to Zhukov's counter-strike plan, Stalin gave it his approval, at the same time allocating three air divisions for support of the operation. He ordered a twenty-four-hour postponement to allow Rokossovsky's army, fighting on Zhukov's right, to complete its preparations. It was essential that operations begin simultaneously in both sectors so as to prevent the Germans from maneuvering their reserves.

At the meeting Belov expressed the urgent need for more automatic weapons, emphasizing the Germans' clear advantage in firepower over the dismounted cavalrymen. Stalin promised Belov fifteen hundred automatic rifles and two batteries of new seventy-six-millimeter guns.

Meanwhile, the Stavka had assigned the Fiftieth Army to the Western *Front* and transferred the defense of Tula to Zhukov. These transfers meant that the *front*'s defense had been significantly expanded, and Zhukov began receiving from the Stavka Reserve new replacement units and tank troops to supplement the line. Some of these forces had just arrived from combat duty in the Ukraine. The Stavka forces were concentrated on the more dangerous approaches, especially in the direction of Volokolamsk, Klin, and Istra, where the main blow of the German armored formations was expected. The men received warm winter clothing—coats, felt boots, heavy quilted jackets, and caps with earmuffs (at the same time the poorly clad German forces were already being thinned by "General Frost").

Although the Western *Front* received large numbers of reinforcements and by mid-November had six armies, the troops were spread out over more than 370 miles. Zhukov hoped to secure the more threatened sectors and to maintain a *front* reserve to maneuver when necessary. His plans were changed abruptly on November 13, when Stalin called on the telephone. Zhukov reports the incident in his memoirs:

"What is the enemy doing?" Stalin asked Zhukov.

"He is finishing the preparation of his strike groups and apparently will soon go over to the offensive," Zhukov replied.

"And where do you expect the main blow?"

"We expect the most powerful strike from the area of Volokolamsk

obstacle in pursuit of the aims for which the war was fought. When he felt himself to be right over some controversial matter, Zhukov could contradict Stalin fairly sharply, which was something that no one else dared do." Sergei M. Shtemenko, *The Soviet General Staff at War, 1941–1945,* 383.

and Novo Petrovskoye toward Klin and Istra. Guderian's army will very likely try to outflank Tula and push on to Venev and Kashira."

"Shaposhnikov and I are in agreement," said Stalin, "that it is necessary to repel the strike the enemy is preparing by preemptive counterstrikes. One counterblow must be delivered by encircling Volokolamsk from the north, and the other from the region of Serpukhov in the flank of the German Fourth Army. It is obvious that powerful forces are assembling in these areas in order to strike toward Moscow."

"And which forces will deliver these counterstrikes?" Zhukov asked. "There are no spare forces in the *front*. We only have forces for holding the occupied lines."

"In the Volokolamsk region use the right-flank units of Rokossovsky's army, the Fifty-eighth Tank Division, the separate cavalry divisions, and Dovator's cavalry corps. In the area of Serpukhov use Belov's cavalry corps, Getman's tank divisions, and part of the forces of the Forty-ninth Army," Stalin proposed.

"That cannot be done right now," Zhukov answered. "We cannot throw the *front*'s last reserves into dubious counterstrikes. We will have nothing with which to reinforce our armies when the enemy begins the offensive with his strike formations."

"You have six armies in the *front*. Isn't that really enough?"

Zhukov replied that the defensive frontage of the Western *Front* had been greatly extended; with its curves it was more than 370 miles long. He had very few reserves in depth, especially in the center of the *front*.

Stalin spoke: "Consider the question of the counterstrikes decided. Report on the plan this evening."

Zhukov again tried to convince Stalin that counterstrikes were unwise —that they would consume the remaining reserves—but the telephone connection was broken. Stalin had hung up.

The conversation depressed Zhukov, not because Stalin had not taken his views into consideration but "because Moscow, which the soldiers had taken an oath to defend to their last drop of blood, was in mortal danger, and we had been ordered preemptorily to throw away our last reserves in an extremely questionable counterstrike. And having expended all of them, we would not be able to reinforce the weak sectors of the defense."

About fifteen minutes later Bulganin entered Zhukov's office and said: "Well, I got it real hard this time. Stalin told me: 'You and Zhukov are giving yourselves airs. But we'll put a stop to that.'* He insisted that I see you at once and that we start organizing the counterstrikes right away."

Zhukov told Bulganin: "Well, that's that. Sit down and let's summon Vasily Danilovich [Sokolovsky] and alert Rokossovsky and Zakharkin, the army commanders."[20]

Within two hours the *front* staff had issued orders for the counter-strike to the commanders of the Sixteenth and Forty-ninth armies and to other major commanders. The blow was struck, but the Germans renewed their offensive against Moscow at almost the same time. They hit the left flank of the Kalinin *Front*'s Thirtieth Army northwest of Moscow and, simultaneously, the right flank and center of the Western *Front*'s Sixteenth Army. More than three hundred German tanks attacked at a time when the Soviets were able to muster only fifty-six tanks, many of them light and poorly armed.

The situation was also critical for other Red Army units. Belov says that the Forty-ninth Army was under strength and incapable of conducting decisive offensive action. Three of its right-flank divisions, all with good combat experience (two had already received the honorary "guards" designation), had suffered heavy losses in recent battles. The 765th Infantry Regiment of the Fifth Guards Infantry Division, for example, numbered only 123 men, and the Sixtieth Infantry Division had only 500 soldiers.

Belov reports that the three aviation divisions which Stalin had promised him for support of the operation were redirected to another sector. His cavalrymen found, too, that their intelligence estimates of German strength had been well below the mark. In the bitter back-and-forth fighting along the Nara River, Belov became separated from his head-quarters. Finding Major General Viktor K. Baranov of the Fifth Cavalry Division, Belov asked him about the progress of the battle. Baranov said the division had been virtually halted by large German forces. Using Baranov's field telephone, Belov called the other divisions and heard similar stories from each. It turned out that, instead of two or three enemy battalions opposing the cavalry-mechanized group, "at least two German divisions were before us." Zhukov was forced to order a dis-

---

* A more accurate translation of Stalin's comment would be: "There with Zhukov you think you're something! But we will find justice for you!"

engagement, which was carried out with much difficulty, and a redeployment in the Kashira area.

On the morning of November 16, having penetrated the defenses of the Thirtieth Army, the Germans began to develop their strike toward Klin, where there were no Soviet reserves to confront them. They also launched an attack from the Volokolamsk region toward Istra, employing 400 medium and heavy tanks; Soviet armor strength consisted of 150 light and medium tanks.

At this point Rokossovsky, commanding the Sixteenth Army, began to feel the increasing enemy pressure toward Klin. In an attempt to improve the condition of his army and check the Germans, Rokossovsky decided that his troops must withdraw from their positions along a line six to seven miles west of the Istra Reservoir to a new line:

> The reservoir itself, the Istra River, and surrounding terrain formed a very advantageous natural line, the timely occupation of which, in my opinion, would have enabled the organization of a solid defense by small forces, the placing of several units in the army's second echelon, thereby creating a deep defense zone and, in addition, sparing a certain amount of troops to strengthen the defenses in the direction of Klin.
>
> Having thought out all sides and having carefully considered them with my assistants, I reported on our concept to the *front* commander and requested that he allow a withdrawal to the Istra line.[21]

Rokossovsky's army had suffered heavy losses in personnel and equipment in an almost uninterrupted series of battles and firefights. Furthermore, the survivors were exhausted, and command and staff personnel, he writes, "literally collapsed on their feet, sometimes succeeding in catching a nap in the vehicles during trips from one sector [of the front] to another."[22] Under these conditions Rokossovsky did not expect his old friend (and former subordinate) to deny his request to withdraw. But, he says, "General of the Army G. K. Zhukov, having listened to our proposal and request, categorically disagreed with them and ordered a stand to the death, not permitting a withdrawal of even a single step."[23]

The disappointed and desperate Rokossovsky decided to go over Zhukov's head:

> I considered the question of withdrawal to the Istra line so serious that I could not agree with the decision of the *front* commander, and in this respect I turned to the chief of the general staff, Marshal of the Soviet

Union B. M. Shaposhnikov, justifying my proposal in detail. After several hours we received an answer from him. We were told that the proposal was correct and that he, as chief of the general staff, approved it.

Having known Boris Mikhailovich Shaposhnikov in the peacetime service, I was certain that this answer was absolutely agreed to by the Supreme Commander in Chief, [and] that in any event the latter had been informed. Having received permission of the chief of the general staff, we immediately prepared the order to the troops for withdrawal of our main forces during the night to the line of the Istra Reservoir. To cover the withdrawal, it was ordered that reinforced detachments be left in the former positions, and, once they had fulfilled their mission, they would withdraw only under enemy pressure.[24]

In any army it is a serious matter when a subordinate bypasses channels, and when the higher echelon sanctions the act, the commander who has been overruled knows his authority has been undermined. Zhukov reacted accordingly. He sent Rokossovsky a terse wire: "I command the troops of the *front*. I rescind the order concerning withdrawal of the troops beyond the Istra Reservoir, [and] I order a defense on the occupied line and no withdrawal, not even one step back. General of the Army Zhukov."[25] Rokossovsky complied.

In an unusual attempt to get to the bottom of the disagreement, the editors of *Voyenno-Istorichesky Zhurnal* asked Georgi Zhukov for his explanation of the episode:

The editor turned to the former commander of the Western *Front*, Marshal of the Soviet Union G. K. Zhukov, with a request to explain why a withdrawal by the Sixteenth Army beyond the Istra River had not been permitted. He answered that the question of the withdrawal of the Sixteenth Army had to be decided on the basis not only of its own interests but also of the situation on the entire *front*. With the withdrawal of this army beyond the Istra, the right flank of the Fifth would have been exposed and the Perkhushkovo direction, where the *front* command was located, would have been unprotected.[26]

The Germans began to apply more pressure on the Sixteenth Army's left flank and finally succeeded in throwing the Soviets back to the east and forcing the Istra. South of the Volga Reservoir they penetrated the Thirtieth Army's defenses, advancing quickly with their tank and motorized formations to expand the breakthrough. Simultaneously they struck in the direction of Solnechnogorsk, circling the Istra Reservoir from the north. On the Klin and Solnechnogorsk axes the situation became desperate as the Germans threw six divisions (three tank, two infantry, and one motorized) against the 107th Motorized Rifle Division of the Thirtieth Army and the 126th Infantry, Seventeenth Cavalry, and Fifty-eighth Tank divisions and the Twenty-fifth Tank Brigade of the Sixteenth Army. "All these troops were extremely weak and understrength," Rokossovsky writes. "It is sufficient to say that the 107th Motorized Rifle Division numbered only about three hundred men; in our Fifty-eighth Tank Division there were no tanks; and there were no more than twelve, four of them T-34's, in the Twenty-fifth Tank Brigade."[27]

On the German side, despite their advances the officers were becoming anxious about their chances of victory. Many ominous signs had appeared, the most disquieting being the deficiencies in supplies, especially winter clothing, and provisions for maintaining equipment in cold weather. The intense cold had made optical tank sights virtually useless, and engines had to be preheated before they would start (the Germans built fires under them). Not to be brushed aside was the changing attitude of the Russian people in territory occupied by the Germans. Guderian describes a conversation with an elderly citizen of Orel:

> As an indication of the attitude of the Russian population, I should like to quote a remark that was made to me by an old Czarist general whom I met in Orel at this time. He said: "If only you had come twenty years ago we should have welcomed you with open arms. But now it's too late. We were just beginning to get on our feet and now you arrive and throw us back twenty years so that we will have to start from the beginning all over again. Now we are fighting for Russia and in that cause we are all united."[28]

On November 23, Guderian visited the commander of Army Group Center, Field Marshal von Bock, to request postponement of the offensive because of the exhausted condition of the troops, the lack of winter clothing, the breakdown of the supply system, and the shortage of tanks and guns. Von Bock reported by telephone to Army Commander in Chief von Brauchitsch, who categorically rejected Guderian's proposal to go over to the defensive until the following spring. Guderian concluded that "in view of the manner in which the Commander-in-Chief of the Army and the Chief of the Army General Staff refused my requests, it must be assumed that not only Hitler but also they were in favour of a continuation of the offensive."[29]

The situation in Zhukov's Western *Front* deteriorated sharply as the Germans approached in separate sectors to within twenty miles of Moscow. Artillery fire could be heard distinctly by Muscovites living in the northwest section of the city. By November 22, German divisions had broken into Klin, north of Moscow, and had reached Istra, on the west. The latter, about fifteen miles from the capital, was the closest point to Moscow the Germans reached, and it was very likely from here that they later recalled they "could look at Moscow through a pair of good field glasses."[30]

After seizing Klin, the Germans turned toward Solnechnogorsk. Rokossovsky's defending Sixteenth Army withdrew, simultaneously bringing up everything possible from other sectors, including antitank platoons, artillery batteries, and antiaircraft battalions from Moscow's air-defense organization. The Sixteenth Army held out until the arrival of the Seventh Division from Serpukhov, and two tank brigades and two antitank artillery regiments from the Stavka Reserve. These reinforcements enabled Rokossovsky to form a strong defensive line.

During the critical fighting north of Moscow, Stalin telephoned Zhukov. "Are you sure we can hold Moscow?" he asked the *front* commander. "I say this to you with a heavy heart. Speak honestly, as a Communist."

"There is no doubt that we will hold Moscow," Zhukov replied. "But we still need no less than two armies and at least two hundred tanks."

"It's good that you have such confidence," Stalin said. "Telephone Shaposhnikov and come to an agreement about where to concentrate the two reserve armies which you have requested. They will be ready by the end of November, but we don't have the tanks yet."

Zhukov and Shaposhnikov decided that the newly formed First Shock Army would be massed in the Yakhroma area and the Tenth Army in the vicinity of Ryazan.

Zhukov's optimism was partly based on recent encouraging developments in other sectors of the front. On November 12, Leningrad *Front* forces counterattacked at Tikhvin. On November 17 a Southern *Front* counteroffensive was launched near Rostov and eventually threw the German First Tank Army back across the River Mius. On November 29, Rostov was recaptured by the Red Army, and the German command quickly began to pull individual divisions from other sectors of the front, transferring them to Tikhvin and Rostov. This occurred just at the moment when the most critical point of the drive toward Moscow had been reached. Soviet counterattacks near Tikhvin and Rostov aided the plan for a massive counteroffensive around Moscow by relieving some of the pressure on the Russian capital. "Our misfortunes began with Rostov; that was the writing on the wall," Guderian wrote in his memoirs.[31]

Halder's journal entry of November 30 is replete with portents of things to come. He first lists the casualties of the Eastern Army from June 22 to November 26, 1941: 24,658 officers and 718,454 noncommissioned officers and enlisted men killed, wounded, and missing. The Eastern Army was short 340,000 men, with half its infantry strength depleted. Combat companies were operating with 50 to 60 men. Hitler became increasingly agitated about the situation. When the First Panzer Army in Army Group South sought to withdraw to the line from Taganrog to Mius to the mouth of the Bakhmut River, Hitler forbade it. Halder recorded that "these people have no conception of the condition of our troops and keep grinding out ideas in a vacuum." The tension at headquarters became unbearable. Halder describes the scene in his journal:

> ObdH [army commander in chief] was ordered to the Führer at 1300 [1:00 P.M.]. The interview appears to have been more than disagreeable, with the Führer doing all the talking, pouring out reproaches and abuse and shouting orders as fast as they came into his head. Regrettably, ObdH yielded to the Führer's insistence and has issued the order not to fall back to the aforementioned line in one move. Field Marshal von Rundstedt's reply was that he could not comply with the order and asked that either the order be changed or he be relieved of his post.[32]

The next day Rundstedt was relieved of his command.

Zhukov continued accumulating reserves near Moscow for the counterstrike. His two new armies were ready for commitment. He placed the Twentieth Army, also newly reorganized from a number of reinforcing units, in the area of Lobna, Skhodna, and Khimok and moved Belov's cavalry corps into position. On November 27, reinforced by infantry and tank units, he launched a counterattack on the German Second Panzer Army and threw it back eighteen miles south of Kashira. On

November 29 part of the First Shock Army counterattacked, crossed the Moscow–Volga Canal near Yakhroma, and by December 1 had thrown the Germans back across the canal. By means of these quick counterattacks the Russians halted Hitler's offensive north and south of Moscow, and his forces were unable to close the pincers east of the Russian capital.

Despite these setbacks the German command did not yet consider that its offensive had failed. In an order dated December 2, Field Marshal von Bock wrote: "The enemy tries to ease his situation, transferring whole divisions or parts of divisions from the less threatened to the more threatened sectors of the front. The arrival of new reinforcements, in small quantity, was noted only in one sector. . . . The enemy defense was on the verge of a crisis."

In the first days of December the Germans committed several divisions of the Fourth Army in a last desperate effort to break through to Moscow from Naro Fominsk. They managed to penetrate the front to a depth of twelve to fifteen miles in the direction of Aprelevka, but their troops were annihilated by K. D. Golubev's Forty-third Army in battles lasting from December 3 to 5.

The German command believed that the Tula salient must be cleared up before other objectives could be undertaken. With this goal in mind Guderian began applying more pressure there. On December 3 the old city of Tula, known for its arms industry, was encircled when the Germans cut both the railroad and the highway to Moscow. General I. V. Boldin, who had been placed in charge of Tula's defense on November 22, describes events on that critical day in December:

> The phone rang from H.Q., and General Zhukov asked for me. I felt it would be an unpleasant conversation. And so it was. "Well, Comrade Boldin," Zhukov said, "this is the third time you've managed to get yourself encircled. Isn't it rather too much? I already told you to move your army headquarters and command post to Laptevo. But you were pigheaded, wouldn't carry out my order. . . ." "Comrade Commander," I said, "if I and my army staff had left, Guderian would already be here. The position would be much worse than it is now."
>
> For a couple of minutes there was a loud crackle in the receiver, and finally I could hear Zhukov again. "What steps are you taking?" he said. I reported that the 999th Rifle Regiment of the 258th Division had gone into action to clear the Moscow highway and that, moreover, an attack was

being mounted against the Germans at Kashira. "What help do you need?" said Zhukov. "May I ask you to move the tanks of Getman's division southward along the Moscow highway to meet the 999th Rifles?" "Very well, I shall," said Zhukov. "But you, too, do your stuff."

Siyazov [commander of the 258th Division] went on phoning hour by hour. The 999th Regiment had been fighting for seventeen hours when another phone call came: An overjoyed, excited Siyazov reported: "Comrade Commander, Vedenin [the regiment's commander] has just phoned to say that his men and the Getman tanks have joined up. Traffic may be resumed along the Tula–Moscow highway."[33]

All attacks on Tula failed. Guderian later attributed the failure to the exhaustion of his troops, the bitterly cold weather, the lack of fuel, and the timely arrival of Zhukov's Siberian reserves.[34]

By the fifth of December, German troops in all sectors opposite the Western *Front* were spent and had begun to go on the defensive. The Soviets were now prepared to launch their mighty counteroffensive against the exhausted and half-frozen enemy. Zhukov explains how the Germans were halted almost before the very gates of Moscow:

> After the war I was asked many times: How did the Soviet troops manage to withstand the onslaught of the stronger German Fascist formations around Moscow? Concerning the course of defensive fighting at Moscow much has been written and is essentially accurate. However, as former commander of the Western *Front*, I want to express my own opinion.
>
> In planning such a complex grand-scale strategic operation as Operation Taifun, the Hitlerite supreme high command seriously underestimated the strength, condition, and capabilities of the Soviet Army to fight for Moscow and grossly overestimated the capabilities of its own forces it had massed to penetrate our defense and to capture the capital of the Soviet Union.
>
> Great miscalculations were also made in setting up the strike groups intended to carry out the second phase of the Taifun operation. The enemy's flank strike groups, especially those fighting in the area of Tula, were weak and were made up of an insufficient number of combined-arms units. To stake [everything] exclusively on the armor units under these specific conditions did not justify itself, as was shown in practice. They were exhausted, had suffered heavy losses, and had lost their fighting strength.
>
> The German command was not able to complete preparations in time to launch a simultaneous attack in the center of our *front*, although sufficient strength was at hand to do so. The absence of such a strike gave us the opportunity to transfer freely from the central sectors all reserves, including

also divisional, to the flanks of the *front* against the enemy's strike groups. Heavy losses, unpreparedness for combat under winter conditions, the stubbornness of the resistance of the Soviet troops sharply affected the enemy's combat capability.

. . . The enemy was not able to breach our defensive front; he did not manage to encircle a single division, to fire a single artillery round on Moscow. By the beginning of December he was exhausted and had no reserves, but by that time the Western *Front* had received two newly re-formed armies and a number of units from the Stavka, from which was formed the third army—the Twentieth. This permitted the Soviet command to organize a counteroffensive.[35]

This seems to be as fair an assessment of the Russian defensive victory as has ever been presented by Soviet sources—in fact, by any source. The Soviet counteroffensive at Moscow, Zhukov notes, was born of defensive fighting. It was simply an outgrowth of Soviet counterattacks on the Germans' flanks begun in late November and early December, and the method of conducting it was determined as the fighting continued.[36]

Until the end of November neither the Stavka nor the *fronts*, particularly the Western *Front*, had worked out a plan for a full-scale counteroffensive. Until that time Zhukov and other leading figures were totally engaged in stopping the German onslaught before Moscow. On November 29, when Zhukov telephoned Stalin about the transfer of the First Shock and Tenth armies from the Stavka Reserve to the Western *Front*, Stalin asked him, "But are you sure that the enemy has reached a critical state and that he does not have the capability to introduce some new powerful force into action?" Zhukov assured him that the Germans were exhausted. Without fresh troops, however, the Western *Front* could not eliminate the dangerous wedges in its lines, and the situation would certainly worsen as soon as the Germans could bring up replacements from Army Groups North and South. Stalin said that he would consult with the General Staff. Zhukov then asked permission for his own chief of staff, Sokolovsky, who shared his conviction that the two armies should be incorporated into the Western *Front*, to telephone the General Staff and explain the need for their immediate transfer. Late that evening Zhukov was informed that the Stavka had decided to transfer the two armies and all the divisions comprising the Twentieth Army to the Western *Front*. He was ordered to present a plan for their deployment.

In the predawn hours of November 30, Stalin called to ask what the Military Council thought about the execution of a counteroffensive along the entire *front*. Zhukov replied that he had neither the manpower nor the matériel to launch such an attack but that it might be achieved by developing the counterattacks already being made on the flanks of the *front*. The rest of the day was spent in working out a plan which would take advantage of the new armies which had been transferred to the *front*.

The essence of Zhukov's proposal was to begin the counteroffensive on December 3–4 after the new armies had been unloaded and concentrated in position. (In fact, it was delayed until December 6 by the necessity to counter a German breakthrough at Naro Forminsk.) The immediate objective was to crush the principal German formations on the right wing by attacking toward Klin, Solnechnogorsk, and Istra and to rout the Germans on the left wing with attacks against Uzlovaya and Bogoroditsk on the flank and in the rear of Guderian's group (see map, page 198). The armies in the center of the *front* were to begin the offensive on December 4–5, with the limited objective of pinning down the opposing forces and preventing the Germans from shifting units. As a preliminary to the counteroffensive, the enemy's forward movement was to be stopped northwest of Moscow and along the Kashira axis.

On November 30, Zhukov reported his plan of operations to the Stavka. It was approved without change by Stalin. Then Zhukov assigned his troops their missions.

The First Shock Army, under the command of Lieutenant General V. I. Kuznetsov, after liquidating German forces which had broken through to the Moscow–Volga Canal, was to deploy in the Dmitrov–Yakhroma area and, together with the Twentieth and Thirtieth armies, strike in the direction of Klin and beyond in the general direction of Teryaeva Sloboda.

The Thirtieth Army was assigned the task of defeating the enemy in the area of Rogachevo and Borshchevo and, together with the First Shock Army, to seize Reshetnikovo and Klin and continue the attack toward Kostlyakovo and Lotoshino.

From Krasnaya Polyana and Belyy Rast the Twentieth Army, coordinating with the First Shock and Sixteenth armies, was to attack in the general direction of Solnechnogorsk, capture it from the south, and strike out toward Volokolamsk. In addition, the Sixteenth Army's right wing was to advance on Kryukovo and beyond toward Istra.

The Fiftieth Army, fighting defensively in the Tula area, was ordered to attack along the Bolokhovo–Shchekino axis and subsequently to fight as the situation required. From Mordves, Belov's operational group was to strike Venev, then Stalinogorsk (Novomoskovsk) and Dedilovo, in conjunction with the Tenth and Fiftieth armies.

The Tenth Army, deployed along the Serebryanyye Prudy–Mikhaylov line, was to attack Uzlovaya and Bogoroditsk and then move south of the Ula River. Thus were the additional forces furnished by the Stavka committed to combat against the Germans' northern and southern formations.

Four armies on the Western *Front*, the Fifth, Thirty-third, Forty-third, and Forty-ninth, which were on the defensive in the center of the battleground, were given the mission of pinning down the Germans and preventing them from freely maneuvering their forces. Since these four Soviet armies were badly under strength, they were incapable of more decisive action.

Writes Zhukov:

> I am not quite sure, but I think it was on the morning of December 2, while on the phone with me, that I. V. Stalin asked: "How does the *front* estimate the enemy and his capabilities?" I replied that the enemy was reaching the point of exhaustion. Apparently he did not have the capability of reinforcing his assault groups with reserves, without which Hitler's forces could not mount an offensive. The Supreme Commander in Chief said, "Fine, I'll call you back." I realized that the Stavka was pondering the further actions of our forces.
>
> In about an hour the Supreme Commander in Chief called again and asked what the *front*'s plans were for the next few days. I reported that the *front* troops were being prepared for the counteroffensive according to the plan already approved.[37]

In a telephone conversation with Zhukov on December 2, Stalin said that the Kalinin *Front* and the right wing of the Southwestern *Front* had been ordered to support Zhukov's Western *Front*, the intention being that all of these major units would strike simultaneously. Two days later, on the evening of December 4, Stalin again phoned Zhukov and asked, "What help does your *front* need in addition to that already provided?"

Zhukov realized that there was not enough time to request and receive substantial new forces. He therefore thought it most important to obtain air support from the Stavka Reserve and the National Air Defense Organization. He believed that rapid exploitation of the strike would require at least two hundred tanks and crews, and the Western *Front* had only a very limited number of them.

"There are no tanks, and we can't give any to you," Stalin replied. "You'll get your aircraft. I'll call the General Staff right away. Keep in mind that the Kalinin *Front* will go on the offensive on December 5 and that the operational group of the right wing of the Southwestern *Front* will also take to the offensive from the area of Yeltsa on December 6."[38]

Zhukov says that in the final days of November and the early days of December, when the Soviets were organizing for battle, they had no idea that they were initiating such a large-scale counteroffensive. Zhukov writes: "As far as I can recall, no special order or directive for the counteroffensive was issued. . . . The counteroffensive around Moscow did not have a clearly defined beginning, as, for example, that at Stalingrad."[39] The attack set up for November 30 had the limited objective of striking about thirty-seven miles to the north and sixty-two miles to the south. It soon became apparent, however, that the enemy was exhausted, so much so that he could neither continue the offensive nor organize a strong defense. Thus when the Germans began retreating on the right and especially on the left flank of the *front*, Zhukov ordered the intensity of the strikes increased, and on December 5–6 the great Moscow counteroffensive became a reality.

Zhukov's account of the operation is precise and appears to be an honest appraisal of a situation which was, at least in the beginning, extremely tenuous. On December 6, after concentrated air strikes and artillery preparation, the troops of Zhukov's Western *Front* began to move north and south of Moscow. As the battle progressed, the initiative proved to be in the hands of the now high-spirited Russians. By this time the units of the Kalinin *Front*, which had begun their attack a day earlier, had driven a wedge into the enemy's defense south of Kalinin.

The offensive at Kalinin began successfully but was hampered by the winter impassability of roads and the lack of a decisive advantage in forces. The Western *Front's* right wing applied heavy pressure, threatening to cut off and surround the concentrations of German forces from

Klin to Solnechnogorsk. The Soviets at Klin forced the German command to begin transferring troops from adjacent sectors, but this only facilitated the Red Army's push against Solnechnogorsk, Krasnaya Polyana, and Istra. By December 13 resistance around Klin and Solnechnogorsk had been broken, and the Germans were withdrawing, abandoning guns and vehicles. Soviet pilots bombed the columns retreating to the west along snow-covered roads, inflicting heavy losses.

Kyrill D. Kalinov saw Zhukov at his headquarters on December 12, less than a week after the counteroffensive had begun. He writes:

> Zhukov gave the impression of being completely tired out. His eyes lay deep in their sockets and were very red. The need for sleep seemed to have overcome him and his voice sounded hoarse. He was still keeping his head above water only by superhuman efforts. Several glasses of tea—black as the ace of spades—were standing before him on the table. He liked tea and consumed it in excessive amounts. [40]

Zhukov was not so fatigued that he lost control of his troops. He still possessed all the energy and forcefulness which helped him accomplish difficult tasks at Khalkhin-Gol and at Leningrad. But, Kalinov noted, he had little patience with certain subordinates.

> He was keeping the reins fast in his hands. In my presence he talked on the phone with General Belov, who, along with the stubbornness of a Don Cossack, had the tendency to want to decide everything by himself without inquiring of the High Command. At that time Belov was commanding the Southern Reserve Group, consisting of two Cossack cavalry divisions and the First Guards Division. Between December 16 and 18, he defeated the Seventeenth Panzer Division and the Twenty-eighth, Twenty-ninth, and Thirtieth Infantry divisions of the Wehrmacht and thus liberated Stalinogorsk and Venev. . . .
>
> Belov was rather popular and was held in high regard by Stalin. But that did not constitute any reason for Zhukov not to tell him his opinion bluntly. "I order you to be here in a quarter of an hour," he roared into the telephone. "You can't? . . . Why not? I don't care; I order you to come here! . . . What? . . . If you're not here I'll have you put in custody until you turn black, do you understand?"[41]

Belov appeared punctually for his conference with Zhukov.

In the meantime, Halder's daily journal was reflecting increased pessimism. On December 12, Halder and Field Marshal von Bock discussed the day's events by telephone. Afterward Halder noted cryptically: "The situation has entered an acutely critical stage. The 134th and 45th divisions are no longer in any condition to fight. No supplies. Bankruptcy of the command of the sector between Tula and Kursk. Army Gp. order envisages withdrawal to the line Tula–Novosiltim in several stages." On the north, he noted, heavy snowdrifts were blocking rail lines, hampering supply and movement.[42]

At the same time Zhukov was reporting good news to Stalin. "On December 6, 1941," he writes, "the troops of the *front*, having exhausted the enemy in previous battles, launched a decisive counteroffensive against his flank strike groups. As a result of this offensive, both of these groups have been defeated and are hastily retreating, discarding matériel and weapons and sustaining enormous losses."[43]

On December 13 the Soviet Information Bureau announced that the Germans had failed in their attempt to encircle the Russian capital. Soviet newspapers also published photographs of Red Army generals who had won the battle of Moscow: Zhukov, Lelyushenko, Kuznetsov, Rokossovsky, Govorov, Boldin, F. I. Golikov, Belov, and A. A. Vlasov. A large picture of Zhukov appeared in the center, surrounded by smaller photographs of the others.

Zhukov's further operational objective, reflected in his directives from December 13 to 24, was to advance the right wing to the Zubtsov–Gzhatsk line and the left wing to the Polotnyanyy Zavod–Kozelsk line. With troops of the center forming the rear echelon along the Mozhaisk–Maloyaroslavets line, the plan was to create a situation whereby the *front*'s left and right wings would encircle the main formations of Army Group Center. As Zhukov explains in his memoirs, the central armies of his Western *Front* (the thirty-third, forty-third, and forty-ninth) did not take part in the counterstrikes and made only slow progress in the subsequent counteroffensive because they were drained of strength to reinforce the wings. Only when the Germans began a hasty withdrawal to the Ruza and Lama rivers did Zhukov advance all three armies.

Zhukov also skillfully employed the *front*'s aircraft, and for the first time in the war the Germans lost their advantage in the air. Three-fourths of the available Soviet aircraft were used to support the combat operations of the *front*'s right-wing troops, while the remainder (including three aviation divisions assigned to the Western *Front* from the Stavka Reserve) assisted the cavalry units of General Belov, as well as the Tenth and Fiftieth armies. The *front*'s aviation command post was collocated with Zhukov's at Perkhushkovo, which helped to maintain close coordination and control.

In his memoirs Zhukov reveals his leadership techniques and his procedures for ensuring firm, uninterrupted control of his troops. Sometimes his methods were unorthodox and contrary to Soviet tactical practices. For example, he defends his choice for the location of his command post near the front lines. While recognizing that such practices were contrary to accepted security procedures, he maintained that constant close touch with his subordinates was the overriding consideration.

Zhukov's mission was facilitated somewhat by the *front*'s proximity to the capital. The use of all the communication lines in the government and civilian network enabled Zhukov and his staff to maintain telephone and telegraph communications with the Stavka, the General Staff, and all the armies comprising the *front*. Emergency communications had also been established for any possible contingency, and, when necessary, a *front* headquarters or command post could even contact a particular division directly.

Zhukov believed it essential that, once operations began, the *front* commander should be at his headquarters to maintain constant communication with his subordinate commanders, adjacent *fronts*, the Stavka, and the General Staff. One day, however, he decided that he must visit one of the divisions of the Sixteenth Army. His brief absence caused him no small amount of anxiety.

Stalin had received information that Red Army troops had abandoned Dedovsk, a town very close to Moscow. Naturally, he was quite disturbed by this news, especially since the Ninth Guards Rifle Division had beaten off fierce German attacks in the area on November 28–29. He telephoned Zhukov.

"Are you aware that Dedovsk has been occupied?" he asked.

"No, Comrade Stalin, I am not."

"A commander should know what's happening on his *front*," Stalin admonished, and ordered Zhukov to go to the area "to organize the counterattack personally and regain Dedovsk."

Zhukov objected, saying that it was unwise for him to leave *front* headquarters during such a tense situation.

"That's all right," Stalin told him. "We'll get along somehow. Let Sokolovsky take your place for the time being."

Zhukov immediately contacted Rokossovsky and demanded an explanation why *front* headquarters had not been notified of the Dedovsk pullout. It turned out that the Germans had not seized Dedovsk but that the village of Dedovo might have been taken.

"Clearly, a mistake had been made," Zhukov writes. "I decided to phone the Stavka and explain that there had been a misunderstanding. But now, as they say, we ran up against a stone wall. Stalin finally became angry and demanded that I go to Rokossovsky and see that this ill-fated populated point was taken from the enemy." Stalin also ordered Zhukov to take with him the commander of the Fifth Army, General L. A. Govorov, to organize artillery fire in support of the Sixteenth Army.

Zhukov saw no point in making further objections, although Govorov agreed that the trip was unnecessary. "Why should he, Govorov, leave his own army in such tense times? I explained to the general that this was Stalin's order."

Zhukov, Govorov, and Rokossovsky drove to General A. P. Beloborodov's division. "The division commander was hardly pleased to see us appear among his units," Zhukov says, since "all that time he was up to his neck in problems, and now he had to offer explanations for the enemy's occupation of a few houses in the village of Dedovo on the other side of a ravine." Beloborodov explained that it was not tactically expedient to recapture the houses, but Zhukov did not want to tell the division commander that he, Zhukov, was having to operate according to considerations far removed from tactics. Accordingly, he ordered Beloborodov to send a rifle company and two tanks to drive off the platoon of Germans who had occupied the houses.

Zhukov telephoned his chief of staff, Sokolovsky, who reported that Stalin had telephoned three times, asking, "Where's Zhukov? Why did he leave?" Stalin had ordered Zhukov to return immediately to *front* headquarters. Only after Zhukov had called the supreme commander in chief and reported on the battle situation did Stalin ask, casually, "Well, how is Dedovsk?" Observes Zhukov, "Thus ended one of my absences from *front* headquarters during defensive fighting at Moscow."[44]

During the counteroffensive Zhukov sometimes found it necessary to visit the various army commanders to coordinate their action, offer guidance, and issue specific directives. About a week after the push began, he issued the following orders:

. . . Pursuit of the enemy must be swift to prevent the enemy from dis-
engaging. Strong advance detachments must be widely employed to seize
road junctions and defiles and to disorganize the enemy's march and combat
formations.

. . . I categorically forbid frontal attacks against reinforced centers of
resistance. Leading echelons, without pausing, are to bypass them, leaving
their destruction to succeeding echelons.[45]

Zhukov issued these orders after his strike forces had become bogged
down in bloody, drawn-out frontal attacks. The situation was complicated by the fact that many of the Soviet commanders lacked experience
in conducting offensive operations. Some of them, fearing encirclement,
hesitated to throw their units into gaps in the lines. The lack of large
armored formations seriously hampered Zhukov's breakthrough plans.
In the absence of tanks he sent ski units, cavalry, and airborne forces to
the enemy's rear to seal off escape routes. Although they fought well,
these forces were a poor substitute for armor.[46]

By December 16, Soviet troops had pushed the Germans out of Kalinin,
Klin, and Yelets. In the next few days the troops of Generals Belov and
Vlasov captured many weapons and vehicles in their drive against the
Germans.

During the night of December 16–17, Guderian received a telephone
call from Hitler, who forbade further withdrawals and promised replacements. Halder, ordered to report to the Führer at midnight, recorded the visit in his journal:

> Order. General withdrawal is out of the question. Enemy has made sub-
> stantial penetration only in a few places. The idea to prepare rear positions
> is just drivelling nonsense. The only trouble at the front is that the enemy
> outnumbers us in soldiers. He does not have any more artillery. His soldiers
> are not nearly as good as ours.[47]

Hitler announced on December 19 that he was taking over the command of the army himself, replacing dismissed Field Marshal von
Brauchitsch. The next day Guderian flew to East Prussia to discuss with
the Führer the situation at the front. Hitler was unfriendly and unsym-
pathetic. He informed Guderian that he, as Führer, was entitled to ask
German soldiers to sacrifice themselves. Guderian replied that sacrifices
could be asked only if the results were worth them. The panzer leader
then complained that winter clothing had not arrived, a statement which

evoked an angry denial from Hitler. The quartermaster general was summoned, and he had to admit that Guderian was correct. "We are suffering twice as many casualties from the cold as from the fire of the Russians," Guderian declared.[48]

On Christmas Day, 1941, the Red Army made significant advances against Guderian's troops, encircling elements of the Tenth Motorized Infantry Division at Chern. After the Germans broke out of the encirclement, Guderian ordered a withdrawal to the Susha–Oka position. Field Marshal von Kluge, who had replaced the ailing Marshal von Bock, was furious and requested that OKH remove Guderian. The next day Hitler did so.

German losses before Moscow were devastating. During the counteroffensive (December 6 to 25) Zhukov's Western *Front* captured more than 1,000 tanks, 1,434 guns, and large quantities of other military equipment. Troops of the Southwestern *Front* captured and destroyed 81 tanks, 491 guns, and other weapons. Tens of thousands of men lost their lives. According to contemporary Soviet sources, the number of German dead and prisoners was about 300,000. The threat which hung over Moscow had been dispelled.

By January 1, 1942, Zhukov's successful counteroffensive had produced the following situation along the *front*: the First Shock, Sixteenth, and Twentieth armies were pushing the Germans back along the Lama and Ruza rivers (the Stavka had transferred the Thirtieth Army to the Kalinin *Front*). In the center the Fifth, Thirty-third, Forty-third, and Forty-ninth armies were carrying out offensive operations along the Ruza, Nara, and Oka rivers in the direction of Mozhaisk, Borovsk, Maloyaroslavets, and Kondrovo. On the left wing the Tenth and Fiftieth armies and Belov's group were successsfully pursuing the Germans toward Yukhnov, Mosalsk, and Kirov (southwest of Moscow). At the same time the Kalinin *Front* was attacking in the general direction of Staritsa and Rzhev, while forces of the newly re-formed Bryansk *Front* were engaged along the Oka line, slightly to the rear of the Western *Front*'s left wing.

At this point the armies of Zhukov's left wing found themselves in an exceptionally favorable position. They had driven a deep wedge into the German lines and were now able to develop a successful offensive. To do so, however, fresh forces were needed, but the *front* had exhausted its reserves, and Zhukov's plea for more was refused by the Stavka. He says that if he had received even four armies (one each for the Kalinin and Bryansk *fronts* and two for the Western *Front*), he could have restored the positions these *fronts* occupied before the German October offensive.

Heady with the success achieved by his armies before Moscow, Stalin believed that the Germans, unprepared for winter fighting, would fall back in other sectors of the Soviet-German Front. He therefore wanted to begin a general offensive as soon as possible along the entire front— from Lake Ladoga to the Black Sea. On the evening of January 5, Zhukov was summoned to Moscow to discuss plans for future operations. Present at the meeting were members of the State Defense Committee, Chief of the General Staff Boris Shaposhnikov, and other members of the Stavka. Shaposhnikov delivered a brief report on conditions at the front and presented a rough outline of a plan of operations. It soon became apparent that Stalin intended to expand the counterstrike already in progress to include all the other sections of the front, with the aim of crushing the enemy at Leningrad, in the region west of Moscow, and in the Ukraine and the Crimea. Thus Zhukov's counteroffensive in the center was supposed to develop into a general offensive along the entire front.

The plan was indeed grandiose. It envisioned the main blow to be directed against Army Group Center by forces of the Western and Kalinin *fronts* and by the left wing of the Northwestern and Bryansk *fronts*. The troops at Leningrad, the right wing of the Northwestern *Front*, and the Baltic Fleet were assigned the mission of routing Army Group North and lifting the Leningrad blockade. The Southwestern and Southern *fronts* were to defeat Army Group South and liberate the Donbas region. The Caucasus *Front* and the Black Sea Fleet were charged with freeing the Crimea. The time for the beginning of this offensive was to be advanced as far as possible.

Summarizing Shaposhnikov's briefing, Stalin said: "Right now the Germans are in a state of confusion following their defeat before Moscow and they are poorly prepared for winter. Now is the most advantageous time for launching a general offensive."

After the plan had been explained, Stalin asked, "Who would like to say something?"

Zhukov realized that such a sweeping offensive was impossible to execute. The tremendous resources it would require were unavailable. He took the floor and declared that the *fronts* had to continue the offensive along the western strategic axis, where the conditions for success were most favorable and where the enemy units had not yet been restored to combat readiness. To achieve even this limited objective, he needed reinforcements in personnel, combat equipment, supplies, and tank units in particular. He argued that any offensive by Red Army troops at Leningrad or in the southwestern area would require an initial breach by heavy artillery through the Germans' impressive defenses. The troops would soon become exhausted and would sustain unjustifiable losses. Therefore, Zhukov urged, the *fronts* west of Moscow (that is, in the center) should be reinforced and the primary offensive carried out in their sectors, while the *fronts* around Leningrad and on the south should stand fast for the time being.

From Stalin's interjections during Zhukov's evaluation, it was obvious that he had already made his decision and that it was not to be changed. Nonetheless, N. A. Voznesensky, who had become chairman of the State Planning Commission (Gosplan) in 1939 and was soon to be elected a member of the State Defense Committee (GOKO) in 1942, took the floor and joined Zhukov in opposing a general offensive. He argued that the Soviet forces did not possess sufficient matériel to support simultaneous offensives on all *fronts*. Stalin countered Voznesensky's argument, saying that Marshal Timoshenko was in favor of the offensive and adding, "We must grind up the Germans in a hurry so that they will not be able to launch an offensive in the spring." Malenkov and Beria also supported Stalin, belittling the difficulties foreseen by Voznesensky, which they held to be surmountable. No one else asked to speak, and Stalin concluded the meeting by saying, "So be it; on that we shall end the discussion."

Once again Zhukov could not fail to conclude that Stalin had summoned military advisers to the Stavka not to discuss the advisability of a general offensive but to "nudge the military," as he was fond of saying.

As Zhukov and Shaposhnikov left the latter's office, Shaposhnikov turned to his friend and said: "You argued in vain. This issue had already been decided by the Supreme Commander in Chief. Directives have been issued to almost all the *fronts*, and they will begin the offensive in the next few days."

"Then why was our opinion asked for?" Zhukov asked.

"I just don't know, my friend," Shaposhnikov answered with a deep sigh.[49]

On the evening of January 7, Zhukov's headquarters received the directive: the Western and Kalinin *fronts* were to attempt to encircle the enemy in the Mozhaisk–Gzhatsk–Vyazma area.

As the Russian offensive began anew, Hitler ordered his forces to hold fast on the Lama River line, where the Soviets had prepared strong defensive positions in October and November. They were still intact, affording the Germans an opportunity to regroup and regain their strength.

On January 10, following a ninety-minute artillery barrage, the Twentieth Army, the cavalry corps of Major General I. A. Pliyev, a portion of the First Shock Army, the Twenty-second Tank Brigade, and five ski battalions attacked with the aim of breaking through the Volokolamsk area. After two weeks of stubborn fighting, the defense was finally penetrated, and Pliyev's cavalry corps, the five ski battalions, and the Twenty-second Tank Brigade were thrown into the breach toward Shakhovskaya. On January 16 and 17 the *front*'s right-wing forces occupied Lotoshino and Shakhovskaya and severed the Moscow–Rzhev rail line.

At this point, Zhukov believed, the Soviet forces should be augmented to expand and exploit their success, but he was to be disappointed. On January 19 he was ordered to transfer the First Shock Army from the combat sector to the Stavka Reserve. He and Sokolovsky immediately telephoned their protests to the General Staff and requested that the First Shock Army be retained. "There was only one answer," Zhukov says. "Such was the order of the Supreme Commander in Chief." Zhukov then telephoned Stalin, who told him, "Transfer [the army] without any further discussion." In response to Zhukov's protest that the departure of the First Shock Army would weaken his strike force, Stalin replied: "You have many troops. Count how many armies you have." Zhukov reminded him that his battle line was very long and that fierce fighting had erupted in all sectors, which prevented regrouping. He requested that the First Shock Army not be taken from the right wing of the Western *Front* until the offensive in progress had been completed, since its removal would lessen the pressure being brought to bear in the sector. "Instead of answering," Zhukov recorded in his memoirs, "Stalin hung up."[50]

On December 16 the Stavka had transferred the Thirtieth Army to the Kalinin *Front,* and now, a month later, the First Shock Army was being placed in reserve. Both moves weakened the Western *Front*'s right wing, with the result that Zhukov had to stretch the Twentieth Army over a wide front. Upon reaching Gzhatsk, the depleted right wing was stopped cold by the Germans.

On January 20 the Fifth and Thirty-third armies, attacking in the center of the front, liberated Ruza, Mozhaisk, and Vereye. The Forty-third and Forty-ninth armies reached the Domanovo and engaged the Germans at Yukhnov. Between January 18 and 22 two battalions of the 201st Airborne Brigade and the 250th Airborne Regiment were dropped into the Zhelanye area, twenty-four miles south of Vyazma, to sever communications lines in the rear.

The Thirty-third Army was ordered to develop the breakthrough and to seize Vyazma in cooperation with Belov's First Cavalry Corps, airborne and Russian partisan detachments, and the Eleventh Cavalry Corps of the Kalinin *Front*. On January 27, Belov's corps broke through to the Warsaw highway twenty-one miles southwest of Yukhnov and three days later linked up with the airborne and partisan detachments. On February 1 three reinforced rifle divisions of the Thirty-third Army, commanded by Lieutenant General M. G. Yefremov, arrived, and fighting broke out on the approaches to Vyazma.

The battle at Vyazma deserves special comment. After pushing the offensive from Naro Fominsk in the general direction of Vyazma, the Thirty-third Army reached the Shansky-Zavod–Domanovo area toward the end of January. Subsequently it was decided to capture Vyazma before enemy reserves could be brought up. With its fall the Germans would be in an extremely precarious position.

General Yefremov decided to lead the shock army himself, making a swift, bold thrust toward Vyazma. On February 3–4, however, when his main forces reached the approaches to the city, the Germans struck through a gap near the Ugra River, cut off part of his forces, and then dug in along the river line. The right wing of the Thirty-third Army, held up at Shansky-Zavod, and its left-flank neighbor, the Forty-third Army at Medyn, obviously were in no position to carry out Zhukov's order to assist Yefremov's group. Consequently, as Belov's cavalrymen reached Vyazma, they were cut off in the rear.

At this crucial point the Stavka acted, although the forces it committed were sent piecemeal. The Fourth Airborne Corps was ordered dropped at Ozerechni to reinforce Belov's corps and coordinate with the Eleventh Cavalry Corps of the Kalinin *Front*. But because few transport planes were available, only the Eighth Airborne Brigade, consisting of two thousand men, was dropped, and then only after several trips.

Belov's corps, Yefremov's group, and the paratroopers were now in the German rear, where they carried out operations for two months. On February 10 the airborne troops, in conjunction with partisan detachments, occupied the Morshanovo–Dyaglevo area, where they killed the German Fifth Panzer Division staff and seized considerable matériel. Zhukov's command post established and maintained communications with Belov and Yefremov and, to the extent possible, supplied their forces with ammunition, medicine, and food. Also noteworthy is the fact that many of the wounded were evacuated by air.

The situation worsened in April, when the Germans decided to remove the "splinter." With the arrival of the spring thaws, which made maneuvering difficult, Zhukov instructed Belov and Yefremov to disengage and reunite with the Western *Front*. They were told to move through partisan territory, through the wooded areas along the Desna, and on toward Kirov, where the Tenth Army had prepared a gap for them at a weak spot in the German lines. But General Yefremov, who considered the route too long for his exhausted men, radioed the General Staff and requested permission to take the shortest route—across the Ugra. Stalin agreed, countermanded Zhukov's decision, and ordered the enemy engaged in the Forty-third Army's zone. The coordinated strike by Yefremov's group never took place. The Germans discovered the group and cut it to ribbons. Yefremov was killed, as was his chief of artillery, Major General P. N. Ofrosimov.

In the meantime, Belov's cavalrymen and the airborne troops carried out Zhukov's order precisely, skirting large enemy formations and making their way back to the *front*. Although they lost many heavy weapons and much combat equipment, most of the troops managed to rejoin the *front* at the end of May.

In a critical examination of events during the winter of 1941–42, Zhukov asserts that the leaders of the High Command erred in their appraisal of the situation at Vyazma. They underestimated the Germans' capability, and, worse, they ordered an offensive (scheduled for March) at a time when the *front*'s manpower and matériel had been exhausted. Zhukov says that the situation was so bad that each time he was summoned to the Stavka he literally begged Stalin for antitank guns, machine pistols, and a minimal quantity of shells and mortar rounds. Whatever Zhukov managed to obtain in this manner was loaded into trucks and hurried to the neediest units.

Zhukov describes the desperate shortage of ammunition, citing statistics to prove his point. Of the ammunition planned for delivery in the first ten days of January, the *front* received only 1 per cent of its 82-millimeter mortar shells and 20 to 30 per cent of its artillery shells. In the entire month it received only 2.7 per cent of its 55-millimeter, 36 per cent of its 120-millimeter, and 55 per cent of its 82-millimeter mortar rounds and 44 per cent of its artillery shells. The February quota was not delivered at all, and of 316 boxcars ordered for the first ten days, not one was received. Ammunition for the rocket-launching artillery was in such short supply that the artillery units had to be withdrawn to the rear. "It may be hard to believe," Zhukov writes, "that we had to establish a limit of one to two rounds a gun a day. And this during the offensive!" On February 14, Zhukov reported to Stalin: "As has been shown by combat experience, the shortage of shells precludes artillery support, and since the enemy's fire system is not destroyed, our troops, in attacking enemy defensive positions which have not been neutralized, suffer very heavy losses without achieving the desired success."[51]

On February 1, recognizing the multiplicity of tasks in the Western Direction and the need for ensuring close coordination between the Kalinin and Western *fronts*, the Stavka reestablished the position of commander in chief of the Western Direction and assigned Zhukov to the post, although he also continued as commander of the Western *Front*.

By the time the Stavka had decided to reinforce the *fronts* of the Western Direction at the end of February and the beginning of March, the Germans had also begun reinforcing their units. German operations toward the end of February took a deadly toll of the defenders, and the battered Twenty-ninth Army, which had been surrounded during German counterattacks at the beginning of February and now numbered only about six thousand men, was extracted with great difficulty and at the expense of its heavy weapons.

It was becoming increasingly difficult for the exhausted Soviet forces to overcome German resistance. Zhukov's frequent requests for permission to allow his troops to stop and consolidate the positions they had gained were refused. Stalin continued to insist upon the offensive. "If you don't have any success today," he said, "then tomorrow you will. If you don't hold the enemy down with your attack, the result will be felt on other sectors of the front."

But no advance whatever was made by either the Kalinin or the Southwestern *Front*. The Leningrad *Front* and the right wing of the Northwestern *Front* were engaged in a prolonged struggle, as were units in the southern part of the country. "Despite the heavy costs and the lack of a strategic result," Zhukov records, "the Stavka again demanded, in a directive dated March 20, that the previously assigned mission be continued with increased vigor. But with the insignificant reinforcements they had received, the *fronts* in the Western Direction were not up to the task."[52] Nevertheless, in late March and early April these *fronts* made another attempt to comply with the directive to destroy the enemy in the Rzhev and Vyazma areas. They failed. Bad roads and uncertain deliveries of supplies complicated troop operations, and the Stavka was forced to order a transition to the defensive along the line extending through Velikie Luki, Velizh, Demidov, Belyy, Dukhovshchina, the Dnieper River, and Nelidovo. Rzhev, Gzhatsk, and Kirov were still in German hands.

During the January–March offensive, the troops of the Western *Front* advanced from about forty to sixty miles in some sectors and improved the general operational situation somewhat. In particular, Moscow gained some breathing room. Zhukov declares, however, that his troops unquestionably could have achieved much better results if he had been permitted to concentrate more forces in his *front* to capitalize on the success of the December counteroffensive. The winter thrusts of the Leningrad, Volkhov, and Northwestern *fronts* bogged down because they lacked the men and matériel needed to crack the German defenses. For the same reason, the offensive by the Southern and Southwestern *fronts* was also short-lived.

Even so, Zhukov concludes, these problems can in no way minimize the importance of the Soviet victory in the Battle of Moscow. The bloody campaign pushed the Germans back one to two hundred miles. The primary reason the Soviets failed to win decisively lay in the shortage of tanks. Says Zhukov: "Without them, as the war showed, it is impossible to carry out modern offensive operations with decisive goals and on a large scale. Only with powerful tank and mechanized formations is it possible to outmaneuver the enemy, outflank him quickly, penetrate his rear, and surround and cut up his units."[53]

Zhukov's opinion of Stalin's contribution seems fair enough:

> The question is often put to me, "Where was Stalin during the battle of Moscow?" Stalin was in Moscow, organizing forces and equipment for the defeat of the enemy around Moscow. He must be given his due. . . . He did a great job in organizing the strategic reserves and the material and technical means needed for armed combat. In the period of the battle around Moscow he was always attentive to advice, but, unfortunately, he sometimes made decisions which the situation did not call for. Such was the case when the First Shock Army was placed in reserve and an offensive was launched with all the *fronts*.[54]

Zhukov notes that in the Battle of Moscow the Red Army for the first time dealt a great strategic defeat to a major German combat group. There had been some earlier local successes, but they could in no way compare with the fighting at Moscow, where a strong defense enabled the Soviets to counterattack with considerable skill, demonstrating the growing maturity of Soviet military leaders. Red Army men, hardened in combat, had been transformed from a retreating defensive force into a mighty offensive force, Zhukov writes, adding that this campaign stands out above all others in his memory.[55]

The occasion was a memorable one for many of the German commanders, too. General Gunther Blumentritt, chief of staff of the Fourth Army during the struggle for Moscow, was bitter in his recollections:

> The Battle of Moscow was the first major German defeat on land during the Second World War. It marked the end of the Blitzkrieg technique which had won Hitler and his Wehrmacht such spectacular victories in Poland, France and the Balkans. It was in Russia that the first fatal decisions were taken. From the political point of view, perhaps the most fatal of all had been the decision to attack that country in the first place. For now we were fighting a very much stronger enemy than we had met before. There were no more easy victories to be gained in the endless East.
>
> Many of our leaders had grossly underestimated the new enemy. This was partly due to ignorance, for some of them knew neither the people nor their soldiers. Several of our responsible senior officers had never campaigned in the East, having spent the whole of the First World War on the Western Front, and had no idea of the difficulties presented by the terrain nor of the toughness of the Russian fighting man. They chose to ignore the warnings of the experts.

With deep feeling Blumentritt described the German forces as they approached the outskirts of the Soviet capital:

> And now, when Moscow was already almost in sight, the mood both of commanders and troops changed. With amazement and disappointment we discovered in late October and early November that the beaten Russians seemed quite unaware that as a military force they had almost ceased to exist. During these weeks enemy resistance stiffened and the fighting became more bitter with each day that passed. Marshal Zhukov had now assumed command of the troops covering Moscow. For weeks his men had been constructing a defensive position in depth which ran through the forests that bordered the Nara from Serpukhov in the south to Naro-Fominsk and thence north. Skillfully camouflaged strong points, wire entanglements and thick minefields now filled the forests which covered the western approach to Moscow.
>
> . . . Within the next few days Marshal Zhukov was to launch the great Russian counteroffensive which began on December 6th and was initially directed against the two panzer groups northwest of Moscow. The turning point in the East had been reached: our hopes of knocking Russia out of the war in 1941 had been dashed, at the very last minute.
>
> . . . Every soldier outside Moscow knew that this was a battle for life or death. . . . In 1941 the choice for the Germans was only to hold fast or to be annihilated.[56]

Zhukov emerged as the *spasitel* ("savior") of Moscow, but he wisely and tactfully attributed his success to the guidance of Stalin and the unconquerable fighting qualities of his men. After Germany had been defeated, Stalin paid high tribute to his warrior. Speaking before an honor banquet on May 25, 1945, he declared:

> The Fatherland and the Party will never forget the role played by the commanders of the Soviet armies in our national defensive struggle. The names of all these generals who gained the victories and saved the Fatherland will stand forever carved on the tablets of honor which history will erect on the battlefields. Of these battlefields, one is of very special significance. That is the field on which the battle of Moscow, the capital of our Soviet Union, was fought. And the name of Comrade Zhukov remains undissolubly connected with this battlefield as the symbol of victory.[57]

For Zhukov, there was no time to rest. As the winter snows melted and the Germans made new plans for their 1942 offensive, he was dispatched to scenes of fresh crises.

IX. THE LURE OF STALINGRAD

What millions died that Caesar might be great!

Thomas Campbell

IN January, 1942, Soviet forces struck new blows against the Germans, penetrating their defenses on the Lama and Ruza rivers and liberating Mozhaisk and Kaluga. But, wrote *Red Star* correspondent Ilya Ehrenburg:

> Towards the end of January it became clear that our advance had been halted. On January 23d I travelled with Pavlenko to GHQ [Stavka] on the Western Front. Zhukov, the general in command, described to us the course of the offensive: the battle for Moscow was over, on certain sectors it might be possible to gain ground, but the Germans had dug themselves

in and to all intents and purposes the war would be of a positional character till the spring.[1]

Zhukov was now commander in chief of the combined Kalinin and Western *fronts*, and neither *front* had sufficient forces and equipment to renew a serious thrust westward. The Stavka had exhausted its reserves on other strategic axes and could not help. Therefore, the commander of the Western Direction had to make a painful decision: to dig in, preserving the gains made in December and January, and use the lull to prepare for summer operations. Nevertheless, despite the extreme cold and lack of replacements, Zhukov was able to make limited advances on certain sectors of the front toward Orel and Vyazma.

According to Vice Admiral Kurt Assmann:

> From about February 23, a noticeable lull set in on the whole eastern front; the striking power of the Russian Army seemed almost played out also. Therewith the long months of winter warfare which had strained the German forces to the utmost came to an end. The German Army survived the ordeal of the Russian assault with untold effort and by giving up valuable territory. The ground lost was not great, relative to the enormous area captured in 1941, but the main objective, the enemy capital, Moscow, vanished beyond reach. Never again was the German Wehrmacht to get as close as it did on December 5, 1941.[2]

The end of the tremendous German effort in the winter snows and spring mud before Moscow and the losses sustained in restoring equilibrium on the central front precluded operations on the grand scale of 1941. Hitler by no means intended to relinquish the initiative, however, even though the forces available for 1942 would limit its scope. With the coming of spring he issued a new directive, dated April 5, praising his troops for their "outstanding bravery and the self-sacrificing effort" and assigning them a new mission. As soon as weather and terrain conditions were favorable, they were to break through into the Caucasus, capture the oil fields there, and push on to Stalingrad.[3]

"The lure of Stalingrad," writes Churchill, "fascinated Hitler; its very name was a challenge. The city was important as a centre of industry and also a strong-point on the defensive flank protecting his main thrust to the Caucasus. It became a magnet drawing to itself the supreme effort of the German Army and Air Force."[4]

Before the attack could be launched, resistance in the Crimea had to be eliminated. Bitter fighting had been in progress there since December, 1941, when the Soviets landed 40,000 troops in an attempt to recapture the Kerch Peninsula. They succeeded in occupying all of it and regaining the important city of Feodosia. The attack caught the German Eleventh Army just as the battle on the northern front of Sevastopol had entered its crucial phase, and the sheer weight of numbers almost knocked the Germans off balance. Colonel General Erich von Manstein, commander of the Eleventh Army at the time, later wrote of the Russian landings: "Behind them, and in the utter ruthlessness with which they were expended, one sensed the brutal will of Stalin."[5] Unfortunately for the Red Army, however, the Kremlin did not exploit its successes, and on May 8, 1942, the Eleventh Army began a new offensive to reconquer the Kerch Peninsula. A few days later the Germans scored a major victory, capturing (if German sources can be believed) up to 150,000 prisoners and a large number of tanks and guns. Even the Russians admitted that the enemy seized almost all of their combat equipment and heavy armament and later used it against the defenders of Sevastopol.

Now Manstein's army, unfettered, was in a position to reduce Sevastopol, completing the attack which had been broken off by the Russian eruption into the Kerch Peninsula. It proved to be no easy task, however, and the contest lasted throughout June. Sevastopol finally fell on July 1, and a grateful Hitler promoted Manstein to field marshal. The Crimea now belonged to the Germans.

In May the Russians were routed in disastrous battles at Kharkov. Simultaneously with the fighting in the Crimea, they undertook an ambitious two-pronged offensive against strong German forces north and south of Kharkov. When it appeared that Timoshenko's Southwestern Direction was moving into a trap, the command asked Stalin for permission to halt the advance and concentrate on blunting the German counteroffensive. But Stalin was adamant, and even the pleas of Khrushchev, who was the direction's Military Council member, fell on deaf ears.* Finally, on May 19, Stalin realized the danger that was

---

* Khrushchev recalls that during the battle for Kharkov in the spring of 1942 he sensed that the Red Army units were headed straight for disaster. From the scene of the fighting he tried to contact Stalin to warn him what would happen if they continued the operation. Vasilevsky answered Khrushchev's telephone

facing the Sixth and Fifty-seventh armies and General L. V. Bobkin's group, which was fighting near Krasnograd, and decided to halt the Red offensive. The decision came too late. In extremely fierce combat the Germans exacted a terrible toll, including the deputy commander of the Southwestern *Front*, General F. Ya. Kostenko; the commanders of the Sixth and Fifty-seventh armies; and General Bobkin.

This victory, added to others in the Crimea, succeeded in using up precious Russian reserves and weakening the southern flank. It allowed the Germans to shift their offensive toward the Don and achieve their immediate goals fairly quickly. Comments a Soviet history of the war:

> As a result of our failures in the area of Kharkov, the situation on the southern wing of the Soviet-German front radically changed in favor of the enemy. By cutting off the Barbenkovo salient, the German troops occupied favorable jump-off positions for their pending offensive. The Soviet command decided to go over to the defensive, in order to frustrate the enemy's move toward the east.[6]

In mid-July the Germans finally began their massive operation toward Rostov and Stalingrad from concentrations around Kharkov. A disgusted Halder recorded in his journal:

> The Führer surprises me by approving my very recommendation which yesterday he rejected in less than gracious manner in favor of a plan which would produce a meaningless concentration on the north bank of the Don at Rostov. And immediately his most lordly order is issued, directing a crossing of the Don on a wide front and the initiation of the battle of Stalingrad.[7]

call and after listening to his plea that the Soviet offensive be called off replied that Stalin had already made up his mind and issued the orders.

Recalled Khrushchev: "Anyone who has ever dealt with Vasilevsky will be able to imagine the steady, droning voice with which he said this. I was on very good terms with him; so after hanging up, I decided to call him back and try again. This time I pleaded with him urgently to help, but he still refused: 'Nikita Sergeyevich, Comrade Stalin has made up his mind and that's all there is to it.' If only Zhukov had been at General Headquarters instead of Vasilevsky. I'm sure he would have driven straight out to the Nearby Dacha [Stalin's residence] and intervened on our behalf."

In desperation Khrushchev tried to telephone Stalin direct, but this time Malenkov intercepted the call and refused to allow Khrushchev to speak to him. After protesting to Malenkov that the offensive would be disastrous, Khrushchev hung up. General Bagramyan, who was with Khrushchev, burst into tears as his nerves began to crack. Khrushchev, *op. cit.*, 184–86.

By July 21, General Friedrich Paulus' Sixth Army was advancing on Stalingrad, while the Russians were moving in new troops from the northwest by rail and truck. A few days later, on July 26, Rostov was in real danger, despite heavy counterattacks by the Red Army, and hard battles were being fought west of Stalingrad. By July 28 the Red Army was pulling back from Rostov. Lack of fuel and ammunition prevented Paulus from exploiting his success, however. In addition, armor was beginning to stack up at Rostov, causing Hitler to explode in a fit of rage, hurling insults against the General Staff and launching tirades about the mistakes of others. On July 30, General Alfred Jodl announced that the fate of the Caucasus would be decided at Stalingrad and that, in view of the importance of the battle, forces might have to be diverted from another army group.

By this time about thirty Axis divisions were pressing toward Stalingrad, including those of the Italian Eighth Army and the Rumanian Third Army. But the Soviets had not been idle. On July 10 the Stavka had sent fresh reserves into the battle area, including the Sixty-second and Sixty-fourth armies, while the local headquarters had sent its reserves to the rear of the Southwestern *Front* along the Don from Pavlovsk to Kletskaya and farther south through Surovikino to Verkhne-Kurmoyarskaya. From these forces, plus the Twenty-first army and the Eighth Air Army, which had been taken from the former Southwestern *Front*, the Stalingrad *Front* was created on July 12. Marshal S. K. Timoshenko was placed in command, Nikita Khrushchev became the member of the Military Council, and P. I. Bodin, who had served for some time on the General Staff as chief of the Directorate of Operations and deputy chief of the General Staff, was named the *front*'s chief of staff. The Stavka immediately moved the First and Fourth Tank armies to the *front*, with orders to reestablish the defenses; simultaneously steps were taken to rush the necessary reserves to Stalingrad from bases deep in the interior of the country. The battle for Stalingrad was about to begin. It would drag on into 1943.

The over-all campaign can be divided into two stages, the defense of the city and the Soviet counterthrust, to be described briefly. The contributions of the Stavka—and those of Zhukov in particular—will be examined in greater detail.

The defensive fighting on the approaches to Stalingrad, in the area around the city, and in the city itself continued from the middle of July to November 18, 1942. On July 23 the Stavka sent General A. M. Vasilevsky to Stalingrad to help the *front* command organize the defenses and prepare counterattacks. A few weeks later he and Zhukov returned to the city with the same mission.

The early phases of the campaign were marked by desperate efforts by the Red Army to slow the German advance, most of the struggle taking place inside the Don Bend. The Russians hoped to gain time to strengthen Stalingrad's defenses, an activity already begun by thousands of the city's inhabitants. Although the defenses were not particularly effective, they did prevent the Germans from capturing the city by storm.

From August 5 to August 18 an enveloping thrust from the south supplemented the advance on the city from the west and northwest. In the period from August 19 to September 3 the fighting between the Don and the Volga reached crisis proportions as the Germans broke through to the Volga north of Stalingrad, forming a five-mile-wide salient. To prevent encirclement (and also to keep the Germans from striking south), the Red Army defenders withdrew to the city. Between September 4 and 13 the Germans broke through to the Volga south of Stalingrad, isolating the Soviet Sixty-second Army in the city proper from the rest of the front. Finally, from September 13 to November 18, a desperate battle raged within the city, while most of the Soviets' artillery was deployed on the far side of the Volga.

It is important at this point to define clearly the role of the Stavka representatives in the defense of Stalingrad, especially since they have no equivalent in American armed forces. Such an understanding is necessary to appreciate fully the power and facility with which they operated. They were in close contact with Stalin and other members of the Stavka and were largely responsible for decisions made at the scene of the fighting. They were empowered to overrule local commanders, to order counterstrikes by entire armies, and to coordinate the activities of entire theaters. For instance, Vasilevsky ordered a counterattack by the First and Fourth armies on July 25 and 27, an action which failed to dislodge the enemy and which was later criticized. Vasilevsky's defense of this move illustrates the authority granted to Stavka representatives: "Being one of the most responsible initiators of these events, one who carried out all negotiations with the Supreme Commander in Chief on this problem, and also an eyewitness to the entire seriousness of the situation which had developed, I believed, and still believe, that the decision for carrying out the counterattack . . . was, under the conditions, the only correct step to take."[8]

An understanding of the organization and leadership of the Stavka itself is essential to an appreciation of Zhukov's role in the Battle of Stalingrad and subsequent campaigns. The Stavka, sometimes referred to as GHQ (General Headquarters) by Western historians, was directly under Stalin and the State Defense Committee* and consisted of a select staff of twelve to fourteen top military officers, advisers to Stalin.[9] It was the highest organ of field direction of the Supreme Command of the Armed Forces of the U.S.S.R. During the war years the Stavka worked out battle plans and directly managed the preparation, organization, and conduct of strategic operations. Representatives of the Stavka continually made trips to the front and, in accordance with the strategic plan, organized important on-the-spot operations, exercising close control over the execution of Stavka orders and coordinating actions of the various *fronts*. The chief of staff served on the Stavka, and the General Staff was directly subordinate to it, having the task of providing information and detailed operational plans.

Zhukov, chief of staff from January to July, 1941, headed the Stavka during most of its existence (June 23, 1941, to 1946) as first deputy commissar of defense, a post he assumed after illness forced Marshal Shaposhnikov to retire. Vasilevsky served as second deputy to Stalin

* The Stavka probably received little help or guidance from the State Defense Committee, which was composed of politicians and "political generals," among them Voroshilov, who had demonstrated his ineptness at Leningrad in 1941.

The Stavka (or GHQ) had certain problems, especially in its early months. Admiral Kuznetsov records in his memoirs:

"The first sittings of the GHQ of the Chief Command of the Armed Forces in June [1941] were not attended by Stalin. Marshal Timoshenko was only nominally its chairman. . . . There was no statute of the GHQ and no one knew its functions. The men on it were not at all inclined to be subordinate to the People's Commissar for Defense. They wanted him to report and provide information, and even render an account of his actions.

"The GHQ and the State Defense Committee, set up on June 30, suffered for a long time from the organizational deficiencies which are inevitable in the initial period. After a year or two, the GHQ, or rather Stalin, had established much closer relations with the *front* commanders, and he paid more and more attention to their opinions. All the major operations, like Stalingrad and Kursk, were at that time prepared jointly with the *fronts*." N. G. Kuznetsov, "Before the War," *International Affairs* (Moscow), January, 1967, 104.

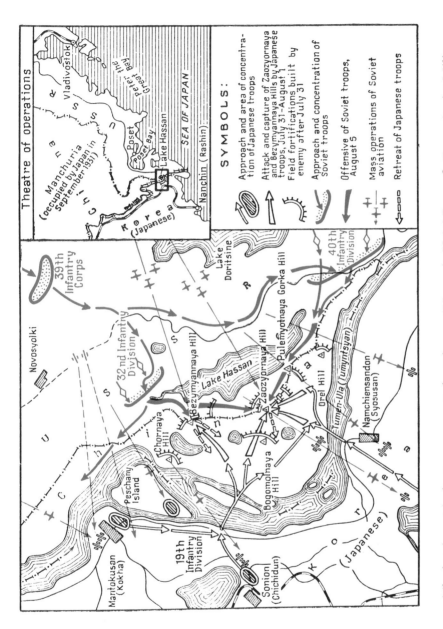

The battles with the Japanese at Lake Khasan (Hassan), U.S.S.R., 1938. From *Soviet Military Review* (Moscow), July, 1968.

This and the subsequent official maps from the English-language monthly *Soviet Military Review* are reproduced as they appeared in the original publication.

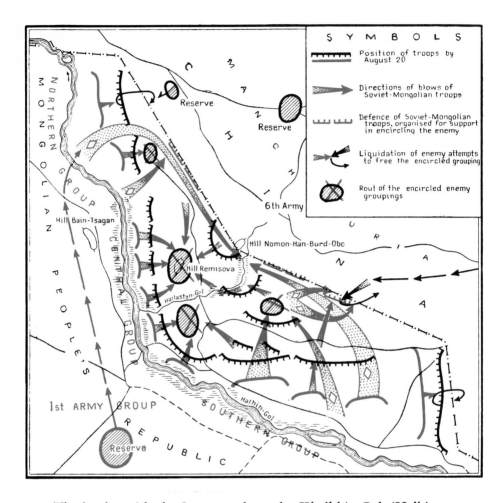

The battles with the Japanese along the Khalkhin-Gol (Halhin-Gol) River in the Great Khingan Mountains, Mongolian People's Republic, August 20-31, 1939. From *Soviet Military Review*, August, 1969.

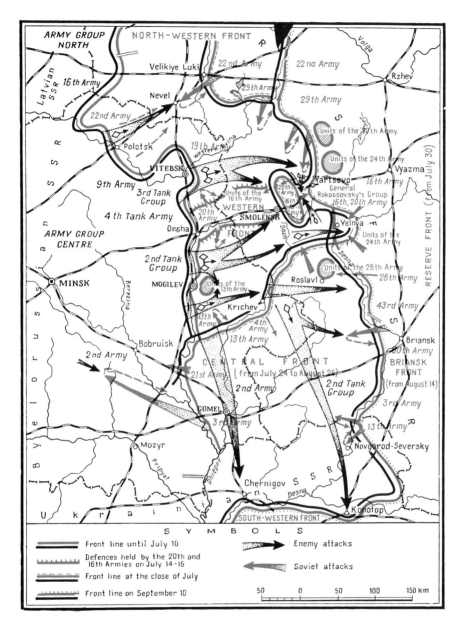

The Battle of Smolensk, July 10–September 14, 1941. From *Soviet Military Review*, April, 1968.

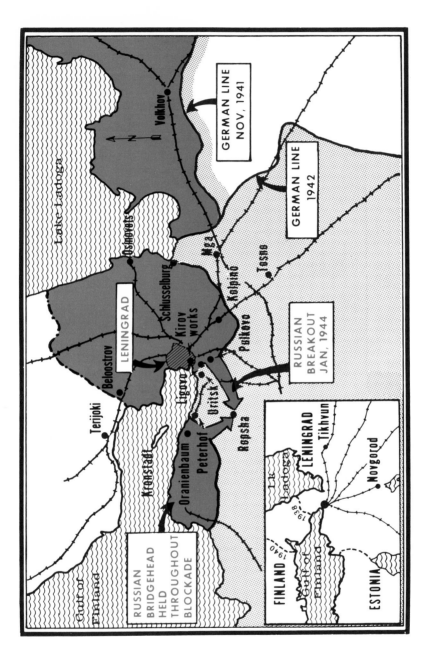

The Leningrad Blockade, 1941–44. Adapted from Alexander Werth's *Russia at War, 1941–1945*, New York, E. P. Dutton & Co., Inc., 1964. Reproduced by permission.

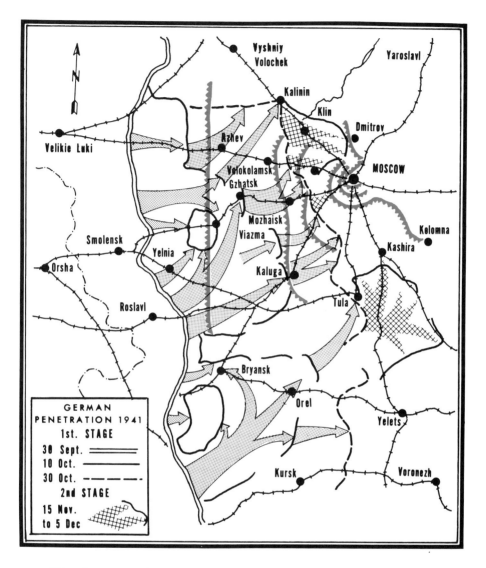

The German offensive against Moscow, September 30–December 5, 1941. Adapted from Alexander Werth's *Russia at War, 1941–1945*, New York, E. P. Dutton & Co., Inc., 1964. Reproduced by permission.

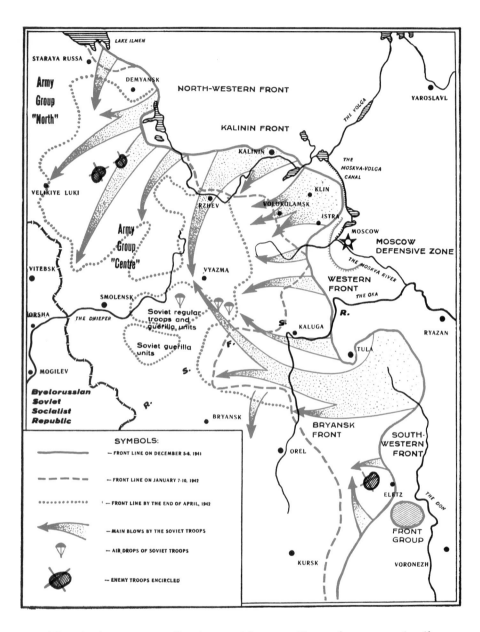

The Soviet counteroffensive at Moscow, December, 1941–April, 1942. From *Soviet Military Review*, January, 1966.

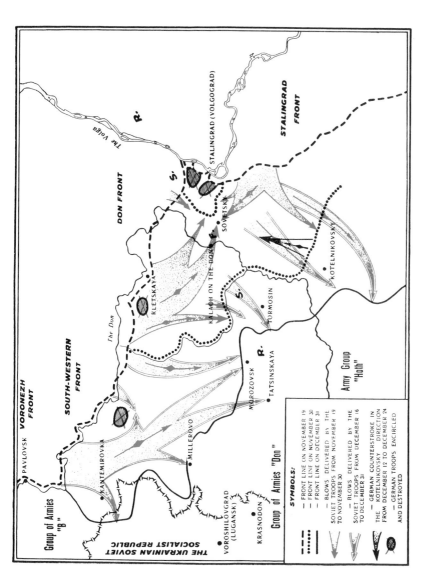

The battle on the Volga. Soviet counteroffensive at Stalingrad, November 19, 1942–February 2, 1943. From *Soviet Military Review*, February, 1966.

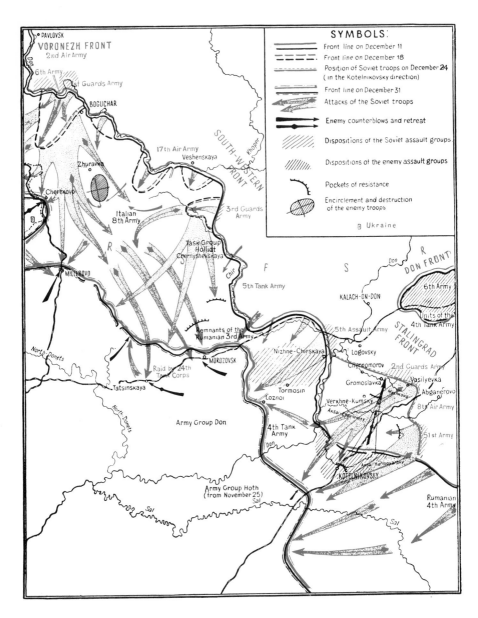

The Battle of Stalingrad. Soviet counteroffensive operations, December, 1942. From *Soviet Military Review*, January, 1968.

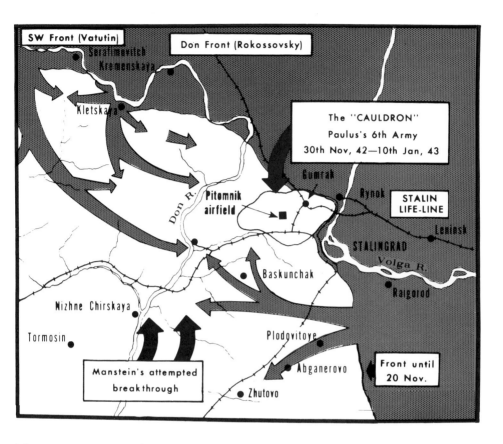

The Germans trapped at Stalingrad, 1942–43. Adapted from Alexander Werth's
Russia at War, 1941–1945, New York, E. P. Dutton & Co., Inc., 1964.
Reproduced by permission.

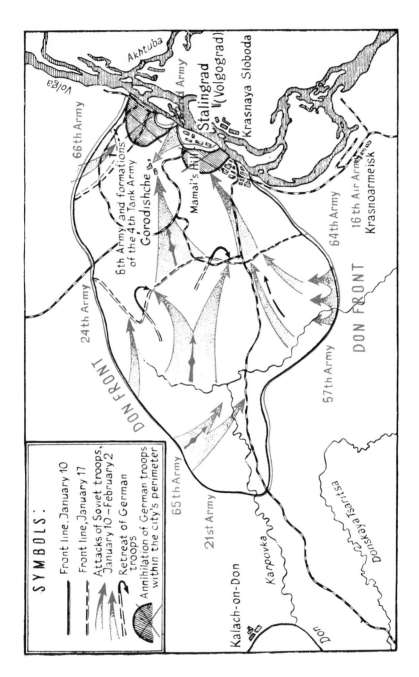

Annihilation of the Germans trapped at Stalingrad, January 10–February 2, 1943. From *Soviet Military Review*, February, 1968.

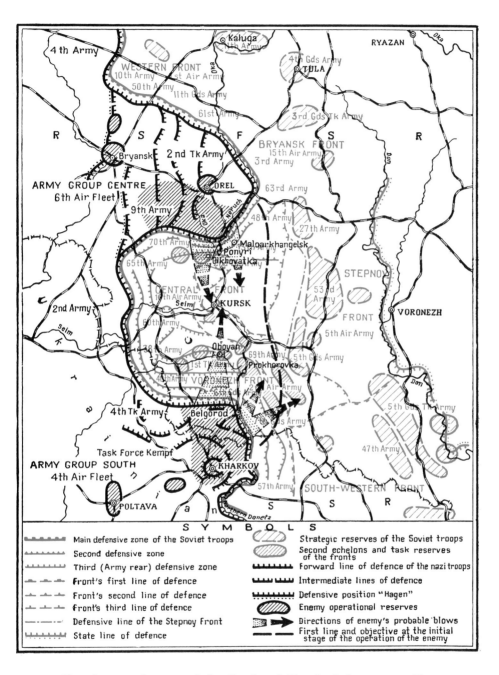

Situation on the eve of the Battle of Kursk, July 5, 1943. From
Soviet Military Review, July, 1968.

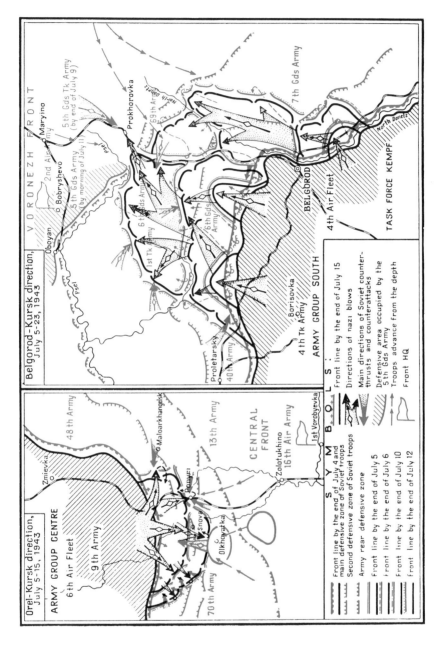

The Battle of Kursk. Defensive fighting, July, 1943. From *Soviet Military Review*, August, 1968.

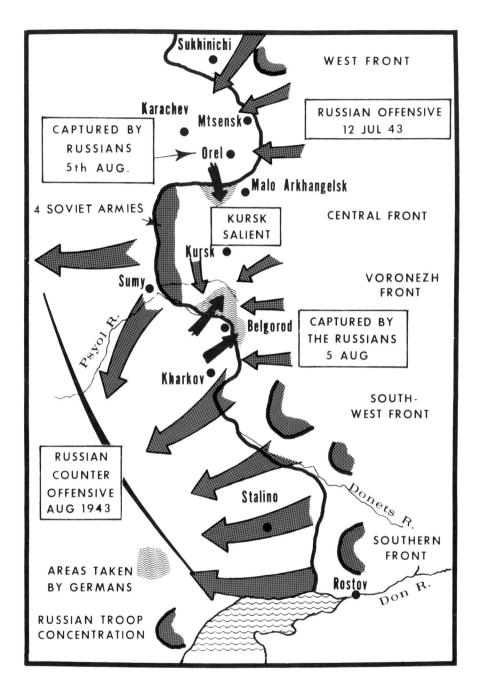

The Battle of Kursk. The Soviet counteroffensive, July 12–August 5, 1943. Adapted from Alexander Werth's *Russia at War, 1941–1945*, New York, E. P. Dutton & Co., Inc., 1964. Reproduced by permission.

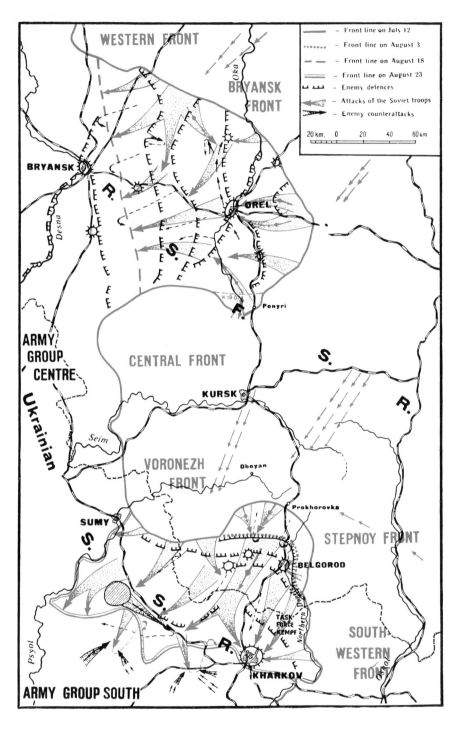

The triumph at Kursk and the liberation of Orel and Belgorod,
July 12–August 23, 1943. From *Soviet Military Review*, July, 1966.

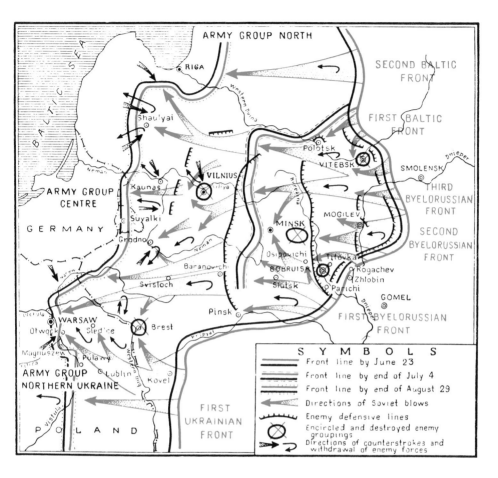

The liberation of the Belorussian Republic, June 23–August 29,
1944. From *Soviet Military Review*, July, 1969.

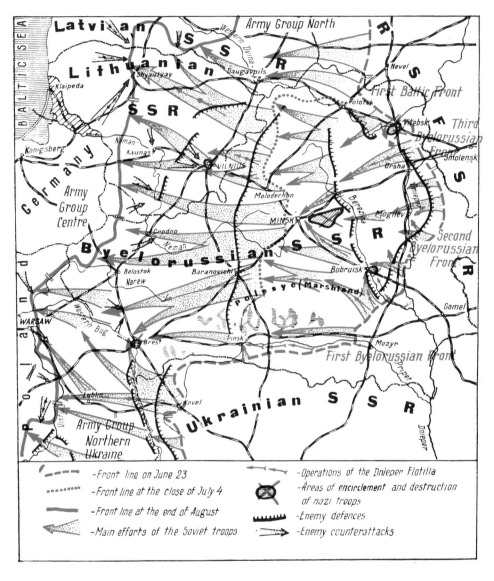

The Belorussian offensive. *Front* operations, June 23–August 29, 1944. From *Soviet Military Review*, March, 1967.

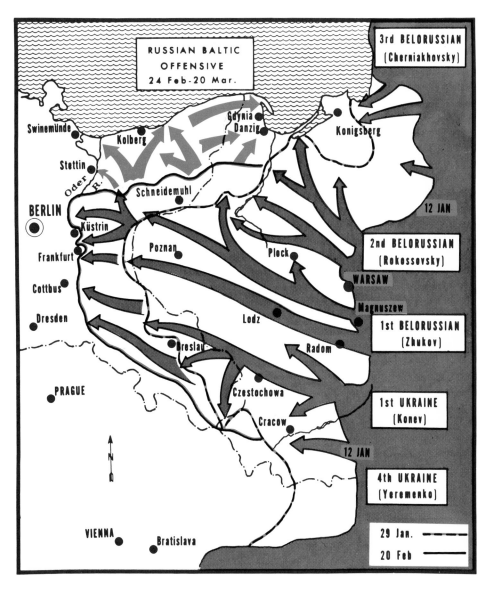

The liberation of Poland and the invasion of Germany, 1945.
Adapted from Alexander Werth's *Russia at War, 1941–1945*, New
York, E. P. Dutton & Co., Inc., 1964. Reproduced by permission.

209

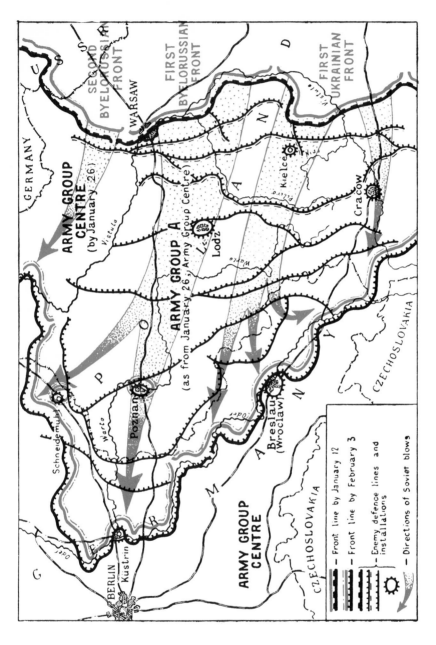

The Vistula–Oder operation. Soviet *fronts* strike across Poland toward Berlin, January 12–February 3, 1945. From *Soviet Military Review*, February, 1970.

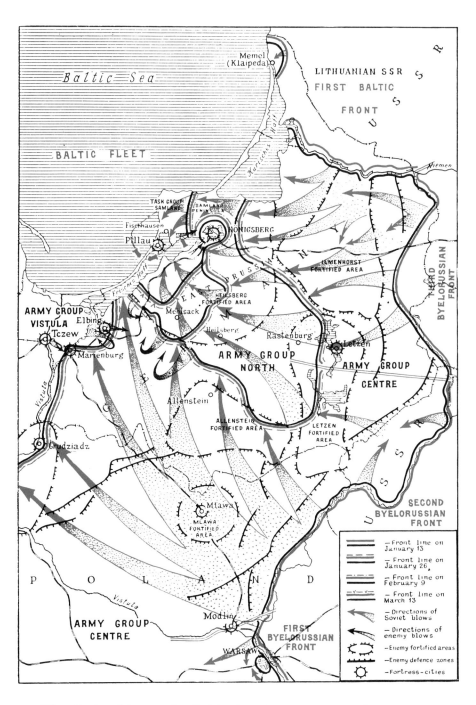

The Soviet drive to the Baltic Sea, January 13–March 13, 1945.
From *Soviet Military Review*, January, 1970.

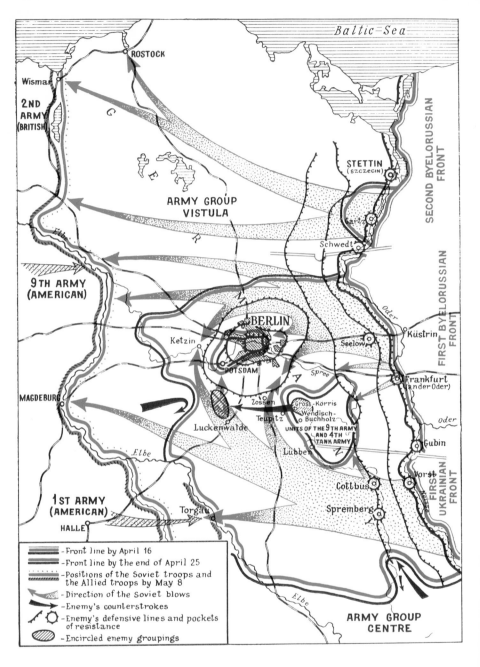

The capture of Berlin and the sweep to the Elbe River, April 16–
May 8, 1945. From *Soviet Military Review*, April, 1970.

and chief of staff after November, 1942, and, with Zhukov, often appeared at the front during critical times. Other members included, at one time or another, Marshal Timoshenko, the Stavka's first chairman in 1943 and 1944; Marshal of Artillery N. N. Voronov; Shaposhnikov, chief of staff from October, 1941, until November, 1942 (the Stavka may well have been his idea); and possibly General A. I. Antonov and General Sergei M. Shtemenko. A number of experts in broad technical fields also served on the Stavka as needed: Marshal of Engineer Troops V. Vorobyev; Marshal of Signal Troops I. T. Peresypkin; General A. V. Khrulev, chief of the rear services; and several leaders of combat arms, including Admiral of the Fleet N. G. Kuznetsov, chief of the naval staff; General (later Marshal) Ya. N. Fedorenko, an armor expert; Marshal Budenny, representing cavalry; and Aviation Generals (later Marshals) A. A. Novikov and A. Y. Golovanov.[10] The old political cronies of Stalin, Voroshilov and Budenny, though early members of the Stavka, soon lost any real influence on decision making. The reason was obvious: "The Stavka was organized, and apparently very effectively, for the planning of war."[11]

Zhukov and Vasilevsky were sometimes detached temporarily from the Stavka to assume command in the field. In March, 1944, when General N. F. Vatutin was killed, Zhukov took over Vatutin's First Ukrainian *Front*. In February of the following year, when General I. D. Chernyakhovsky was fatally wounded outside Königsberg, Vasilevsky took over command of the Third Belorussian *Front*.[12]

On many occasions *front* commanders were given the operational plan worked out by the Stavka and then adapted it to their own situations. Communication between the Stavka and the *front* commands was close, smooth, and even welcomed. In Soviet histories the titles "High Command" and "Supreme Command" refer interchangeably to Stalin and the Stavka. Stalin frequently called its members together for discussions of proposed operations, listening to the pros and cons of a particular strategy before ruling on the matter and cutting off discussion.[13]

Stavka planning even extended to the selection of personnel, as illustrated in this account of a telephone conversation between Vasilevsky and A. I. Yeremenko on August 9, 1942:

VASILEVSKY: Comrade Stalin has directed me to get in touch with you and obtain your opinion on the following matters.

First. Comrade Stalin considers it to be expedient and timely to combine the problems of Stalingrad's defense under one command, with the objective of placing the Stalingrad *Front* under your command; at the same time you would remain as commander of the Southeastern *Front*. Lieutenant General Golikov will be assigned as your deputy on the Southeastern *Front*. Major General Moskalenko will be named to replace Comrade Golikov as commander of the First Guards Army.

Second. Comrade Stalin also believes it expedient to appoint Comrade Sarayev of the NKVD, who is also in command of the NKVD Division presently in Stalingrad, as commandant of the garrison of the city of Stalingrad. What are your ideas on these matters?

YEREMENKO: My reply is that there is no wiser comrade than Stalin, and I consider [the decision] absolutely correct and timely.

VASILEVSKY: What are your views on the appointees Golikov, Moskalenko, and Sarayev?

YEREMENKO: I consider all the candidates to be suitable. They are worthy candidates.[14]

In mid-August, General Vasilevsky once again rushed to Stalingrad to investigate the situation. On August 23 (incidentally, the third anniversary of the notorious Ribbentrop-Molotov agreement), Vasilevsky was with the troops of the Sixty-second Army, which had that very day been cut off from the main forces of the Stalingrad *Front* by enemy armor. For the next two days the Germans conducted a massive aerial bombardment of the city, reducing much of it to rubble. Vasilevsky was forced to communicate with Stalin by open radio until high-frequency telephone communications could be reestablished. On the night of August 24 he called Stalin again, and the supreme commander severely rebuked him and the other Red Army commanders for the general calamity at Stalingrad.

At about the same time Hitler was berating his military commanders, charging them with "intellectual conceit, mental inadaptability, and utter failure to grasp essentials."[15] During the next few weeks the Führer displayed annoyance, worry, and finally bitter disappointment as the German forces began to tire and lose momentum at Stalingrad. On September 24 he dismissed his army's Chief of the General Staff Franz Halder, who had served in that post since August, 1939, replacing him with General Kurt Zeitzler. In Halder's final journal entry he said that his nerves and those of the Führer were worn out. Hitler, he wrote, "is determined to enforce his will also in the Army."[16]

The Lure of Stalingrad

Zhukov writes:

On August 27, 1942, when I was conducting offensive operations in the area of Pogoreloye Gorodishche, I received a phone call from A[leksandr] N[ikolaevich] Poskrebyshev [head of Stalin's personal secretariat, who disappeared shortly after Stalin's death]. From the conversation with him it became clear that the day before, that is, August 26, the State Defense Committee—examining the situation in the southern part of the country—had decided to appoint me deputy supreme commander in chief. Aleksandr Nikolaevich informed me that I was to be at my command post at 2:00 P.M. to await a call from Stalin. Not wasting any words, he answered all my questions with "I don't know. He himself will apparently tell you about it." However, even from these words I understood that the State Defense Committee was very much alarmed over the course of the war in the region of Stalingrad.

Soon Stalin called on the high-frequency ("V Ch"—Vysoko Chastotny) telephone. After asking about the situation on the Western *Front*, he said: "You should come right away to the Stavka. Let the Chief of Staff take your place there." And then he added: "Think about who should be assigned commander in your place."

The conversation ended on that. Stalin did not say anything about my appointment as deputy supreme commander in chief. Apparently, he wanted to announce that when we met personally. It should be said that Stalin generally said on the telephone only what was absolutely necessary at that moment. He also demanded from us extreme caution in the use of the telephone, especially during conversations in the combat zone, where there were no means for making the transmissions secure.

Without returning to the *front* headquarters, I left for Moscow.

Late in the evening of the same day I arrived in the Kremlin. Stalin was working in his office. Also there were several members of the State Defense Committee. Poskrebyshev announced my arrival, and I was immediately received.

Stalin said that the situation in the south was bad and that the Germans might take Stalingrad. The situation in the northern Caucasus was not much better. The State Defense Committee had decided to appoint me deputy supreme commander in chief and send me to the Stalingrad area. Already in Stalingrad were Vasilevsky, Malenkov, and Malyshev. Malenkov would remain with me, but Vasilevsky was to fly back to Moscow.

"When will you be able to leave?" Stalin asked me.

I answered that I needed a day to study the situation, and I could fly to Stalingrad on the twenty-ninth.

"Well, that's fine. But aren't you hungry?" Stalin asked. "It wouldn't hurt to have a little refreshment." Over tea Stalin briefly informed me of the complex situation as of 8:00 P.M. on August 27. Having told me quickly what had transpired at Stalingrad, Stalin said that the Stavka had decided to transfer the Twenty-fourth, the First Guards, and the Sixty-sixth armies to the Stalingrad *Front*.

General Kozlov commanded the Twenty-fourth Army, Moskalenko the First Guards Army, Malinovsky the Sixty-sixth Army. The First Guards Army of General Moskalenko was to be transferred to the Loznoye region. On September 2 it was to launch a counterstrike on the enemy groups which had penetrated toward the Volga and link up with the Sixty-second Army. Under the protection of Moskalenko's army the Twenty-fourth and Sixty-sixth armies were to be sent to the departure positions and quickly introduced into the fighting. Otherwise Stalingrad could be lost, the Supreme Commander in Chief said.

It was clear to me that the battle for Stalingrad was of the greatest military and political significance. If Stalingrad fell, the enemy command would be able to cut off the south of the country from the center. We could lose the Volga—the important water artery, along which a large amount of goods flowed from the Caucasus.

The Supreme Command had sent everything possible to the Stalingrad area, except for the newly formed strategic reserves designated for subsequent fighting. Urgent measures were taken to increase the production of aircraft, tanks, guns, ammunition, and other matériel, in order to have them in time to defeat the enemy groupings in the Stalingrad region.

On August 29 I took off from the Central Airport; four hours later we touched down on an airstrip in the area of Kamyshin [near Stalingrad]. Vasilevsky met me and then and there informed me about the latest developments. After a short conversation we drove to the headquarters of the Stalingrad *Front* at Malaya Ivanovka.

We arrived at the *front* headquarters about noon.

Lieutenant General V. N. Gordov was at the forward positions. Chief of Staff Nikishev and Chief of Operations Rukhle reported on the situation. Listening to their reports, I felt that they did not sufficiently understand the situation and were not sure that the enemy could be halted in the area of Stalingrad.

Telephoning the headquarters of the First Guards Army, where General Gordov was located at that time, I told him to wait for us at the headquarters of Army Commander K. S. Moskalenko, where I would come with Vasilevsky.

At the command post of the First Guards Army we met Generals Gordov and Moskalenko. Their reports and they themselves reassured us. I felt that they well knew the strength of the enemy and the capabilities of their own troops.

Having talked over the situation and the condition of our units, we concluded that we could prepare the troops of the concentrated armies for a counterstrike no earlier than September 6. We immediately informed Stalin of this on the high-frequency "V Ch" phone. He listened to me and said that he had no objections.

Since Vasilevsky had been ordered to return immediately to Moscow, he—if my memory doesn't fail me—flew from Stalingrad on September 1.[17]

Because of fuel shortage, Moskalenko's First Guards Army was unable to launch the attack ordered for September 2 by the Stavka. The next morning, the army attacked, but the advance was soon halted. On that same day Zhukov received a telegram from Stalin ordering that the Germans be struck without delay.*

Zhukov telephoned Stalin immediately and reported that he could order an attack the next morning (September 4) but that the troops of the three armies would have to attack without sufficient ammunition since the artillery positions could not be resupplied until that evening. Zhukov also said that he needed time to work out the coordination of the artillery, tanks, and aviation.

"Do you think," Stalin asked, "that the enemy will wait while you are running around doing all these things? Yeremenko maintains that the

---

* Although Vasilevsky paints a glowing picture of Soviet optimism in the early days of September, 1942, saying that the Germans' plans had been frustrated and "any renewal of a serious offensive . . . was out of the question . . . before the beginning of the summer of 1943," Zhukov's September 3 directive reveals the desperation of those days. Zhukov writes: "The situation at Stalingrad has worsened. The enemy is three versts [10,500 feet] from the city. Stalingrad could be seized today or tomorrow if the northern group of forces is not rendered immediate assistance. The troop commanders north and northwest of Stalingrad are to strike the enemy quickly. . . . No procrastination will be tolerated. Delay now is regarded as criminal. Throw all aviation to help Stalingrad." K. K. Rokossovsky (ed.), *Velikaya Pobeda na Volge*, 155. One realizes immediately that the Soviets themselves were far from optimistic at the time. The Sixty-second and the Sixty-fourth armies had retreated to their last position inside Stalingrad. Pressure from the Germans was steady, although their advance could now be measured in hundreds of yards a day, and the Soviet troops were defending along the city's inner ring.

enemy can seize Stalingrad with little effort if you don't strike quickly from the north."

Zhukov answered that he did not share that point of view and asked permission to begin the offensive on September 5, as had been ordered earlier.

> "Oh, well, all right," Stalin replied. "If the enemy begins a general offensive against the city, attack him at once, but don't wait while putting the finishing touches on troop preparations. Your main task is to divert the German forces from Stalingrad and, if successful, to liquidate the German corridor separating the Stalingrad and Southeast *fronts*."

At dawn on September 5 the Soviet artillery and air preparation began, but the density of fire was insufficient and failed to achieve the desired result. Watching the action from an observation point of the First Guards Army, Zhukov noted that the enemy fire on the attacking Red Army infantry was so intense that no significant forward movement was possible. An hour or two later it became clear that the Germans had halted the Soviets and were counterattacking with infantry and tanks. Soviet aerial reconnaissance revealed that large groups of tanks, artillery, and motorized infantry were moving north from Gumrak, Orlovka, and Bolshaya Rossoshka. German bombers appeared and began bombing the Soviet positions. Later in the day enemy reinforcements entered the battle and in several sectors succeeded in throwing the Soviets back to their original positions.

By evening the Russians had been resupplied with shells, mines, and other ammunition. Zhukov decided to plan a new attack, based on new information about the enemy which had been gathered during the day, as soon as the Soviet forces could achieve a night-time regrouping. Late that evening Stalin phoned Zhukov to ask about the situation at Stalingrad. Zhukov replied that the day's fight had been difficult and that the enemy had shifted some forces from the area of Gumrak.

"That's good," Stalin said. "That will be of great assistance to Stalingrad."

"Our forces achieved only insignificant advances," Zhukov said, "and in some cases they remained in their starting positions."

"For what reason?"

"Because of lack of time, our troops were unable to prepare sufficiently for the offensive, to carry out an artillery reconnaissance, and to plan counterbattery fire, and therefore we naturally were unable to suppress their fire. When our units went into the attack, the enemy stopped the attack with his fire and counterattacks. Besides, the enemy aviation had air superiority and bombed our units all day."

"Continue the attacks," Stalin ordered. "Your main task is to divert as many enemy forces as possible from Stalingrad."

On the next day the fighting resumed with even greater ferocity. Soviet aviation units bombed the enemy positions during the night. "Besides frontal aviation, long-range aviation bombed all night," Zhukov writes. The long-range bombers were under the command of Lieutenant General Golovanov who was stationed with Zhukov at the command post of the First Guards Army.

On September 6 the Germans introduced new units, and on a number of commanding heights they dug in their tanks and assault guns and thoroughly organized their fire points. These positions were vulnerable only to very powerful artillery strikes, but, as Zhukov recalls, "at that time we had very little large artillery."

On the third and fourth days the fighting for the most part consisted of artillery exchanges and aerial combat.

"On the 10th of September, having visited the army units," Zhukov writes, "I came to the conclusion that penetration of the enemy formations and liquidation of his corridor by our available forces was not possible." Generals Gordov, Moskalenko, Malinovsky, and Kozlov shared Zhukov's opinion. On the same day Zhukov reported to Stalin:

With those forces which are available to the Stalingrad *Front*, we cannot penetrate the corridor and link up with the troops of the Southeastern *Front* in the city. The defenses of the German troops have been significantly strengthened by units coming from Stalingrad. Further attacks by our same forces would be without purpose, and the troops would inevitably suffer large losses. We need reinforcements and time to regroup for a more concentrated frontal strike. The strikes by the army cannot dislodge the enemy.

Stalin told Zhukov that "it might not be bad" if he flew to Moscow and reported on these problems in person. On September 12, Zhukov took off for the capital and four hours later was in the Kremlin.

Vasilevsky, who had also been summoned to the Kremlin, made a report on the movement of new enemy units from Kotelnikovo, on the course of the fighting around Novorossisk, and also on the battles toward Grozny.

After carefully listening to Vasilevsky's report, Stalin said, "They would give anything to get at Grozny's oil. Well, now let's hear Zhukov concerning Stalingrad."

Zhukov repeated what he had said on the telephone and added that the Twenty-fourth, First Guards, and Sixty-sixth armies had proved to be efficient fighting units. Ther basic weaknesses were lack of good reinforcements and insufficient howitzer and tank units, which were necessary for close support of the infantry. Zhukov spoke of the terrain around Stalingrad: open, cut by deep ravines which offered good cover for the enemy, it was unfavorable for offensive actions by the Red Army. Having occupied a number of commanding heights, the Germans had long-range artillery observation and a capability of placing fire in any direction. Under these conditions, Zhukov concluded, the three armies of the Stalingrad *Front* were unable to penetrate the enemy defenses.

"What does the Stalingrad *Front* need to liquidate the enemy corridor and join forces with the Southeast *Front*?" Stalin asked him.

"A minimum of another full-strength combined-arms army, a tank corps, three tank brigades, and no less than four hundred howitzers. In addition, at the time of the operation it will be necessary to reinforce with at least an air army." Vasilevsky supported Zhukov's estimate.

Stalin took up his map showing the location of the Stavka reserves and studied it for a long time. Vasilevsky and Zhukov left the table and walked over to the corner, where in a low voice they discussed the need to find some other solution.

"And what kind of 'other' solution?" Stalin asked, lifting his head from the map. (Zhukov writes that he was unaware that Stalin had such sharp hearing.) He and Vasilevsky returned to the table.

"See here," Stalin said, "go to the General Staff and consider thoroughly what has to be done at Stalingrad. From where and which troops can be transferred for strengthening the Stalingrad group, and together consider also the Caucasus *Front*. Tomorrow evening at nine we will meet here."

Zhukov and Vasilevsky spent the entire next day trying to decide how to carry out such a large operation without using up all their reserves in piecemeal actions. In another month they would complete the formation of the strategic reserves, which would include large, well-equipped tank units. By that time Soviet industry would have significantly increased production of new models of aircraft and artillery ammunition.

Having considered all possible alternatives, Zhukov and Vasilevsky decided to propose to Stalin that the Soviets continue an active defense to wear down the enemy and then launch a counteroffensive of such magnitude that the strategic balance in the south would be shifted to the side of the U.S.S.R.

Zhukov admits that the details of the counteroffensive could not be worked out in a single day but that the main blows would be launched against the flanks of the Stalingrad groupings, which were held by the Rumanians. A rough estimate showed that it would be at least mid-November before a counteroffensive could be launched. Zhukov based his assessment on the assumption that the Germans could not fulfill their strategic plan for 1942 and that they had insufficient forces available to carry out their goals either in the northern Caucasus or in the region of the Don and Volga.

The forces which the Germans could employ in the Caucasus or the Stalingrad area had been bled white and would undoubtedly be forced to go over to the defensive. The Soviets knew too that Paulus' famed Sixth Army and Hoth's Fourth Panzer Army, which had participated in the exhausting and bloody battles around Stalingrad, were in no condition to seize the city.

For the Soviet side, the future held promise, Zhukov believed. The formation and training of Soviet strategic reserves were nearing completion. They consisted of large tank and mechanized units equipped with medium and heavy tanks. "By November," Zhukov recalled, "the Stavka would have mechanized all tank formations, armed with the world-famous T-34 tanks, which would permit us to assign our troops deeper, more important missions. Moreover, our higher-echelon command cadres had learned much in the first period of the war, had comprehended much and, graduating from the difficult school of combat with a powerful enemy, had become masters of the art of war."

Zhukov reveals how the Soviets took advantage of the Axis weaknesses:

The General Staff—on the basis of information of the *fronts*—studied the strong and weak sides of the German, Hungarian, Italian, and Rumanian troops. In comparison with the Germans their satellites were less well armed, less experienced and less efficient, even in defense. And more important—their soldiers, and even many of the officers, did not want to die for interests alien to them in the distant fields of Russia, where they had been thrown by the will of Hitler, Mussolini, Antonescu, Horthy, and other fascist leaders.

The Germans' situation was aggravated by the fact that they had few operational reserves in the area of the Volga and Don—no more than six divisions scattered over a broad front. To pull them together in a concentrated force in a short time was not possible. The Soviets were also favored by the configuration of the front: Red forces occupied flanking positions and could easily improve their bridgeheads near Serafimovich and Kletskaya.

Zhukov writes:

In the evening [September 13] Vasilevsky telephoned Stalin and said that we were ready to make our report. Stalin said that he would be occupied until 10:00 P.M. and that we were to arrive then. At 10:00 P.M. we were in Stalin's office.

Greeting us with a clasp of the hand (which seldom happened with him), Stalin said with indignation: "Tens, hundreds of thousands of Soviet people are giving up their lives in the fight with fascism, and Churchill is haggling over twenty Hurricanes [an outstanding British fighter aircraft which figured in winning the air war over England in 1940, before Soviet Russia entered the war]. And their Hurricanes—rubbish! Our pilots don't care for this machine." And in an absolutely calm tone without any transition he continued, "Well, what did you decide? Who is going to report?"

"Whomever you say," Vasilevsky replied. "We share the same opinion."

Stalin went up to our map. "What do you have here?"

"These are preliminary outlines of a counteroffensive in the Stalingrad area," answered Vasilevsky.

"What about these troops in the Serafimovich region?"

"That's a new *front*. It was necessary to create it to inflict a powerful blow on the operational rear of the enemy in the Stalingrad area."

"Right now we do not have enough forces for such a big operation."

I reported that we had calculated that in forty-five days we would have the necessary forces and means and would have prepared them.

"Would it not be better to organize a strike from the north to the south and from the south to the north along the Don?" Stalin asked.

I said that in this case the Germans could quickly swing their panzer divisions from Stalingrad and parry our strikes. A thrust by our troops west of the Don would deny the enemy the opportunity to maneuver quickly because of the river obstacle and run into our groups with his reserves.

"Aren't your strike groups too far out?"

Vasilevsky and I explained that the operation was divided into two main stages: penetrating the defenses, surrounding the German Stalingrad grouping, and creating a strong outer front to isolate this group from forces on the outside; and then annihilating the surrounded enemy and suppressing enemy attempts to break out of the blockade.

"It will be necessary to think about the plan some more and count up our reserves," Stalin said. "But right now the main task is to hold Stalingrad and not allow the enemy to advance on Kamyshin."

At this point, Zhukov recalls, Poskrebyshev entered the room and reported that Yeremenko was on the telephone. After a brief absence while he talked with Yeremenko, Stalin rejoined his military chiefs and told them that according to Yeremenko the Germans were moving up tank units toward Stalingrad and a new attack could be expected the next day. Then, turning to Vasilevsky, Stalin directed: "Issue orders immediately for a rapid crossing of the Volga by Rodimtsev's Thirteenth Guards Division and see what else can be put there tomorrow."

Zhukov writes:

> Turning to me, Stalin said: "Telephone Gordov and Golovanov and order them to set the aviation into motion right away. In the morning have Gordov attack to pin down the enemy. You yourself fly back to the Stalingrad *Front* and start studying the situation around Kletskaya and Serafimovich. In several days Vasilevsky will have to visit the Southeastern *Front* to study the situation on the left wing. We will continue the discussion about our plan later. Only the three of us here who have talked it over need know about it."
>
> An hour later I was in a plane and was flying to the headquarters of the Stalingrad *Front*.
>
> September 13, 14, and 15 were difficult, much too difficult days for Stalingraders. The enemy—despite everything—step by step penetrated the ruins of the city near the Volga. It seemed that our people were on the point of not being able to hold him back.

But, Zhukov writes, the gallant men of the Sixty-second and Sixty-fourth armies converted the ruins into a fortress.

The turning point of those difficult days was the surprise counterstrike by Rodimtsev's Thirteenth Guards Division, which had crossed over to Stalingrad. On September 16 the division recaptured Mamayev Kurgan. Again the Stalingrad defenders were assisted by air strikes by Golovano's long-range aviation and by artillery attacks against the German Eighth Army Corps.

At this point in his account Zhukov subtly reminds his reader that only three persons—Stalin, Vasilevsky, and Zhukov himself—had detailed knowledge of the Stalingrad counteroffensive plans, a reminder which serves to rebuff those memoirists who would later claim a main role in the planning. Zhukov notes that Yeremenko visited him to discuss the situation, but, "inasmuch as Stalin had warned me about keeping in strictest secrecy the projected counteroffensive, our conversation dealt mostly with reinforcing the Southeastern and Stalingrad *fronts*." As he wrote these words, Zhukov undoubtedly was thinking of the postwar attempts by the field commanders, including Yeremenko, to detract from the on-the-spot Stavka representatives.* As will be shown, Zhukov returns again and again to the question of the identity of the chief architects of the Stalingrad victory.

Zhukov continues:

> At the end of September I was again summoned by Stalin to Moscow for a discussion of the counteroffensive plan. By that time Vasilevsky, who had studied conditions for a counteroffensive by the armies of the left wing of the Southeastern *Front*, had also returned to Moscow. Before appearing before Stalin, Aleksandr Mikhailovich [Vasilevsky] and I met to discuss the results of his study of the conditions for carrying out the plan.

During the meetings with Stalin, the supreme commander in chief asked Zhukov what he thought of General Gordov. Zhukov replied that he was a good operations man but unable to get along with his com-

---

* Another slap at Yeremenko was dealt by Vasilevsky, who wrote that the Stavka instructed him not to involve Yeremenko in the "practical work" of preparing the offensive until November, "thereby allowing him to devote his full energies to the job at hand, the defense of Stalingrad." A. Vasilevsky, "Nezabyvaemiye Dni," *Voyenno-Istorichesky Zhurnal*, October, 1965, 20. In all fairness to the field commanders, it should be pointed out that the Stavka representatives often asked them for their ideas on a particular operation, and it seems only natural that the commanders would take some credit for the over-all planning. Zhukov's digs at Yeremenko and others can be more fully appreciated when one realizes that many highly placed detractors took advantage of his two periods of disfavor to remove his name from Soviet histories of the war. Zhukov is seeking to reassert his place in the Soviet Union's greatest victories.

mand personnel. Stalin said that in that case a new *front* commander should be appointed. Zhukov suggested Rokossovsky, a choice agreed to by Vasilevsky. It was also decided that the Stalingrad *Front* would be renamed the Don *Front* and the Southeastern *Front* changed to the Stalingrad.

After a detailed discussion of the forthcoming counteroffensive, Stalin turned to Zhukov and said:

> "Fly back to the front. Take all steps to wear down and weaken the enemy further. Look again at the areas selected by the plan for concentrating the reserves and the jump-off areas for the Southwest *Front* and the right wing of the Stalingrad *Front*, especially around Serafimovich and Kletskaya. With this same objective Comrade Vasilevsky will go again to the left wing of the Southeastern *Front* and there study all problems outlined in the plan."

After Zhukov and Vasilevsky made their on-the-spot study, they returned to the Stavka, where their plan was approved. The map depicting the counteroffensive was signed by both men, and then Stalin wrote on it, "I approve," and signed his name. Stalin then instructed Vasilevsky to seek the views of the *front* commanders on future operations, being careful not to divulge the closely guarded plans.

On September 28 the Stalingrad *Front* became the Don *Front*. Zhukov was ordered to brief the *front*'s Military Council in person about certain aspects of the Stalingrad operation. Zhukov gave his briefing in a bunker in a gully north of the city where Moskalenko's command post was set up.

Zhukov writes:

> Replying to my orders that active operations must not be reduced—so that the enemy could not transfer forces from the sector of the Don *Front* to attack Stalingrad—Konstantin Konstantinovich [Rokossovsky, who had taken over command of the *front**] said that the *front*'s strength was so

---

* In 1968, Rokossovsky described his appointment as commander of the Don *Front*. Zhukov and Rokossovsky had flown to the Stalingrad area, and Zhukov had informed Gordov of the Stavka decision to replace him with Rokossovsky. Rokossovsky later turned to Zhukov and said: "I ask you for the opportunity to direct—fully and personally—my troops, that is, to resolve the tasks assigned by headquarters, taking into consideration the actual development of the combat situation."

"In brief, what you want to say is that there is nothing for me to do here now?" Zhukov asked.

diminished that we could not accomplish anything here. Of course, he was right. I was of the same opinion, but with the active help of the Southeastern *Front* (now Stalingrad) it was impossible to hold the city.

On October 1, Zhukov returned to Moscow for further work on the counteroffensive plan. He flew in the cabin of a plane piloted by General A. Y. Golovanov. On the way to the capital the plane suddenly made a turn and began to descend, a maneuver which made Zhukov think that they were changing course. A few minutes later General Golovanov landed the plane on an airfield unfamiliar to Zhukov. He asked the pilot, "Why did you land the plane here?"

"We should be thankful that we were close to an airfield, or we could have crashed."

"What happened?"

"Icing."

During this discussion Zhukov's own plane, which had been following, touched down, and Zhukov soon took off in it for Moscow's Central Airfield.

Zhukov remarks that it was only natural that such flights, conducted under complex conditions and carried out on the spur of the moment, could not always be without incident. On another occasion he again almost lost his life:

> It was on a flight from Stalingrad to Moscow several days later. We did not have good flying weather and a rain fell. Moscow reported that fog lay over the city and visibility was limited. But fly we must—Stalin had called.
>
> On the way to Moscow it was not bad, but on the approaches to the city visibility did not exceed 110 yards. On the radio the pilot ordered the airforce flight section to go on to an alternate airfield. If we had done that, we would have surely been late at the Kremlin, where Stalin awaited us.
>
> Taking all responsibility on myself, I ordered the pilot to put down at the Central Airfield, and I remained in the cabin. Flying over Moscow, we suddenly saw a factory chimney off our left wing at a distance of ten to fifteen yards. I glanced at the pilot, who, without batting an eye, pulled

---

Rokossovsky, smiling, nodded, and Zhukov declared, "I shall fly to Moscow this very day."

Rokossovsky paid his respects to his friend: "Georgi Konstantinovich Zhukov and I are old fighting comrades. We have had occasion to experience together side by side many of the ordeals of the war." *Literaturnaya Gazeta*, January 31, 1968, 1–2.

the plane up a little and two or three minutes later landed it. When we were on the ground I said, "It seems we came out of that situation O.K. That was a close call."

Smiling, he replied: "In the air anything can happen if flying personnel ignore weather conditions."

"It was my fault!" I told the pilot, firmly gripping his hand.

Over the expanse of time I unfortunately have forgotten the name of the pilot. Unless I am mistaken, it was Belyaev, a fine man and a very experienced pilot. I flew with Comrade Belyaev more than 130 hours. Regrettably, he perished in an air crash.

In the meantime, from mid-September the Stalingrad battle had taken on the character of positional, or "fortress," war. Wrote the German general Hans Doerr in *Der Feldzug nach Stalingrad* (*The Campaign for Stalingrad*):

> The time for carrying out large operations had finally passed. From the broad steppes the war now changed over to the Volga Heights, cut by ravines and gullies, to the industrial region of Stalingrad, built on uneven, rugged, jagged terrain, with its buildings constructed of iron, concrete, and stone. A kilometer as a measure of length was replaced by a meter, and the General Staff's map was a town plan. For every house, workshop, water tower, railway embankment, wall, cellar and finally for each mound of rubble, bitter fighting raged, unequaled even in the period of World War I by the gigantic expenditure of ammunition. The distance between our forces and those of the enemy was almost incapable of measure.

Doerr wrote that attempts by German aviation and artillery to widen this zone of "close combat" were futile. He also observed that "the Russians surpassed the Germans in taking advantage of the terrain and in the use of camouflage, and they were more experienced in barricade fighting and in combat for individual houses; their defense was steadfast."[18]

In October the Stavka ordered six full-strength divisions to cross the Volga to Stalingrad to reinforce the Sixty-second Army, because, in Zhukov's words, "as a matter of fact nothing was left of this army except rear units and headquarters." Rokossovsky's Don *Front* was also reinforced somewhat.

Also about this time Hitler ordered Army Group B and Paulus' Sixth Army to take Stalingrad. For the thrust against the city the German command moved German troops from defensive positions on the flanks and sent Rumanian units to take their place. This shift of forces greatly weakened the Axis defense near Serafimovich and south of Stalingrad.

In mid-October the Germans unleashed a fierce attack on the Stalingrad defenders. Three infantry divisions and two panzer divisions, deployed on a three-mile front, were thrown into the fray. German aircraft flew about three thousand sorties on October 14, bombing and strafing the Russian troops almost without interruption. By midnight of that day the Germans had surrounded the Dzerzhinsky Tractor Factory and were fighting in its workshops, with three thousand of their number dead along its walls. The Russians also suffered great losses, especially from the bombings. Some units were so hard hit that they were no longer combat effective. On October 15, for example, two divisions in V. I. Chuikov's Sixty-second Army had lost 75 per cent of their personnel.

About this time Stalin took a direct hand in events. He informed Vasilevsky that he was dissatisfied with the actions of the Stalingrad *Front* commander, Colonel General Yeremenko, who, according to information in Stalin's possession, had not concentrated his attention on aiding the troops of the Sixty-second Army but instead—apparently fearing a possible enemy crossing of the Volga—had continued to reinforce the defensive sector on the left bank of the river. For this reinforcement, Stalin said, Yeremenko had used troops sent by the Stavka specifically for the Sixty-second Army. Vasilevsky was ordered to instruct Yeremenko, in the name of the Stavka, to go to Chuikov, learn the true situation in detail, and explain what steps would have to be taken to render effective assistance to the Sixty-second Army. That part of the city still remaining in its hands was to be held at all costs.[19] Yeremenko immediately made his way across the Volga (some members of his staff were killed along the way) and arrived at Chuikov's battered headquarters. Saying good-by at dawn the next morning, the *front* commander promised Chuikov that he would obtain the supplies he needed. But a day later Chuikov learned that instead of a month's supply of ammunition he was to get but a single day's allotment. He protested and managed to obtain a little more.*

* This interesting account reveals another aspect of Stavka power: control of the vitally important Stavka reserves. The Stavka not only decided when a unit would revert to its strategic reserves or be taken from them but also informed the *front* commander which of his armies was to receive them and how they were to be used.

The Russians held fast, although houses, buildings, and entire blocks of the city exchanged hands many times. They quickly formed companies from rear-area citizens—tailors, cobblers, workshop and stable hands—and rushed them into the inferno. As soon as they reached Stalingrad, these poorly trained men fast became expert street fighters or perished. Finally, as both sides became exhausted, the fighting began to lose its ferocity. On the evening of October 29 the battle abated, and on the following day there were only sporadic exchanges of fire. Paulus' Sixth Army appeared incapable of continuing the attack on a large scale.

At this point Zhukov, Vasilevsky, and Voronov visited Stalingrad to continue on-the-spot planning for the counteroffensive. Before their departure for the front the Stavka established tentative target dates for the beginning of the operation: November 9 for the Southwestern and Don *fronts* and November 10 for the Stalingrad *Front*. As it turned out, these dates had to be postponed for several days because of delays in bringing up combat supplies, fuel and lubricants, and the necessary air support for the operation.

In preparing the troops, primary attention was given to disrupting the enemy's tactical rear, which entailed careful planning to coordinate action by all the participating forces. A study was also made of the assignments that would fall to the mechanized and tank units in the hoped-for rapid encirclement and destruction of the Axis groups in the operational rear.

On November 3, Zhukov held final conferences with the forces of the Fifth Tank Army on the Southwestern *Front*. Present at the sessions were commanded personnel of the *front* and the army, as well as the corps and division commanders. Zhukov satisfied himself that all commanders clearly understood their assignments and the means for carrying them out. He then discussed his plans with each of the commanders in turn, reviewing once more all aspects of coordinated operations by artillery, tanks, and aviation. He was especially concerned that all commanders thoroughly understand the role of the tank and cavalry divisions in approaching the intended breakthrough area and that they know how to capitalize on their successes once they had penetrated deep inside the enemy's defenses. He reviewed the problems of flank protection in the course of the operation and the handling of troops. Conference participants reported on the status of their troops, supplies and matériel, and the combat readiness of all major units. Similar discussions were carried out on November 4 with the command personnel of the Twenty-first Army (part of the Southwestern *Front*, although the Don *Front* commander was also asked to be present) and on November 10 with the command personnel of the Stalingrad *Front* at the command post of the Fifty-seventh Army.

Following the conferences Zhukov, accompanied by Vasilevsky, toured the *fronts* and formulated a report to the Stavka about the combat readiness of the troops. The plan of operations, worked out in detail during the briefing, was put into map form for the Stavka. In their report, delivered orally, Zhukov and Vasilevsky said that the strength of both sides in the Stalingrad area was, on the whole, equal but that in the most critical sectors the Soviets, having repositioned Stavka reserves, had a significant advantage. No sizable enemy reserves had been detected moving toward Stalingrad, nor had any regrouping among enemy troops been observed. Zhukov and Vasilevsky expressed confidence that the missions were clearly understood by all command personnel and that coordination of infantry with artillery, tanks, and aircraft had been worked out down to the regimental level. In short, they foresaw success for the counteroffensive.

After discussion of several points the Stavka gave final approval to the plan and the timing of the offensive. Vasilevsky was assigned the responsibility of coordinating operations on all three *fronts*. The final draft, now given the code name "Uran" (Uranus), was, according to the *Istoriya*, "noteworthy for its clarity of mission, boldness of concept, and breadth of scope."[20]

"After Stalin's death," Zhukov writes, "there was considerable vagueness concerning who actually authored the plan for the counteroffensive, which was significant for its size, effect, and results. Although in our [society] this question has no special importance, and information concerning work on the plan has already been provided, I shall nevertheless make some additional remarks here." Zhukov points out that every *front* commander was called on to submit operations plans for his *front*, as well as any other recommendations he cared to make, and turn them over to the Stavka in Moscow or to one of its representatives in the field. But only the Stavka and the General Staff had detailed knowledge of available reserves and matériel, and only they were able to work out plans for large-scale campaigns. "The basic and decisive role in the detailed planning of and providing for a large strategic operation," he repeats, "unquestionably belongs to the Stavka of the Supreme High Command and the General Staff." The Stavka and the General Staff analyzed all factors of the Stalingrad campaign and foresaw how the battle would develop and end, he says. "Hence it should not be said that any one individual was responsible for the concept of the counter-offensive."

The counteroffensive would unfold along a 250-mile front, and the pincer movement was to embrace an area with a radius of about 60 miles. As the Axis defenses were penetrated, the Soviets would advance along two converging lines to Kalach and Sovetsky and then cut the Germans off from most of their reserves and supply bases and sever their lines of communication. The main attacks, to be delivered against the more vulnerable Rumanians, were timed to allow completion of preparations, thus weighting the axes of main efforts and catching the enemy forces at the very moment when their offensive had failed but before they had succeeded in going over to the defense along the entire Stalingrad sector and in shifting their forces. Subsequent events demonstrated that timing was a significant element in the over-all success of the counteroffensive.

During this time Zhukov was busily engaged in last-minute arrangements for the counteroffensive. On November 11, after visits with the troop commanders, he cabled Stalin that two infantry divisions assigned to Yeremenko by the Stavka had not arrived because of transportation problems. He noted that he had ordered everything to be ready by November 15. He also urged Stalin to help expedite the shipment of one hundred tons of antifreeze for Yeremenko's mechanized units and warm uniforms and ammunition for the troops.

On the morning of November 13, Zhukov returned to Moscow to deliver a progress report. He found Stalin in a good humor:

Stalin listened attentively. It was obvious that he was satisfied, since he unhurriedly smoked his pipe, stroked his mustache, and not one time interrupted our report. The Stalingrad operation signified the transfer of initiative to the Soviet troops. All of us had faith in the forthcoming counteroffensive, which could be very important for our country.

While we were making our report, members of the State Defense Committee and several Politburo members gathered in Stalin's office. We had to report the basic questions which had been discussed in their absence. After a short discussion of the counteroffensive plan, it was completely approved.

Vasilevsky and I pointed out to Stalin that, as soon as the German Command found the going rough in the Stalingrad area and in the northern Caucasus, they would feel compelled to transfer part of their troops from other areas, in particular from the Vyazma region, to help the southern group. So that this would not happen, it was necessary right away to prepare and carry out an offensive operation north of Vyazma and first defeat the Germans in the Rzhev salient. For this operation we proposed using troops of the Kalinin and Western *fronts*.

"That would be fine," Stalin said, "but which of you will take care of this matter?"

Aleksandr Mikhailovich [Vasilevsky] and I had already agreed on this, and I therefore said: "The Stalingrad operation in all respects is already prepared. Vasilevsky can handle the coordination of the operations at Stalingrad, and I can take care of preparing the counteroffensive of the Kalinin and Western *fronts*."

Agreeing with this proposal, Stalin said: "Tomorrow morning fly to Stalingrad. Check one more time on the readiness of the troops and commands for beginning the operation."

On November 14, Zhukov was back at Stalingrad with Vatutin's troops. He was there only a few days, for on November 17, Stalin again summoned him to Moscow to start planning the counteroffensive on the Kalinin and Western *fronts*.

A curious event occurred two days before the offensive was to begin. Stalin ordered Zhukov and Vasilevsky to Moscow to participate in a meeting of the State Defense Committee. Vasilevsky was shown a letter from General B. T. Volsky, commander of the Fourth Mechanized Corps, which had been assigned a decisive role in the Stalingrad operation. Volsky had written Stalin that the strike not only did not warrant any hope of success but was indeed doomed to failure. Volsky claimed that other responsible participants held similar views and asked the commander in chief to give the matter immediate attention, postpone the operation, and consider canceling it. Vasilevsky replied by reminding the State Defense Committee that while the offensive was being planned Volsky had never once expressed any doubts about its success or the tasks assigned his corps. Stalin ordered Vasilevsky to connect him with Volsky by telephone. After a short and (to the amazement of all present) restrained conversation, Stalin announced that Volsky would remain with his corps and carry out his assignment, no matter what happened.

Volsky's fate would be decided after the results of the first days of the operation were known. Fortunately for all concerned, Volsky and his corps performed well and heroically.

On the morning of November 19 the thunder of artillery heralded the start of the Soviet counteroffensive by the Southwestern and Don *fronts*. Just before 9:00 A.M. the artillery shifted its fire to the depths of the Axis defenses, and the Red infantry, accompanied by supporting tanks and artillery, began the attack (see map, page 199).

The Southwestern *Front*, under Vatutin, penetrated the defenses of the Rumanian Third Army in two areas, and the Rumanian sector soon crumbled under the combined blows of tank, mechanized, and cavalry forces. Major General P. L. Romanenko's Fifth Tank Army completed the rupture of the Axis positions, leaving mop-up actions to the infantry units moving up. In the meantime, Major General A. G. Rodin's Twenty-sixth Tank Corps broke through into Perelazovsky, a large town and highway junction, inflicting a costly defeat on the Rumanian Fifth Corps. According to Soviet sources, the attack was so swift that the Rumanians left documents on desks, files open, safes with keys in the doors, and blouses on coat racks.

When they reached the vicinity of Perelazovsky, the tanks of the Twenty-sixth Corps wheeled southeast to link up with forces of the Stalingrad *Front*. On November 21 the Germans attempted to halt the advancing Red armor, failed, and began withdrawing to the Don. In a bold move the Twenty-sixth Corps commander took advantage of darkness to seize the only remaining bridge across the Don, near Kalach. At three o'clock in the morning, with vehicle lights blazing, an advance detachment of the corps moved in a column along the road from Ostrov to Kalach, passing through the German defenses and heading for the crossing site. The Germans mistook the column for their own, and the detachment rumbled along unchallenged. Reaching the bridge, it crossed to the left bank of the Don, where flares were fired to signal the remainder of the force to attack.

The Twenty-first Army, having ripped into the Rumanian Thirteenth and Fifteenth Infantry divisions, sent its mobile group, consisting of the Fourth Tank and Third Guards Cavalry corps, through the hole in the line to exploit the penetration. In coordination with the Fifth Tank Army the group was ordered to destroy the enemy reserves, headquarters and rear-area units; cut off withdrawal routes to the west and southwest; and prevent the approach of deep reserves. By November 23 the Fourth Tank Corps was to link up with forces of the Stalingrad *Front* rear Sovetsky, southeast of Kalach, and complete the encirclement.

The terrain, criss-crossed by streams and river beds, and the poor roads severely limited the armor's maneuverability, forcing it to operate only on well-defined axes. The Germans exploited these conditions to slow the tanks' forward movements. After some anxious moments, during which the inexperienced tankers halted and began to fire in place, inviting annihilation, a young Russian commander, Lieutenant N. A. Lebedev, rallied them and ordered them forward. Breaking the resistance of the Axis units, the armor column moved into Grimki and destroyed two regimental headquarters of the Rumanian Thirteenth Infantry Division.

On November 23 the Fourth Tank Corps speeded up the tempo of the advance, crossing the Don on the bridge seized by the Twenty-sixth Corps and overcoming German defenses around Kamyshin before surging ahead toward Sovetsky.

In four days the Soviets had closed the ring around the German Fourth Panzer and Sixth armies, numbering twenty-two divisions and about 330,000 men. Zhukov and other Stavka members, aware that the Axis forces would try to break out, decided that the exterior front of investment should be pushed about 95 to 125 miles westward to prevent the German High Command from relieving the encircled troops.

Paulus was ordered to stand and fight while the German High Command planned the rescue of the Sixth Army. Field Marshal von Manstein, who was given the task, has said that in the critical days at the end of November the Russians could have destroyed Army Group A and the Sixth Army with a quick thrust down to the Lower Don at Rostov.[21]

At that moment Zhukov, headquartered with the Kalinin *Front*, was proposing to split the surrounded Germans into two parts, collect as much strength as possible at Samofalovka and Kotluban, and strike in a southerly direction to Bolshaya Rossoshka. Converging there, the Red forces would quickly mass and strike in a northern direction on Dubinin and Hill 135.6.

To carry out this operation, additional forces would have been required. Furthermore, the strike forces would have been restricted along their way by deep ravines running mainly west to east. Therefore, the Stavka rejected Zhukov's plan, which also failed to receive support from the *front* commanders and the Stavka representatives stationed with combat units between the Volga and the Don. It is nevertheless significant that Zhukov, many miles away on another *front*, was asked to help direct this particular stage of the Stalingrad operation. Moreover, German leaders later admitted that an aggressive Russian stroke at that moment might have proved fatal to their groupings. Also noteworthy is the fact that Zhukov made a very important contribution to the plan which was finally accepted.*

On December 9, Vasilevsky and Rokossovsky proposed to the Stavka that the Second Guards Army, which had arrived from the Stavka Reserve, be joined with the forces on hand to defeat the encircled Axis forces. Operation Koltso ("Ring"), as it was called, was to be carried out in three stages. First, the Don *Front* would annihilate four infantry divisions west of Rosseshki. Next, through strikes by the Don *Front* in a southeast direction toward Voroponovo and by the Sixty-fourth Army

---

* On November 28, Zhukov was at the headquarters of the Kalinin *Front*, where he was discussing with the commanders the forthcoming offensive in that sector. Late in the evening Stalin telephoned him and asked whether he was aware of the latest information on conditions at Stalingrad. Zhukov said that he was. Then Stalin told him to give him his thoughts on how to finish off the Germans trapped there. The next morning Zhukov telegraphed Stalin a recommendation that the Soviet forces should make one thrust toward Bolshaya Rossoshka and another toward Dubininsky and Hill 135 to cut the German forces into two parts. Elsewhere in the area Soviet troops should go over to the defensive to wear down and exhaust the Germans. After cutting them in half, Zhukov concluded, the weaker half should be annihilated first, and then all forces should join in to attack the remaining group. After dispatching this message, Zhukov called his friend Vasilevsky on the secure line and told him of his proposal. Vasilevsky agreed with it.

On December 8, Zhukov and Stalin issued a directive to the Western and Kalinin *fronts* calling for elimination of the Rzhev salient by the third week of December. When the Western *Front* was unable to breach the German defenses, Stalin sent Zhukov to General Konev's headquarters to find out what had gone wrong and try to correct it. Arriving at the *front*, Zhukov decided that it was useless to repeat the operation, since the enemy had moved forces from other sectors to reinforce the defenders. The Kalinin *Front* also had problems: the Germans had cut off General M. D. Solomatin's mechanized corps. Zhukov quickly sent for a rifle corps from the Stavka Reserve to help relieve Solomatin's forces, and four nights later Siberian relief troops succeeded in rescuing them. Zhukov writes that, although the Soviets failed to eliminate the Rzhev salient, their offensive combat prevented the German command from sending significant reinforcements from that area to Stalingrad. To hold the Rzhev–Vyazma positions, the Germans had to bring up four tank divisions and one motorized division.

of the Stalingrad *Front* south toward Voroponovo, enemy troops in the southern part of the encirclement would be isolated and then captured. Finally, all armies of both *fronts* would strike in the general direction of Gumrak to break the enemy resistance.

By December 11 the Stavka had communicated with its members, including Zhukov, and studied the proposal. It reworked the plan (or, as Soviet historians are wont to say, it subjected the plan to "more precise defining"), finally issuing a directive calling for a two-stage operation. The first phase would consist of an advance on Basargino and Voroponovo to destroy the Germans' western and southern groups. The second phase would be a general assault west and northwest of Stalingrad by all armies of the two fronts. The initiation of Operation Koltso was to be announced to the command by telephone, and at least the first phase was to be completed no later than December 23.

Meanwhile, on December 12, in what Manstein describes as a "race with death," the Fourth Panzer Army struck out desperately for Stalingrad and counterattacked again and again in attempts to regain ground earlier won by German armor. By December 19 the Fifty-seventh Panzer Corps had crossed the Aksai River, thrusting northward as far as the Mishkova River, the last natural barrier before Stalingrad. The German spearhead, now within thirty miles of the southern siege front, succeeded in gaining a foothold on the north bank of the river. From there the lead troops could see the flash of artillery around Stalingrad. Success seemed possible if the Sixth Army could create a diversion by attacking and preventing the Soviets from throwing fresh forces in the path of the Fourth Panzer Army.

But the Sixth Army's attack never materialized.[22] At this juncture the Soviets unleashed a massive offensive against the Italian Eighth Army on the Middle Don, compelling Manstein to draw heavily on General Hermann Hoth's Fourth Panzer Army to cover Rostov. This move may have decided the fate of Paulus' Sixth Army. An eyewitness, General F. W. von Mellenthin, chief of staff of the Fourth Panzer Army, writes that the Sixth Panzer Division, Hoth's best, was rushed northwest to try to stem the Russian flood. If this division, still intact, had remained under his command, he might have been able to break through to Paulus.[23]

The Soviets hurled new forces into the fray. Lieutenant General R. Y. Malinovsky's Second Guards Army, for example, made a forced march of twenty-five to thirty miles a day across the snow-covered steppe to reach the area. As Soviet units were thrown into battle, the Germans withdrew to Kotelnikovo, abandoning it on December 29 and retreating to Zimovniki and beyond the Manych River, about sixty miles southwest of Kotelnikovo, where Manstein had started his offensive on December 12.[24]

When Mainstein's breakthrough attempt failed, he and Paulus consoled themselves with the thought that German troops in the cauldron were serving a useful purpose in tying down large Soviet forces. The airlift which Hermann Göring had guaranteed would adequately supply the surrounded Sixth Army until the spring of 1943—when the whole area would supposedly be reconquered by the Germans—was obviously failing. Göring's promises to fly five hundred tons of food, fuel, and ammunition a day to Stalingrad proved to be overoptimistic; in fact, by the end of December fewer than one hundred tons a day were being brought in. By mid-December the starving troops began to slaughter the horses of the Rumanian cavalry division for food.[25]

Zhukov and the Soviet High Command now prepared to execute the final offensive against the trapped Sixth Army. Operation Koltso, carefully worked out by Zhukov, Vasilevsky, and others, was now, in the last days of December, 1942, ready for implementation (see map, page 200).*

---

* Toward the end of December, during a meeting of the State Defense Committee, Stalin proposed to simplify operations by placing the effort to annihilate the trapped Germans in the hands of a single commander. Stalin asked who should be appointed to the post, and someone suggested Rokossovsky. Turning to Zhukov, Stalin asked, "Why are you not saying anything?"

"In my opinion," Zhukov replied, "both commanders are capable. Of course, Yeremenko would be hurt if his Stalingrad *Front* was turned over to Rokossovsky."

"Now is not the time to feel hurt," Stalin snapped. "Telephone Yeremenko and tell him the decision of the State Defense Committee."

That same evening Zhukov telephoned Yeremenko on the high-frequency telephone and told him of the committee's decision—to charge Rokossovsky with the final liquidation of the German groups at Stalingrad and to transfer Yeremenko's Fifty-seventh, Sixty-fourth, and Sixty-second armies to Rokossovsky's Don *Front*. As Zhukov expected, Yeremenko was offended, and Zhukov tried to explain what lay behind the decision.

Soon afterward the Stalingrad *Front* was renamed the Southern *Front* and was sent against the Germans at Rostov. The three armies from the Stalingrad *Front* were transferred to the Don *Front* by a Stavka directive dated December 30. By

Only in the early 1960's were the roles of Zhukov and the Stavka in the counteroffensive first described in accurate detail by Soviet historians. One of the more useful accounts is Colonel F. Vorobyev's article in *Voyenno-Istorichesky Zhurnal,* in which he accuses Marshal Voronov of poor scholarship in his earlier article on the offensive. After paying tribute to the work of Vasilevsky, Zhukov, and Voronov in the over-all planning of the operation, Vorobyev takes Voronov to task:

> Let us pause now on the criticism of N. N. Voronov of the Stavka directive of December 28. In his memoirs he writes: "The Stavka directive required many regroupings, reinforcements and additional significant expenditures of artillery rounds. . . . It was clear to us that the 'Moscow Version' was extremely slow and required many forces and equipment. . . . It surprised us that the decision of the Stavka was accepted without a thorough study of the situation and without preliminary talks with us [the Stavka representatives in the zone of operations]. . . ."
>
> Regrettably, the author of the memoirs did not cite factual arguments for corroboration of his critical remarks.

Vorobyev goes on to prove that the Stavka directive did not require "many regroupings," as alleged by Voronov, by comparing the *front*'s concept of operations with that of the Stavka. He shows that in the zones of the Sixty-fifth and Sixty-sixth armies there were only insignificant differences in the plans submitted by the *front* and by the Stavka. Further, he notes that no serious changes were required in the dispositions of the other armies. "What the Stavka actually changed in the plan of the *front* was the direction of strikes of the main forces of the Sixty-fifth, Fifty-seventh, Sixty-fourth, and Sixty-sixth armies. [Thus] . . . the tasks of the army were decreased, which corresponded more to the actual correlation of forces."[26]

Colonel Vorobyev acknowledges that the Stavka made some mistakes. For example, in launching counterstrikes in July–September in the large bend of the Don and along the Yerzovka–Samofalovka line, the Stavka unwarrantedly used its strategic reserves in a piecemeal manner which not only failed to produce the desired results but led to heavy

---

January 1, 1943, the Don *Front* numbered 212,000 men, about 6,500 guns and mortars, more than 250 tanks ("in good condition," Zhukov notes), and about 300 combat aircraft. Zhukov, "Razgrom Nemetskikh Voysk v Rayone Dona, Volgi i Stalingrada," in *Stalingradskaya Epopeya,* 68–69.

losses. Nor did it provide reserves for liquidating the encircled Axis forces and developing the offensive after gaps had been opened in the German lines. But, Vorobyev declares, the Stavka's decision to destroy the trapped Germans was expedient and correct. He chides Voronov for claiming that it was his plan and that of the Don *Front's* command which was adopted. Vorobyev is, he says, eager to set the record straight, for the controversy has "an educational significance, since in it emerges the matter of interrelationships—on the one hand, the Stavka, and on the other, the Stavka representative and the *front* command."[27]

After citing a number of documents, Vorobyev says that Operation Koltso was carried out in accordance with the Stavka directive of December 28, 1942. "In conclusion," he writes, "the desire must be expressed that participants of the Great Patriotic War in preparing their memoirs should not rely on their notes and memory, especially in examining serious questions. A check of the facts in archive documents would more greatly assist in accurately establishing the true picture of events."[28] Thus Vorobyev's critique represents another refreshing effort to arrive at historical accuracy, giving credit where it is due: to the Stavka and its representatives, including Georgi Zhukov.

Alexander Werth declares that Zhukov was "the real brain behind the operation,"[29] despite Soviet efforts in various postwar histories to minimize his contributions. Another brilliant military historian, Hanson W. Baldwin, notes in his account of the Battle of Stalingrad that the Soviet counterblow "was the conception of the Stavka . . . and particularly of General Georgi K. Zhukov, . . . aided by Generals Alexander M. Vasilevsky (Chief of the General Staff) and Nikolai N. Voronov."[30] He accurately records that

> the Stavka formulated Soviet strategy and directed its implementation. It operated, in a sense, as a committee, but Marshal Georgi Zhukov, perhaps Russia's greatest World War II soldier, the savior of Moscow and at various times Army Chief of Staff and First Deputy Commissar of Defense, was, after Stalin, its most notable member. Zhukov was a member throughout the war, and more than any other one man was responsible for the formulation and implementation of Soviet strategy.[31]

Baldwin reiterates that Zhukov, Stalin, Voronov, and Vasilevsky share the major credit for planning the Stalingrad counteroffensive.[32]

It is interesting, though certainly not surprising, that Soviet writers in the postwar period heaped accolades on Nikita Khrushchev for his role in the victory at Stalingrad. Taking advantage of Zhukov's ouster in November, 1957, a group of so-called historians tried to exalt Khrushchev and themselves by creating the legend of the Battle of Stalingrad.[33] When Zhukov left the scene, Soviet historiographers were given new guidelines concerning the role of the Party in wartime successes. The instructions stated that

> a most important task [of historians] is the scientific analysis of the role of the Communist Party of the Soviet Union as the organizer of the national struggle with the enemy, of its many-sided activities in directing the front, the partisan warfare behind the enemy lines, and the economic and political life of the country. The research work must thoroughly portray the superiority of the socialist economic system, the Soviet social and state systems.[34]

After showering almost endless flattery on Khrushchev, even those who had been patronized by the premier discovered that their fawning and adulation had limits. In a *Pravda* article of February 2, 1963, marking the anniversary of the victory at Stalingrad, Malinovsky himself finally revived Zhukov's name as one of the three (together with Vasilevsky and Voronov) Stavka representatives who played key roles in conceiving and planning the Stalingrad operation.[35] Thomas W. Wolfe comments:

> Why Malinovsky chose on this occasion to slight Khrushchev's Stalingrad role and to make favorable public reference to Zhukov, whose name had become synonymous with professional military flouting of Party supremacy, remains one of the minor mysteries of internal Soviet politics. It should be noted, however, that Malinovsky's position with respect to the subtle and touchy problems of political-military relations has never been altogether clear and consistent. In a figurative sense at least, he has seemed to suffer a split personality, being at once the titular guardian of military interests within the Soviet bureaucracy and the chief executor of Khrushchev's policies within the armed forces. While he himself was a member of the "Stalingrad group," he has not always identified himself with it as a claimant of Khrushchev's favor, as in the case of the 1963 anniversary article.[36]

As new histories of the Stalingrad campaign appeared, it became obvious that their authors were courageously attempting to give credit to Zhukov, Vasilevsky, and other members of the Stavka for the Stalingrad counteroffensive. Reviewing the one-volume *Velikaya Otechest-vennaya Voina Sovetskogo Soyuza* (*The Great Patriotic War of the Soviet Union*) in the July 10, 1965, issue of *Izvestia*, Colonel V. Morozov noted that it was free of exaggeration or underestimation of the roles of certain important military leaders and political figures in elaborating military plans. In particular, he said, its authors made substantial interpretative corrections in earlier accounts of the elaboration of the counterattack plan. Observing that some historical works and memoirs tried to create the impression that the work was done by the Military Council of the Stalingrad *Front* (that is, Khrushchev), Morozov declared that the authors of the new history showed more comprehensively and objectively the parts played by the highest bodies of strategic leadership and by specific individuals. They give proper credit, he said, to Zhukov and Vasilevsky by name and to the Stavka, General Staff, and the various front-line headquarters.[37] Other works reiterated that the strategic counteroffensive was conducted according to the plan of the Supreme Command, with consideration for the proposals of the *front* commanders, and that preparations for the operation were carried out under the leadership of Zhukov and Vasilevsky.[38]

Many of the military historians appear to have rebelled against the incessant Party prattle which apotheosized the political figures at Stalingrad and downgraded the professional military leaders. Wartime tensions between uniformed politicians and Red Army commanders were reflected in postwar memoirs and histories.* More illustrative than any

---

* In 1968 Zhukov himself finally had his say. "The defense of Stalingrad," he wrote, "the preparation of the counteroffensive and participation in working out the operational problems in the country's south had a special importance for me. Here I received significantly greater experience in the organization of the counteroffensive than in 1941 at Moscow, where our limited forces did not permit us to organize the counteroffensive with the objective of surrounding the enemy groupings.

"For successfully carrying out the general leadership of the counteroffensive at Stalingrad and for the great results achieved during it, I was among those who were awarded the first Order of Suvorov, First Class. To receive the first Order of Suvorov signified for me not only a great honor but also a demand by the Motherland to work even more to bring nearer the hour of complete defeat of the enemy. The second Order of Suvorov, First Class, was awarded to A. M. Vasilevsky. [Other] Orders of Suvorov, First Class, were presented to N. N. Voronov, N. F. Vatutin, A. I. Yeremenko, K. K. Rokossovsky. A large group of generals, officers, sergeants, and soldiers were also awarded high government decorations." *Ibid.*, 72.

historical summary of the struggle between combat leader and Party overseer is the dialogue of a battalion commander and a Party representative in Viktor P. Nekrasov's novel *V Okopakh Stalingrada* (*In the Trenches of Stalingrad*). The scene is the battalion command post just before an attack. The Party hack speaks first:

"You have thought through the course of the operation," he asks, lifting his colorless eyes. His long front teeth protrude over his lower lip.

"Yes, I have thought it through."

"The command attaches great significance to it. You know this?"

"I know it."

"How about your flanks?"

"Flanks?"

"When you advance, how will you cover your flanks?"

"I won't. The adjacent battalions will support me. I don't have enough men. We're taking a chance."

"That's bad."

"Sure, it's bad."

He writes something in his notebook.

"What resources do you have?"

"I have no resources except for a handful of men. Fourteen will jump off in the attack."

"Fourteen?"

"Yes, fourteen. And fourteen will remain on the line. Twenty-eight men in all."

"If I were you, I wouldn't do it that way."

He glances at his notebook. I can't take my eyes off his teeth. Do they always stick out like that? I slowly draw a cigarette case from my pocket.

"If you were in my place, you could do as you like, but in the meantime allow me to act according to my own judgment."

He compresses his lips as much as his teeth will permit him.

". . . I ask that you remember that you're talking to a superior."

"I forget nothing. I ask that you leave this place. That's all."

"I disturb you?"

"Yes, you do."

"How?"

"By your very presence. Your tobacco. You see what's happening here. It's impossible to breathe."

I feel I am beginning to speak foolishly.

"My place is at the battalion observation post. I'm supposed to follow your work."

"That means you intend to be with me at all times?"

"Yes, I do."

"And you'll attack the hill with me?"

For several seconds he looks at me fixedly, unblinking. Then he rises demonstratively, deliberately folds his newspaper, thrusts it into the map case, and, turning to me, carefully choosing each word, he says:

"Very well. In another place we will talk."

Then he crawls through the bunker. At the door he catches his mapcase on a nail and for a long time cannot free it.[39]

With this inglorious exit, the Party representative removes himself to a safe position.

The Red Army's distaste for its political watchdogs reached such proportions that in October, 1942, the Presidium of the Supreme Soviet again restored *yedinonachalie*. The order stated that an enormous number of new and experienced officers had emerged, that they had proved their devotion to their country, and that the dual control system was abolished. The political commissar became the commander's deputy in the political field. "All this was, in a sense, a clear victory of the 'Army' over the 'Party,' " observes Alexander Werth.[40]

Paulus' Sixth Army was dying. Characteristically, Hitler assured the encircled Germans that OKH was preparing to reorganize the airlift, which had broken down by this time, on a broader basis and that those trapped at Stalingrad could expect to be relieved in the second half of February, 1943. The preliminary condition for the rescue was restoration of the Southern Front, and if the Sixth Army could hold out, what seemed to be disaster could be turned into a great German victory.[41] But there was no hope, and many of the men knew it. One soldier wrote:

I was horrified when I saw the map. We're quite alone, without any help from the outside. Hitler has left us in the lurch. Whether this letter gets away depends on whether we still hold the airfield. We are lying in the north of the city. The men in my battery already suspect the truth, but they aren't so exactly informed as I am. So this is what the end looks like. Hannes and I have no intention of going into captivity; yesterday I saw four men who'd been captured before our infantry re-occupied a strong point. No, we're not going to be captured. When Stalingrad falls you will hear and read about it. Then you will know that I shall not return.[42]

Another soldier wrote:

> For a long time to come, perhaps forever, this is to be my last letter. A comrade who has to go to the airfield [probably Gumrak, which fell on January 22] is taking [the letter] along with him, as the last machine to leave the pocket is taking off tomorrow morning. The situation has become quite untenable. The Russians are only two miles from the last spot from which aircraft can operate, and when that's gone not even a mouse will get out, to say nothing of me. Admittedly several hundred thousand others won't escape either, but it's precious little consolation to share one's own destruction with other men.[43]

The stranglehold tightened. With the fall of the Gumrak airstrip, the Germans' last physical link with the outside world was lost (see map, page 201). Winter was taking a deadly toll, and, to add to their agonies, an epidemic of typhus broke out. Still Paulus rejected a January 8 ultimatum to surrender. By January 22, Red Army troops had pushed the Germans to the outskirts of the city, pinning the Sixth Army in an oblong strip only four miles deep and eight miles long. They now pounded it with artillery and aerial bombardments (see map, page 202).

Various German units began to surrender, and on January 31 the Red Army began its final drive from all directions to seize central Stalingrad. Alexander Werth heard the story of Paulus' surrender from a young Russian lieutenant who participated in the negotiations. After a heavy artillery and mortar barrage the square in front of the Univermag was captured. The Russians learned that Paulus was in the building. Risking his life, the young lieutenant responded to a signal from a German officer inside the Univermag and rushed into the building while shells were still pounding it. Ushered into Paulus' room, the Russian found him, dressed in his uniform, lying on an iron bed. "Well, that finishes it," the lieutenant remarked. Paulus only nodded. The Russian sent for a car, and Paulus was taken to Rokossovsky's headquarters. Two days later, on February 2, the capture of the Sixth Army was completed.[44] Only about ninety thousand Axis soldiers had survived.

Criticism of Hitler's conduct of the Stalingrad campaign came from every quarter. One critic, Colonel General Zeitzler, chief of the Army General Staff from 1942 and later a figure in the plot to assassinate Hitler, was bitter in his attack on the Führer:

> In November I had told Hitler that if a quarter of a million soldiers were

to be lost at Stalingrad, then the backbone of the entire Eastern Front would be broken. I was to be proved right, for the Battle of Stalingrad was the turning point of the entire war.[45]

The January 8 ultimatum to Paulus did not bear Zhukov's name, and some foreign observers circulated rumors that he had fallen into disfavor. The stories were not true; Stalin had other plans for him. He sent Zhukov to Leningrad to begin preparations for another Soviet counteroffensive. While the U.S.S.R. was cheering the victory at Stalingrad, Zhukov was coordinating operations of the Leningrad and Volkhov *fronts*, setting the stage to break the sixteen-month blockade of Leningrad.

On January 18, 1943, Zhukov was made marshal of the Soviet Union, the first field commander of World War II to be so recognized. An *Izvestia* editorial entitled "Skill of Red Army Leaders" listed the new marshals and generals, and Zhukov's name led them all. He was acclaimed a "highly talented and brave leader" who had carried out Stalin's plans for repulsing the Germans at Moscow, Stalingrad, and Leningrad.[46]

At Stalingrad many of the Soviet Union's most promising younger generals were put to the test for the first time, and their degree of success certainly influenced their future in the Red Army. They were carefully selected, the most important criterion being, in most cases, a good record during the first fifteen or sixteen months of the war. By early 1943 they had fully justified the trust which the High Command had placed in them, and two of their number, Zhukov and Voronov, were rewarded by promotion to the rank of marshal.[47] Vasilevsky became general of the army.*

The victory at Stalingrad boosted morale in the Soviet Union. Werth described a party held in the city:

Our hosts had, I think, got tired of waiting for us; they had started on the supper. Here was a big spread, and with plenty of vodka, and my neighbor

---

* The January 19 issue of *Izvestia* announced that an order of the Supreme Soviet of the same date had promoted Zhukov to marshal of the Soviet Union. Colonel General Voronov became marshal of artillery, Vasilevsky was promoted to general of the army, and A. A. Novikov was awarded the rank of colonel general of aviation. It was also announced on the front page that the Leningrad blockade had been broken and that Zhukov, Meretskov, Voroshilov, and Govorov received credit for this feat.

was a red-nosed colonel who had already had a good number of drinks. "We've done them in," he cried, "half a million of them! Here, come on, drink to the heroes of Stalingrad—'Do dna,' bottoms up!" . . . He beat his chest. "Look," he cried, pointing at his Red Star, "yesterday I received this from our Great Government! Zhukov—I worship Zhukov. He planned the whole thing, he and our Great Stalin. Halkin Gol, where we routed the Japs—that was just a rehearsal. But Stalingrad, *that* was the real stuff! Hitler's best divisions were destroyed there. And who destroyed them? We Russian people did it! Why is Stalingrad important, I ask you? Because he who won the Battle of Stalingrad has also won the war. That's why."[48]

X. THE END OF *DRANG NACH OSTEN*

The idea of a war against Russia is in itself popular, inasmuch as the date of the fall of Bolshevism should be counted among the most important in civilization. . . . The Germans believe it will all be over in eight weeks. . . . But what if this should not be the case? If the Soviet armies should show the world a power of resistance superior to that the bourgeois countries have shown, what results would this have on the proletarian masses of the world?

Count Galeazzo Ciano

WHILE General Paulus was surrendering the remnants of his Sixth Army at Stalingrad, the chief architect of that great Soviet victory, Georgi K. Zhukov, was far away at Leningrad, laying plans for another Red Army victory. From September 8, 1941, when the Germans completed the land blockade of the city, until early 1943 the courageous Leningraders had clung desperately to the hope that relief would come, that somehow the Red Army would rescue them. Months passed and thousands died, many of starvation and sheer physical exhaustion, amid some of the most horrible conditions ever faced by man since the dawn of recorded history. The German siege had almost accomplished Hitler's fanatic purpose.

On December 2, 1942, the Stavka ordered the commanders of the Volkhov and Leningrad *fronts* to prepare to break through the German stranglehold. Given the code name "Iskra" ("Spark"), the operation called for the creation of strike groups by each *front*. The Second Shock Army of the Volkhov *Front* comprised one group, and the Sixty-seventh Army of the Leningrad *Front* formed the basis of the other. The two, less than ten miles apart at some points, were to push toward each other, the Volkhov *Front* moving westward while the Leningrad *Front* attacked east and southeast. Responsibility for coordination of the actions by both was given to Voroshilov and Zhukov.

On December 8 the Stavka issued more concrete instructions to both *fronts*, and reinforcements were sent in to assure the success of the break-out. The Volkhov *Front* received about 22 per cent more troops, 20 per cent more guns, and about 30 per cent more mortars. The Leningrad *Front* was reinforced with 10 per cent more troops. On December 28, Zhukov and Voroshilov worked out their final plan for the converging strikes. The two groups were to meet along a line running from Workers' Settlement No. 2, near the southern shores of Lake Ladoga, to Settlement No. 6, about six miles south. The commander of the Baltic Fleet, Vice Admiral V. F. Tributs, was to support the action with gunboats positioned along the Neva River. By January 1, 1943, both *fronts* were ready for the operation, but because of unfavorable weather the Stavka granted them permission to postpone the offensive for ten to twelve days.

On the morning of January 12, while the thermometer stood at twenty-three degrees below zero, more than two thousand Red Army guns and mortars broke the icy silence. For the next several days, especially between January 14 and 18, fighting was exceptionally bitter as the Soviet troops tried to break through defenses which the Germans had carefully prepared over the past year. The ingenuity of the Soviet command was clearly demonstrated by the daring maneuver of the

Twelfth Ski-mounted Infantry Brigade, which was sent across frozen Lake Ladoga to strike the Germans from the rear at the village of Lipka. Finally, on January 18, troops of the Leningrad and Volkhov *fronts* linked up at Workers' Settlements No. 1 and No. 5. The blockade of Leningrad had been broken.

Zhukov was now available for assignment elsewhere. Elsewhere proved to be the Kursk salient. The Germans were concerned about how they should continue the struggle in the approaching summer. Writes Erich von Manstein:

> Obviously, after so many major formations had been lost, there would no longer be forces available to mount another crucial offensive on the scale of 1941 and 1942. What did seem possible—given proper leadership on the German side—was that the Soviet Union could be worn down to such an extent that it would tire of its already excessive sacrifices and be ready to accept a stalemate. At the time in question this was far from being wishful thinking.[1]

Manstein believed that the German command staffs and fighting forces were still superior to their Red counterparts:

> The German command thus had very little time left in which to force a draw in the east. It could only do so if it succeeded, within the framework of a—now inevitable—*strategic defensive*, in dealing the enemy powerful blows of a localized character which would sap his strength to a decisive degree—first and foremost through losses in prisoners.[2]

A large bulge had developed in the Russian line, beginning at a point south of Orel and extending south to Belgorod (see map, page 203). To the German High Command this broad salient posed a serious threat, in that it could serve as a jumping-off place for attacks against the flanks of the two German army groups positioned along that sector. The Germans decided to pinch off this salient, believing that if the attack was launched early enough the Red Army units would be caught unprepared and forced to commit armored units which had been severely battered toward the end of the winter campaign. For the operation, assigned the code name "Citadel," Army Group South was to provide two armies, Fourth Panzer and Army Detachment Kempf, comprising eleven armored or panzer-grenadier divisions and five infantry divisions. To supply these forces the Donetz and Mius dispositions had to be thinned out. Army Group Central was to furnish the Ninth Army, composed of six armored or panzer-grenadier divisions and five infantry divisions. The army would have to assemble in the salient around Orel, where the Soviets might attack it in the rear and from the east and north.[3]

While Citadel was still in the planning stage (the Germans hoped to launch it in the first half of May), the Stavka sent Georgi Zhukov to the Kursk salient to study the situation. Before he left, however, Stalin summoned him to Moscow. Arriving late on a mid-March evening, he conferred with Stalin and members of the Politburo until three o'clock the next morning. After all the participants had departed, Stalin turned to Zhukov and asked if he had eaten. Zhukov replied that he had not, whereupon Stalin told him, "Well, then, come with me, and at the same time let's talk about the difficult situation in the area of Kharkov."

During the meal maps were brought from the General Staff, showing the situation along sectors of the Voronezh and Southwestern *fronts*. A briefing officer pointed out that matters were especially grave southwest of Kharkov, where German units had gone over to the offensive from Poltava and Krasnograd and were putting heavy pressure at the junction of the two *fronts*.

After the meal Zhukov departed to assume his new duties. "About seven o'clock I was already at the Central Airport and was flying to the headquarters of the Voronezh *Front*. It was necessary to analyze the situation which had developed there and render help on the spot. As soon as I had taken my seat on the plane, I fell into a deep sleep and was only awakened by the bump during the landing at the airfield."[4]

Later the same day Zhukov reported to Stalin on the high-frequency telephone. He urged his chief to rush everything possible from the Stavka reserves and neighboring *fronts* to prevent the Germans from seizing Belgorod and developing a strike along the Kursk axis. An hour later Zhukov learned from the chief of the General Staff that Stalin had already ordered the First Tank, the Twenty-first, and the Sixty-fourth armies into the Belgorod region. When enemy units broke into Belgorod on the eighteenth of March, they were unable to move farther north. Nor were they able to penetrate the Soviet defenses in repeated attempts toward the end of March.

In the meantime, Stalin had appointed General Vatutin commander of the Voronezh *Front*, and he and Zhukov spent the last days of March and the first few in April visiting almost all the major units of the *front*, assisting their commanders in evaluating the situation and planning future operations.

On April 8, Zhukov reported to Stalin:

> Evidently the enemy, collecting a maximum of his forces, including up to 13–15 tank divisions, supported by a large amount of aviation, will deliver a strike by his Orel-Kromy groupings to envelop Kursk from the southeast. . . . One must expect that this year the enemy will count on tank divisions and aviation for the offensive, since his infantry is considerably weaker for carrying out offensive actions than last year.

Zhukov recommended that the Soviets not go over to the offensive, since "it would be better if we wore the enemy down on our defenses, knocked out his tanks, and then, introducing fresh reserves, by going over to the general offensive finally finish off his main forces."

A day or so later Vasilevsky arrived on the scene, and Zhukov discussed with him the details of his report to Stalin. "There were no differences of opinion between us about anything," Zhukov says. The two men drafted a Stavka directive on the disposition of its reserves and the creation of the Steppe *Front* in the Kursk area and sent it to Stalin. On the evening of April 12, Zhukov and Vasilevsky arrived in Moscow to brief Stalin on the Kursk operation. Writes Zhukov:

> We concluded that it was necessary to construct a strong, deeply echeloned defense on all important axes, especially in the area of the Kursk bulge. In connection with this the *front* commanders were issued appropriate instructions. Troops began digging in deeply on the winter line. The Stavka strategic reserves which had been formed and trained were still not committed, but were concentrated closer to the most threatened areas.

For the remainder of April the Soviet command continued almost feverish planning and preparations for the forthcoming battle.

In the first days of May, Zhukov returned to the Stavka from a tour of the North Caucasus *Front*; the basic plans for the summer and fall campaign were being completed by the General Staff. Meanwhile, the Stavka had carried out careful reconnaissance (by agents and aircraft) which positively established that the main flow of German troops and military supplies was toward Orel, Kromy, Bryansk, Kharkov, Krasnograd, and Poltava. Zhukov writes: "This confirmed our April estimates. Both in the Stavka and in the General Staff it was assumed that the German troops might possibly start their offensive in the next few days."

About this time the Voronezh *Front* commander, General Vatutin, and the Military Council member, Khrushchev, proposed to Stalin that a preemptive strike should be carried out against the German dispositions in the Belgorod–Kharkov area. Zhukov, Vasilevsky, Antonov, and a number of General Staff members disagreed with the proposal, and Zhukov reported that fact to Stalin. To Zhukov's dismay, Stalin wavered, unable to decide whether to meet the enemy with a strong defense or anticipate his attack with a preemptive strike. "Stalin said that our defense could not contain a German strike, as if it were 1941 or 1942," Zhukov complains. "At that time he was not sure that our troops would be able to defeat a strong, well dug-in enemy. This vacillation continued, as I recall, almost until mid-May." Finally, after repeated discussions and arguments, Stalin agreed to allow the Germans to wear themselves down on a deeply echeloned Soviet defense and then hit them with a powerful counteroffensive on the Belgorod–Kharkov and Orel axes.

Things were shaping up poorly for the Germans. In early May, Hitler decided to postpone Citadel until June, by which time, he hoped, his armored divisions would be equipped with new tanks. But by the time the new tanks arrived, the operation had been delayed until the beginning of July, and the essential advantage of striking the Russians before they could recover from the winter campaign was lost forever.[5]

Acting on Zhukov's advice, the Stavka quickly began concentrating forces to stop the German attack. The Central and Voronezh *fronts* would bear the brunt of the assault. As a reserve and counterstrike force, the Stavka formed, under Colonel General I. S. Konev's leadership, the Reserve *Front* (later the Steppe *Front*), consisting of combined-arms armies and tank and mechanized formations. The terrain over which these troops would operate—open steppe with infrequent ravines and gullies—was highly suitable for the use of massed tanks. Five tank armies, several tank and mechanized corps, and a number of infantry corps and divisions were assembled in the Stavka Reserve and in the second echelons of the *fronts*. Not only could these mobile formations be rushed in to plug any gap that might be made in the line but also they represented a significant counteroffensive force which could be committed at the proper time. The Stavka assigned to the commanders of the Western and Bryansk *fronts* the responsibility of planning an offensive operation against the Germans around Orel, but it was to be initiated only after the German initial offensive had been halted.

For the first time since the start of the war, the number of Russian artillery regiments with troops on the defense now exceeded the number of rifle regiments, by one and a half times. The heaviest artillery density lay along the most probable axes of enemy advance. The Thirteenth Army of the Central *Front*, for example, which was covering the most seriously threatened sector, along the Orel–Kursk rail line, was supported by about 148 artillery weapons and mortars for each mile of front, far more than the Germans were able to muster for their offensive.

During their defensive preparations, the Central and Voronezh *fronts* received more than 9,000 additional artillery pieces and mortars; in all, they were reinforced by an additional 92 artillery regiments from the Stavka Reserve. More than 6,000 antitank guns were dug in, and almost 400,000 mines and charges were laid along the more important axes. Stalin ordered Zhukov to remain at Kursk to coordinate the actions of the Central, Bryansk, and Western *fronts*, while Vasilevsky was to give direction to the Voronezh *Front*.

At three o'clock on the afternoon of July 4, after a short artillery attack and aerial bombardment, the Battle of Kursk erupted (see map, page 204). That evening, according to General von Mellenthin, German grenadiers and riflemen, supported by assault guns and engineers, penetrated the forward edge of the Red defense. Mellenthin continued:

> On the second day of the attack we met our first setback, and in spite of every effort the troops were unable to penetrate the Russian line. "Gross Deutschland" [a very strong division, mustering about 180 tanks], assembling in dense formation and with the swamp on its immediate front, was heavily shelled by Russian artillery. The engineers were unable to make suitable crossings, and many tanks fell victims to the Red Air Force— during this battle Russian aircraft operated with remarkable dash in spite of German air superiority. Even in the area taken by the German troops on the first day Russians appeared from nowhere, and the reconnaissance units of "Gross Deutschland" had to deal with them. Nor was it possible to cross the stream and swamp on the night 5/6 July. On the left flank the attacks of the 3rd Panzer Division against Sawidowka were as unsuccessful as those of "Gross Deutschland" against Alexejewka and Luchanino. The entire area had been infested with mines; and the Russian defense

along the whole line was supported by tanks operating with all the advantage of high ground. Our assault troops suffered considerable casualties, and the 3rd Panzer Division had to beat off counterattacks. In spite of several massive bombing attacks by the Luftwaffe against battery positions, the Russian defensive fire did not decrease to any extent.[6]

Fighting along the entire Kursk sector was hard and uninterrupted, and after a week of bitter combat the Germans were concluding that Russian reserves were inexhaustible. By July 14 it was obvious to the more astute German leaders, among them Mellenthin, that "the timetable of the German attack had been completely upset." There were many reasons for this. Mellenthin writes:

> At the very beginning of the offensive, the piercing of the forward Russian lines, deeply and heavily mined as they were, had proved much more difficult than we anticipated. The terrific Russian counterattacks, with masses of men and material ruthlessly thrown in, were also an unpleasant surprise. German casualties had not been light, while our tank losses were staggering. The Panthers [new tanks] did not come up to expectations; they were easily set ablaze, the oil and gasoline feeding systems were inadequately protected, and the crews were insufficiently trained. Of the eighty Panthers available when battle was joined only a few were left on 14 July.[7]

On July 13, when the battle was at its climax, Hitler summoned the commanders of Army Group South and Army Group Central to tell them that the Allies had landed in Sicily that day and that the Italians were putting up a very poor fight. The gravity of the situation was increased by the possibility of an Allied invasion elsewhere—the Balkans or lower Italy.* Therefore, Operation Citadel must be discontinued.[8] That was easier said than done. After all, as Mellenthin observed, "We are now in the position of a man who has seized a wolf by the ears and dare not let him go."[9]

Military historians have generally failed to describe the immediate effects of Hitler's decision. Manstein dismisses it with the laconic observation that "when 'Citadel' was called off, the initiative in the Eastern theater of war finally passed to the Russians."[10] One might suggest that by the time Hitler canceled the operation the fate of the German divi-

* Too often Soviet historians play down the role of the Western Allies in defeating the Germans. The impact of the landings in Sicily on Operation Citadel should not go unnoticed.

sions had already been sealed. The German High Command had made a colossal blunder in allowing the Soviets time in April, May, and June to regroup and build up their strength.

In an exceptionally hard battle fought around Prokhorovka, German losses in armor and men were very high; Soviet records place the total at 350 tanks and 10,000 officers and men in one day's engagement. And the fury of the struggle on the southern face of the salient is also attested by great losses. The Seventy-third Panzer Regiment of the Nineteenth Panzer Division, for example, had only two companies left by the fifth day of the offensive. The 332d Infantry Division had lost 3,700 men, and the Sixth Panzer Division had also suffered great losses of men and could muster only 47 tanks. At that point Zhukov and Vasilevsky, in their capacity as local Stavka representatives, ordered the Western and Bryansk *fronts* to begin their offensive, and three days later, on July 15, the Central *Front* opened the attack along the Orel axis (see map, page 205).

The German command was faced with an urgent decision whether to withdraw troops attacking along the Belgorod–Kursk axis to their former positions. By consolidating there, the Germans counted on being able to employ some of their forces operating in the Orel bridgehead. On July 16, therefore, Fourth Panzer Army and Army Detachment Kempf began a withdrawal, covered by strong rear-guard forces. Simultaneously Zhukov ordered a swift counterblow by the Sixth Guards and First Tank armies along the Oboyan–Belgorod highway on the south. On July 18 he committed the Steppe *Front* to action, and by July 20 all armies of the Voronezh and Steppe *fronts* were aiming converging blows on the retreating Germans. By the end of the day the positions that had been occupied by the Soviet forces before the offensive began on July 5 were retaken.

At the end of July troops of the Eleventh Guards, Fourth Tank, and Sixty-first armies were approaching the Orel–Bryansk highway and rail line, and by early August the fight was carried to the approaches to Orel. Seemingly endless columns of withdrawing German troops and wagons stretched along roads and fields, and frustrating bottlenecks developed along main highways. Soviet ground-attack fighters and bombers went after these chokepoints and troop formations piled up at crossing sites on the Oka River.

As Soviet troops approached Orel, they found the city, which before the war had had a population of more than 100,000, lying in ruins. Plants and factories had been blown up and the rail yards destroyed. Only a few shattered walls of multistoried apartment buildings remained. The Germans put up stiff resistance, but by August 5, Red Army forces had cleared the city (see map, page 206).

With the triumph at Kursk and the liberation of Orel and Belgorod, the first of the victory salutes began in Moscow. "There was nothing fortuitous or arbitrary in the Russian decision to celebrate the victory of Kursk with those first victory salvoes and fireworks," observes Alexander Werth. "The Russian command knew that by winning the Battle of Kursk Russia had, in effect, won the war."[11] Or, as Stalin put it: "If the battle of Stalingrad foreshadowed the decline of the German Fascist army, the battle of Kursk confronted it with disaster."

On July 31 the Presidium of the Supreme Soviet announced the award of decorations "for skillful and gallant command of operations, and for success in fighting against the German invaders": to Marshal Zhukov, the Order of Suvorov, First Class; to Colonel General Konev, the Order of Kutuzov, First Class; to Lieutenant General Bulganin, the Order of the Red Banner.

Honors and recognition did not slow Zhukov's pace. He continued his personal direction of crucial battle areas. An interesting, though biased, account of a visit Zhukov made to a tank unit having difficulties near Kursk is given by Nikolai K. Popel in his book *Tanki Povernuli na Zapad* (*The Tanks Turned to the West*), published in 1960. The relationship between Zhukov the professional soldier and General Popel, an army political commissar and future Khrushchev apologist, was probably a very cool one. Popel described Zhukov's arrival at General A. L. Getman's headquarters:

> Slamming the door, Marshal Zhukov got out of his vehicle. While he walked to Getman's tent, quickly glancing all around, the news spread like a breeze through the headquarters. The commanders looked on Zhukov with apprehension and hope. With apprehension, for they knew that the rare visit of Zhukov would not be without just and unjust dressings down, dismissals, demotions. With hope, because the representative of the Stavka, vested with authority, was able to get units moving and at any time—since he knew the situation well—could prompt a decision.

This time the reasons for Zhukov's indignation were understandable. The situation was actually turning tragically; Leonov's brigade had got itself cut off. But why must he, without grasping the meaning, accuse someone and give vent to his impetuous irritation? They say a commander's rebukes are supposed to get the subordinates working better, moving faster and thinking. I don't believe this. Not five minutes ago, Getman was decisive and firm; now he had lost his nerve.[12]

At this point Popel became vitriolic in his attack on Zhukov:

> The rudeness [*grubost*], which many commanders of my generation connected with the name of Marshal Zhukov, was not his only self-indulgence. His belief in his right to insult, to humiliate his subordinate was transmitted like an infection. Martinet-like arrogance, which is alien to the truly democratic nature of our army, was adopted by some of the commanders, and at times even became their style.[13]

Then, possibly without knowing it, Popel touched on the crux of the matter, at the same time making it clear that Zhukov's *grubost* was especially reserved for army political hacks: "Zhukov's hostility toward the political workers—at times completely open—could be explained, we thought, by the fact that they opposed to the extent of their power petty tyranny of such 'Napoleons.' "[14] Popel's path as a historian, if he can be called that, was to prove a rocky one. His criticism of Zhukov would later be attacked. At the time his book was published, however, the Party line called for condemning Zhukov's "Bonapartist" tendencies.

On August 23 troops of General Konev's Steppe *Front*, aided by the adjacent Voronezh and Southwestern *fronts*, liberated the Ukrainian city of Kharkov. That victory, added to the brilliant successes at Kursk and Orel, marked the ruin of the German army on the Eastern Front. Soviet operations never outran their resources, and the Red Army now had a decided superiority in numbers. Soviet air strength was by this time twice that of the Germans, and the rapidly changing situation kept German aircraft constantly moving from one battle area to another to deal with fresh crises.

Throughout the closing months of 1943 the Germans retreated along all of the southern front, with the Red Army in full pursuit. Having hoped to make a stand on the Dnieper, the Germans watched almost helplessly as the Soviets crossed it in October, leaving only the river mouth in German hands. The land approach to the Crimea, Perekop, was recaptured, cutting off the Germans on the Crimean Peninsula. Kiev fell in November, and, one by one, the towns and cities of the

Ukraine were reclaimed by the Soviets.* By December, after a three-month push, the Germans in central and southern Russia had been driven back more than two hundred miles. Then both sides settled down for the hard winter campaign.

In accordance with the over-all plan of the Soviet Supreme Command, the four Ukrainian *fronts* resumed their offensive at the end of December, 1943, and the beginning of January, 1944. In the early weeks of 1944, Zhukov was rushed to the Ukraine to coordinate the operations of General Vatutin's First Ukrainian *Front* and General Konev's Second Ukrainian *Front*. Near Kanev and the Korsun–Shevchenkov region, at the bend in the Dnieper, a salient about eighty miles wide had been developed by ten German divisions and a motorized brigade, commanded by General Wilhelm Stemmerman. On January 24 troops of the Second Ukrainian *Front* attacked the salient, followed two days later by an offensive of the First Ukrainian. These forces penetrated the German defenses, and by January 29 the two *fronts* had converged near Zvenigorodka, trapping the Axis divisions. On February 8, Zhukov sent General Stemmerman an ultimatum demanding his surrender. The Germans rejected the offer, and the battle was resumed with renewed vigor. The condition of the encircled German divisions deteriorated day by day, and after February 10 the entire pocket was under Soviet artillery fire. On the night of February 17 the Germans made one last desperate attempt to break out but were only partly successful. According to Russian figures, 55,000 Germans were killed and 18,200 captured in the Korsun–Shevchenkov operation, while German sources claim that, of the 50,000 men trapped at Korsun, Manstein managed to extricate about 35,000, though a large amount of matériel, especially artillery, was lost. Whatever the actual statistics, the outcome was a great victory for the Red Army and the Zhukov-Vatutin-Konev triumvirate.

Early in March the Soviet Supreme Command decided to launch a large-scale offensive involving the First, Second, and Third Ukrainian

---

* The Soviets entered Kiev on November 21, 1943. Khrushchev recalls the triumphal hour as the Red Army reached the west bank of the Dnieper and prepared to liberate the Ukrainian capital. Zhukov came from the Stavka for the great event. "An underground bunker was prepared for him and me to sleep in," Khrushchev said. "During the day we sat around joking and discussing the situation. On the second or third day we didn't even bother to use the dugout any more." Khrushchev, *op. cit.*, 211.

fronts to complete the liberation of that part of the Western Ukraine known as the Right Bank. The Stavka began regrouping its *fronts* in this area, establishing new demarcation lines among them. The Fourth Tank Army was transferred from the Stavka Reserve to the First Ukrainian *Front*. With the recapture of Rovno and Lutsk it was now possible to pursue the attack on the wing of the First Ukrainian *Front* toward Kovel and farther to Brest and Lublin. (On February 24 the Second Belorussian *Front* had been formed by the Stavka in the area between the First Belorussian and the First Ukrainian *fronts*.)

The basic strategy of the offensive called for powerful, simultaneous strikes along a wide front from Polesye to the Dnieper Estuary, breaking the enemy into small groups to be destroyed piecemeal. The Second Belorussian *Front* was to attack toward the Kovel–Brest region, while the First Ukrainian *Front* was to launch its strike from Shepetovka toward Chertkov and Chernovtsy and cut the retreat routes of Army Group South in the zone north of the Dniester River. The Second Ukrainian *Front* was to attack from the Zvenigorodka area toward Uman and Iași, and the Third Ukrainian *Front* from Krivoy Rog toward Nikolayev and Odessa. The Fourth Ukrainian *Front* would not participate in the Western Ukraine operations but was to begin preparing for the offensive in the Crimea.

The various Soviet commands began regrouping their forces and concentrating troops in the area of the main thrusts. Despite inclement weather and a poor network of roads, the preparations were completed on schedule. Although efforts were stepped up to reinforce the Red Army units with men, equipment, ammunition, fuel, and food, because of the poor roads some divisions did not receive their supplies until after the offensive had begun.

During the final preparations the Red Army suffered a serious loss. On February 29, while General Vatutin was on the way to visit his troops, he was wounded when the car in which he and members of his staff were riding was ambushed by Ukrainian nationalists. Vatutin lived about a month and a half, dying during surgery on April 15.

On the first day of March, Georgi K. Zhukov replaced Vatutin as commander of the First Ukrainian *Front*. He left the previous combat missions of the troops unchanged, except that he ordered the Thirteenth Army to use its main force to defend its current line, while its left-flank division was to attack southwest, in conjunction with the Sixtieth Army.

On the morning of March 4, in almost impassable fields of mud, Zhukov's troops, inspired by his presence, began the Chernovtsy offensive. They broke through strong German defenses along a front about 110 miles long and in two days advanced 15 to 30 miles. On March 5, Stalin ordered 20 artillery salvos fired from 224 guns in a salute to the troops of the First Ukrainian *Front*.

Between March 7 and 11, Zhukov's assault groups trudged through morasses of Ukrainian mud to capture the Volochisk–Cherny–Ostrov area and cut the Lvov–Odessa rail line, in an advance which carried them sixty-two miles. Meanwhile, General of the Army R. Y. Malinovsky's Third Ukrainian *Front* had gone over to the offensive, forcing the Ingulets River and breaking through strong German defenses along its western bank.

Several adroit German commanders managed to stay out of Zhukov's clutches. To avoid encirclement, the Forty-eighth Panzer Corps began to withdraw toward Tarnopol in a very risky march across the front of Zhukov's advancing armies. General Hermann Balck adopted the principle of fighting by day and moving by night. To ensure uninterrupted control of the corps, he placed his headquarters far behind the front so that it could remain in one place for several days before making another long move to the rear. Since it appeared to Balck that every Red Army attack was aimed at large towns (possibly, by capturing them, to attract Stalin's notice and earn salvos in Moscow in a Special Order of the Day), these towns were carefully avoided. Writes Mellenthin:

> Many disasters were caused in the Russian campaign by locating higher headquarters in large towns, or by putting them too near the front for reasons of misplaced bravado. In consequence headquarters were frequently "sucked" into the battle, and command and control completely broke down. Balck avoided this error, and took care to site his H.Q. away from the main roads.[15]

The Forty-eighth finally succeeded in concentrating west of Tarnopol, where it became a part of the front in that area.

Dubno, the old fortress on a steep riverbank where Cossack Taras Bulba had fought, fell to Zhukov's First Ukrainian troops on March 17, and on the following day the important rail junction Zhmerinka was seized. Kremenets was recaptured on March 19 through a combined flanking maneuver and frontal attack, and on the next day the large railway junction Mogilev Podolski fell. (At the same time Konev's troops were seizing the industrial center of Vinnitsa on the Southern Bug.) Zhukov's assault groups continued their offensive on March 21. Spring floods, deep ravines, and water-filled gullies slowed but did not stop the groups as they made their way to the Dniester River. The First Tank Army forced the river, while other tank units were crossing the Prut River and liberating Chernovtsy.

Zhukov's troops were now advancing so rapidly that the Soviet Information Bureau sometimes had to resort to catch-all descriptions, such as the one which appeared on March 27: "240 Places Freed." The capture of larger, more important locations was cause for twelve to twenty artillery salvos during the evening hours in Moscow. Chertov, Proskurov, Kamenets Podolski, and Kolomyya fell in quick succession, and on April 5 an *Izvestia* article declared that "the brilliant operations of the troops of the First Ukrainian *Front*, commanded by Marshal of the Soviet Union Comrade Zhukov, have brought the Red Army to the foothills of the Carpathians, and have split the German front in two, depriving the enemy of his main communications." Furthermore, the article said, "the southern German grouping has now been compelled to base itself solely on roads leading through Rumania." Summarizing the recent victories of Zhukov's men, *Izvestia* noted that "in less than a month of the offensive the troops of the First Ukrainian *Front* have routed 28 German divisions, five German divisional groups and one Rumanian division." The casualty figures and weapons losses may have been exaggerated: more than 200,000 officers and men, 2,187 tanks and self-propelled guns, 4,602 guns, 2,676 mortars, and almost 54,000 trucks and prime movers.[16] A special communique issued by the Soviet Information Bureau on April 3 noted that "Zhukov's Twenty-Eight Days" had liberated 16,173 square miles of Soviet territory, three regional centers of the Ukraine—Vinnitsa. Kamenets Podolski, and Chernovtsy— and fifty-seven towns.[17]

Nevertheless, the *Istoriya* is critical of Zhukov's conduct of the offensive in the last days of March. It claims that he did not take the necessary measures in time to reinforce troops on the outer front in the Eighteenth Guards Rifle Corps sector or on the inner front in the Fourth Tank Army area. He was not successful in denying the enemy use of the air space over Soviet units.* Reconnaissance was poorly carried out, and command posts were separated from the units.[18] Taking advantage of these mistakes, the German First Panzer Army, which had been surrounded on March 28 near Skala, southeast of Tarnapol, concentrated a large force of seven tank and three infantry divisions and at the end of March launched a strong attack in the Lyantskorun–Chertov sector and had advanced to Buchach by April 7. On April 4, employing one tank and two infantry divisions transferred from France and Yugoslavia, the Germans launched an attack near Podgaytsy against the Eighteenth Guards Rifle Corps and forced it to withdraw to the south. On April 7 these German units joined forces with the First Panzer Army at Buchach and at the cost of heavy casualties succeeded in breaking out of the encirclement and even managed to carry out most of their heavy equipment. Nevertheless, the episode produced the final crisis between Hitler and Field Marshal von Manstein. At first Hitler refused to let the First Panzer Army try to break out, insisting on a last-ditch defense. But Manstein flew to the Berghof, Hitler's Berchtesgaden villa, and, after threatening to resign, finally received permission to plan the move. A week later, however, before the breakout was achieved, Manstein was removed from command.

Zhukov's First Ukrainian troops continued their westward push, defeated the Germans in the Carpathian foothills, and reached the frontiers of Czechoslovakia and Rumania. To commemorate the event, on April 8 in Moscow 24 artillery salvos from 324 guns saluted the First Ukrainian *Front*. Malinovsky's Third Ukrainian *Front*, continuing its offensive, captured Razdelnaya, an important strongpoint on the approach to Odessa, cutting off the Germans' Odessa forces from the main route of retreat to Rumania. Troops of Marshal Konev's Second Ukrainian *Front* forced the River Prut north of Iaşi and captured Dorokhoi and Botoshang. Zhukov's men went on to take the important town of Tarnopol, and on the evening of April 15, Muscovites heard the now-familiar artillery salvos honoring the First Ukrainian *Front*.

---

* Zhukov could not be blamed for shortcomings in air operations. *Istoriya Velikoy Otechestrennoy Voiny Sovetskogo Soyuza* (*IVOVSS*) admits that flooded spring roads prevented Soviet aviation from shifting to other airfields to carry out effective combat operations in the encirclement area. Several major units being resupplied by air were short of fuel and ammunition as a result of the forward airfield problem (IV, 79).

Weeks earlier, the Stavka and the staffs of the various *fronts* had begun preparations for an offensive against Army Group Center to liberate the Belorussian Republic. During the course of their work General Staff members debated the question of operational deception and decided to try to convince the Germans that the Red Army's major attacks would be made in the south and in the Baltic States. On May 3, 1944, the General Staff issued an order to the commander of the Third Ukrainian *Front* to concentrate behind his right flank eight to nine infantry divisions, reinforced by tanks and artillery, for which the necessary forces would be provided. Mockups of tanks and artillery were to be set up, antiaircraft positions were to be deployed, and fighter planes were to patrol a carefully selected location north of Kishinev. The commander was to check the concentrations from the air to ensure that the deceptive measures were adequate. To maintain secrecy, only a limited number of persons were informed of the plans. The operational camouflage was to extend from June 5 to June 15. A similar directive was issued to the commander of the Third Baltic *Front*, calling for camouflage and deception east of the Cherekha River.

Other measures were taken to safeguard Soviet intentions. For example, only five persons had detailed information about the Belorussian offensive: Zhukov, as first deputy to Stalin; the chief of the General Staff, Vasilevsky, and his first deputy, General Antonov; Shtemenko, chief of the Directorate of Operations, and his deputy. Any correspondence on questions of operations was strictly controlled, and sensitive discussions by telephone and telegraph were absolutely forbidden. Radio traffic was tight; even low-power radios were not permitted within about thirty-five miles of the forward edge of the battle area.

After study and analysis of the considerations submitted by the *front* commanders in the first half of May, the Stavka worked out a preliminary plan for the Belorussian operation. Given the code name "Bagration" (named for the hero of the 1812 campaign), the operation called for liquidation of the bulge in the Vitebsk–Bobruisk–Minsk area and an advance toward Desna, Molodechno, Stolbtsy, and Starobin. The flanks of the German troops defending the salient were to be attacked by two forces: Group A, consisting of the First Baltic and Third Belorussian *fronts*, and Group B, made up of the First and Second Belorussian *fronts*. They would include seventy-seven infantry divisions and three tank, one mechanized, and one cavalry corps. The operation was planned to a depth of about 125 to 155 miles and was to last forty to fifty days. It was examined and elaborated at a May 22–23 Stavka conference attended by Stalin and *front* representatives. The over-all purpose of the plan remained unchanged, although specific tasks of the *fronts* were spelled out in greater detail or altered. On May 31, the Stavka issued its directives outlining the specific duties of the *fronts*.

The First Baltic *Front* was to advance toward Beshenkovichi and Shvenchenis, coordinating its operations with the Third Belorussian *Front* to defeat the enemy around Vitebsk and Lepel, before forcing the Southern Dvina River and advancing to the Lepel–Chashniki area. This advance called for penetration of the German defenses southwest of Gorodok by two armies and seizure of Beshenkovichi. Certain units were to advance jointly with the right-flank army of the Third Belorussian *Front* to occupy Vitebsk.

The Third Belorussian *Front* was given the task of coordinating its operations with the First Baltic and Second Belorussian *fronts* to defeat the Vitebsk and Orsha groups and advance to the Berezina River. Troops of the Third Belorussian *Front* were to mount two attacks, the first by two armies toward Senno, with part of these forces advancing in the northwest to coordinate their operations with the First Baltic *Front* in capturing Vitebsk, and the second by two armies along the Minsk highway toward Borisov. After seizing Senno and Orsha, these troops were to employ their impressive mobile forces to rout the Borisov groupings and advance to the western bank of the Berezina in the Borisov area.

The Second Belorussian *Front* was ordered to coordinate its operations with those of the First and Third Belorussian *fronts* and to destroy the enemy around Mogilev before advancing to the Berezina.

Troops of the First Belorussian *Front* were to destroy the enemy formations at Bobruisk and then advance to the area of Osipovichi, Pukhovichi, and Slutsk. This operation called for two attacks by two armies each, one from the Rogachev area toward Bobruisk and Osipovichi, the other from Ozarichi toward Slutsk.

More than a thousand long-range planes were to attack German airfields at Orsha, Minsk, Bobruisk, Baranovichi, Luninets, Brest, and Belostok and also disrupt the enemy's rail shipments. On the night before the offensive long-range bombers were to hit the major centers of German defenses in those sectors destined for penetration.

The Belorussian partisans were instructed to intensify their attacks on the enemy's communications and seize advantageous positions, river-crossing sites, and bridgeheads, holding them until Red Army units could effect a linkup.

The Stavka also took a number of steps to reinforce the *fronts*, particularly the First and Third Belorussian, with troops and equipment. The Second Guards and Fifty-first armies, having completed their operations on the Crimean Peninsula, were placed in the Stavka Reserve and sent to Belorussia. The Stavka appointed Vasilevsky to coordinate the operations of the First Baltic and Third Belorussian *fronts* and Zhukov to coordinate the First and Second Belorussian. (Konev had taken command of Zhukov's First Ukrainian *Front* on May 15.)

Zhukov's successes in the Belorussian campaign can be attributed to his remarkable personal and professional qualities, described in a November, 1966, article:

> In preparing an operation G. K. Zhukov always sought to work not only with the commanders of the *fronts* and armies but also with the commanders of [other] formations, personally familiarizing himself with the actual situation, especially in the sectors of penetration of the enemy's front. Colonel General S. M. Shtemenko, recalling the work of Zhukov when he was representative of the Stavka for coordinating the actions of the First and Second Belorussian *fronts* in the Belorussian operation, wrote: "The Stavka Representative worked on the terrain in the zone of each army. He considered all possibilities, so that by joint efforts all variants of the operation could be examined and reckoned with over and over again; finally it was recognized that the best method of carrying out the mission of the First Belorussian *Front* would be the surrounding of the enemy in the area of Bobruisk and subsequently destroying the encircled enemy. The preparation of the offensive for carrying this out was not delayed and was executed in accordance with the approved plan and on instructions from the Representative of the Stavka, which sent troops from its reserves to help the *front* command."[19]

Additional information about Zhukov's and Vasilevsky's procedures has been provided by General Shtemenko in an article describing the preparations for the Belorussian offensive: "The activity of the Stavka, then as always, had a very strenuous character and was not confined to the walls of its offices. By this time the Stavka representatives had already amassed experience on the most important *fronts*, where they, together with the local command, solved problems of preparing and conducting operations of great significance."[20] Shtemenko says that after the war certain *front* commanders complained that the constant presence at the *fronts* of the chief of the General Staff and the first deputy to the supreme commander reflected unfavorably on the leaders of the front-line formations. Shtemenko declared:

> In some measure this was actually so, but, it seems to us, basically, in spite of the criticism (for the most part postwar), the activity of the Stavka representatives in those circumstances justified itself. The situation required the presence on the *fronts* of persons who would possess experience and authority permitting a quick decision jointly with the *front* command of the most important of combat actions and to help ensure carrying out the operation.

Shtemenko pointed out that Zhukov's very position as Stalin's first deputy justified his frequent trips to the *fronts*, while Vasilevsky would normally have remained at the General Staff, which he headed. "But the Supreme Commander did not confer with anyone regarding this. Apparently considering such a situation normal, almost every time they returned, he asked when they thought they would go back."[21]

By June 20, 1944, the Soviets had amassed an impressive array of forces in their *fronts*, including 166 divisions and 9 rifle brigades, supported by more than 31,000 large-caliber guns and mortars, 5,200 tanks and self-propelled guns, and 6,000 planes. They had a three-to-one superiority over the Germans in numbers of infantry and cavalry divisions and almost a three-to-one advantage in guns and mortars. To add to the Germans' woes, the Soviet advantage in tanks and self-propelled artillery was fourfold, with a somewhat better advantage in combat aircraft. The First and Third Belorussian *fronts* had two-thirds of the manpower and three-fourths of all the tanks and self-propelled guns and planes on the four *fronts*.

Zhukov and Vasilevsky chose a single-echelon formation for the First and Third Belorussian *fronts*, while the battle formation of the rifle corps was massed in depth, making it possible to intensify the attack while breaching the enemy's tactical defense zone.

By June 22 preparations for the offensive were completed. Immediately before the attack, advance battalions carried out a reconnaissance in force to obtain last-minute information on the state of the German defenses. Their successful operations in some sectors resulted in improved tactical positions of certain Red Army units, and in a number of sectors the reconnaissance probes developed into general offensives.

The First Baltic *Front* sent most of its armies into the attack on June 23 (see maps, pages 207 and 208), but progress was slow because of poor roads and stubborn enemy resistance. After artillery and air preparation, troops of the Third Belorussian *Front* joined in. The greatest initial successes were achieved by the Fifth and Thirty-ninth armies, which broke through the German defenses to a depth of about six miles along a thirty-mile-wide front. The offensive was a little slower in the Orsha sector, where, in the face of strong resistance, the Eleventh Guards Army was able to advance only one-half to a little less than two miles a day. The Thirty-first Army was not successful. The advance of Soviet units along the Minsk highway was slowed, primarily because the very strong German defenses in the area had not been neutralized by artillery and aerial bombardment. The German fire system had been inadequately reconnoitered. Further, poor camouflage discipline by Soviet artillery units led to their discovery and denied them the surprise they had hoped to achieve. After three days of fighting, however, troops of the Third Belorussian *Front* had reduced the enemy's defenses along a sixty-two-mile strip between the Southern Dvina and the Dnieper and had advanced eighteen to thirty miles. Vitebsk and Orsha fell on the morning of June 27.

The First Belorussian *Front* began its offensive on June 24, although, owing to poor weather and inadequate reconnaissance, some of its major units made rather slow starts. The southern assault group was more successful, and as infantry units punched holes in the defenses, tank troops were thrown into the breach. Fighting around Bobruisk was especially bitter, the Germans fighting to avoid encirclement and the Russians hurling artillery shells and bombs into the area to trap them. Soviet sources admit that at least five thousand Germans succeeded in breaking out before Bobruisk was seized on June 29. In five days of fighting, troops of the First Belorussian *Front* penetrated the German lines along a 125-mile front and advanced to a depth of 68 miles.

Troops of the Second Belorussian *Front* went into action on June 23, and by June 26 the advance units had forced the Dnieper River, seizing several bridgeheads on the right bank north of Mogilev. Three days later Soviet troops had liberated Mogilev and reached the confluence of the Prut and the Dnieper.

The Germans now began a withdrawal along the entire front from the Southern Dvina River to the Pripyat. The Stavka issued new instructions to the four *fronts* calling for an advance toward Minsk, the liberation of that city, and the destruction of approaching enemy reserves, thus preventing the Germans from stabilizing their positions. The three Belorussian *fronts* converged on Minsk, and by July 3 the capital of Soviet Belorussia, a city in ruins, had been cleared of Germans. In the days which followed, the Soviets began the systematic destruction of the German formations east of Minsk, and on July 9 the commander of the Second Belorussian *Front* was ordered to destroy the many small units which had been disrupting Soviet communications and operations.

The Red Army was now given new missions: to complete the liberation of Belorussia and drive the Germans from Lithuania and Poland. The First Baltic *Front* aimed its major thrust toward Daugavpils and Kaunas, while the Third Belorussian was ordered to attack toward Vilnyus and Lida and seize a bridgehead on the western bank of the Neman. The Second Belorussian was to move toward Novogrudok, advance to the Neman, and then resume the attack toward Belostok. Troops on the right wing of the First Belorussian *Front* were to mount their major attack toward Baranovichi and Brest, advance to the Southern Bug River, and establish bridgeheads on its west bank. For the most part these tasks were achieved in the second half of July. The operations against Brest, which Zhukov directed, involved a tank army and nine combined-arms armies, including the First Polish Army. In this phase of the campaign a feeling of mutual respect and admiration developed between Zhukov and the leaders of the Polish forces.

On July 20 the offensive got off to a successful start as the assault groups on the left wing of the First Belorussian *Front* advanced to the Southern Bug along a wide front, crossed it in three places, and entered Polish territory. Lublin fell on July 23, and Zhukov's armies reached the Vistula on July 25. The advance made it possible to encircle the Brest units on July 27. The next day, Brest, the fortress which had felt the first blows of the war in June, 1941, was recaptured by the Red Army.

At this point the Stavka issued fresh directives aimed to carry the four *fronts* to the borders of East Prussia and the Vistula River. The two *fronts* under Zhukov's command had specific missions. The Second

Belorussian was to press the offensive toward Lomzha and Ostrolenka, establish a bridgehead on the west bank of the Narew River by about August 10, and then consolidate its positions before advancing into East Prussia. The First Belorussian was to attack in the general direction of Warsaw, capture Praga, on the outskirts of the Polish capital, by August 8, and establish bridgeheads on the west banks of the Narew and the Vistula.

Although the offensive was slowing down, the Second Belorussian *Front* reached the Avgustov–Lomzha line in the second half of August, while the armies of the First Belorussian attained the Narew between its estuary and Pultusk. The Germans, however, succeeded in restoring their strategic front, and that setback, coupled with overextension of the Soviet lines of communication and the troops' fatigue, made it necessary for the Soviets to break off the offensive. On August 29, Stalin ordered all four *fronts* to take up defensive positions on a front from Jelgava to Jusefuv. Zhukov's First and Second Belorussian *fronts* were allowed to continue limited offensive operations in September to establish bridgeheads on the Narew and to liberate Praga before taking up defensive positions.

In the meantime, the Polish Underground seized upon the German retreat and the Russian advance and ordered a general insurrection, to begin in the evening of August 1. Although a detailed examination of the Warsaw uprising is not within the scope of this book, it should be pointed out that the martyrdom of the Polish capital was one of the most controversial episodes of World War II, and, of course, it had far-reaching political implications.* Debate continues today concerning the ability and willingness of the Red Army to come to the aid of the Warsaw fighters, and this question at least must be discussed, albeit only briefly.

Was Zhukov capable of continuing his advance and driving the Germans from the Polish capital? The leader of the uprising, General Tadeusz Bor-Komorowski, believed so, since Red Army units had

---

* George F. Kennan has described the Warsaw affair as "the most arrogant and unmistakable demonstration of the Soviet determination to control eastern Europe in the postwar period." George F. Kennan, *Russia and the West Under Lenin and Stalin*, 365. For observations twenty-five years after the uprising, see Andrzej Korbanski, "The Warsaw Uprising Revisited," *Survey*, No. 76 (Summer, 1970), 82–98.

crossed the Vistula on the same day they reached its eastern bank.* To him this was clear proof that the Soviets had encountered no serious German opposition and that the Vistula was no longer a major obstacle to their advance. He noted, too, that Red Army patrols were pushing deep into the country from their bridgehead without meeting any opposition, while German units appeared to be evacuating Warsaw in a chaotic rout.[22]

Zhukov tells quite a different story, and it should be examined in the light of the Soviet penchant for halting an offensive along a riverbank for consolidation and regrouping. After the war Zhukov admitted to Brigadier General John Spruling, of the United States Seventh Armored Division in Berlin: "When we reached Warsaw, we could not see how we could get beyond the Vistula unless the German forces on our front were considerably weakened." According to Zhukov, the Soviet Supreme Command believed that Hitler was so fanatical in his hatred of Communism that he would concentrate everything he could against the Red Army, despite the demands of the other fronts. The Germans' fear of

* General Shtemenko writes that in early September Stalin became concerned about possible courses of action available to the Second and Third Ukrainian *fronts*. Since Timoshenko, the Stavka representative to these *fronts*, had fallen ill, Stalin sent Zhukov to determine conditions in their sectors. As soon as Zhukov had returned, Stalin sent him to the First Belorussian *Front*, "to find out what is with Warsaw and to take the necessary measures." Stalin told Zhukov to give the Poles their assignment in person and help them organize it, since "they are still inexperienced." On September 15, Zhukov flew to the First Belorussian *Front*, and on the next morning he and Rokossovsky visited the Zelena sector of Praga, the command center of the First Polish Army. They discussed the situation with the Polish commander, who had already started sending infantry units across the Vistula to aid the insurgents. Shtemenko fails to elaborate on Soviet support except to say that "everything possible was done for the successful crossing of the Vistula." A few days later Stalin ordered the General Staff to consult Zhukov and Rokossovsky about how to help Warsaw. On September 20, Zhukov and Rokossovsky submitted their proposals to the General Staff, but little is known about them; Shtemenko is again vague about what the two men suggested. He notes that "political intrigues promoted by the leadership of the Armiya Krayova [the Polish Underground Army loyal to the Polish government-in-exile in London] led . . . Rokossovsky to express the firm opinion favoring the cessation of combat operations in Warsaw. This suggestion was supported by G. K. Zhukov." Stalin agreed, and the First Polish Army was ordered to go over to the defense along the eastern shore of the Vistula. S. Shtemenko, "Na Puti k Pobede," *Znamya*, June, 1970, 135–40.

the Slavs, the concentration of much of the German war factories in eastern Germany, and the fact that this area was the stronghold of the Prussian military caste—all these factors led the Soviets to assume that Hitler would yield ground in the west rather than weaken his forces on the Eastern Front.[23]

Churchill quotes a statement by General Guderian at the Nürnberg Trials that his front "was hardly more than an agglomeration of the remains of our armies which were endeavoring to withdraw to the line of the Vistula."[24] Guderian says in his book, however, that fighting along the river was bitter and that "we Germans had the impression that it was our defense which halted the enemy rather than a Russian desire to sabotage the Warsaw uprising."[25]

At the same time, it is obvious that Stalin, whether capable or not, did not want to go to the aid of the Poles. He considered the fighting in Warsaw a "reckless and terrible adventure" by a "group of criminals" greedy for power.[26] Further, Stalin categorically refused the United States and Britain permission to use Soviet air bases after resupply missions. On August 16, Andrei Vishinsky, deputy minister of foreign affairs, read the following statement to the U.S. ambassador in Moscow:

> The Soviet Government cannot of course object to English or American aircraft dropping arms in the region of Warsaw, since this is an American and British affair. But they decidedly object to American or British aircraft, after dropping arms in the region of Warsaw, landing on Soviet territory, since the Soviet Government do not wish to associate themselves either directly or indirectly with the adventure in Warsaw.[27]

On the same day Prime Minister Churchill received a message from Stalin: "In the situation which has arisen the Soviet Command has come to the conclusion that it must dissociate itself from the Warsaw adventure."[28] When President Roosevelt and Churchill appealed to Stalin on August 20 to drop supplies and munitions to the Polish patriots in Warsaw, Stalin's reply was that "sooner or later the truth about the group of criminals who have embarked on the Warsaw adventure in order to seize power will be known to everybody." He assured them that, in the meantime, "the Red Army is not sparing its efforts to break the Germans round Warsaw."[29] Yet Soviet sources admit that on August 29 the Stavka ordered the troops of the four *fronts* to go over to the defense.[30]

Finally, in mid-September, the Soviets began dropping supplies to the beleaguered Poles, although the Red Army still made no attempt to march into Warsaw. "They wished to have the non-Communist Poles destroyed to the full," concluded Churchill.[31] In early October the Polish forces in Warsaw surrendered. The struggle had lasted more than sixty days, and almost half the Polish Underground Army and ten thousand German soldiers had perished—figures which attest to the hand-to-hand nature of the fighting. When the Russians entered Warsaw three months later, they found a city in ruins and many of its dead yet unburied.[32]

Elsewhere events were unfolding rapidly. By the end of August, 1944, Italy, Finland, Rumania, and Bulgaria—all former allies of Germany—had quit the struggle.

The Red Army had suffered heavy losses in its summer offensive, and in October, Georgi Zhukov became concerned about his westward advance. The Russians' fears that Hitler would yield ground in the west to intensify the fight in the east subsided somewhat as they witnessed the character of the German defense in the west. The Allies began penetrating German territory, capturing Aachen and threatening the Ruhr. Although the Germans assembled their remaining armored forces in the west and hurled them into a bloody counteroffensive which almost reached the Meuse, the attack was stopped by the end of the year, and the Allies once more pushed the Germans back.

In 1944, Zhukov received the highest Soviet military decoration, the Order of Victory. Created in 1943 by the Presidium of the Supreme Soviet, it was awarded "for skillful leadership of large-scale military operations, resulting in the achievement of outstanding success in defeating the German Fascist troops." Three persons ultimately received the Order of Victory twice—Vasilevsky, Zhukov, and Stalin. The following military leaders received one such award: Govorov, Rokossovsky, Konev, F. I. Tolbukhin, Timoshenko, Malinovsky, Meretskov, and Antonov. It was indeed a small and distinguished group of men who were so honored.

The year 1944, marked by many Soviet successes, was now drawing to an end. On September 5 the Russians declared war on Bulgaria, but on September 9, after the Bulgarians declared war on Germany, the Stavka ordered all military actions halted in that country. On October 3 troops of the Second Ukrainian *Front* crossed the Yugoslav border and began to liberate towns near the frontier. On October 20 the Soviets and

Yugoslavs freed Belgrade while the Second Ukrainian *Front* was seizing the Hungarian city of Debrecen. By the end of December the Second and Third Ukrainian *fronts* had surrounded Budapest and the provisional government of Hungary had declared war on Germany.

Plans were being made for the assault on Germany, and Georgi Zhukov was destined to play a great role in that undertaking. When he and Konev arrived in Moscow on November 7, 1944, to celebrate the twenty-seventh anniversary of the Bolshevik Revolution, they heard Stalin announce that Berlin was to be taken by forces of the First Belorussian *Front* under Zhukov's command. "Stalin's arbitrary decision to reserve for Zhukov the plum of all Soviet military operations and victories," writes Roman Kolkowicz, "dismayed the planners of the General Staff and deeply offended Konev, who wanted to have a part in the conquest of Berlin."[33] How Konev reacted to this decision will be examined in the next chapter, and the long-term effects of his dislike of Zhukov will be evident throughout the remainder of this book.

XI. THE THIRD REICH PASSES
INTO HISTORY

On the battered streets and crossings or from the windows of their houses,
the befuddled inhabitants stared, overwhelmed at this roaring, endless tide
of soldiers and machines. Even I had the sensation that these were no mere
brigades and divisions but the whole of Russia pouring in.

Konstantin Simonov

AS the new year began, the Red Army was poised in East Prussia, at
the walls of Budapest, in the mountains of Czechoslovakia and
Yugoslavia, and along the Vistula River facing the ruins of Warsaw.
The Soviet High Command was completing preparations for one of
the greatest offensives of the war, designed to carry the Red Army across

Poland to Berlin.* Earlier, in November, 1944, plans had been drafted for the gigantic thrust, which came to be known as the Vistula–Oder Operation (see map, page 209).

A valuable account of the planning has been provided by Lieutenant General N. A. Antipenko, Zhukov's chief of rear services. On November 19, K. K. Rokossovsky left the First Belorussian *Front* to take command of the Second Belorussian, and Georgi Zhukov arrived to replace Rokossovsky.[1] Antipenko describes Zhukov's trip to Moscow in the last week of November, 1944:

> It was then that he informed me about the impending arrival in the First Belorussian *Front* of four new combined-arms armies, about the contemplated dispositions of our troops before the offensive and about the proposed date for the beginning of the offensive. . . .
>
> Just as important for the correct organization of the rear was the operational war game carried out by the *front* commander in the period from December 8 through 10, that is, a month before the offensive. All the army commanders and also the chiefs of the branches of service of the *front* were brought in for the game. I also participated in it. Essentially, the actual version of the operation was played, which contributed still more to working out measures for the rear.[2]

Antipenko adds that strict orders were given to conceal the arrival of the reinforcing armies, and they were forbidden to detrain in the attack positions. Two base areas were therefore established: one where the

---

* Khrushchev has acknowledged that American material aid, Lend-Lease, was vital to the Berlin operation. "Just imagine," he declares, "how we would have advanced from Stalingrad to Berlin without them [American cars and trucks]! Our losses would have been colossal because we would have had no maneuverability." Khrushchev notes that even after Stalin's death almost all the artillery of the Group of Soviet Forces—Germany was mounted on American Studebakers. "Just look how many years have passed since the war ended, and we're still driving around in American equipment." Khrushchev, *op. cit.*, 225–26. I remember from my own tour of duty in East Germany that as late as 1959 Studebakers were still in evidence with Soviet units.

During the war the United States sent the Soviet Union more than 400,000 jeeps and trucks, more than 12,000 armored vehicles (including more than 7,000 tanks—enough to equip over 20 armored divisions), more than 14,000 aircraft, and about 2 million tons of food. See Charles B. MacDonald, *The Mighty Endeavor; American Armed Forces in the European Theater in World War II*, 514; Robert Huhn Jones, *The Roads to Russia: United States Lend-Lease to the Soviet Union*.

army itself would unload and another, the main one, where all the heavy freight was sent.[3]

Now, in early January, troops of the Red Army were poised for a strike across east-central Europe. Seven Soviet *fronts* opposed the Germans. From north to south they were positioned as follows: Chernyakhovsky's Third Belorussian was located along the Neman; Rokossovsky, who had succeeded M. V. Zakharov, commanded the Second Belorussian along the Narew; Zhukov, with his First Belorussian, and Konev, leading the First Ukrainian, were on the Vistula; the Fourth Ukrainian, commanded by General of the Army I. E. Petrov, was on the San, and Malinovsky's Second Ukrainian and Tolbukhin's Third Ukrainian were in Hungary.

The Vistula–Oder Operation was to be conducted in the main direction of Warsaw and Berlin by Zhukov's First Belorussian troops, Konev's *front*, and some forces from the Fourth Ukrainian *Front*, with support by part of Rokossovsky's *front* (see map, page 210). The First Polish Army was also to participate.

Zhukov knew where the drive would end—in Berlin itself—and he was probably eager to command the *front* that would spearhead it. Indeed, he may have had himself assigned to this important post, which promised much glory and honor. Observes Lauterbach, "Zhukov was to enjoy the pleasure, seldom experienced by staff officers, of translating his own strategical concepts into tactical reality."[4]

The political objective of the operation, according to Soviet sources, was to liberate Poland from the Germans and "render aid in forming a strong, independent, democratic state." The strategic objective was to rout German Army Group A, which was covering the vital centers of Germany, to emerge on the Oder, and to prepare for the final drive on Berlin. Furthermore, the operation was "to divert enemy forces from the West European front and to ease the situation for the American and British armies which had developed in connection with the offensive by the German fascist troops in the Ardennes and the Vosges."[5] The concept of the offensive was to strike two powerful blows against the Germans toward Poznań and Breslau, dividing the defenders into isolated groups and destroying them piecemeal.

The Stavka assigned specific missions to the various *fronts*. Zhukov's First Belorussian was to destroy the Warsaw–Radom groupings and, no later than the eleventh or twelfth day of the offensive, to take the

Red soldiers on the attack.

Strategy sessions. Above: Zhukov (left) with General P. I. Batov (center) and Rokossovsky (far right, nearest the camera), at Sixty-fifth Army headquarters. Below: Field officers plan the forcing of the Dnieper River.

Above: Red Army men ford a water obstacle. Below: Russian T-34 tanks on the attack.

The famed Katyusha (Little Kate) multiple free rockets along the Oder River, 1945.

Front commanders in the final stages of the war, 1945. Seated, left to right: Marshals of the Soviet Union Konev, Vasilevsky, Zhukov, Rokossovsky, Meretskov. Standing, left to right: Marshals of the Soviet Union Tolbukhin, Malinovsky, Govorov; Generals of the Army Yeremenko and Bagramyan.

Wrecked vehicles lie in the rubble-littered grounds of the shattered Reichstag,
Berlin, 1945.

Vehicles destroyed in Allied air raids lying in the streets in front of the Brandenburg Gate, 1945. On the far right is the Reichstag.

Above: German prisoners of war are marched to the rear along the center island of the Autobahn, near Güsen, Germany, as vehicles of the U.S. Sixth Armored Division, Third Army, roll past them to the front, March 29, 1945. Below: German soldiers of the Twenty-first Army crowd the road with horse-drawn wagons, fleeing from the advancing Red Army, Grabow, Germany, May 5, 1945.

In front of a sign symbolizing the historic meeting of the American and Russian armies, Second Lieutenant William D. Robertson, Sixty-ninth Infantry Division, U.S. First Army, greets Red Army Lieutenant Alexander Sylvashko on April 25, 1945. Earlier that day Robertson was one of the first Americans to meet a Russian soldier, as both men were climbing across the twisted and sloping girders of a blown-out bridge over the Elbe River, at Torgau, Germany.

Marshal Konev (center), commander of the First Ukrainian Front, presents his war horse, a handsome Don stallion, to General Omar N. Bradley (far right) at Torgau, Germany, May 5, 1945. Bradley presented Konev the Legion of Merit and an American jeep. Bradley had crossed the Russian lines to meet Konev.

Lieutenant General Alexander M. Patch, Jr., commanding general of the U.S. Seventh Army, with Field Marshal von Rundstedt, May 5, 1945, shortly after the latter was captured by the Seventh Army.

Allied participants after the signing of Germany's unconditional surrender at Reims, France, SHAEF Forward Headquarters, May 7, 1945. Left to right: Major General of Artillery Ivan Susloparov, of the Red Army; Lieutenant General Sir F. E. Morgan, deputy chief of staff, SHAEF; Captain Harry C. Butcher, SHAEF naval aide; General Dwight D. Eisenhower, supreme Allied commander (holding the pens used in the signing of the surrender document); Sir Arthur Tedder, deputy supreme Allied commander; Admiral Sir Harold M. Burrough, Allied naval chief.

The Germans surrender at Berlin, May 9, 1945. Zhukov (above) watches as German officers enter the room at Russian headquarters to sign the ratified surrender terms. Below, left to right: Colonel General P. F. Stumpf, commander in chief of the Luftwaffe; Field Marshal Keitel; and General Admiral Hans Georg Friedeburg, commander in chief of the German fleet, prepare to sign the surrender documents.

Above: Field Marshal Keitel signs the surrender documents in Berlin, May 9, 1945. Below, left: Field Marshal Zhukov signs for the Red Army. Below, right: Keitel salutes as he prepares to leave Russian headquarters after the surrender.

Above: Zhukov reads the citation for the Order of Victory awards before presenting the medals to General Eisenhower and Field Marshal Sir Bernard L. Montgomery (right), commander of the Twenty-first Army group, in Frankfurt, Germany, June 10, 1945.

The Order of Victory (inset) is the highest Soviet military decoration of World War II. It is a five-pointed platinum star, two inches in diameter, encrusted with 135 diamonds and 5 rubies. Only five non-Russians were awarded the medals: Eisenhower, Montgomery, Marshal Josip Broz Tito, Polish Marshal Mikhail Rola-Zymierski, and King Michael of Rumania.

Montgomery (left), Eisenhower, and Zhukov offer a toast to the "victory of the United Nations" after presentation of the Order of Victory awards.

Eisenhower and Zhukov watch an air show performed by seventeen hundred Allied airplanes during Zhukov's visit to Frankfurt, June 10, 1945. Behind them (center) is Lieutenant Colonel O. Pantuhoff, Eisenhower's interpreter.

Tedder, Montgomery, Eisenhower, Zhukov, and Andrei Y. Vishinsky (far left) before SHAEF headquarters, Frankfurt, Germany, June 10, 1945.

line from Zychlin to Łódź. Then it was to begin the attack on Poznań. The main blow was to be delivered toward Kutno by four combined-arms and two tank armies and one cavalry corps from the Magnuszew bridgehead. Zhukov was to send part of these forces northwest to smash the German defenses opposite his *front*'s right wing and, cooperating with the Second Belorussian *Front*, liberate Warsaw. A supplemental strike was planned from the area north of Warsaw by the Forty-seventh Army, situated on the right flank of Zhukov's *front*. This army, in conjunction with the left wing of the Second Belorussian *Front*, was to clear the Germans from between the Vistula and the Western Bug and then surround Warsaw from the northwest. At the same time, Rokossovsky's Second Belorussian troops, having attacked from the line of the Narew River to Marienburg, were to use part of their forces to surround Modlin from the west so as to be ready to force the Vistula and prevent the Germans from escaping from Warsaw.

It was the task of Konev's First Ukrainian *Front* to cooperate with Zhukov's troops in routing the Kielce–Radom group and, by the tenth or eleventh day of the offensive, seize the Piotrków–Radomsko–Częstochowa–Miechowice line and then attack toward Breslau. The main blow was to be delivered by five combined-arms and two tank armies and four tank and mechanized corps, which would move out from the Sandomir bridgehead toward Radom. The First Ukrainian was to break through the enemy defense in the center of the bridgehead, using the forces of three armies, supplemented by six artillery divisions. Two combined-arms armies in the second echelon would exploit the penetration, one to attack Szydłowiec and surround the Ostrowiec grouping, the other to be used to intensify the attack along the main axis.

The Fourth Ukrainian *Front* was to prepare its right-flank Thirty-eighth Army for attacking in the direction of Cracow to liberate that city in cooperation with the First Ukrainian *Front*. The troops on the left wing and in the center of the *front* had the mission of continuing the offensive in Czechoslovakia.

The Stavka sent large numbers of reinforcements to Zhukov and Konev. The combined forces of the First Belorussian and First Ukrainian *fronts* were staggering: 163 divisions, 32,143 guns and mortars, 6,460 tanks and self-propelled guns, 4,772 planes, and 2,200,000 men. The Soviets had a significant superiority of forces over the Germans in the approaching offensive: 5.5 to 1 in manpower, 7.8 to 1 in guns and mortars,

5.7 to 1 in tanks, and 17.6 to 1 in aircraft. The average operational density of troops along the entire zone of attack of the *fronts* amounted to one infantry division for each 1.3 miles. Artillery density reached 103 guns and mortars for each mile of front, while the number of tanks and self-propelled guns averaged 19 a mile. In a classic of understatement, the authors of the *Istoriya* concluded that

> the strategic situation on the central sector of the front was favorable for the Red Army. . . . Having a great advantage over the enemy troops and occupying favorable positions for the offensive, the Soviet armed forces firmly held the initiative in their hands. The enemy, though he also had strong forces, was nevertheless unable to establish a sufficient density in artillery and tanks in the directions of the main strikes by Soviet troops. All this created favorable prerequisites for the successful offensive by the Red Army on the territory of Poland and for its final liberation.[6]

Now Zhukov and his staff worked out the details of the offensive. It was decided to lay down a two-and-a-half-hour artillery barrage to a depth of two miles in preparation for the attack by the First Belorussian troops. Engineers cleared passageways through minefields and set up obstacles to slow or halt counterattacks. They built new roads, repaired old ones, and constructed bridges across the Vistula. Great quantities of supplies, ammunition, and fuel were stockpiled at the Magnuszew and Puławy bridgeheads, while medical teams prepared facilities for treatment and evacuation of the wounded. In Zhukov's *front* alone, 180 field hospitals with 60,300 beds were set up, and an additional 68,000 beds were prepared in the rear. Blood was readied for transfusions; there were 32,500 donors in the First Belorussian *Front*, including more than 4,000 Polish donors. In the political-military sphere negotiations were carried out between representatives of the Polish and Soviet governments to place Colonel General Mikhail Rola-Zymierski's First Polish Army under the operational control of Zhukov.

The *Istoriya* provides almost no details about the influence of individual commanders on the over-all conduct of operations, and since Zhukov was out of favor when it was published, the authors dealt with him rather hurriedly. Fortunately, his rehabilitation in the mid-1960's was accompanied by some honest appraisals of his leadership, including this description by a Party spokesman, Lieutenant General K. F. Telegin, the one-time member of the Military Council of the First Belorussian *Front*:

From the first steps of his work in the post of commander of the First Belorussian *Front*, G. K. Zhukov in every possible way encouraged a high spirit of creativity and solidarity of the entire leading collective, skillfully directing its efforts to the accomplishment of the mission. Operations were prepared by him with scrupulous care. He grasped all their aspects, worked them out in detail, calculated, checked with the commanders of the branches of service, chiefs of services, with the army commanders; he played them on maps and relief tables. During the course of the operation the commander attentively followed its development, and he strictly controlled and rigidly demanded the fulfillment of the plan and orders, making those responsible answer for lack of organization and lack of administrative abilities. And it is true that not all military chiefs were pleased. It must not be forgotten that the success of even the smallest operation depends on many factors, and hitches on one sector immediately tell on others. . . . In general and on the whole our *front* collective paid honor to the energy, persistence and decisiveness of G. K. Zhukov, his great organizing abilities and his leadership talents, so fully developed in the final battles of the Great Patriotic War.[7]

The offensive began on January 12, when troops of the First Ukrainian *Front* moved out from their positions along the Vistula. Two days later, after a short but intense artillery concentration, Zhukov's First Belorussian troops launched simultaneous attacks from the Magnuszew and Puławy bridgeheads. By the end of the day the troops attacking from the Magnuszew bridgehead had forced the Pilica River and driven an almost seven-and-a-half-mile wedge in the German positions. The attack from the Puławy bridgehead met with even greater success as the Red Army troops crossed the Zwolenka River (a branch of the Vistula halfway between Radom and Puławy), seized the Zwolen strongpoint, and engaged the Germans in a battle for Radom. On January 13 fresh artillery barrages signaled the resumption of the Russian offensive. Zhukov sent the First Guards Tank Army to exploit a breakthrough in the Eighth Guards Army's area. In the days which followed, the First Belorussian *Front* won impressive victories as it occupied Nowy Miasto and advanced on Łódź. Radom was taken on January 16, and on the next day Zhukov's troops, including the First Polish Army, liberated what was left of Warsaw.

Only recently has Zhukov been given proper credit for victories in the opening rounds of the Vistula–Oder offensive. The occasion was

Zhukov's seventieth birthday (at which time he also received his fifth Order of Lenin):

... In conducting the Vistula–Oder Operation Zhukov, calculating that the enemy had uniformly stretched his forces along the front, made his decision to launch three attacks—two from the bridgeheads on the western bank of the Vistula in the region of the cities of Magnuszew and Pulawy and the third, north of Warsaw. The success of the operation depended on the rapid breakthrough of the tactical zone of the enemy's defense and the subsequent bold exploitation of the success in depth. ...

For achieving decisive objectives in the operations and increasing the speed in carrying them out, G. K. Zhukov skillfully employed armored and mechanized troops. For example, by the start of the Vistula–Oder Operation the composition of the First Belorussian *Front* included two tank armies [the First and Second Guards], two separate tank corps and five separate tank brigades. By the decision of G. K. Zhukov the tank armies, which were a basic factor for a rapid development of the offensive, were introduced in the fighting on the second and third day of the operation, that is, only after the complete penetration of the enemy's defense. This permitted preserving the forces of the mobile groups for prolonged and tense fighting in the operational depth of the defense. The tank corps and separate tank brigades were used in this textbook operation in the role of army mobile groups and tanks in direct support of infantry. After the breakthrough of the enemy's tactical zone the tank units, supporting the infantry, withdrew from subordination to commanders of infantry divisions and were combined into specially constituted army mobile detachments for pursuing the enemy. These detachments fulfilled the function of a connecting link between the tank and combined-arms armies.

Thanks to the correct use of tank troops in the Vistula–Oder Operation an unusually high speed of offensive was achieved. After breaking through the enemy defense, the offensive by the tank armies achieved an average rate of 28 miles and on some days up to 43.5 miles in a twenty-four-hour period, and when disengaged from the combined-arms armies, up to 62 miles.[8]

With the liberation of Warsaw an important stage in the Vistula–Oder Operation was concluded. In four to six days troops of Zhukov's First Belorussian and Konev's First Ukrainian *fronts* had broken through the German defenses along a zone 310 miles wide and 60 to 100 miles deep, reaching the Sochaczew–Tomaszów-Mazowiecki–Częstochowa line.

Exceptionally favorable conditions had been created for further development of the offensive, and so, on January 17, the Stavka defined more precisely the missions for the next few weeks. The First Ukrainian troops were to continue moving toward Breslau, arriving no later than January 30 on the Oder south of Leszno and establishing bridgeheads on the left bank of the river. The First Belorussian *Front* was ordered to attack toward Poznań, seizing the Bydgoszcz-Poznań line by about February 4. Zhukov and Konev placed their mobile detachments ahead of the main forces of their tank and combined-arms armies, which advanced in columns. When it was necessary to repel flank counterattacks and destroy large enemy groups left in the rear of the attacking forces, separate units were selected to carry out these missions and, upon completion of the engagement, were returned to the main forces.

On January 19, Konev's troops took Cracow and three days later fought their way across the Oder River and began establishing bridgeheads along the left bank. On January 18, Zhukov's First Belorussian troops destroyed the surrounded German units west of Warsaw and on the following day took the large industrial city of Łódź before the Germans could destroy anything or even evacuate the valuable lathes and other equipment already packed for shipment to Germany. In two days (January 22 and 23) the *front* advanced from about 60 to 90 miles. On the right wing, after a circling maneuver by the Second Guards Tank Army and the Second Guards Cavalry Corps, the fortified city of Bydgoszcz, part of the Poznań defensive line, was occupied.

Zhukov's memoirs* have provided valuable insights into the planning of the Polish campaign. By that account, when the First Belorussian *Front* reached the Bydgoszcz–Poznań line, it was to establish a link with the First Ukrainian *Front*. The Stavka had delayed a decision about further operations for the First Belorussian *Front* until it arrived at the line. "However," Zhukov points out, "in the course of the operation the troops of the First Belorussian *Front* significantly overfulfilled the Stavka timetable, and by January 23 the *front's* right wing had already seized Bydgoszcz and had developed the offensive toward Schneidemühl and

---

* All references to Zhukov's memoirs in this chapter are from the June, 1965, installment in *Voyenno-Istorichesky Zhurnal*. The Moscow memoirs, already cited, were not published until the summer and fall of 1966. The memoirs of the Vistula–Oder and Berlin campaigns were Zhukov's first public writings after he was ousted from his post as defense minister in the fall of 1957.

Deutsch-Krone [Wałcz]. On January 25 the center of the *front* surrounded the powerful forces at Poznań, and the left wing, closely coordinated with the First Ukrainian *Front*, advanced to the region of Jarocin."[9]

At noon on January 25, Stalin telephoned Zhukov. After listening to a report on the situation, he asked what Zhukov intended doing next. Zhukov replied that since the enemy was demoralized and incapable of serious resistance he had decided to continue the attack and advance to the Oder. The main objective would be Küstrin, where the Soviets would try to seize a bridgehead. The *front*'s right wing would turn north and northwest against the East Pomeranian groupings, which still did not present a serious direct threat.

Stalin objected that once Zhukov's forces reached the Oder they would be separated from the Second Belorussian *Front* by more than ninety miles. "This cannot be done now. It is necessary to wait until the Second Belorussian *Front* completed its operations in East Prussia and regroups its forces on the Vistula."

Zhukov asked when that operation would be completed, and Stalin told him it would take about ten to fifteen days. He further stated that Zhukov could expect no support on his left flank by the First Ukrainian *Front*, since it would be tied down for some time cleaning up resistance in the Oppeln and Katowice areas.

Zhukov tried to persuade Stalin not to halt the offensive, arguing that later it would be more difficult to penetrate the fortified line at Meseritz (Międzyrzecz). He also asked for one additional army to reinforce the right wing of the *front*. Stalin promised to think about it, but Zhukov's headquarters received no answer that day.

On January 26 a patrol of the First Guards Tank Army reached the Meseritz line, where it captured a large group of prisoners. Through interrogation it was learned that many sectors of the line had not yet been occupied by German troops and that many units were only now beginning to move up. Zhukov decided to speed his main forces to the Oder and quickly try to establish a bridgehead on the west bank. To protect his main advancing forces (the First and Second Guards Tank armies and the Fifth Shock, Eighth Guards, Thirty-third, and Sixty-ninth armies) from German attacks out of East Prussia, Zhukov proposed sending the Third Shock, First Polish, Forty-seventh, and Sixty-first armies and the Second Cavalry Corps (in that order) north and northwest. He would leave part of the Eighth Guards and First Guards Tank armies at Poznań to destroy the German garrison there. (The Russians believed that there were no more than twenty thousand enemy troops at Poznań, but actually there were more than sixty thousand, and the struggle stretched to February 23.)

After much discussion Stalin finally agreed to Zhukov's proposal, although he would not allot Zhukov additional forces. "The concern of the Supreme Commander in Chief to protect our right flank was well grounded," Zhukov notes. "As subsequent events proved, the threats of strikes from eastern Pomerania grew constantly."[10]

The offensive developed rapidly. The front's main forces broke through the Meseritz line and by February 3 had advanced to the Oder. A small bridgehead was seized on the western bank near Küstrin. "By this time," Zhukov writes, "the enemy's resistance against our right flank had significantly increased. Air reconnaissance disclosed the approach and concentration in Pomerania of large enemy forces. Troop patrols confirmed this intelligence. To meet the imminent danger from the north quick and decisive actions were needed."[11] Zhukov took those decisive actions, ordering the First and Second Guards Tank armies to relinquish their sectors on the Oder to adjacent units, make a forced march, and regroup on the north near Arnswalde (Choszczno). He also transferred to that point the reinforced Seventh Cavalry Corps and a large portion of his artillery, engineer units, and matériel. Troops of the Second Belorussian *Front*, on Zhukov's right, were directed by the Stavka to go over to the offensive on February 10 and occupy all of eastern Pomerania from Danzig to Stettin and advance to the Baltic Coast (see map, page 211).

On February 10 the Second Belorussian troops attacked but were unable to carry out their mission. On February 24 the Stavka sent the Nineteenth Army from its reserve, and the troops renewed the drive. On March 1, Zhukov's troops went on the offensive, assisting the Second Belorussian units in their advance. They reached the Baltic on March 5, captured Köslin (Koshalin), and turned east again to attack Gdynia and Danzig.* Zhukov's First Tank Army was temporarily transferred

---

* According to A. S. Zavyalov and T. E. Kalyadin, *Vostochno-Pomeranskaya Operatsiya Svetskikh Voysk, Fevral–Mart 1945 g.*, 7–10, an excellent source, the reasons for the slow start of the second Belorussian offensive were the transfer of four armies to the Third Belorussian *Front*, bad roads, and poor terrain conditions.

to the Second Belorussian *Front* to help defeat the Germans in the Gdynia area.

At this point in his memoirs Zhukov lashes out in a strong attack on Marshal V. I. Chuikov.[12] In the spring of 1964, Chuikov had written several articles in which he had accused Zhukov, V. D. Sokolovsky, and others of delaying the capture of Berlin for lack of skill and initiative. Had Zhukov not dragged his feet, Chuikov charged, the Soviet Union would have seized a much larger share of Europe.[13]

In March, 1965, Zhukov's defenders opened their attack on the claims of Chuikov and other Khrushchevites. General Antipenko accused Chuikov of falsifying the facts and citing data to which he could not have had access. General Telegin, who had been on Zhukov's staff, attacked Chuikov's claims after reminding his readers that Chuikov's benefactor, Khrushchev, was not around any longer to protect him.[14] In 1966, Zhukov joined the dialogue:

> It is appropriate, in my opinion, to dwell on a question in more detail, one which is now being raised by several authors of memoirs, in particular Marshal of the Soviet Union V. I. Chuikov. Why did the First Belorussian *Front* command, after its arrival at the Oder in the first days of February, not get permission from the Stavka to continue the attack on Berlin without a pause?
>
> In [Chuikov's] memoirs . . . he asserts that "Berlin could have been taken even in February. And this, naturally, would have brought the end of the war nearer."
>
> In our press a number of comrades have come out against such a point of view of Comrade Chuikov, but he considers that "arguments come not from the active participants of the Vistula–Oder Operation, but either from those who participated in working out the orders of the Stavka and *front* concerning halting the offensive against Berlin and the conduct of the East Pomeranian operation, or from those authors of several historical works." It must be said that with regard to the offensive against Berlin everything was not as simple as V. I. Chuikov thinks.[15]

Zhukov then points out that on January 26, 1945, when it had become clear that the Germans would not be able to halt the Russian offensive against the fortifications on the Oder approaches, he and his staff made a preliminary proposal to the Stavka, the substance of which follows:

By January 30, Zhukov's First Belorussian *Front* was to advance to the line from Berlinchen (Barlinek), to Landsberg (Gozhuv Velikopolsky), to Grets (Brudzisk), moving up the rear and building up the reserves and force the Oder by the morning of February 2. Later the *front* was to move rapidly toward Berlin, concentrating the main forces to envelop the city from the northeast, north, and northwest. The Stavka approved Zhukov's proposal on January 27. The next day Marshal Konev presented his own proposal to the Stavka, providing for defeat of the Breslau groupings and an advance to the Elbe by February 25 to 28. At the same time he planned to use the right wing of his *front*, in coordination with Zhukov's First Belorussian, to seize Berlin. Konev's proposal, which was somewhat in the form of an announced decision, precipitated heated debates in the General Staff on how to reconcile Konev's plans with Stalin's earlier dictum that the First Belorussian *Front* would take Berlin. General Antonov agreed that Konev's *front* should be allowed to participate in the assault on Berlin; but the Stavka, which was Zhukov's domain, while concurring in principle, recommended drawing a dividing line between the *fronts*. Using Zhukov's guidelines, the Stavka relegated Konev's *front* to the territory south of Berlin, while Zhukov's First Belorussian *Front* was to dominate the main offensive axis.[16]

Zhukov omits these details, merely saying that Konev's proposal was approved on January 29. He then resumes his reply to Chuikov's allegation that Berlin could have been captured earlier except for Zhukov's unfounded fears. Zhukov admits that at that time the Germans had deployed only limited forces along the Berlin approaches but repeats that by early February the danger of counterattack from eastern Pomerania had begun to pose a threat on the *front*'s flank and rear. To prove his case, Zhukov cites statements by Field Marshal Wilhelm Keitel and Chief of Staff Guderian that the Germans were indeed planning to launch attacks against the Russians from Pomerania.

At the beginning of February the German Second and Eleventh armies, composed of sixteen infantry, four tank, and three motorized divisions, four brigades, and eight battle groups, were active between the Oder and the Vistula. Soviet intelligence indicated that the flow of forces to the area was continuing. In addition, the Third Panzer Army was deployed near Stettin, and the German command could (and did) commit this force both to defend Berlin and also to reinforce the eastern Pomeranian groups. Zhukov asks: "Could the Soviet command run the risk of continuing the offensive against Berlin with the *front's* main forces under those conditions when a serious danger threatened from the north?" He writes that Chuikov thought such a risk justified, since Red Army troops had covered more than three hundred miles in the Vistula–Oder Operation and it was only forty to fifty miles from the Oder to Berlin. Zhukov's reply is that, while the Russians could have disregarded the danger, sending both tank armies and three or four combined-arms armies straight toward Berlin, the Germans, with a blow from the north, could have severed the Russian covering force advancing to a crossing point on the Oder, thereby endangering the entire *front*. Zhukov reminds his readers of a historical precedent, when overzealous Red Army forces greatly extended themselves and paid the consequences: "The experience of history shows that risk is expected, but it is not to be overdone. In this respect the lesson was well demonstrated with the Red Army's offensive against Warsaw in 1920, when a precarious, indiscriminate advance forward led not to success but to a hard defeat of the troops of the Western *Front*."

In his 1964–65 articles Chuikov asserted that an objective evaluation of enemy strength in Pomerania should have shown that any threat to the Soviets along the Berlin axis could have been contained by the troops of the Second Belorussian *Front*. Zhukov retorted that "actual fact refutes this assertion." Furthermore, the forces of the Second Belorussian *Front* had proved insufficient to defeat the Germans in eastern Pomerania. The Second Belorussian troops began their offensive February 10 and after ten days had advanced only thirty to forty miles. At the same time the Germans launched a counterstrike south of Stargard, pushing back Soviet troops and advancing five to seven miles southward. The Stavka, concerned about the ever-growing German forces in eastern Pomerania, now forty divisions, decided to bring up four combined-arms and two tank armies of the First Belorussian *Front*. The joint combat actions of the two fronts were concluded only at the end of March. "It was a tough nut," Zhukov says.

Chuikov estimated that in February, 1945, the First Belorussian and First Ukrainian *fronts* could have detached eight to ten armies, including three to four tank armies, for the offensive against Berlin. Zhukov disagreed. In early February, of the eight combined-arms and two tank armies of his *front* which had been on the Berlin axis, only four under-strength armies remained (the Fifth Shock, Eighth Guards, Thirty-third, and Sixty-ninth). Two corps (one each from the Eighth Guards and Sixty-ninth armies) were fighting around Poznań, while the rest of the *front* had turned toward eastern Pomerania to cope with the threat from that direction. The First Ukrainian *Front*, on the other hand, had mounted an offensive northwest of Breslau between February 8 and 24 in which the main forces of the *front* participated (four combined-arms and two tank armies, plus the Second Airborne Army). The Germans, bringing up considerable reinforcements, managed to put up a very stubborn resistance. In seventeen days the First Ukrainian troops had advanced sixty-two miles, bringing the *front* up to the Neisse River. Attempts to cross the river failed, and so the Soviets went on defense.

To complicate matters, the Red Army had suffered serious losses in the Vistula–Oder Operation. By February 1 the strength of the infantry divisions averaged about 5,500 men, although the Eighth Guards numbered from 3,800 to 4,800. Zhukov's two tank armies had 740 tanks, or about 40 tanks for each armor brigade, although in many there were only 15 to 20. A similar situation existed in Konev's First Ukrainian *Front*.

Thus in February, 1945, neither Konev's nor Zhukov's *front* was able to carry out the final push toward Berlin. "To exaggerate the capabilities of one's troops and to underrate the strength and ability of the enemy are equally dangerous," Zhukov says. "Such the many-sided experience of war has taught, and it is impossible to ignore it." He further observes that the logistical aspects of the situation cannot be disregarded. The troops had advanced more than 300 miles in twenty days, and supplies had naturally lagged behind. The Russian units were in need of combat matérial, especially fuel. Similarly, the aviation units had not yet been able to shift their bases forward to support the front line.

Chuikov, says Zhukov, failed to analyze all the complications of the situation in the rear but resorted to a number of qualifications: "If the Stavka and the *front* staffs had been able to deliver the necessary amount of ammunition, fuel, and rations; if aviation had been shifted forward to airfields near the Oder; if pontoon-bridge units had provided crossings at the Oder—then our four armies could have developed an offensive against Berlin in early February." Zhukov declared that "such reasoning, with references to 'if it had been,' cannot be seriously considered even by a writer of memoirs. The very acknowledgment by Chuikov that resupply was in disorder, that aviation and pontoon-bridge units were lagging behind indicates that undertaking an offensive against Berlin under such circumstances would have been pure adventurism."[17]

How did the Germans react to Zhukov's drive? In early February, General Guderian urged Hitler to postpone a planned offensive in Hungary and instead use forces from the Balkans, Italy, Norway, and especially from Kurland (Courland) to attack the Soviet spearhead, which had reached the Oder at a point between Frankfurt and Küstrin. Guderian writes that the flanks of the spearhead were still vulnerable to attack from a line between Glogów and Gubin on the south and Pyrzyce and Arnswalde on the north. Such an attack would, he hoped, give increased protection to Berlin and the interior of Germany and win time for armistice negotiations with the Allies.

The Führer listened to Guderian's suggestion but turned it down. Guderian persisted: "You must believe me when I say it is not just a pig-headedness on my part that makes me keep on proposing the evacuation of Courland. I can see no other way left to us of accumulating reserves, and without reserves we cannot hope to defend the capital. I assure you I am acting solely in Germany's interests."

With that, Hitler, trembling down the left side of his body, jumped to his feet and shouted: "How dare you speak to me like that? Don't you think I'm fighting for Germany? My whole life has been one long struggle for Germany." He continued to berate Guderian until Göring took him from the room while tempers cooled. When the Führer summoned him back into the conference room, Guderian resumed his argument but only evoked a new outburst of rage from Hitler. He stood in front of Guderian shaking his fists until Guderian's chief of staff pulled the general away, "lest I be the victim of a physical assault."

Guderian did not get the Kurland troops, even though General Reinhardt Gehlen's Intelligence Section—Foreign Armies East estimated that the Soviets could increase their forces on the Oder by about four divisions a day. "If our attack was therefore to make any sense at all," Guderian was convinced, "it must be launched with lightning speed, before further Russian troops had arrived and before they became aware of our intentions."

A few days later, on February 13, a second meeting was held at the Chancellery, and after another violent outburst, Hitler finally agreed that the Russians must be attacked, but without the reserves Guderian needed. The offensive began on February 16 and made good progress for a day or two. Unfortunately for the Germans, however, the man who was in charge of it, General Walter Wenck, was seriously injured in a car accident as he was returning from an evening briefing with Hitler. Without his leadership the attack bogged down and never regained momentum.[18]

Zhukov notes in his memoirs that Chuikov described a February 4 meeting at the headquarters of the Sixty-ninth Army at which the plan for the offensive against Berlin was discussed. Chuikov said that Stalin telephoned Zhukov during the discussion and, after being told that the Berlin offensive was the subject of the conference, demanded (to Zhukov's surprise, Chuikov added) that the participants instead occupy themselves with a plan to defeat the Germans in Pomerania.

According to Zhukov, this was not the first occasion on which his former subordinate had taken liberties with historical fact. Citing official archives of the Ministry of Defense, Zhukov declared that there was no such conference and that therefore the talk with Stalin could not have taken place. On February 4 and 5 Zhukov was, he said, at the headquarters of the Sixty-first Army, which was preparing operations against the Germans' Pomeranian forces. Did Chuikov intentionally falsify the record, or was he confused about the date and place of the meeting? Was Zhukov correct, or was he clouding the issue in a further attempt to discredit Chuikov as a historian of the campaign? With the limited available evidence, no definite conclusion is possible.

With the advantages of historical perspective and serious studies of this phase of the Russian campaign, there is no question that Zhukov's reasons for delaying the final drive toward Berlin were valid ones. In *Vostochno-Pomeranskaya Operatsiya Sovetskikh Voisk* (*The Eastern Pomeranian Operation of the Soviet Forces*) published, incidentally, while Zhukov was out of favor, Zavyalov and Kalyadin assert that before the last, decisive strike toward Berlin "it was necessary first of all to defeat the enemy groups in eastern Pomerania which threatened the Soviet forces along the Berlin axis from the north and at the same time to put an end to the German Fascist command's plan to prevent our blow on this axis. Besides this, it was necessary to liquidate the enemy group cut off in East Prussia."[19]

The *Istoriya*, which is generally rather offhand in its treatment of Zhukov, lends support to his account. It reports that Zhukov decided to move the Third Shock Army and the First Polish Army to his right flank to counter the threats from Pomerania. Further, "at the end of January and the beginning of February the most intense fighting developed on the right wing and the center of the First Belorussian *Front*. Germans in position on the Pomeranian rampart west of Bydgoszcz showed especially stubborn resistance," continuously counterattacking troops of the Forty-seventh Army and pushing them back in some areas. On January 29 the First Polish Army entered the fray; two days later the Third Shock Army was brought in.[20] The *Istoriya* also supports Zhukov's statement that resupply difficulties arose as the retreating Germans destroyed railroads, highways, and bridges. Railroad and road-building units were put to work restoring essential rail lines and roads as soon as possible, while engineer troops were ordered to begin building bridges across the Vistula immediately.

Despite delays and setbacks the Vistula–Oder Operation was a brilliant success. Soviet sources claim the capture of 147,000 soldiers, 1,377 tanks and self-propelled artillery pieces, 5,707 mortars, and 1,360 aircraft. The twenty-three-day operation carried Soviet and Polish units 310 miles at an average rate of 12 to 14 miles a day.

Now with his First Belorussian *Front* along the Oder, Zhukov was ready for the final assault on Germany (see map, page 212). On April 1 he and Konev were summoned to Moscow for a meeting with Stalin. Generals Antonov and Shtemenko were also present. "We were hardly through with our greetings," Konev writes, "when Stalin asked us, 'Do you think you have a clear idea of the latest situation?'" Zhukov and Konev said that they thought they had, based on the data available at their *fronts*. "Read them the telegram," Stalin told Shtemenko. The operations chief read a telegram containing information that the Anglo-American command was preparing an operation to capture Berlin. The main strike force had been set up under Field Marshal Sir Bernard Law Montgomery. The major attack was planned north of the Ruhr, along the shortest route separating most of the British troops from Berlin. Several preliminary measures adopted by the Allied command were enumerated, including the organization of the strike force and the concentration of troops. The telegram concluded with the report that the Allies considered the plan to take Berlin before the Red Army could reach it perfectly realistic and that preparations were well under way.

When Shtemenko finished reading, Stalin turned to Zhukov and Konev: "Now who is going to take Berlin, we or the Allies?"*

---

* In the several available accounts of this conversation only Konev's point of view is presented. Cornelius Ryan was given the same story in April, 1963, when he

Konev replied first, assuring him that the Soviets would take Berlin.

"So this is the sort of man you are," Stalin said with a half smile, and then asked point blank: "How will you be able to get up a strike group for this purpose? Your main forces are on your southern flank, and apparently you'll have to do a lot of redeployment."

"Comrade Stalin," Konev replied, "you can rest assured that the *front* will carry out all necessary measures and that we will regroup for the offensive on Berlin in proper time."

Then came Zhukov's reply. He was fully prepared for the capture of Berlin, he said, and his First Belorussian *Front*, now "saturated" with troops and equipment, was aimed directly toward Berlin and was the shortest distance from it.

"Very well," Stalin said. "Both of you should prepare your plans right here in Moscow at the General Staff and report them in a day or two to the Stavka so that you can go back to the *fronts* with fully approved plans in your hands."[21]

Konev wanted desperately to share the honor of seizing the German capital; more precisely, he wanted to steal the show from Zhukov by getting there first. He disliked Zhukov intensely, and Stalin took advantage of this enmity to play one man against the other.* According to Boris I. Nicolaevsky, Stalin, with his great talent for exploiting human weaknesses,

> quickly sized up Konev and cleverly used his feelings toward Zhukov. If we trace the history of Stalin's treatment of these two soldiers, the chronology of their promotions and awards, we shall see that as early as the end of 1941, Stalin was grooming Konev, the politician, as a rival, whom he could play off against the real soldier, Zhukov. This was typical of Stalin's foresight and bears all the marks of his style. He conferred honors on Zhukov only when he had no choice, but on Konev he bestowed them even when there was no particular reason for doing so. This was necessary in order to maintain the balance between the indispensable "organizer of victory" and the even more indispensable political counterweight to him.[22]

interviewed Konev in Moscow. The Soviet government allowed Ryan and John Erickson to interview a number of participants in the Battle of Berlin, including Konev, Sokolovsky, Rokossovsky, and Chuikov, but the two historians were not permitted to interview Zhukov. See Cornelius Ryan, *The Last Battle*, 248n.

* Konev's vitriolic attack on Zhukov in 1957 will be examined in the final chapters of this book.

Now in Moscow each of these strong-willed men hoped to convince Stalin that his plan for the final assault on Germany should be adopted. Zhukov believed that his First Belorussian troops could capture Berlin by themselves, while Konev continued his campaign to overturn an earlier Stavka decision relegating his forces to securing the territory south of the city. Members of the General Staff suggested a pincer movement by both *fronts*, a proposal which clashed with Zhukov's concept of a frontal assault, as well as with Konev's suggestion of a coordinated frontal assault. When the meeting resumed early on the morning of April 3, Stalin listened to the plans of both commanders and then resolved the impasse by walking up to the map and drawing a line between the First Ukrainian and the First Belorussian *fronts*. The line ended at Lübben, on the Spree River, about thirty-seven miles southeast of Berlin. According to General Shtemenko, Stalin then declared, "Whoever gets there first will also take Berlin."

Cornelius Ryan notes that had Stalin continued the line from Lübben right across Germany, thereby marking a boundary that Konev was not to cross, the First Ukrainian *Front* would clearly have been denied any participation in the Berlin attack. Although "Stalin did not say anything, the possibility of a show of initiative on the part of the command of the *front* was tacitly assumed." Without a word being spoken, the green light to Berlin had been given to Konev's *front*. He felt that Stalin had read his mind. With what Konev was to term a "secret call to competition . . . on the part of Stalin," the meeting closed.[23]

Zhukov's account of the meeting, though not as imaginative as Konev's, is probably the more accurate one. He says that the offensive on the Berlin axis and the seizure of the city itself were charged to the troops of the First Belorussian *Front*. Konev's First Ukrainian *Front* was to attack from the Neisse River and destroy the enemy south of Berlin, isolating the main forces of Army Group Center from the Berlin units and thereby supporting Zhukov's attack. But, Zhukov writes, "right here in the conference in the Stavka, I. V. Stalin issued instructions to Marshal of the Soviet Union I. S. Konev: In the event of stiff enemy resistance on the eastern approaches to Berlin and the possible delay of the First Belorussian *Front*'s offensive, the First Ukrainian *Front* will be ready to deliver a strike on Berlin from the south."[24]

Zhukov's memoirs reveal his anxiety about the final drive on the German capital. "The unusual and extremely complex offensive operation

against Berlin demanded from all the *front* and army command echelons exceptionally cautious preparations." His concern was well founded:

> In the experience of war we had not yet had the occasion to take such a
> strongly fortified city as Berlin. Its total area was almost 350 square miles.
> The city's subway and well-developed underground engineering structures
> gave the enemy maneuvering capability. The city and its suburbs were
> carefully prepared for a stubborn defense. Every street, square, alley, house,
> canal, and bridge constituted a part of the over-all defense of the city.[25]

Zhukov ordered reconnaissance aircraft to undertake six photographic
missions over Berlin, the approaches to the city, and its defensive lines.
From the aerial photographs, captured documents, and information
from prisoners of war the Russians prepared detailed maps and descrip-
tive reports, which were issued to command echelons down through
company level. In addition, engineering units prepared an exact scale
model of the city and its suburbs for Zhukov and his staff.

From April 5 to 14 the First Belorussian *Front* conducted meetings and
command exercises on maps and scale models, with participants from
the armies, corps, army and *front* artillery, and all major service elements.

As the day of the offensive approached, last-minute preparations were
made. Zhukov decided to employ another of his well-known innovations
to "stun the enemy and morally overwhelm him." Taking into account
that troops defending at night are more susceptible to confusion and
panic, he decided to launch his attack two hours before dawn. His own
forces would be assisted by 140 searchlights, which would be used to
illuminate the enemy positions and facilitate control over the attacking
Red formations.

Meanwhile, the Germans had been feverishly preparing defenses
along the Oder. Colonel General Gotthard Heinrici, who had been
recalled from the inactive list in the summer of 1944, was given command
of Army Group Vistula with orders to hold the Russians on the Oder
and save Berlin. His specialty was defensive operations. In the final days
of January, 1942, he had been given command of Fourth Army remnants holding ground near Moscow. There he had developed a highly
successful defensive technique. As soon as he determined that a Soviet
attack was imminent in a particular sector, he ordered his units to withdraw during the night to new positions one or two miles to the rear.
The Red artillery barrages, normally so devastating, would fall on an

abandoned front line. Wrote Heinrici: "It was like hitting an empty bag. The Russian attack would lose its speed because my men, unharmed, would be ready. Then my troops on sectors that had not been attacked would close in and reoccupy the original front lines."[26]

In early April, 1945, Heinrici inspected the two defensive lines he had created along the Oder. Just before Zhukov's artillery barrage was to begin, the German units were to evacuate the easternmost line so that the artillery rounds would fall on empty trenches. The critical problem obviously was to determine the exact moment of the Russian attack. Several feints made Heinrici's task more difficult. Nevertheless, the greatly burdened general believed that the offensive would not begin until mid-April.

Shortly after 8:00 P.M. on Sunday, April 15, Heinrici made his decision. After analyzing reports from the field, he was convinced that Zhukov's attack would begin early the next day. He issued a one-line order to General Theodor Busse, commanding the Ninth Army: "Move back and take up positions on the second line of defense." The Germans immediately began pulling back under cover of darkness, a stratagem which took most of the night.

By now Zhukov was impatient to begin his mighty offensive. In the early predawn hours of April 16, he surveyed the German positions from his bunker atop a hill in the Küstrin bridgehead. At exactly four o'clock in the morning, he gave the order: "Now, Comrades, now!" Instantly, three red flares appeared in the black sky, and Zhukov's 140 searchlights, supplemented by tank and truck lights, were turned on, illuminating the German positions.* Three green flares were fired, the

---

* Soviet memoirists have debated Zhukov's use of searchlights. Some are critical of the innovation, while others praise Zhukov's imagination. Konev writes that he intentionally did not employ any artificial illumination on his own *front*. "Our First Ukrainian *Front* decided on an entirely different method. We were to cross the Neisse, and we planned a longer artillery preparation intended to secure two stages: the crossing of the Neisse and the breakthrough of the enemy main line of defense, which stretched along the Neisse's western bank. To conceal the crossing as much as possible it was not to our advantage to illuminate the breach zone. On the contrary, we wanted to prolong the night as much as possible." I. Konev, "Nineteen Forty Five," *International Affairs* (Moscow), August, 1965–April, 1966, 8. Chief Marshal of Artillery Voronov wrote that "I liked the decision of . . . Zhukov to begin the Berlin offensive with an artillery preparation and an attack by infantry and tanks even before daybreak and to blind the enemy by use of searchlights." N. N. Voronov, "Podvig Sovetskogo Naroda," *Istoriya SSSR*,

signal for the start of the artillery barrage. In an earthshaking bombardment which had never been equaled on the Eastern Front, entire villages disintegrated and forests erupted in flames. The holocaust was so intense that it created a fire storm. German survivors still talk about the strange, hot wind which suddenly whipped up, blowing dust and debris across the countryside.[27]

As the earsplitting barrage continued, Zhukov's troops began moving toward the German positions. Chuikov, commanding the Eighth Guards Army, says that in the first half hour after the start of the attack there was almost no German fire, except from a few machine guns and self-propelled guns well protected in stone buildings and isolated bunkers. These were very likely defenders Heinrici had left on the forward battle line. As the Soviet barrage lifted and the Germans emerged to meet the onslaught, Zhukov's troubles began. German flak and antitank guns began pouring deadly fire into the Soviet formations, blowing infantrymen off tanks and setting fire to armored vehicles. John Toland interviewed several survivors of this terrible fight, including Gerhard Cordes, an eighteen-year-old airman at the time of the battle. Basing his account on the interview, Toland wrote the following description of the Soviet attack along one sector of the battlefield:

Now Cordes could see more shapes. The din of motors and clank of treads was tremendous. The earth trembled. He picked up a *Panzerfaust* [bazooka]. From behind came an abrupt, heavy-throated chorus; 88-mm shells screeched overhead and smashed into the first tanks. Flames shot up, parts of metal and shell fragments rained over the foxholes. At least six tanks were on fire, but others kept coming on and on. In the reddish glare they stood out with clarity and were helpless before the withering fire of big guns. Red Army infantrymen began erupting from the middle of this massive conflagration. There must have been 800, and they scrambled up the hill shouting, Cordes thought, like madmen.

The airmen fired rifles and burp guns, and hundreds of Russians toppled over. The rest came on, still yelling. More fell and at last, like a

July–August, 1965, 21. Chuikov, who was under Zhukov's command at the Küstrin bridgehead, was highly critical of the artificial illumination, claiming that it played havoc with the soldiers' night vision "and in fact did more harm than good." V. I. Chuikov, "Konets Tretego Reykha," *Oktyabr*, April, 1964, 145. The United States Army successfully employed searchlights in the Korean War to create "moonlight" for attacking troops.

great wave that has shattered its strength against a jetty, the attackers fell back.[28]

Zhukov could not believe that his forces had been stopped. After staring incredulously at Chuikov, he exploded: "What the hell do you mean—your troops are pinned down?" Chuikov, who had seen Zhukov angry before, answered, "Comrade Marshal, whether we are pinned down temporarily or not, the offensive will almost certainly succeed. But resistance has stiffened for the moment and is holding us up." Chuikov explained that heavy artillery fire from the Seelow Heights had hit the troops as they advanced. Moreover, the terrain was proving extremely difficult for the tracked vehicles. In the marshes and irrigation canals along the Oder self-propelled guns and tanks were miring down and being raked by devastating fire.[29]

Zhukov soon learned that the first-echelon attack had proved inadequate. He knew that the sheer weight of his armies could overwhelm the German defenders, but he did not want the offensive slowed. He therefore decided to change his tactics. He sent bombers to blast the enemy gun positions, and ordered his artillery to pulverize the heights. Zhukov's original plans had called for committing his tank armies only after the Seelow Heights had been taken, but now the marshal decided to throw them in immediately. By this time Zhukov was livid with anger. He did not intend to be slowed by a few well-placed German guns—nor did he intend for Konev to beat him to Berlin. As he made his way out of his bunker, brushing by his staff officers, he turned to General M. Y. Katukov, commander of the First Guards Tank Army, and snapped: "Well! Get moving!"[30]

In his memoirs Zhukov confirms that his armies ran into difficulties that forced him to commit his tank armies and air support. The Germans threw reinforcements into the fray, and the fighting grew even fiercer. By April 17, Zhukov's forces had managed, by sheer weight of numbers, to smash the defenses on the Seelow Heights and begin moving forward. More German units and matériel arrived, including antiaircraft artillery pulled from the Berlin defenses, and Zhukov's offensive was slowed again.

In the meantime, Konev's *front* was making excellent progress, and one can surmise that Konev was not unhappy about Zhukov's troubles on the road to Berlin. On April 17 Stalin telephoned Konev: "Zhukov is having a difficult time. He is still trying to break through the defenses." Stalin was silent for a few moments, and Konev, too, said nothing. Finally Stalin asked: "Is it not possible to transfer Zhukov's mobile forces and let them move toward Berlin through the gap you have created on the sector of your *front*?" Konev replied: "Comrade Stalin, this will take much time and will cause great confusion. It is not necessary to transfer tank troops from the First Belorussian *Front* into the gap we created. Events in our sector are developing favorably, our forces are adequate, and we are in a position to turn both our tank armies toward Berlin." He discussed the direction in which his armies would be turned, naming Zossen as an orientation point. This town, about sixteen miles south of Berlin, was the headquarters of the German General Staff.

Stalin asked Konev the scale of the map he was using. He answered that he was working with a 1:200,000-scale map.

After a short pause, during which he apparently was trying to find Zossen on the map in Moscow, Stalin answered: "Very well. Do you know that the headquarters of the German General Staff is at Zossen?"

"Yes, I know."

"Very well," Stalin said. "I agree. Turn your tank armies toward Berlin."

Konev's exultation was probably not lost on Stalin. As soon as Stalin hung up the telephone, Konev immediately called the commanders of both tank armies on the high-frequency radio and ordered them to turn toward Berlin. More specific directives followed. The Third Guards Tank Army was ordered to force the Spree during the night of April 17–18 and move rapidly toward Fetshau, Holsen, Baruth, Teltow, and the southern edge of Berlin. On the night of April 20–21, the army was to break into Berlin from the south. The Fourth Tank Army was to force the Spree on the night of April 17–18 and move rapidly toward Drepkau, Kalau, and Luckenwalde in order to capture the region around Beelitz, Treuenbrietzen, and Luckenwalde by April 20. Potsdam and the southwestern sector of Berlin were objectives for the night of April 20–21.

In later years, with no trace of bitterness, Zhukov wrote that "in those days Stalin displayed serious anxiety, fearing a delay of our troops' offensive. Therefore, he ordered the commander of the First Ukrainian *Front* to strike with part of his forces from south of Berlin, as provided for in the operational plans approved in the Stavka on April 3."[31] But in those critical days of April, 1945, Zhukov reacted strongly to the possibility that his First Belorussian troops, so close to victory, would have their glory snatched from them at the last minute. Lieutenant Colonel Pavel Troyanosky, senior correspondent for the military paper *Red Star*, spoke of the incident: "The attack had stalled and Stalin reprimanded Zhukov. It was a serious situation and a reprimand from Stalin was often couched in not very mild language." Troyanosky could plainly see that "Zhukov, a man with all the marks of an iron will about his face and a man who did not like to share his glory with anyone, was extremely worked up."[32]

After tense battles on April 20 the German defenses on the approaches to Berlin were overcome. During his interrogation after the war, German General Karl Weidling, commander of the Fifty-sixth Tank Corps, declared that "the twentieth of April was the most difficult day for my corps and very likely for all the German units. They had suffered terrible losses in previous battles, were extremely exhausted and unable to withstand the great onslaught of the superior Russian troops."[33]

In the early afternoon of April 20 the long-range artillery of the Seventy-ninth Infantry Corps of the Third Shock Army, part of Zhukov's *front*, became the first to open fire on Berlin proper. On April 21 units of the Second Guards Tank, Third Shock, and Forty-seventh armies broke through to the edges of the city. Zhukov realized that the wide sweeps in which armor was best employed were not possible in the narrow, easily barricaded streets of the city, and he therefore decided to use his tank armies, along with the combined-arms armies, in a sweeping movement which, by its sheer shock action and massed firepower, would overwhelm the city's defenders.

Meanwhile, Konev was frantically racing to his objective. By April 20, General P. S. Rybalko's Third Guards Tank Army had overrun Zossen and was advancing toward Berlin, while other units were involved in stubborn battles with the German units at Cottbus. The next day Konev's tankers approached the Berlin defensive ring at a point about fifteen miles from the southern edge of the capital. By evening the Berlin belt-line road had been crossed in several spots. The same night Konev made a number of new decisions. One was to put the Tenth Artillery Breakthrough Corps, the Twenty-fifth Breakthrough Division, and the Twenty-third AAA Division under Rybalko to reinforce the

Third Guards Tank Army, now meeting very strong resistance on Berlin's southern approaches. The Second Fighter Aircraft Corps was also transferred to Rybalko's command.

April 22 was an important day for both *fronts* as Zhukov's Eighth Guards, Thirty-third, and Sixty-ninth armies and Konev's Third Guards and Third Tank armies and part of the Twenty-eighth Army began closing the ring around the forces near Frankfurt and Gubin. Rybalko's troops, advancing on Berlin from the south, were separated from Chuikov's Eighth Guards Army, advancing on Berlin's southeastern edges, by a narrow strip measuring about seven and a half miles. Two rings of encirclement had thus been formed and were being closed: one around the German Ninth Army east and southeast of Berlin, the other west of Berlin around those units which were defending the city itself.

Konev's forces encountered a major obstacle when they reached the Teltow Canal: the Germans had prepared strong defenses on its northern bank. Along it were massed large quantities of guns, mortars, tanks, and *Panzerfauste*. A number of bridges had been destroyed, and others were prepared for demolition. On April 24, Rybalko's troops, supported by artillery, infantry, and bombers, began crossing the Teltow. Heavy-caliber artillery brigades hit the houses lining the northern side of the canal and demolished many of them at once. Along a narrow front the Soviets had concentrated 966 guns a mile, and under their fire leading detachments began to force the canal without waiting for the barrage to lift. Several forward units which crossed the canal near Linquist were counterattacked by German tanks and infantry, and the Russians were forced to abandon their bridgehead. Along other sectors of the canal the bridgeheads held, and by afternoon Soviet engineers had thrown bridges across. While Konev was observing this action from the roof of a large building, word reached him that elements of the First Belorussian and First Ukrainian *fronts* had joined behind Busse's Ninth Army.

The crossing of the Teltow continued throughout the day and into the night, allowing Rybalko's troops to penetrate the German inner defensive lines covering the central part of Berlin from the south.

Stalin's Order No. 11074, addressed to both Zhukov and Konev, stated that, as of April 23, Berlin was divided between them as follows: "Lübben, thence to Teupitz, Mittenwalde, Mariendorf, Anhalter Station." Ryan records the impact of this new boundary between the *fronts*:

Although he could not complain publicly, Konev was crushed. Zhukov had been given the prize. The boundary line, which ran straight through Berlin, placed Konev's forces roughly 150 yards *west* of the Reichstag—which the Russians had always considered the city's prize plum, the place where the Soviet flag was to be planted.[34]

The Third Reich was in its death throes, but Berlin's defenders continued to resist the Russian onslaught. In the heavy fighting now raging within the city, the German troops were pushed back to the belt-line railroad and beyond. By April 30 only the government sector, the immediate vicinity of the Tiergarten, and a strip extending westward from the zoo to the Havel River were still in German hands.

The Soviets employed a methodical procedure in their attack, preceding each fresh assault with bombing and artillery strikes. Infantrymen were supported by tanks and engineer troops with flame-throwing and demolition equipment. The Red infantry advanced in small sectors —street by street and house by house, infiltrating through back yards, cellars, subways, and sewers. Often the German defenses were stormed from behind or below. Gradually, the defenders gave ground, falling back to the large air-raid bunkers and flak towers. German artillery soon began taking up firing positions in open squares, parks, and rail yards. Finally, the remaining German guns were massed in the Tiergarten.[35]

Stalin had challenged the Soviet troops to hoist a "banner of victory" over the Reichstag, and every Russian unit in the city hoped to earn this honor. At 5:00 A.M. on April 30 the Soviets turned their artillery on the building. In the early afternoon Zhukov's troops poured through holes in the building walls, and for the next hour fighting raged inside. At 2:25 P.M. the Soviets emerged victorious, leading out twenty-five hundred prisoners, and the Red flag was run up over the ruined structure.

While Zhukov's troops were hoisting the Soviet flag over the Reichstag, Hitler was in the air-raid shelter under the Chancellery. He had put his affairs in order, secretly married Eva Braun, and made out a will. After hearing of Benito Mussolini's death, Hitler lunched quietly. At the end of the meal he shook hands with those present and then retired to his room. At half-past three he shot himself in the mouth. His wife poisoned herself.* "The bodies were burnt in the courtyard," wrote

---

* Khrushchev says that one day in Kiev he received a call from a jubilant Zhukov: "Soon I'll have that slimy beast Hitler locked up in a cage. And when I

Sir Winston Churchill, "and Hitler's funeral pyre, with the din of Russian guns growing ever louder, made a lurid end to the Third Reich."[36]

Before his death Hitler had informed General Karl Weidling, now in charge of the defense of Berlin, that he would permit a breakout by small units but stressed that capitulation was out of the question. Shortly after the Führer's death Joseph Goebbels intervened and ordered that no one was to leave the city and that he would begin negotiations with the Soviet command. Orders were published and countermanded; proposed breakouts were canceled. This vacillation produced great confusion among the troops and resulted in the capture of most of the defenders.

Goebbels' attempts to negotiate with the Soviets failed. Zhukov would discuss only unconditional surrender. Goebbels then poisoned his six children and ordered an SS guard to shoot him and his wife. That evening Admiral Karl Dönitz, at his headquarters in Holstein, received a telegram appointing him the Führer's successor.

Early on May 2, General V. A. Glazunov, at the command post of the Forty-seventh Guards Division, called General Chuikov, of the Eighth Guards Army, to report that "the front line says that they see German troops forming into columns." At 6:00 A.M. General Weidling, accompanied by two generals from his staff, crossed the line and surrendered. Weidling identified himself as commander in chief of the Berlin defenses. When asked whether Goebbels had consented to the surrender, Weidling answered that he had made the decision himself.[37] By three o'clock that afternoon the rest of the Berlin garrison, numbering more than seventy thousand troops, had surrendered.* The war with Germany was over.

Stalin claimed in his May Day speech that the final sweep of the war had cost the Germans more than 1,000,000 men killed and 800,000

send him back to Moscow, I'll ship him by way of Kiev so you can have a look at him." "I wished Zhukov every success," Khrushchev continues. "I knew that with him commanding the front, our offensive was in good hands. Then, after Germany capitulated, Zhukov called me again and said, 'I won't be able to keep my promise after all. That snake Hitler is dead. He shot himself, and they burned his corpse. We found his charred carcass." Khrushchev, *op. cit.*, 218–19.

* On May 9, Weidling and a number of other German generals and colonels were put on a plane bound for Moscow. Weidling died in a Soviet prison in November, 1955. See John Toland, *The Last Hundred Days*, 551.

prisoners. Red Army troops had captured or destroyed 6,000 enemy aircraft, 12,000 tanks and self-propelled guns, more than 23,000 field guns, and enormous quantities of equipment.

Meanwhile, American and British forces were sweeping across Germany. By April 22 they were along a line from Hamburg through Magdeburg, Leipzig, Chemnitz, Nürnberg, and Stuttgart—well into what was to be the Soviet Zone. As the Americans rushed toward the east, they encountered thousands of Germans fleeing from the Russians. Soon prisoner-of-war camps were overflowing. On April 25 a patrol from the U.S. Sixty-ninth Division met a Russian horseman near the village of Leckwitz, two miles from the Elbe River. Later the same day another patrol from the Sixty-ninth fashioned a crude American flag and made its way across a damaged bridge at Torgau. As the Americans crawled across the remains of the bridge, a Russian soldier began to climb toward them. Meeting over the Elbe, the American patrol leader and the Red soldier grinned and slapped each other good-naturedly.[38]

Soon American and British leaders were meeting their Russian counterparts, and for a brief time, at least, there was genuine warmth and good feeling between East and West. In early May, Marshal Konev dined with General Omar N. Bradley. After dinner Bradley presented Konev the Legion of Merit, and also gave him a jeep. Konev had a personal gift for the American general, too—his war horse, which had accompanied him everywhere since he assumed command of the Steppe *Front* in 1943. The handsome Don stallion was presented complete with saddle, bridle, and trappings.[39]

The war was over in Europe. It now remained for the Allied representatives to draw up the instrument of unconditional surrender and work out the problems of peace. That, as the world would soon find out, was no easy task.

XII. A BRIEF HONEYMOON

If the United States and Russia will only stand together through thick and thin, success is certain for the United Nations. If we are partners there are no other countries in the world that would dare to go to war when we forbade it.

Georgi K. Zhukov to Dwight D. Eisenhower

TENSIONS between the U.S.S.R. and its wartime allies were mounting long before the smoke faded from the skies over defeated Berlin. General Alfred Jodl, representing the German High Command, signed the unconditional surrender of all German land, sea, and air forces to the Western Allies and simultaneously to the Soviet High Command on May 7, at 1:41 A.M., Central European Time, in Reims,

France. General Walter Bedell Smith signed for the Allies, Major General Ivan Susloparov signed as a witness for the Soviets—apparently without clear authority to do so, as subsequent events indicated. The cessation of hostilities was to be effective on May 8, at 11:01 P.M., Central European Time. Later the same day, however, General Dwight D. Eisenhower's headquarters received a message from General Antonov saying that the Soviets had decided that General Susloparov had not been an acceptable Soviet representative at the Reims ceremony.* They demanded the signing of a more formal Act of Military Surrender, to take place in Berlin, with Marshal Zhukov representing the Soviet government.[1]

General Eisenhower was deeply concerned by what he felt was a questioning of the sincerity of the Allies' part in the German surrender. He immediately replied, assuring Antonov that he had scrupulously adhered to the stipulation that there would be no separate truce and that he was willing to come to Berlin the following day, May 8, at an hour specified by Marshal Zhukov. If bad weather prevented his arrival at the specified time, Eisenhower said, the chiefs of the British and American military missions in Moscow could sign for him.[2] He later decided not to go to Berlin but instead sent his deputy, British Chief Marshal Arthur W. Tedder, to sign for him. American General Carl A. Spaatz and French General Jean de Lattre de Tassigny also journeyed to Berlin for the ceremony. John R. Deane, head of the United States Military Mission to the U.S.S.R., flew from Moscow to participate.

Since the Soviets were expecting General Eisenhower, Zhukov's entire staff, headed by Marshal Sokolovsky, was on hand at the airport to

---

* Stalin was livid when he learned that Susloparov had signed the surrender protocol. On May 7 he telephoned Artillery Chief of Staff N. N. Voronov, asking, "Who the hell is the 'famous' General of Artillery Ivan Susloparov?" He berated Voronov for failing to educate artillery officers properly and said that Susloparov had been recalled to Moscow and would be punished harshly. (General Susloparov —despite rumors to the contrary—was not shot.) N. N. Voronov, "Podvig Sovetskogo Naroda," *Istoriya SSSR*, No. 3 (1965), 24–26; cited in Seweryn Bialer, *Stalin and His Generals*, 557–58, 625n. As Bialer points out, Stalin was upset because the surrender ceremony took place on territory occupied by Western, not Soviet, armies and the document was signed by Eisenhower but not by a senior Soviet officer. It served to accentuate the Western contribution to the victory over Germany. Also, unfortunately, through an error by Eisenhower's chief of staff, the surrender document was different from the one agreed upon by the Allies in March, 1945. The suspicious Soviets believed the worst.

greet him. When, instead, Admiral Archer and General Deane, the first to arrive, alighted from the plane, the Russians' "jaws dropped as though at a command," wrote Deane. However, "they recovered quickly and were most gracious to us."[3] About eleven o'clock Tedder and his party arrived. As soon as the guard of honor had completed its ceremony, the German representatives were allowed to deplane. They included Field Marshal Wilhelm Keitel, Admiral Hans von Friedeburg, and General P. F. Stumpf of the Luftwaffe.

The representatives were driven through debris-filled streets to Karlshorst, a small suburb cast of Berlin.[4] In his memoirs Tedder describes his frustrations during the surrender negotiations. He was eager to sign the surrender and return to his headquarters. He asked to see Zhukov at once but was told that the marshal was very busy. Tedder replied that he was equally busy, and "a little quiet insistence was necessary before I obtained entry to the General's office." Zhukov expressed his apologies for keeping Tedder waiting.

Tedder brought with him a draft instrument of surrender similar to the one signed at Reims. "Zhukov had obviously never seen such a document or anything like it," writes Tedder, "so when one remembers the deeply suspicious nature of the Russians it is not surprising that it took the best part of twelve hours, most of it spent standing in Zhukov's office, to sort out the outstanding issues, each of which had to be argued out *ad nauseam*." Tedder observes that "the presence, or absence, of M. Vishinsky was a potent factor which determined the progress, or lack of it, in our negotiations." Once when Vishinsky was out of the room, Zhukov pat a hand on Tedder's shoulder and said, "Please believe me, I am not trying to be difficult, but we must get this right; otherwise there will be trouble later."[5]

Other writers have confirmed that Vishinsky was deciding matters that had political implications,[6] but it would be incorrect to assume that he was dictating *military* policy to Zhukov. Further, Zhukov certainly did not allow himself to be dominated by his political adviser. Eisenhower's *At Ease*, published in 1967, provides an interesting insight into the relationship between Vishinsky and Zhukov in the days following the war:

> The Marshal had scant patience with political men.
> Once, when I told him that I wanted to talk about a military matter and had not brought along my political adviser, I added that he could have

his present if he liked. "No," he replied, "if you're not going to have yours, I'm going to throw mine out." He turned to Andrei Vishinsky, his adviser, and said, "Get out, I don't want you here."[7]

During the afternoon meeting de Tassigny complicated the proceedings by producing a letter from Charles de Gaulle empowering de Tassigny to sign the surrender document on behalf of the French High Command. Tedder objected, since Eisenhower had authorized him to sign for all the Western Allies. If the French signed, then all the other Allied nations should also participate as separate entities. The issue was argued for several hours before being settled by preparing the instrument for the signatures of Zhukov and Tedder as principals and de Tassigny and Lieutenant General Carl Spaatz as witnesses. "The argument," writes Deane, "developed some heated discussions, with Zhukov, probably at Vishinsky's instigation, taking sides with de Tassigny. It was the first strong Soviet bid for a closer postwar relationship with France, and this became more pronounced as the day wore on."

The surrender ceremony was to take place in the assembly hall of a small engineering college across the street from Tedder's quarters. The various representatives assembled there about 8:00 P.M. although the surrender document itself was not ready in its final form until about 12:30 A.M., May 9. Vishinsky suggested a number of changes in wording, none of which were radical departures from the document signed at Reims on May 7. But each small change necessitated a complete rewriting of the document in Russian and in English, and the revised version in turn had to be checked carefully by the interpreters to ensure that its meaning was the same in both languages.

Finally the surrender documents were ready for signing. At one end of the assembly hall was a long table at which the principal Allied representatives were to sit. Zhukov took his place at the center, an arrangement which Tedder found not altogether satisfactory, believing that he should share the central position. He let the matter rest, however, on the grounds that Berlin was in Soviet hands, which might be sufficient justification for Zhukov to act as representative of the host nation and chairman. Tedder sat on Zhukov's right, and Vishinsky was seated on Tedder's right, although Vishinsky "might just as well have remained standing as he was constantly bobbing up to whisper instructions in Zhukov's ear."[8]

During the proceedings, the Soviet journalist Konstantin Simonov recalls, Vishinsky fidgeted, Spaatz appeared placid, Tedder seemed to regard the ceremony with some irony, and de Tassigny "looked like someone who had come a bit late, was anxious about it, and eager to come to grips with the matter at hand." Zhukov was beaming, but his expression was both benign and ominous. "Watching Zhukov's heavy but handsome features, I recalled my meetings with him during the fighting against the Japanese at Khalkhin-Gol, when he held the rank of corps commander and was in charge of our forces in Mongolia. I had not seen him for six years and would never have dreamed that I would see him next in Berlin, accepting the surrender of the Nazi army."[9]

As the noise in the hall subsided, Zhukov rose and called the meeting to order. After about ten minutes, during which a list of the participants was read, Zhukov stood up again and told the officers at the door: "Let the German delegation in." Keitel, Friedeburg, and Stumpf entered, followed by their aides. Keitel took only about three steps to reach the table, where he raised his field marshal's baton in salute, pulled out the middle chair, and sat down.[10] Captain Harry C. Butcher, Eisenhower's naval aide, says that Keitel surveyed the room as he might have looked over the terrain of a battlefield. "His attitude contrasted sharply with that of the German civilians I had seen during the day, all of whom appeared completely whipped and cowed."

Tedder rose and asked whether the Germans accepted the terms of surrender, a copy of which had been handed them earlier. An interpreter translated his remarks, and Keitel replied that he accepted the terms as written in the paper, which he held up.[11] Simonov describes the scene:

> The ceremony went on. I had my eyes on Keitel. His gloved hands lay on the table in front of him. Stumpf seemed to be calm. Friedeburg froze, but there was something about his immobility which bespoke utter despair. Keitel was at first perfectly placid, then turned his head and looked at Zhukov. His eyes kept shifting between the table and the Soviet marshal. Oddly enough, it was curiosity that I read in his eyes whenever he looked up. It was as though he were looking at a man who had interested him for a long time and whom he could now view a few steps away.[12]

The German representatives were now to sign the document. "Keitel's face darkened," Simonov writes, and he became rigid as he awaited his turn to sign. Soon "he tossed his head back as though to contain the tears about to roll from under his lids."[13]

"It is proposed that the German delegation sign the unconditional surrender act," Zhukov said firmly. Before the interpreter had finished translating the sentence, Keitel seemed to grasp the meaning and moved his hand over the table as if requesting that the document be laid in front of him. Zhukov, however, remained on his feet and curtly gestured the German representatives to the table. "Let them sign it here!" he snapped.[14]

Keitel was the first to come forward. He took the several copies and quickly signed each of them with an air of disdain. As he returned to his seat, Friedeburg (who committed suicide two weeks later) and Stumpf walked to the table and signed. Zhukov and Tedder then signed as representatives of the Allies, and Spaatz and de Tassigny signed as witnesses.

"The German delegation may leave the hall," Zhukov announced. Keitel rose promptly, snapped to attention, rendered a salute with his baton, pivoted, and strode from the room, followed by the other German officers. As the door closed behind them, the tension suddenly broke, and those remaining in the hall heaved a collective sigh of relief. The war in Europe was now officially over.

After the Germans had filed out, Zhukov announced that the delegation would assemble again in about an hour for a victory celebration. "The banquet was one never to be forgotten," General Deane declares. "British-American-Soviet friendship was at its peak. Zhukov paid a glowing tribute to Eisenhower, characterizing him as 'the greatest military strategist of our time.' "[15] Moreover, Zhukov asserted, "General of the Army Eisenhower has given the most magnificent performance of any general of the current time. His great strides in the West helped me in the East."[16] The affair lasted until six o'clock that morning. General Deane writes that, upon his return to Moscow in the afternoon, his heart was warmed by the "spontaneous spirit of friendship being shown by thousands of Russian people in the square outside my window. I had great hopes for the future."[17]

It now remained for the Allied commanders to meet and draw up a basic proclamation announcing the formation of the Allied Control Council and assumption of joint responsibility for the administration of Germany.[18] On the eve of the council's organization, General Eisenhower shared his hopes for the future with Captain Butcher. Eisenhower, Butcher recalls, talked about the Soviet Union. He believed American and British relations with the U.S.S.R. were at about the same arm's-length stage which had marked American-British dealings early in the war. Later, as representatives of the two nations worked together, a common understanding developed, and they eventually became allies "in spirit as well as on paper." The more contact the Soviets had with Americans, Eisenhower felt, the more they would understand the United States and the greater would be their cooperation. The Soviets were blunt and forthright in their dealings, and any evasiveness aroused their suspicions. It should be possible to work with them, Eisenhower thought, if the United States followed the same pattern of friendly cooperation which had resulted in the outstanding record of Allied unity during the war, demonstrated first by the Allied Force Headquarters (AFHQ) and subsequently at the Supreme Headquarters of the Allied Expeditionary Forces (SHAEF).[19]

On May 30, President Roosevelt's special assistant Harry Hopkins sent word to Eisenhower that Stalin had appointed Georgi Zhukov the Soviet member of the Allied Control Council. The Americans interpreted the appointment to mean that a joint military government could be installed in Berlin without further delay. On June 5, therefore, General Eisenhower, General Lucius D. Clay, Robert Murphy, American political adviser for Germany, and others flew to Berlin to participate in the signing of the Declaration on the Assumption of Supreme Authority in Germany by the Allies and to take part in the organizational meeting of the Allied Control Council.

Eisenhower insisted on an exact time schedule, to be prepared in advance and accepted by all concerned, including the Soviets.[20] The American delegation arrived in Berlin on time, and since the meeting was not scheduled to begin until the middle of the afternoon, Eisenhower took the opportunity to call at Zhukov's headquarters and present him with the Legion of Merit, Chief Commander Grade, awarded him by the American government. "I thought Marshal Zhukov an affable and soldierly-appearing individual," Eisenhower writes.[21] Thus began a friendship between the two men which was to last for some time.

Nevertheless, on this particular day, unfortunate tensions were created by an irritating Russian delay in convening the meeting, at which Zhukov was to act as host. No explanation was forthcoming, and Eisenhower became increasingly restive and finally asked Robert Murphy: "What's going on here? Do you think these people are giving us the runaround?" Murphy asked his counterpart, Vishinsky, for an explanation and was told that one of the three proclamations which were on the agenda for that day contained a clause pledging the Big Three to intern Japanese within their respective jurisdictions. Since the Soviets were not yet at war with Japan, they could not publicly agree to such cooperation. "But this is an obvious error," Murphy told Vishinsky. "I am sure that General Eisenhower will agree to eliminate the clause without reference to Washington or London." Vishinsky merely replied that he must await word from the Soviet government. Murphy thought that he seemed embarrassed by the episode. Perhaps Vishinsky and Zhukov were being especially cautious because of the trouble stirred up when General Suslaparov signed the Reims surrender document.[22]

In midafternoon, word came from Moscow, and the three commanders in chief then assembled to sign the proclamations, followed by Zhukov's informal convening of the first meeting of the Big Three military governors in Berlin. Eisenhower requested an immediate effort toward establishing the Allied Control Council, adding that he wanted to leave Murphy and General Clay in Berlin for that purpose. After consulting with Vishinsky, Zhukov politely rejected the proposal, saying that each occupying power must withdraw its troops into its own zone before international controls could be put into operation. Thus the Americans were being asked to evacuate all portions of the Soviet Zone which they still held in Thuringia, Saxony, and Pomerania without any quid pro quo. Murphy again realized that Vishinsky, rather than Zhukov, was making all the political decisions, decisions of a nature which Eisenhower could and did make on his own authority. Since it was evident that Zhukov was not empowered to accept Eisenhower's proposal for immediate entry into Berlin, Eisenhower decided not to press the matter.[23]

Marshal Zhukov had arranged a lavish banquet for his guests, and he expected Eisenhower to delay his departure to participate in the celebration. The Soviets had spared no expense and had brought a number of their finest dancers, musicians, and entertainers. But, writes Murphy:

Eisenhower had not liked the whole procedure of the day and he insisted upon returning to Frankfurt with his entire staff at the scheduled hour.

Zhukov, amazed and uncomprehending, could not believe that Eisenhower was determined to leave. "I shall arrest you and make you stay!" he exclaimed jovially. But Eisenhower remained only long enough to drink the first toasts, explaining that he had not been informed about the dinner and had made other arrangements. On the way back to the airport, he graciously invited Zhukov to visit Allied Headquarters. So, feeling rather deflated, we came back to Frankfurt only a few hours after we had left. Eisenhower had an uneasy feeling that he had been pushed around, despite Zhukov's flamboyant hospitality and personal amiability, and the immediate outlook was confused.[24]

Murphy claims that the Soviets got everything they wanted at that first Eisenhower-Zhukov meeting. The three proclamations served Russian purposes admirably. Proclamation No. 1, which dissolved the last vestiges of the national German government, entrusted supreme authority in Germany to the commanders in chief of the victorious powers. Proclamation No. 2 stipulated that unanimous agreement among the victorious powers must be reached in matters affecting Germany as a whole, and in case unanimous agreement was not possible, each commander in chief would be supreme in his own zone. In effect, this proclamation gave each occupying power an absolute veto and resulted in the indefinite division of Germany between the zones of the Eastern and Western conquerors. Proclamation No. 3 fixed the boundaries of the zones and confirmed the London agreement that Berlin should be divided into sectors, each to be occupied by a victorious power. The third proclamation, together with the London protocols of September 12 and November 14, 1944, remains the chief legal basis for maintaining Western garrisons in Berlin.[25]

Just before Eisenhower left the meeting, Zhukov told him that he had just received a message from Stalin instructing him to confer upon Eisenhower and Field Marshal Montgomery the Russian Order of Victory. The award had never before been presented to a foreigner. Zhukov asked Eisenhower when he would like the decoration bestowed upon him, and Eisenhower suggested that Zhukov conduct the ceremony at his headquarters in Frankfurt. Zhukov agreed, and Montgomery said that, since he had served under Eisenhower's command throughout the European campaign, he too would like to receive his decoration at Eisenhower's headquarters.[26] When Zhukov arrived on June 10, a simple ceremony was held. Zhukov first decorated Eisenhower, then Montgomery. The Order of Victory, a platinum base covered with diamonds and rubies, impressed the few witnesses to the ceremony.

Deane believes that the United States bungled the presentation of awards to foreigners. Less than a week earlier, the American government had presented Zhukov with a Legion of Merit, hardly comparable to the Order of Victory. Rather late in the war American authorities decided that the highest decoration which could be given to foreigners was Chief Commander Grade of the Legion of Merit. The decision was not made, however, until several British officers had been presented with the more-coveted Distinguished Service Medal. Deane comments:

> The Russians set much store on decorations in general and are the greatest students in the world on the relative importance of each. They had presented Eisenhower with the "Order of Victory," their super-super award, and I suspect they were a little hurt when their leaders such as Zhukov, Konev, Rokossovsky, and Antonov were awarded something that was not considered by Americans to be the best they had in the bag.[27]

After the ceremony in Frankfurt a luncheon was held, during which toasts were raised to various leaders and the Allied victory. Marshal Zhukov first toasted General Eisenhower: "I want to raise a glass to General of the Army Eisenhower, due to whose abilities and talents the Allied armies attained their great and brilliant successes." He said that he had watched Eisenhower's brilliant campaigns "with amazement." He was especially impressed by the massive use of planes, artillery, tanks, and naval forces. He added:

> Our Soviet officers and generals are watching and studying all the operations that General Eisenhower has conducted. I personally, and the forces under my command, have the deepest respect for General Eisenhower, and I am expressing the hope that in the future work of the four Allied Commanders in the Control Council, that we will be just as unified in our future work. If we had good cooperation in time of war, I am sure that the same cooperation that was shown before will show itself in peace. I raise my glass to General Eisenhower—to his health, his success, and his future work.[28]

In reply, Eisenhower said that, although he raised his glass primarily to speak a word of admiration for Marshal Zhukov on behalf of the Allied forces, he was "going to wander a bit afield" before arriving at his final toast. He noted that Zhukov had praised him in extravagant terms, but, he said, his success had been due in part to skillful soldiers and diplomats who, realizing that only in unity is there strength, had subordinated themselves to his commands with perfect loyalty, "regardless of the claims made upon them from within their own countries." He declared that those who had fought now wanted peace and an opportunity for their peoples to live a little better:

> All of us who are right-thinking want the common man of all United Nations to have the opportunities that we fought to preserve for him. They want the opportunities that will let all nations that have been engaged in this war go forward together to greater prosperity—not for us, sitting around this table, but for the masses that we represent. That means peace. Speaking for the Allied forces, we are going to have peace if we have to fight for it.

He had, Eisenhower continued, met high Soviet officials and "in this basic desire" for peace had found them one with the Western Allies. "Regardless of the methods by which we arrive at that goal, that is what we are struggling for." Glancing around him, the general declared: "There is not a single man around this table that would not give back all the honors, all the publicity, and everything else that this war has brought to him if he could have avoided the misery and suffering and debt that have been brought to the populations by reason of this war." Yet, he noted, the war was a holy war, with forces of evil arrayed against those of righteousness. No matter what the cost, the war had to be won. Concluding his speech, Eisenhower heaped praise on Zhukov:

> To no one man do the United Nations owe a greater debt than to Marshal Zhukov. As our honored guest today he has come down and very courteously conferred certain honors of the Soviet Union upon members of the Allied forces. But Marshal Zhukov, a modest man, probably underrates the standing that he holds in our hearts and minds. One day, when all of us here at this board are gathered to our fathers, there is certain to be another order of the Soviet Union. It will be the Order of Zhukov, and that order will be prized by every man who admires courage, vision, fortitude, and determination in a soldier. Gentlemen, I deem it a very great honor to ask you to rise and drink to Marshal Zhukov.[29]

After Eisenhower had said farewell to Zhukov and his party, he looked back with satisfaction on the events of the day. Zhukov's friendliness and apparent sincerity had impressed the Americans in Frankfurt, and Eisenhower himself had great hopes for closer relations with the Russians, which might bring about a better world. He wrote:

> On the part of Zhukov and his assistants there was discernible only an intense desire to be friendly and cooperative. Looking back on it, that day still seems to have held nothing but bright promise for the establishment of cordial and close relations with the Russians. That promise, eventually lost in suspicion and recrimination, was never to be fulfilled. But so far as the friendly association between Marshal Zhukov and myself was concerned, it continued to grow until the moment I left Europe in November 1945. That friendship was a personal and individual thing and unfortunately was not representative of a general attitude.[30]

Four days after Eisenhower's visit to Berlin, Harry Hopkins stopped in Frankfurt on his way from Moscow to Washington. Robert Murphy recalls that "he was bubbling with enthusiasm about his meeting with Stalin, and his confidence in Soviet-American cooperation was impressive. With obvious sincerity Hopkins said to us in Frankfurt, 'We can do business with Stalin! He will cooperate!'"[31]

Hopkins described the concessions Stalin had supposedly made, and his optimism made Churchill's warnings about Soviet intentions seem exaggerated and possibly even hysterical. He told of his stop in Berlin on the way from Moscow, when the Soviets had been almost embarrassingly hospitable and had even allowed him to carry off some books from Hitler's private library. Hopkins' next comment was revealing. According to Murphy, Hopkins said that Vishinsky had answered political questions addressed to Zhukov, and it became obvious that

> no Russian military man, however high in rank, would have authority in political affairs. Hopkins said that Stalin frankly told him that Zhukov could decide only questions of military import. The Soviet dictator seemed more determined than Americans to observe the principle of military subordination to civilian authority. Hopkins said Stalin always was thinking of how Napoleon had run away with the French Revolution.[32]

Eisenhower was quite interested in this portion of Hopkins' remarks, since General George C. Marshall had insisted throughout the war that American field commanders must have supreme, over-all authority in their own combat theaters. "Roosevelt had supported this policy, even when decisions involved international affairs," Murphy writes.[33]

Eisenhower told Hopkins that he was determined to withdraw all American troops from the Soviet Zone as soon as possible, and Hopkins heartily approved. He also agreed that definite arrangements must be made to assure access to Berlin and promised to call this matter to the personal attention of the President and General Marshall as soon as he reached Washington. On June 14, President Truman sent a message to Stalin requesting that, in the program of mutual transfer of Soviet and American troops in Germany and Austria, provision be made for "free access for U.S. forces by air, road and rail to Berlin from Frankfurt and Bremen." Churchill sent a similar request, but when Stalin replied to both men, he made no mention of access. Both Washington and London must have assumed that unrestricted access to Berlin could be taken for granted. On June 25, Marshall sent Eisenhower's headquarters the draft of a proposed directive for troop transfers with this comment: "It will be noted that the proposed directive contains no action to obtain transit rights to Berlin and Vienna on a combined basis. . . . In accordance with the President's message to Stalin [June 14], these should be arranged with Russian commanders concerned simultaneously with arrangements for other adjustments." It appears, then, that Washington still regarded the access problem as a military detail to be worked out by Eisenhower and Zhukov.[34]

In the meantime, Eisenhower had flown to the United States to participate in victory celebrations across the country and take a well-deserved rest. He would not return to his Frankfurt headquarters until July 10, a week before the opening of the Potsdam Conference. In his absence General Clay laid the foundations for American military government in Germany.

One of Clay's first tasks was to settle the final details for the transfer to the Soviets of a large portion of Germany which had been seized by American troops in the final weeks of the war. On June 29 he flew to Berlin to confer with Zhukov. Unfortunately, he agreed to use only one railway and one highway to supply the American garrison in Berlin and did not obtain written assurances of access to Berlin at that time, while the Americans still controlled a large part of the Soviet Zone. Clay told Murphy that, since Zhukov was so reasonable about everything, it seemed best to assume, as the American and British governments had already done, that all the occupying powers would have unrestricted access to Berlin as soon as the occupation zones were firmly established.[35]

When the Western Allies moved in to occupy their individual sectors of Berlin in early July, 1945, there were some tense moments. The Russians seemed to be resisting transfer of half the German capital to their wartime partners. During the night of July 3–4, the British commander in Berlin, Major General L. O. Lyne, was summoned to Zhukov's headquarters and informed that a bridge on the highway assigned to the British was unsafe. Zhukov suggested that they might use the route allotted to the Americans. The main body of troops who were to occupy the British Sector was scheduled to move into the city on July 4, and careful plans had been drawn up for an impressive entry. General Lyne suspected that the Soviets were intentionally trying to divert the party at this late hour to cause disruption and confusion, and his strong protests to Marshal Zhukov induced the Soviet commander to restore permission to use the original route. Nevertheless, there was much delay in the move on the following day, and by evening the situation was still so unsatisfactory that General Lyne ordered Brigadier William R. N. Hinde to refuse to take over the military government of the British Sector the next day.[36]

On July 4, the day before the meeting of the Allied Control Council, the Americans prepared to occupy their sector. Colonel (later Brigadier General) Frank Howley received orders from the first American commandant of Berlin, Major General Floyd Parks, to occupy the American Sector, with its six boroughs and city halls, by midnight. As Howley was issuing the necessary orders to his military-government units, he received an urgent message from General Parks to report immediately to Parks's headquarters at Babelsberg. When he arrived, Parks handed him a note signed by Marshal Zhukov: "In view of the fact that Berlin is to be ruled by an Allied Kommandatura [Control Council] and that Kommandatura is not yet set up, your sector will not be turned over to you until the Kommandatura is set up." Howley saw in the note an attempt by the Soviets to gain time to finish looting the United States Sector before American troops moved in. He asked for permission to go ahead with Parks's earlier orders to occupy the American Sector according to the original agreement. Parks gave his permission, reminding him not to "get into too much trouble."

Howley moved in at daybreak, while the Soviets were still asleep. Each American detachment was responsible for one of the six boroughs.

The mayor of each borough gave up his house as headquarters for the United States Military Government, and the American flag was placed outside. When the Soviets awakened to find the Americans in possession of the United States Sector, they were quick to react. They sent an officer to each of the headquarters, informing the Americans that they must leave because Zhukov had ordered that they were not yet to take over their sector. The replies from all the headquarters were similar: "Your General Gorbatov gave a clearance to our general. Our general ordered us to come here, and here we shall remain. We are soldiers, as you are. Therefore, we obey our orders." The Soviets were stymied. They left. Friction worsened the next day. The Russians began tearing down American posters in the city. Further, they prevented the complete occupation of the American Sector until July 12, when they finally moved out, in some cases under compulsion.[37]

On July 7, General Clay and his British counterpart, General Ronald Weeks, met with Marshal Zhukov to make preliminary arrangements for the establishment of the Kommandatura. At the same time Zhukov undertook to prepare a charter to be considered at a subsequent meeting. The representatives of the three powers agreed that the date for the transfer of military-government responsibility within the British and American sectors should be decided by the Kommandatura itself when it met.[38]

Then Zhukov turned to other business. He announced to the American representatives: "Now, gentlemen, we will discuss the question of the food and coal you will supply for the maintenance of Berlin." This was the first word that the Americans were expected to feed and supply the fallen capital. SHAEF had earlier said that the task of feeding the Berliners was the responsibility of the Soviets, since they controlled Brandenburg and Pomerania, the two provinces which normally supplied food to the city. In addition, the Americans had just relinquished Thuringia and Saxony, two rich agricultural provinces.

General Clay replied to Zhukov: "It is not our plan to bring food into Berlin. For one thing we don't have food to bring in. Everything Berlin needs should come either from the territory we've just turned over to you, or from the surrounding areas of Brandenburg and northeast Pomerania, where it always has come from."

Zhukov said flatly: "Let's be realistic, gentlemen. What have you come for anyway? Let me tell you frankly, we are not going to supply food to Berlin. Our warehouses are almost exhausted. We must have food, and we must have it quickly."

General Clay was on the defensive. "There are difficulties of transportation and organization," he protested. "Even if we were willing to bring in food and coal, it would be difficult, because there is no big bridge across the Elbe."

Sokolovsky, sitting on Zhukov's right, asked pointedly: "What have you been doing since the Yalta Conference? Why don't you clean up the bridges and use them? That's what we do."

"We didn't realize the situation until a few days ago," Clay answered.

Sokolovsky commented, "It is unfortunate that these matters were not decided previously."

Clay pleaded that the American and British zones had no surplus food or coal. "I can give you mountains," he said, "but no coal."

Zhukov smiled but put an end to the dialogue. "What I want to know, gentlemen, is when you will start bringing in supplies. I think there should be no ambiguity in this arrangement."[39] Weeks and Clay replied that they would have to consult their governments on the matter.

Another meeting was held on July 10. The French were represented at this session and all future ones. Zhukov's charter was accepted, and it was decided that the Kommandatura would hold its first meeting the next day. Weeks and Clay had been informed by their governments that the responsibility for providing food and fuel to Berlin was to be discussed at the approaching Potsdam Conference. Meanwhile, they agreed —as a temporary measure and without prejudice to any decisions that might be reached at the conference—to provide wheat, potatoes, sugar, and salt for their respective sectors for one month, beginning on July 15. General Weeks also agreed to supply twenty-four hundred tons of coal daily for the city.[40]

The first meeting of the Kommandatura was held on July 11, and it was decided that the American and British commandants would assume responsibility for governing their sectors the following day. Despite occasional tensions which developed in these sessions, the warmth and sincerity of Zhukov and his chief assistants made a strong impression on many of the Americans and British. "It was different with their civil representatives," notes S. V. Donnison. "Perhaps the Russians felt this equally. After one meeting Marshal Zhukov said to General Weeks that he thought they had achieved a great deal. When General Weeks agreed, Marshal Zhukov added: 'I think we will go on achieving a great deal so long as the politicians keep out.' "[41]

The personal rapport which had been established between Eisenhower and Zhukov often served to ease strained relations among the occupiers of Berlin. The problem of the air corridor is a case in point. The Soviet authorities wrote the American Military Government frequent letters complaining about what they claimed to be unauthorized flights of American aircraft over Soviet-occupied Germany. The Soviets had authorized the Allies to use a narrow corridor for flights in and out of Berlin, and aircraft were not to venture out of it. Sometimes in bad weather or under other circumstances an American plane would violate the corridor's limits. The Soviets periodically submitted a detailed list of these alleged violations, always in such numbers that investigation of specific instances was impossible. Finally General Eisenhower visited Zhukov and told him that he thought the violations were too inconsequential to cause so much attention. Zhukov agreed that they were minor matters but said that Moscow heard of each violation from anti-aircraft units not under his command, and he was required to request a reply from Eisenhower's headquarters. Eisenhower saw this as another example of Soviet overcentralization, but he told Zhukov to keep sending the complaints and he would continue to send the same stereotyped answers. Zhukov replied that this was satisfactory with him.[42]

General Walter Bedell Smith, Eisenhower's chief of staff, has summed up very well the strange mixture of friendly feelings and polite distance between the Soviets and Americans at that time:

> Our principal contacts were with Marshal Zhukov and General Sokolovsky, both of whom we admired very much, and who, I felt, would be great men in any country. These two, and their principal subordinates, impressed us not only by their ability, but by their frank and straightforward attitude. In spite of the language barrier—and it is very difficult to feel close to a man whom you can only address through an interpreter—we believed that we had reached with them an honest basis of mutual confidence and understanding.

> Marshal Zhukov was obviously sincere in his statement that world peace depended entirely upon the ability of the Russians and the Americans to continue and to perpetuate the cooperation and understanding which they had reached during the course of the war. However, despite the warm feelings which we entertained toward Marshal Zhukov and General Sokolov-

sky, and which we felt were reciprocated, there still was an arm's length between us in our dealings. . . . We had no informal opportunities to meet as friends and come to know each other well. Our contacts were on the official level—whether transacting business or participating in social functions.[43]

Problems of a postwar settlement in Europe and the surrender of Japan brought the Allies together in July. Zhukov writes in his memoirs that Berlin was considered for the site of the conference, but he told a group of security men from the Soviet Union that "the conditions in Berlin were not appropriate for convening a conference of the heads of state. I proposed that they acquaint themselves with the area of Potsdam and Babelsberg." Soviet officials approved Zhukov's recommendation, as did the British and the Americans, and Zhukov's engineers began working around the clock preparing the buildings and roadways. By July 10 everything was ready.

On July 13 and 14 the Soviet delegation, including advisers and experts, arrived in Potsdam. Among them were Chief of the General Staff Antonov, Naval Chief Kuznetsov, representatives from the Commissariat of Foreign Affairs Vishinsky, Gromyko, Maysky, and K. V. Novikov. On July 16 a special train was to arrive with Stalin, Molotov, and members of their staffs. On the evening before, Stalin telephoned Zhukov: "Don't get it in your head to meet us with an honor guard and band. Come to the station yourself and bring with you anyone you consider necessary." The next day Zhukov went to the station with Vyshinsky, Antonov, Kuznetsov, Telegin, Sokolovsky, M. S. Malinin, and several other military men.

"I met Stalin near his car," Zhukov recalls. "He was in good spirits. He approached the group meeting him and gave a greeting with a short raising of the arm." After looking around the station, he slowly got into the car, and then, again opening the door, he invited Zhukov to ride with him. Along the way he asked about the preparations for opening the conference.

When he arrived at the villa where he was to stay, Stalin asked who had been its former owner. He was told it had belonged to General Erich Ludendorff. "Stalin," Zhukov notes, "did not like an excess of furniture. After making the rounds of the premises, he asked that the excess furniture be removed."

On the same day Winston Churchill and President Harry Truman arrived in Potsdam, and the two leaders paid a visit to Stalin. The next morning he returned their visit.[44]

The conference opened the afternoon of July 17. It was scheduled to last until August 2. President Truman brought with him Secretary of State James F. Byrnes; Joseph E. Davies, former ambassador to Russia; Fleet Admiral William D. Leahy; and Truman's interpreter, Charles Bohlen. Prime Minister Churchill was accompanied by Anthony Eden, Clement Attlee, and several others.[45]

Toward the end of July the delegates adjourned for several days. When the conference resumed, Churchill and Eden were no longer members of the British delegation. Their party had suffered a defeat in the elections, and Clement Attlee had become prime minister. Ernest Bevin was the new foreign minister. Although Truman regarded this event as a dramatic demonstration of peaceful change under democracy, the conference would not be the same without the wisdom and experience of Winston Churchill.

At Potsdam it was agreed that Germany should be administered as a unit by the Allied Control Council in Berlin. Germany was to be decentralized, de-Nazified, and demilitarized, but beyond those goals the council's mission was vague. The issue of reparations was not settled, but each power was authorized to satisfy its own demands from its zone of occupation. The Soviet Union and Poland were to receive 10 per cent of the war-industry equipment in the French, British, and American zones. The Soviet Union was to assume control over Königsberg and part of East Prussia, while Poland was to take over the remainder of East Prussia and "administer" a large region each of the Oder–Neisse line. The big powers agreed to a mass, "humane" deportation of Germans from Poland, Czechoslovakia, and Hungary, a process which in fact would be far from humane.

On two occasions during the conference the Japanese secretly asked Stalin to mediate in concluding peace in the Pacific, but the Soviet leader rejected both overtures before informing Churchill and Truman about them.[46] He obviously wanted Soviet troops to enter the war against Japan (though Russia had signed a neutrality pact with that country in April, 1941). There were Far East territories he planned to annex.

In a lighter vein, Zhukov tells the story of a round of toasts after one of the sessions: "Absolutely unexpectedly Churchill proposed a toast to me. There was nothing left for me to do except to propose a toast in reply. Thanking Churchill for this courtesy extended to me, I inadvertently called him 'comrade.' At that moment I noticed a bewildered expression on V. M. Molotov's face, and several appeared embarrassed. Improvising, I proposed a toast to comrades-in-arms, our allies in this war—soldiers, officers and generals of the armies of the anti-Fascist coalition, who had so brilliantly completed the defeat of Fascist Germany. Thus, I didn't commit an error. The next day, when I was with Stalin, he and all those present laughed about the fact that I had quickly acquired a 'comrade' in the person of Churchill."[47]

In June Eisenhower had been invited to visit the Soviet Union, but he had to decline because of the trip to the United States. Back in Europe, in the first week of August, he heard from Washington that Stalin had sent another invitation and that the American government hoped he would accept. Stalin suggested that Eisenhower arrive in Moscow in time to attend the National Sports Parade on August 12. The American commander promptly accepted and learned that Marshal Zhukov would accompany him to Moscow and act as his official host during his stay.

Upon his arrival in Moscow, Eisenhower was quartered in Spasso House, the ambassador's residence, with his friend W. Averell Harriman. His first conference was with General Antonov, Red Army chief of staff, who took him into the war room and explained the disposition of the Soviet armies in the Far East and plans for the campaign there.[48]

The day of the parade arrived, and Eisenhower and his party made their way to Red Square. The Soviet press, apparently following the Party line that too much emphasis must not be placed on the general's importance, had printed only a brief announcement of his presence in Moscow. But as Eisenhower walked to the reviewing stand on that Sunday morning, the crowds broke out in spontaneous cheering which followed him the entire distance to the stand. "It takes some sort of spontaneous combustion," wrote General Deane of this event, "to highlight the differences between the Party line and the will of the people, and it is only occasionally that one is aware that differences do exist."[49]

About twenty thousand people were on hand to watch the parade. Everyone had to stand for the performance, and the American ambassador and his party were allotted a raised section of concrete at the stadium. Just after the Americans arrived, General Antonov came to Eisenhower with an invitation from Stalin to join him in his viewing stand atop Lenin's tomb. "The Generalissimo says that if you would like to come he also invites two of your associates, if you would like to bring them," Antonov said. Harriman quickly informed Eisenhower that this was a precedent-setting courtesy—that he had never known of a foreigner being invited to set foot on top of the tomb. The general accepted the invitation and asked Ambassador Harriman and General Deane, military chief of the mission, to accompany him.

The group stood atop the tomb for five hours, during which time Stalin and Eisenhower conversed intermittently through an interpreter. Stalin repeated several times that it was necessary for the Soviet Union and the United States to remain friends. He also stressed that there was much the American people could do to help the U.S.S.R. "At that time," Eisenhower wrote, "Marshal Zhukov was patently a great favorite with the Generalissimo. Zhukov was included in every conversation I had with Stalin and the two spoke to each other on terms of intimacy and cordiality. This was highly pleasing to me because of my belief in the friendliness and cooperative purpose of Marshal Zhukov."[50]

When Stalin mentioned the work of the Allied Control Council, Eisenhower decided to urge for more authority for the Russian representatives. The problem had weighed heavily on his mind since the council's inception and stemmed from the unwillingness of the Soviet government to allow Zhukov to make any independent decisions. He frequently seemed to be in agreement with some proposal of local importance, but he could never answer on his own authority.

Eisenhower knew that everything he and his associates did was reported instantly to the Soviet capital, and he knew, too, that "national pride would impel the Russians to watch the comparative prestige and authority of their Berlin representative." So he adopted a simple plan: to make Zhukov aware, whenever possible, that Washington accorded to him, Eisenhower, a degree of independence in dealing with all matters which did not run counter to fixed policy. When he had anything to discuss with Zhukov, he made it a point to see him just before or just after a formal meeting of the Allied Control Council. He then outlined the suggestion and placed it before Zhukov in the form of a definite proposal. With this he would remark: "If this project looks well to you, I am ready to put it into effect whenever you say. If you want some time for study, or if you would like to refer the matter to Moscow, I am quite content to await your answer. But I am ready to act instantly." Once or twice, Eisenhower wrote, Zhukov was prompted to ask, "What will your government say about this?" To which Eisenhower replied, "If I sent such small details to Washington for decision I would be fired and my government would get someone who would handle these things himself."

Whether this personal campaign had any effect Eisenhower did not know, but he observed that Zhukov began to evince a greater independence at the meetings. "He discarded the practice of keeping his political adviser by his side and he would meet with no one present except an interpreter. Moreover, he became much more prone to say yes or no to a proposal than merely to ask for a delay in order to consider it."[51]

Now, in Moscow, atop Lenin's tomb, when Stalin mentioned the council, Eisenhower decided to continue his campaign to secure more powers for Zhukov. He said to the generalissimo:

Of course Marshal Zhukov and I get along splendidly. This is because great and powerful countries like yours and mine can afford to give their proconsuls in the field a sufficient amount of authority to achieve accord in local details and administrative matters. Smaller or weaker countries might possibly find it impossible to do this and difficulties would arise. But because Marshal Zhukov and I have such great leeway in reaching agreement we two usually overcome the little obstacles we encounter.

Stalin agreed with Eisenhower emphatically, saying, "There is no sense in sending a delegate somewhere if he is merely to be an errand boy. He must have authority to act."[52]

After the parade had ended and Eisenhower and Zhukov prepared to leave, the crowd gave them a noisy ovation. Then Eisenhower threw his arm over Zhukov's shoulder, and the burly marshal responded by embracing Eisenhower. With that, pandemonium broke loose, and the two leaders stood for some time waving to the screaming crowd. The only way they could end the demonstration was by leaving the box, and after about ten minutes they did so. "There was nothing rehearsed about this," asserts General Deane, "and it had nothing to do with ideologies or political aspirations. It was a sincere demonstration by a representative cross-section of the Russian people of their affection for the American people as embodied in Eisenhower. It was heart-warming and reassuring to us Americans who were there."[53]

The next day Eisenhower and Zhukov visited a collective farm outside

Moscow. The American general's familiarity with farming and his interest in it enhanced his popularity with the Soviet farmers. When the two men left, they returned to Spasso House, and Eisenhower invited Zhukov to lunch. No Soviet official was allowed to accept invitations to homes of foreigners without approval by higher authority, and Zhukov was caught in an embarrassing situation. Since he could not bear to tell Eisenhower that he would have to get permission, he went on in and had lunch with his friend. General Deane remarked that "Eisenhower has never achieved a greater victory and I hope he fully appreciates it."[54]

After lunch the two commanders had a friendly debate about the pros and cons of freedom of the press. Zhukov was not impressed by the American position. He was, Deane writes, "the product of generations that had never known individual freedom of any sort, and to him no argument could justify an individual expressing sentiments or thoughts either in writing or orally that were opposed to the interests of the state."[55]

Eisenhower and Zhukov spent the next few days visiting various points of interest. While they were attending a reception given by Ambassador Harriman, the news of Japan's surrender arrived. World War II was over.

Zhukov accompanied Eisenhower and the general's son, John, a young army lieutenant who had come to Moscow with his father, to Leningrad. At a luncheon in their honor Marshal Zhukov called upon John to propose a toast. The lieutenant rose to his feet and spoke: "I have been in Russia several days and have listened to many toasts. I have heard the virtues of every Allied ruler, every prominent marshal, general, admiral, and air commander toasted. I have yet to hear a toast to the most important Russian in World War II. Gentlemen, will you please drink with me to the common soldier of the great Red Army." Eisenhower commented that his son's toast "was greeted with greater enthusiasm and shouts of approval than any other I heard during the days when we heard so many." Marshal Zhukov was especially pleased and remarked to Eisenhower that they both must be getting old when they had to wait for a young lieutenant to remind them "who really won the war."[56]

Eisenhower's visit drew to a close, and Zhukov accompanied him back to Berlin. The flight to Germany was extremely enlightening to Eisenhower, and doubtless to Zhukov as well. What Eisenhower learned helped shed light on the Russian conduct of the war:

> Because of his special position for several years in the Red Army he had had a longer experience as a responsible leader in great battles than any other man of our time. It seems that he was habitually sent to whatever Russian sector appeared at the moment to be the decisive one. By his descriptions of the composition of the Russian Army, of the terrain over which it fought, and of his reasons for his strategic decisions, it was clear that he was an accomplished soldier.[57]

The two leaders discussed the strength of combat units. American divisions were maintained, Zhukov learned, at a strength of seventeen thousand men. The marshal said that Soviet divisions tried to keep their numbers at about eight thousand but that during a long campaign some were depleted to three or four thousand men.

Zhukov described to Eisenhower the Soviet method of attacking through minefields. The German minefields, always covered by defensive fire, had caused many casualties among the Allied armies. Zhukov told Eisenhower that when Red Army troops approached a minefield they moved forward exactly as if it were not there, Soviet theory being that losses from antipersonnel mines would be no greater than those which would have been inflicted by machine guns and artillery if the enemy had chosen to defend the area with troops. When the infantrymen had passed through a mined area, they established a bridgehead, after which combat engineers cleared out the vehicular mines.

The differences between American and Soviet views on war were immediately apparent to Eisenhower: Americans assess the cost of war in terms of human lives, while the Soviets are concerned with the over-all drain on the nation. To Eisenhower, Zhukov appeared to have little concern for methods, considered important by Americans, of maintaining morale: rotation of units, passes, furloughs, recreational facilities, and, most important of all, avoidance of unnecessary battlefield risks. The marshal felt, however, that the destruction of the enemy's morale must always be a goal of the high command.

Zhukov showed complete unconcern for Russian soldiers who had been captured. "What did you care," he asked, "about men the Germans had captured? They had surrendered and could not fight any more."[58] Nor did he show much interest in measures to protect the foot soldier, such as getting him into battle without the fatigue of long, exhausting marches. He viewed such measures as too costly. The Soviets seemed to think that great victories inevitably require high casualties, Eisenhower concluded.

After Eisenhower returned to Germany, he received President Truman's approval to invite Marshal Zhukov to the United States. Zhukov promptly accepted and asked that General Clay or General Eisenhower accompany him to America. Because of pressing circumstances Eisenhower was not able to make the trip, and Zhukov asked that the general's son, John, go along as an aide. Eisenhower told him that John would be honored to serve in this capacity and his own C-54, the *Sunflower*, would be placed at the marshal's disposal. Zhukov had confidence in the C-54, for he had flown in it across the U.S.S.R. "With the general's plane and the general's son along, I know I shall be perfectly safe," he remarked.

About this time Zhukov fell ill. Many expressed doubt that he was actually sick, speculating that it was a "diplomatic illness." However, when Eisenhower saw him later at an Allied Control Council meeting in Berlin, he noticed that Zhukov appeared to have indeed suffered a serious illness. The marshal's visit to the United States was postponed, and since winter was approaching, he expressed a desire to go in the spring. By then, however, the Soviets had no further interest in sending him to the United States.

General Eisenhower saw Marshal Zhukov for the last time that year on November 7, 1945, at a reception in Berlin given by the marshal in honor of the twenty-eighth anniversary of the Bolshevik Revolution. When he arrived, he found Zhukov, the marshal's wife, and a number of aides standing in the receiving line. As soon as Zhukov had greeted Eisenhower, he left the line. He, his wife, an interpreter, and Eisenhower retired to another room, where, over refreshments, they talked for two hours.

The marshal said he believed that he and Eisenhower were helping promote mutual understanding between two nations so politically and culturally different. But still more could be done. "If the United States and Russia," he said, "will only stand together through thick and thin, success is certain for the United Nations. If we are partners there are no other countries in the world that would dare to go to war when we forbade it."[59] Zhukov reaffirmed his belief in Communism. As he saw it, the Soviet system of government was based upon idealism, the American system upon materialism. Eisenhower recalls:

> In expanding his idea of this difference he remarked—and introduced an apology because of his criticism—that he felt our system appealed to all that was selfish in people. He said that we induced a man to do things by telling him he might keep what he earned, might say what he pleased, and in every direction allowed him to be largely an undisciplined, unoriented entity within a great national complex.
>
> He asked me to understand a system in which the attempt was made to substitute for such motivations the devotion of a man to the great national complex of which he formed a part. In spite of my complete repudiation of such contentions and my condemnation of all systems that involved dictatorship, there was no doubt in my mind that Marshal Zhukov was sincere.[60]

Another matter brought up during the conversation put Eisenhower on the defensive. Walter Kerr, an American correspondent in Moscow during the war, had written that Zhukov's wife was taller than her husband and that the couple had two sons and a daughter.[61] "This story," according to Eisenhower, "irritated him because he saw in it personal disparagement and belittlement. He and his wife stood up for a moment and he said, 'Now you see what kind of lies some of your writers publish about us. Also, we have no sons. We have two daughters.' "[62]

Zhukov also told Eisenhower about an undignified picture of Stalin which had appeared in an American magazine. "If a picture of you like this one should appear in a Russian magazine," fumed the marshal, "I would see that the magazine ceased operations at once. It would be eliminated. What are you going to do?" General Eisenhower explained about the American free press but seemed to make no impression on Zhukov, who said, "If you are Russia's friend you will do something about it." Eisenhower could only expound the virtues of free enterprise, saying that state ownership would involve dictatorship. The desire to escape dictatorial rule was responsible for America's founding and growth, Eisenhower concluded. Zhukov only smiled.[63] The two men said good-by. They would not meet again for nearly ten years.

The friendship of the two wartime leaders did not eliminate the incidents, problems, conflicts, and irritations attending the occupation of Berlin. But for a glorious moment in history there was hope that the two world powers might somehow rise above their differences and that "on earth peace, good will toward men" might become a reality.

XIII. OBSCURITY . . . AND REAPPEARANCE

To the subscriber of the Bolshaya Sovetskaya Entsiklopediya: The State Scientific Press . . . recommends that you remove from the fifth volume of the encyclopedia pages 21, 22, 23, and 24, as well as the portrait inserted between pages 22 and 23, exchanging them with the pages with a new text which are being sent to you. With scissors or razor blade the pages indicated should be cut out, preserving part of the inside margin, on which the new pages can be pasted.

> Instructions issued to the subscribers to the encyclopaedia after Beria's arrest in 1953. Beria's biography was replaced with an article on the Bering Sea and other items.

THE year 1945 drew to a close, and the new year seemed to hold even more promise for Georgi Zhukov. On the front page of the January 1 issue of *Krasnaya Zvezda* (*Red Star*) appeared a large, flattering drawing of a uniformed Stalin. On his right and slightly behind him was a broadly smiling Zhukov. On Stalin's left was Voroshilov, flanked by Rokossovsky, Konev, Budenny, Timoshenko, and others.

On January 2 meetings were held throughout the country to select candidates for deputies of the Supreme Soviet. The workers and engineers of the Rubezhnoye Chemical Combine, the locomotive-repair plant in Lvov, and the farmers of the Krasny Ostrov Collective Farm in the Moscow Province nominated Georgi Zhukov. Those who put forward his name took note of his outstanding wartime services. Headlines proclaimed that "the Soviet people with joy and enthusiasm nominate their best sons and candidates to the Supreme Soviet of the U.S.S.R.," including, besides Zhukov, Stalin, Molotov, M. I. Kalinin, Beria, Malenkov, A. I. Mikoyan, Zhdanov, A. A. Andreev, L. M. Kaganovich, Khrushchev, N. M. Shvernik, Voznesensky, Vasilevsky, Bulganin, A. I. Pokryshkin, S. I. Vavilov, and A. G. Sereginoy. The next day more nominations were announced, including such well-known military figures as Rokossovsky, Konev, Meretskov, Bagramyan, Admiral N. G. Kuznetsov, and Marshal of Aviation Novikov.[1]

Zhukov, the wartime symbol of victory, was second only to Stalin in popularity. A nominating speech by an engineer in the State Optical Plant expressed the feelings of Russians everywhere:

> The Soviet people know well the famous military leader Marshal Georgi Konstantinovich Zhukov. His name is connected with many celebrated victories of the Red Army.
>
> . . . Now, when the day has arrived, giving us the right to put forth our candidate for the deputies of the Supreme Soviet, we naturally paused on the name of one of those closest to us, one of the most worthy representatives of the people.[2]

Other individuals at the plant spoke on the nomination. Support for Zhukov also came in from "N" units (a designation used for security reasons) of the Red Army.[3]

In the next few weeks *Krasnaya Zvezda* was filled with articles on the approaching elections. There were more than sufficient reminders that Stalin was the chief architect of World War II victories and that the military chieftains had simply carried out his plans. As military nominations came in, front-page articles provided the proper mood, with such article titles as: "The Genius of Stalin Gave Us Victory"; and "Beloved

Leader, Teacher, Military Chieftain." Readers were not to forget that "the Great Stalin led us to victory."[4]

Zhukov's name also appeared in many issues, and it was announced on January 9 and 10 that Special Election District No. 660 had registered Zhukov as a candidate to the Soviet of the Union, one of the two chambers of the Supreme Soviet.[5] On January 24 a long biographical sketch was reproduced in *Krasnaya Zvezda*, describing the commander of the Soviet occupation forces in Germany as the hero of Khalkhin-Gol, Elnya, Leningrad, Moscow, Warsaw, and Berlin. Now the "remarkable military chief of the Stalin school has been selected as a candidate for the Supreme Soviet."[6] A few days later Zhukov met with voters of Special Election District No. 660. He probably enjoyed the occasion. Heroes of the war praised him in speeches and applauded him with cries of "Ura!" Zhukov spoke, saying that the Soviet Union, which had played a decisive role in defeating the Germans, now must take the lead in the struggle for peace. He appealed especially to the veterans in his audience to work for the Soviet Union, for peace, and for the security of freedom-loving peoples.[7]

The elections were held on February 10, 1946, and the results were announced on February 14: "A victory for the Stalinist bloc of Communists and non-Party members." Zhukov was the victor from Special Election District No. 660. The list of winners[8] from such districts pointed up that they were representing military units, probably military districts and groups of forces.*

The newly selected Supreme Soviet met in Moscow on March 18, and Zhukov left his post in Berlin to attend. He posed for cameramen with two other deputies of the Supreme Soviet: Guards Colonel Pokryshkin and Guards Major I. N. Kozhedub. These three men were the only three-time winners of the Hero of the Soviet Union award.[9]

On April 10, Zhukov again left Berlin, this time to become commander of all Soviet ground forces.[10] On May Day he appeared atop Lenin's tomb with other military and political leaders.[11] A few weeks later, on May 25, he attended a reception honoring a Polish delegation headed

* The list of winners from the special election districts numbered twenty-six and included other well-known military leaders, among them Antonov, Batov, S. S. Biryuzov, Voronov, Konev, Rokossovsky, and Chuikov. Soviet forces outside the Soviet Union are designated "groups": the Northern Group of Forces (Poland), Southern Group of Forces (Hungary), Central Group of Forces (Czechoslovakia, as of 1968), and Group of Soviet Forces—Germany (East Germany).

by President Boleslaw Bierut.[12] Then, suddenly, in July, *Pravda* announced that Zhukov had been transferred to the Odessa Military District,[13] a relatively unimportant post.

Speculation and rumors were rife: (1) Zhukov had fallen from Stalin's grace; (2) he had become a troubleshooter for the Soviet High Command; (3) he had assumed the capacity of adviser to the Chinese Communists in their conquest of China; (4) he had clashed with Bulganin and lost; (5) he had been ousted because of Inspector General L. A. Govorov's dislike for him; (6) he had been sent to Odessa to prepare an imminent march against Iran, the Middle East, Greece; and so on. There were some who insisted no "disgrace" was involved. But any doubts about that were dispelled in November, 1957, when Zhukov said: "I could not admit and did not admit my *expulsion* from the Central Committee [in 1946] as being correct."[14]

It remains for us to speculate why he was in disfavor for those six or seven years. Dwight D. Eisenhower wrote in 1952:

> One of the speculative reasons given for his virtual disappearance was his known friendship with me. I cannot believe that such was the case because, in spite of that friendship, he always seemed to be profoundly convinced of the essential rectitude of the Communist theory. He knew that I was an uncompromising foe of Communism because I believed it was synonymous with dictatorship; he would listen patiently when I said that I hated everything that smacked of statism, and that our whole Western tradition was devoted to the idea of personal liberty. But his own adherence to the Communistic doctrine seemed to come from inner conviction and not from any outward compulsion.[15]

Yuri A. Rastvorov, a former lieutenant colonel in Soviet intelligence, has claimed that Zhukov had become increasingly derisive about Stalin's insistence on crediting the war victories to his own military genius. According to Rastvorov, the secret police brought Stalin word of Zhukov's comments, and the marshal was jerked up before a Party commission. He was roughly handled by the chairman, who contemptuously addressed him as "ty," the familiar form of "you," generally used when speaking to inferiors. "The credit for our victory," shouted the chairman, "does not belong to you, but to the Party and its leaders!" Zhukov was thereupon demoted to the Odessa Military District.[16]

Nikita Khrushchev substantiated the view that Stalin was jealous of Zhukov and wanted the glory of World War II victories for himself.

Speaking before the Twentieth Communist Party Congress held in Moscow on February 24–25, 1956, Khrushchev said:

> All the more shameful was the fact that after our great victory over the enemy which cost us so much, Stalin began to downgrade many of the commanders, who contributed so much to the victory over the enemy, because Stalin excluded every possibility that services rendered at the front should be credited to anyone but himself.
>
> Stalin was very much interested in the assessment of Comrade Zhukov as a military leader. He asked me often for my opinion of Zhukov. I told him then, "I have known Zhukov for a long time; he is a good general and a good military leader."
>
> After the war Stalin began to tell all kinds of nonsense about Zhukov, among others the following: "You have praised Zhukov, but he does not deserve it. It is said that before each operation at the front Zhukov used to behave as follows: he used to take a handful of earth, smell it and say, 'We can begin the attack' or the opposite, 'the planned operation cannot be carried out.'" I stated at that time, "Comrade Stalin, I do not know who invented this, but it is not true."
>
> It is possible that Stalin himself invented these things for the purpose of minimizing the role and military talents of Marshal Zhukov.[17]

Later Khrushchev affirmed that "I did not disguise my admiration for Zhukov after the war when he fell out of favor with Stalin."[18]

Colonel G. I. Antonov, who served with Zhukov, gives several reasons for the marshal's fate. First, in the entire period of his dictatorship Stalin never tolerated around him people in the Party ranks who were very popular, as Zhukov had undoubtedly become. Stalin's position as generalissimo and Party-recognized inspirer of victory in World War II was not to be threatened. Moreover, it is possible that Stalin seemed to see the ghosts of the Red Army leaders he had annihilated—Tukhachevsky, Uborovich, Yegorov, Yakir, and others—standing dimly behind Zhukov. Perhaps other political motives forced Stalin to push his yesterday's favorite into the background. Nor can one exclude the possibility that the secret dissatisfaction and jealousy of other Red Army marshals and generals played some kind of role, for they, too, had distinguished themselves in the war. Little about them was officially remembered, and most victories were attributed only to Zhukov.* Whatever the cause,

---

* In this observation Antonov was not accurate. Zhukov usually shared the honor with a group of military leaders. And always the military leaders were credited with carrying out the orders of the genius Stalin.

there is no question that Antonov was right when he wrote: "It can be asserted with full certainty that Zhukov was for some period of time in disgrace."[19]

Another possible reason for Zhukov's fall from grace, not mentioned by Antonov, was his continued campaign to lessen the Party's role in the army. Stalin had yielded to Zhukov during the war and disposed of the commissars. By 1946, the Soviet dictator, no longer needing Zhukov to fight his wars, probably found the marshal's attitude toward Party hacks intolerable. As Malcolm Mackintosh writes in his history of the Red Army:

> Stalin showed his bitter jealousy of the man who had done more than any other soldier to hold the Soviet Army together during the worst years of the war. . . . Marshal Zhukov's removal was designed to frighten the military leadership into absolute obedience. In this it succeeded: from late 1946 to 1953 the Soviet Army High Command was paralyzed by fear of Stalin and the NKVD.[20]

Odessa was Zhukov's home for two or three years. Only bits of news about his life during this period made their way out of the country. Then he was abruptly transferred to a still more obscure post.

The reasons for his transfer are unknown, but rumor has it that they stemmed from a long-standing antagonism between Zhukov and Marshal L. A. Govorov. When Zhukov was sent to Leningrad during the siege, he and Govorov, who was soon to become commander of the Leningrad *Front*, clashed over some detail of the defense. Govorov nourished his resentment about the disagreement and avenged himself after the war, when he was named inspector of the Soviet armed forces. Govorov's duties included inspecting units of his choosing, to check on political as well as military preparedness, and reporting his findings to the defense minister for action. Govorov led an inspection tour of the Odessa Military District. The report he turned in is said to have been very unfavorable, and Zhukov was soon transferred to a post in the Ural Mountains.[21]

This story may or may not be true, but there is no doubt that Zhukov's banishment to the Urals signified deep disgrace. From that time only occasional references to him were to be found in the Soviet press. On December 31, 1948, *Krasnaya Zvezda* noted briefly that the marshal had attended graduation exercises at Voroshilov Military Academy.[22]

It must have been a period of bitterness and frustration for Zhukov. Kyrill D. Kalinov, who defected to the West in 1949, reports a conversation he had early the same year with Colonel Tulpanov, a propaganda chief. Tulpanov told him that Zhukov wanted to leave the service. His reasons were threefold: the silence imposed on him about his military accomplishments, nervous tension brought on by constant secret-police checks, and the absence of any private life.[23]

The few clues to Zhukov's activities during this period are mostly negative ones. By January, 1950, his name had been dropped from the election lists—the same lists in which his name had earlier appeared as chief military candidate. Although Zhukov appeared in Moscow occasionally while Bulganin was minister of defense, his position continued to worsen. On Stalin's orders his portraits were removed from all army garrisons.[24] And General Eisenhower heard nothing directly from him for a long time.[25]

When the Korean War broke out in June, 1950, the slow reemergence of Marshal Zhukov began. He reportedly attended a meeting of the Supreme Soviet that month, and it was rumored that he advised the Chinese Communist forces in their winter offense of 1950 from a secret headquarters in Mukden. Several broadcasts reported that Zhukov met with Mao Tse-tung, Kim Il Sung, and other high-ranking Chinese and North Korean leaders, perhaps to determine the degree to which Russia would involve herself militarily in the Korean War.[26]

In 1950 and 1951, Zhukov was permitted several public appearances. At the Nineteenth Party Congress an unprecedented number of senior professional officers were made members of the Party's Central Committee, and twenty-six marshals, generals, and admirals were given candidate status. Zhukov was among those selected as a candidate member.[27]

Unrest in the satellite nations sent Zhukov and Molotov to Warsaw to address the seventh-anniversary celebration of the Polish Communist government. Zhukov delivered a speech praising the Polish army. Nine days later nine high Polish army officers were arrested and charged with spying for the United States. Zhukov was said to have figured in the incident. Then the marshal disappeared again for another year.[28]

In the early 1950's, Stalin must have become convinced that his ill-treatment of the military cadres was damaging Soviet national security and over-all defensive readiness. When the United States hastened to develop its military power as a result of the Korean War, the Soviet dictator also apparently became convinced that his tactics of aggression in foreign policy should give way to more subtle moves. Therefore, in 1952 he tooks steps to put to better use Soviet military resources, including the wealth of personal combat experience and leadership of his officers.[29] Writes Mackintosh:

> First among these changes was Marshal Zhukov's half-concealed but definite return to active duty with the High Command. Exactly when or why this occurred is impossible to say; but it seems certain that Stalin decided to use Zhukov's unmatched experience within the High Command rather than continue to waste it in the Ural Military District.[30]

Zhukov reemerged from obscurity in the summer of 1952 to assume two posts, those of deputy defense minister and of inspector general. He probably returned to Moscow when his friend Sokolovsky replaced General Shtemenko as chief of the General Staff.

For some time it was believed that Shtemenko was removed from his post in February, 1953, but it now appears that Sokolovsky replaced him in June, 1952. *Bolshaya Sovetskaya Entsiklopediya* says that Sokolovsky assumed the post in 1952.[31] A book published in 1968, *50 Let Vooruzhennykh Sil SSSR (50 Years of the Armed Forces of the U.S.S.R.)*, cited by Chief of the General Staff Marshal Matvei V. Zakharov, confirms that General Shtemenko held the position from November, 1948, until May, 1952, and that Sokolovsky succeeded him, leaving his post as first deputy minister of defense in June of that year. Interestingly, Zakharov does not say who was first deputy minister of defense from June, 1952, to March, 1953, when both Zhukov and Vasilevsky were appointed to the position.[32] One can only speculate that the appointment was not confirmed by Stalin, who was ill and was to pass from the scene on March 5, 1953.

Certainly Zhukov was coming back into favor, albeit slowly and almost secretly. In August, 1952, he went to Prague for the annual meeting of the Military Coordination Board of the Soviet Bloc.[33] His name was occasionally mentioned in obituaries of old military comrades. But a sure sign of his reemergence was his election, on October 15, 1952, as an alternate member of the Party's Central Committee.[34]

Regrettably, the West knows little of Zhukov's position during "Stalin's last act of megalomania."[35] In January, 1953, a group of Russian and Jewish doctors were arrested on charges of murdering two political leaders, A. S. Shcherbakov and Andrei Zhdanov, in 1945 and 1948, respectively, and attempting to assassinate Konev, Govorov, Shtemenko, and Gordey I. Levchenko (the last a deputy commander of the navy). The Soviet High Command reacted characteristically:

> Marshals, generals, and admirals who were *not* mentioned as alleged victims noted with apprehension that those who were had been among Stalin's particular favorites. Were the others going to be accused of ordering the doctors to poison their service colleagues, in a sort of grisly flashback to the time of Ivan the Terrible? Had Stalin fabricated this plot as a diabolical move to dispense once and for all with Marshal Zhukov, whom he had agreed to recall, lulling him into over-confidence while he prepared a new 1937 purge?[36]

Since most of the victims of the plot were to be military men:

> Were the military pointedly being told that they would benefit by acquiescing in the coming purge of the Party and the police? Was the military leadership itself divided? Conspicuously absent were Marshal Zhukov, now secretly returned to be Deputy Minister and Inspector General; Marshal Sokolovsky, who appeared in February as Chief of the General Staff; and Admiral Kuznetsov, Minister of the Navy. With all these questions still unanswered, the purge died with the purger.[37]

In her memoirs Svetlana Alliluyeva, Stalin's daughter, sheds little light on these events. She simply writes that after V. N. Vinogradov—the only physician Stalin trusted—was arrested in the "doctors' plot." Stalin would allow no other doctor near him. His housekeeper told her that he was exceedingly distressed about the "plot" and had remarked that he did not believe the doctors were "dishonest." Further, the sole evidence against them was the "report" of one Dr. Timashuk, while everyone else, as usual, remained silent.[38]

Zhukov reappeared publicly on the day of Stalin's funeral, serving as a member of the honor guard around the generalissimo's bier. Thus did he return to Moscow to provide dynamic leadership to the army apparatus and to add color to an otherwise drab governmental coterie which was well aware of its lack of popular appeal. On March 6, 1953, Zhukov was named deputy minister of defense under Defense Minister Nikolai Bulganin, and he probably commanded the Soviet ground forces at the same time.

One of the first major events affecting the role of the military after

Stalin's death was the arrest of Beria and a number of senior secret-police officers. Colonel Rastvorov claims that Zhukov was particularly resentful of Beria, one reason being that the secret police had "informed" on him in 1946 and caused his subsequent banishment. When Beria's plans to take over the government became known, Bulganin, Vasilevsky, and Zhukov discussed the situation with Premier Malenkov. Since no groups in the Moscow Military District could be trusted to help arrest Beria, two Guards divisions in the Urals (probably well known to Zhukov, who had so recently been their commander) were secretly summoned.

A plenary session of the Central Committee was scheduled by Malenkov for June 26, and it was decided to arrest Beria at this meeting.

Khrushchev has described Beria's arrest in his recently published "memoirs." Having decided to get rid of the hated secret police chief, Khrushchev and his associates had to decide how to detain him without being arrested themselves. The Presidium bodyguard was loyal to Beria, and his men would also be sitting in the next room during the session, from where Beria could easily summon them. Says Khrushchev:

> We would have been quite helpless because there was a sizable armed guard in the Kremlin. Therefore we decided to enlist the help of the military. First, we entrusted the detention of Beria to Comrade [General K.S.] Moskalenko, the air defense commander, and five generals. This was my idea. Then, on the eve of the session, Malenkov widened our circle to include Marshal Zhukov and some others. That meant eleven marshals and generals in all.

Since in those days all military personnel were required to check their weapons upon entering the Kremlin, Bulganin was instructed to see that the marshals and generals were allowed to bring their sidearms with them. They were to wait in a separate room while the meeting was taking place. A signal by Malenkov was to bring them into the room to seize Beria.

Although Khrushchev does not mention it in his account, the meeting may have been held in a different location as an additional security precaution. When the session opened, Malenkov proposed that "we discuss the matter of Beria." Beria, sitting on Khrushchev's right, gave a start, grabbed Khrushchev by the hand, and with a startled expression asked "What's going on, Nikita? What's this you're mumbling about?"

Khrushchev replied, "Just pay attention. You'll find out soon enough."

He then took the floor and reviewed Beria's criminal activities and his attempts "to legalize arbitrary rule." Bulganin followed with similar damning accusations, and finally everyone had had his say. Malenkov at this point was supposed to summarize the charges, but he lost his nerve. Khrushchev says:

> After the final speech, the session was left hanging. There was a long pause. I saw we were in trouble, so I asked Comrade Malenkov for the floor in order to propose a motion. As we had arranged in advance, I proposed that the Central Committee Presidium should release Beria from his duties as Deputy Chairman of the Council of Ministers and Minister of Internal Affairs and from all the other government positions he held. Malenkov was still in a state of panic. As I recall, he didn't even put my motion to a vote. He pressed a secret button which gave the signal to the generals who were waiting in the adjacent room. Zhukov was the first to appear. Then Moskalenko and the others came in. Malenkov said in a faint voice to Comrade Zhukov, "As Chairman of the Council of Ministers of the U.S.S.R., I request that you take Beria into custody pending investigation of charges made against him."
> "Hands up!" Zhukov commanded Beria.

The generals and marshals opened the flaps on their holsters in case Beria decided to resist. The deposed secret police chief did reach for his briefcase, and Khrushchev grabbed his arm. Later Beria's briefcase was checked, but no weapon was found. "His quick movement had simply been a reflex action," Khrushchev recalls.

Now that Beria had been arrested, the group had to decide what to do with him. He could not be handed over to officials in the Ministry of Internal Affairs, since their loyalty was uncertain. It was agreed finally that General Moskalenko would transfer Beria to a bunker at the general's air-defense headquarters.[39] His arrest was announced on July 10, 1953, and his execution and that of his officers were made public on December 24, 1953.

Soon thereafter Zhukov was raised to full membership in the Party's Central Committee by the plenum which had sanctioned Beria's arrest. After that, events moved rapidly. The importance of the political police declined, and the army's new role as a strong supporter of the regime began to be recognized. In the three months following Beria's arrest the first postwar high-level promotions were made; ten generals, marshals, and admirals were named.[40] On July 16 a meeting of service chiefs was held under the chairmanship of Colonel General A. S. Zheltov, head of the Main Political Administration (MPA). There the military leaders expressed their support of the action taken against Beria. Writes Mackintosh:

> The significance of this meeting lay in the fact that for the first time Party leaders had called upon the army to show publicly that it approved of something they had done, instead of relying upon stock anonymous articles in the military press to commit the forces to Party policy. This act was clearly understood in the army as recognition of its special position in the state, and of its value as support to any ambitious Party leader who intended to make a bid for the supreme power.[41]

Another manifestation of renewed faith in the loyalty of the Soviet armed forces was the diminished influence of the political officers. Actually, this development had begun in 1951 when a secret decree reemphasized unified command. Marshal Zhukov's reemergence led to a trend in favor of full authority for professional officers, and by late 1955 the post of political officer was abolished at the company level.

In a speech before the Supreme Soviet in August, 1953, Malenkov promised that a new economic policy would soon be introduced, with more emphasis on consumer goods. The announcement picked up immediate public support, and the Soviet press continued to stress the importance of increasing goods and services for the people. Investment in heavy industry would have to be reduced somewhat to allow for the new program, but *Pravda* explained that successes in that area had made it possible to increase the production of consumer goods.

Malenkov's program met with opposition from Khrushchev, who received support from the military establishment. Among the first indications of divergence from the Malenkov line were two discussions in a restricted General Staff journal in September and October, 1953, which emphasized that the country's defensive strength was based on heavy industry. The articles barely mentioned the new consumer-goods policy.[42] In 1954 it became an open issue when Khrushchev inaugurated a campaign for renewed emphasis on heavy industry. "Only on the basis of further development of heavy industry," he declared, "will we be able successfully to promote all branches of the national economy . . . and ensure the inviolability of the frontiers of the Soviet Union."[43] The military press introduced the additional theme that heavy industry was needed to raise the level of armaments.

In 1953 and 1954, Premier Malenkov reduced the announced military budget (the total for each year was about ten billion rubles), but actual military spending fell still further. When deliberations on the 1955 budget began, the conflict between Malenkov and Khrushchev was intensified. On January 24, 1955, *Pravda* attacked those who advocated priority for consumer goods, and in a speech the following day Khrushchev described such individuals as resembling the "right" deviation of Aleksei Rykov and Nikolai Bukharin. Under such withering fire, Malenkov resigned as premier on February 9.[44]

Malenkov had had other problems with Khrushchev and the professional military leadership. In March, 1954, for example, he had declared that a thermonuclear war "would mean the end of world civilization." To army leaders this view implied that neither the Soviet Union nor the United States would risk such destruction and that both sides would use their forces in limited actions. Since the danger of full-scale nuclear war was remote, he believed, military expenditures could be reduced. On April 26, Malenkov seemed to reverse his position when he publicly endorsed the view that nuclear war would inflict enormous damage to both sides but that only capitalism would be annihilated. Mackintosh observes: "It is unlikely that Mr. Malenkov really changed his views so radically in six weeks, and he may have agreed to make this particular recantation purely on grounds of Communist orthodoxy. His earlier view regrettably placed capitalism and communism on the same level— a disastrous error to those claiming the inevitability of Communist victory."[45] Zhukov entered the debate two days before he became defense minister when he answered a question about the validity of the theory of mutual deterrence: "I consider this to be an incorrect point of view. . . . Unfortunately, such irresponsible statements have been made by many prominent military leaders—for instance, Montgomery and Gruenther."[46]

Another issue which alarmed the marshals and placed them firmly in the anti-Malenkov camp was the retrenchment in military appropriations. Budgetary allotments and actual expenditures dipped in 1953 and 1954, and Malenkov and his associates, Maxim Saburov and M. G. Pervukhin, pointedly failed in their election speeches to mention increasing the country's military strength. In a speech on November 6, 1954, Saburov restated the Malenkov line and again slighted the issue of military strength, but on the next day Bulganin, noting the omission, called for improving the defensive capability. In the Supreme Soviet session in which Malenkov bowed out, the military budget was increased more than 12 per cent.[47]

The new premier, Bulganin, drew increasing support from the army press and individual marshals for his thesis that heavy industry and defense were closely tied. In his acceptance speech of February 9, 1955, he reassured the marshals that state stockpiles, or reserves, would be increased to strengthen the nation's defensive capacity. Malenkov had wanted to use these stockpiles to accelerate his consumer-goods program.[48]

Zhukov replaced Bulganin as minister of defense, and Vasilevsky remained as first deputy until March, 1956. With Zhukov's ascendance, new emphasis was placed on the study of modern strategic doctrine based on nuclear weapons and delivery systems. Between 1947 and 1953 little creative work had been done by the men charged with the nation's defense; Stalin seemed to be more preoccupied with the past than with the future. When he died, the Soviet Union was left in the incongruous position of having in its arsenal atomic weapons which its military forces had not been allowed to master.[49]

Beginning in late 1953, Soviet military doctrine and training began to reflect the impact of the new weapons on strategy and tactics. With Zhukov's rise came new vitality in Soviet military theoretical writings as the Russians began to realize that Soviet military history and thought had not always been infallible. Published doctrinal revisions which appeared after Zhukov's appointment represented a long-overdue response to the military "new look" begun in the United States in 1953 and 1954.[50]

In his budget message of January, 1954, President Eisenhower had called for the "creation, maintenance, and full exploitation of modern air power." Of the total $29.3 billion proposed for the three military services, the United States Air Force was to receive $11.2 billion, or about 38 per cent—the first time in postwar years that congressional appropriations were not divided among the armed forces in relatively equal amounts. The Strategic Air Command thus became a primary instrument of American military strength and national policy.[51]

On April 30, 1953, President Eisenhower told reporters that the United

States would begin to concentrate on the latest weapons—that "our strength, which is already very real, must now be made stronger." Further, as he recalls in his memoirs, "that remark of April 30 foreshadowed the later unveiling of a change in American defense: a greater reliance on deterrent nuclear weapons which could be delivered by the Strategic Air Command and later by intermediate and long-range ballistic missiles."[52]

Meanwhile, the Soviets had decided to develop their own long-range striking force. There was evidence in 1954 that the Soviet Union was engaged in series production of two long-range four-jet bombers and a twin-jet medium-range bomber. At the same time the Soviets were developing a fleet of in-flight refueling tankers and expanding the airfield and dispersal facilities for long-range bombers in those Arctic regions which would provide the U.S.S.R. with the shortest air route to North America.[53]

Although he acknowledged the importance of air power and nuclear weapons, Zhukov continued to emphasize massive, extended land campaigns, even in nuclear war. He declared that "air power and nuclear weapons by themselves cannot decide the outcome of armed conflict. Along with atomic and hydrogen weapons, in spite of their tremendous destructive power, large armies and a tremendous quantity of conventional arms inevitably will be drawn into military operations." Zhukov did not mean the mere masses of men which so often were the Red armies of World War II, says Garthoff. Instead he had in mind the large, modern, nuclear-armed land and supporting air and sea forces which the Soviets maintain today. When asked whether nuclear weapons would necessarily be used in a future war, Zhukov replied: "No one, including I, can answer now with completeness because all wars, major and small, arise, are waged, and end, under different political, geographical and economic conditions."[54]

In January, 1955, a month before he became defense minister, Zhukov addressed a secret meeting of "the leading personnel of the armed forces." He told them that there was "need for further systematic perfection of their knowledge on the basis of a deep study of contemporary military technology and advanced military theory." Three months later an editorial in *Voyennaya Mysl* (*Military Thought*) mentioned the meeting and acknowledged that "Soviet military science is working out [too] slowly many important theoretical problems of the present time." Therefore, "in planning work on military science it is necessary to obtain formulations of sharp, burning issues having exceptionally great significance for practical actions" and "to publish only fresh, original articles advancing new scientifically based questions or containing valuable generalizations and conclusions." The journal acknowledged "the fear to say something new," although, as Garthoff points out, recognition of the problem did not mean that it was solved. Moreover, the editors confessed to having held up, "without basis," the publication of an article by Marshal of Tank Troops P. A. Rotmistrov, "On the Role of Surprise in Contemporary War," thereby "displaying a lack of necessary boldness in raising a new and timely question having important significance for a correct understanding of the character of contemporary war."[55]

Zhukov's speech appears to have called for more honest and objective military appraisals. While Stalin lived, Soviet military history reflected the application of all-perfect Stalinist military science and admitted no failures. With Zhukov's rise to power it finally acknowledged its failings, and the Red Army its reverses. "The war record," writes Garthoff, "while hardly candid, is no longer completely idealized. Again the *Military Thought* [*Voyennaya Mysl*] article in March, 1955, reflecting at least in part the views expressed by Zhukov in his secret address, marked the significant step in this 'de-idealization' of Soviet military history."[56] From 1955 on, the Soviets encouraged objective writing by military historians.

It was doubtless due to this change in policy that the monthly Ministry of Defense historical publication, *Voyenno-Istorichesky Zhurnal,* (*Military-Historical Journal*) was revived in 1959 (it had suspended publication before World War II). Today it provides candid, and often controversial, accounts of battles and events. Although he was in retirement when the journal resumed publication, Zhukov was probably the force behind its revival. It was in that publication that his memoirs first appeared, and it was there that he lashed out at Marshal Chuikov for his comments on the Berlin campaign.

During Zhukov's tenure as defense minister Soviet military writing flourished. Russian military theorists, many of whom were given high positions in the defense establishment, slowly but perceptibly began to dwell on the theories and techniques of modern warfare. Zhukov himself joined in the discussions:

The success of war depends on a series of factors, in particular the technical level and condition of the arms of the armed forces, the combat ability and mastery of the troops, the art of the supreme command, commanders, and operational-tactical officer cadres, and the main thing—whether the people and the army recognize the just aims of the war because of which the government has led them into the given war. . . . The factors which have been noted above display their decisive influence on the character of the war and the means of its conduct.[57]

Thus did Zhukov sponsor candid discussion of the military arts and sciences. He insisted that Soviet military history be honest and objective and emphasized the necessity of greater flexibility, personal initiative, and imagination in the practical application of strategic theory.[58] Meanwhile, he was emerging as a political figure on the Soviet scene. The professional soldier was about to enter the dangerous political arena, where enemies were often not clearly identifiable.

XIV.   THE SOLDIER-POLITICIAN

Ambition, the soldier's virtue.

Shakespeare, Antony and Cleopatra

ZHUKOV's many speeches on military policy and wartime history, his presence at important receptions and events, his standing in the Party Presidium (which had violated the usual alphabetical order to make Zhukov first candidate member), and the publicity he was receiving in *Pravda* and *Krasnaya Zvezda* made it unmistakably clear that he was one of the top Soviet political leaders. Never before had a professional soldier risen so high. This appeared to Bertram D. Wolfe to be due to the "lack of any popular figure among Stalin's heirs; to the importance of the armed forces in this era of 'peaceful coexistence'; to the dependence of Khrushchev and Company on the army when they executed Poskrebyshev and Beria."[1]

In late April, 1955, President Eisenhower revealed that during the month he had personally corresponded with Marshal Zhukov for the first time since 1946. He declined to disclose what had passed between them, nor would he say who had initiated the correspondence. At a news conference, however, he said that he entertained a "slim hope" that it might "lead to some betterment of the world situation." The President explained that when he worked with Zhukov in Berlin he believed the marshal "intently devoted to the idea of promoting good relations between the United States and the Soviet Union at that time."[2] There appeared in the American press considerable speculation about whether the warm relationship between Zhukov and Eisenhower might be used to ease tensions between the United States and Russia. The President was quoted as saying that he and Zhukov had set a pattern in Berlin to show that two nations could get along if both recognized the folly of not doing so.[3]

Also in April, Zhukov in a message to the Overseas Press Club, made an indirect appeal to Eisenhower for peaceful coexistence with the Soviet Union. Clearly, the marshal was replacing Molotov as the spokesman for Soviet diplomacy as it related to the United States.

The stage was set. Questions were raised around the world. Could the friendship of the two leaders provide the basis for a genuine easing of tensions between the two great powers? Did Zhukov represent a new force in Soviet affairs? Had the military assumed a new and stronger role in Soviet policy making?

Similar questions were being raised in Russia. The post-Stalin leaders were pursuing a fairly consistent effort to effect a détente in international relations. Very likely the Soviet hierarchy looked upon Zhukov as a possible instrument for bringing about a rapprochement with the West. Had not Eisenhower and Zhukov amicably untangled occupation problems in 1945? Was not the friendship genuine?

Zhukov had been a popular figure in the United States since 1941. He appeared on the cover of *Time* in December, 1942, and was given flattering attention in many leading American magazines. In March, 1955, *U.S. News & World Report* featured him on its cover and published two articles about him. In September, 1956, the Russians responded by placing a smiling, fatherly Zhukov on the cover of one of the early numbers of the English-language publication *USSR Illustrated Monthly*. The lead article in this issue provided American readers with a benign glimpse of the marshal; the accompanying photographs showed him with his family, chatting with his soldiers, and directing operations in his wartime headquarters.

In the early months of the Khrushchev-Bulganin era there were several indications of an effort to relax tensions. For one thing, foreign correspondents in Russia found censorship of their press reports eased, and the Soviet government embarked on a large-scale exchange of visitors with Western nations. When two Soviet fighters shot down an American patrol plane over the Bering Strait, injuring seven crew members, the Soviets offered partial compensation. Winston Churchill, attentive to the new developments in the Soviet Union, pressed for a conference of the Great Powers to discuss mutual problems. After correspondence between East and West, a summit conference was scheduled for Geneva, Switzerland, in July, 1955.[4]

President Eisenhower did not favor meeting with the Soviet leaders unless there were concrete hopes for easing world tensions. He had developed a stock answer to any question about a possible summit: "I would not go to a Summit merely because of friendly words and plausible promises by the men in the Kremlin; actual deeds giving some indication of a Communist readiness to negotiate constructively will have to be produced before I would agree to such a meeting."[5] The "actual deed" which persuaded him to attend the conference was the Russians' announcement that they intended to sign the Austrian State Treaty after years of seemingly fruitless negotiations.[6] But Eisenhower had no great hopes for the meeting. "Personally I do not expect any spectacular results from the forthcoming 'Big Four' Conference," he wrote to a friend. "Nevertheless, I should think that [John] Foster [Dulles] and I should be able to detect whether the Soviets really intend to introduce a tactical change that could mean, for the next few years at least, some real easing of tensions."[7]

Khrushchev says that because Eisenhower planned to bring Secretary of Defense Wilson with him to Geneva, the Soviet leaders decided to include Zhukov in their delegation:

Zhukov had been a friend of Eisenhower's during the war, and we thought their acquaintance might serve as the basis for conversations between our countries. We hoped that Eisenhower and Zhukov might have a chance to talk alone together and that they would exchange views about the need for peaceful coexistence. But that vicious cur Dulles was always prowling around Eisenhower, snapping at him if he got out of line.

Khrushchev claims that Dulles could not tolerate the idea of peaceful coexistence between the two countries.[8]

On July 14, a few days before the conference, the Soviet government announced that Party Secretary Khrushchev and Defense Minister Zhukov would accompany Premier Bulganin to the meeting. Later in the day Bulganin explained that Zhukov's participation was necessary if any discussion of disarmament was to be fruitful. "How can questions of disarmament be solved without him?" Bulganin asked United States Chargé d'Affaires Walter N. Walmsley, Jr., adding, "Zhukov might not agree with the decisions we took without him, but if he is there we can all agree together." In an official statement Tass listed the members of the Soviet delegation in the following order: Bulganin, Khrushchev, Zhukov, and First Deputy Foreign Minister Andrei A. Gromyko.

During a Bastille Day reception at the French Embassy, Bulganin asked the American chargé what he thought of the Soviet delegation, remarking that the representatives were "at the very summit." Walmsley replied that it appeared to him one member was not at the highest level.

Bulganin quickly asked, "You mean Zhukov?" and proceeded to describe the marshal's importance in disarmament talks.

The American diplomat politely demurred. "I should think Zhukov would perhaps be more interested in maintaining the present level of arms since he is a military man," he said.

To this Bulganin replied, "I think not, because as a soldier he knows the horrors of war better than anyone."

Bulganin left the door open for personal talks between President Eisenhower and Marshal Zhukov when, answering a reporter, he declared that it was Zhukov's "personal affair" whether he decided to see the President privately, adding, "My government cannot regulate anyone's personal contacts."[9] It is interesting to note that, *before* the White House learned who the Soviet delegates were to be, Eisenhower said he would welcome an opportunity to renew his acquaintance with Zhukov if he attended the conference.[10] Zhukov told reporters that he did, indeed, expect to meet President Eisenhower outside working sessions. "After not seeing my old friend for so many years," he said with a smile, "that would be only natural." The defense minister did not elaborate on what he wanted to discuss with the President.[11]

On July 18, Eisenhower and Zhukov spent some time together, talking about the prospects of easing East-West tensions and about personal matters—their children and grandchildren. Zhukov asked about the President's son, John, whom he had met ten years before. Their talk was described by White House Press Secretary James C. Hagerty as a "very enthusiastic meeting."

Eisenhower and Zhukov met again at the end of the afternoon session while refreshments were being served near the conference chamber. Leonid F. Ilyichev, a Soviet press spokesman, described this meeting as "very warm." Bulganin and Khrushchev joined in the conversation, which, according to Ilyichev, was conducted in a friendly atmosphere and "in a spirit of understanding."[12]

That evening, the President gave a small dinner for the Soviet delegation. He writes of it:

> Promptly at 8 P.M. the Soviets arrived in a group: Khrushchev, Bulganin, Molotov, Zhukov, Gromyko, and their interpreter, Troyanovsky. It was relatively easy and an interesting silent exercise to categorize them: Bulganin, a genial public-relations type, slightly buoyant; Khrushchev, head of the Communist Party and new to international conferences, rotund and amiable, but with a will of iron only slightly concealed; *Zhukov, on hand as a friendly catalyst, but frightened*; Molotov, studiously maintaining his reputation as "the Hammer," and Gromyko, stern, unapproachable, unhappy, with little taste for the whole performance.
>
> . . . Their first tactical move involved Zhukov. Within a few moments after their arrival, I found myself talking to Zhukov alone; the others had faded into the background. My son, John, joined us. We reminisced about days in Germany and our visit ten years before in Moscow. Then Zhukov said: "There are things in Russia which are not as they seem." Without explaining the meaning of this strange remark, he spoke of personal matters; he announced that his daughter had been married the day before in Russia, and that he had missed the wedding. To my protest over this sacrifice on his part, he said that he would much rather be with me, his old friend and military comrade. Such a statement seemed to me a bit unrealistic; I took it with a grain of salt. Upon learning of this event in his family I

sent for and presented to him a pen set and a portable radio to take back to his daughter, a gesture which genuinely seemed to touch him.[13]

During dinner Eisenhower tried to stimulate his guests to speak candidly. Pointing out that modern weapons could easily destroy the entire Northern Hemisphere, he declared, "War has failed. The only way to save the world is through diplomacy." All nodded vigorous assent, the President recalled, but nothing much of consequence was said.[14]

The Soviet leaders presented a solid front, he wrote, and it was not possible to think of one of them without thinking of all five together. "Whoever was boss," the President observed, "concealed his identity, and each seemed to exercise surveillance over the others."[15]

On July 20, Eisenhower again entertained Zhukov, this time at a luncheon meeting. The only others present were Charles E. Bohlen, the American ambassador to Russia, and Oleg A. Troyanovsky, the interpreter. Eisenhower explained what he hoped to learn from the meeting:

Zhukov, a great personal friend of Stalin's immediately following World War II, and acclaimed as a Soviet hero, had been recalled in 1946 from Berlin for service in Moscow. Then, inexplicably, something cost him his standing with the Soviet hierarchy. Whatever his offense, he was sent into virtual exile and was almost unheard of until long after Stalin's death. For a time I suspected that he was dead. However, a number of years later his name began again to appear in the Soviet news, and before the conference in Geneva he had been appointed Defense Minister of the Soviet Union. Whether this was the result of another reversal of Soviet opinion or whether he was being groomed for Geneva because of his anticipated influence in presenting the Soviet case to me, we did not know. In any event, several members of my staff, early in the conference, began to receive veiled but far from subtle suggestions, usually couched in the form of speculation and seemingly prompted by sheer curiosity, about whether "the President might want to see his old friend Zhukov." I decided to follow up on these heavy-handed hints in the hope that the marshal might be able to give me some explanation of the inconsistencies that seemed always to characterize Russian attitudes and pronouncements.[16]

The first part of the meeting, which Eisenhower termed "interesting and revealing," was given over to reminiscences about the war years and immediate postwar events. Eisenhower recalled that

once we began to talk about serious subjects engaging the attention of the conference, however, it became crystal clear that Zhukov was no longer the same man he had been in 1945. In our wartime association he had been an independent, self-confident man who, while obviously embracing Communist doctrine, was always ready to meet cheerfully with me on any operational problem and to cooperate in finding a reasonable solution. This he did on his own; on one occasion he even abruptly dismissed his political adviser, Andrei Vishinsky, telling him to leave the room so that the two of us might talk confidentially. In many ways it was evident that Zhukov was just what he appeared to be—a highly important man in the Soviet government, perhaps second only to Stalin himself. During my visit in Moscow in 1945 this evaluation of his position and influence was many times reaffirmed. Now in Geneva, ten years later, he was a subdued and worried man. In a low monotone he repeated to me the same arguments that had been presented to the conference by the chairman of the Soviet delegation. This was not ordinary talk; he spoke as if he was repeating a lesson which had been drilled into him until he was letter perfect. He was devoid of animation, and he never smiled or joked, as he used to do. My old friend was carrying out orders of his superiors. I obtained nothing from this private chat other than a feeling of sadness.[17]

On July 23 the Big Four pronounced the summit conference a success and instructed their foreign ministers to return to Geneva to begin detailed negotiations on the future of German and European security. On July 28, upon his return to the United States the President held a news conference. According to the *New York Times* report, he said that he had received

> an amazing personal briefing on inside Kremlin secrets from Marshal Georgi Zhukov.
>
> The President revealed at his White House news conference today that the Soviet Minister of Defense had offered him a first-hand account of what has been going on within the inner barriers of the Iron Curtain.
>
> General Eisenhower did not outline in detail the report Marshal Zhukov made to him. But he implied it had been a persuasive account, particularly in the stress that it laid on the current doctrine of collective leadership.
>
> ... The President had a number of conversations with Marshal Zhukov in Geneva. He indicated, however, that the principal briefing he had received had been in a two and a half hour talk that apparently covered the whole scope of Soviet affairs from Marshal Zhukov's personal fortunes to the present policy of the Soviet government.[18]

What was the "amazing personal briefing on inside Kremlin secrets" that Zhukov gave the President? He may well have talked about his ouster in 1946, the Beria episode, and the de-Stalinization moves. The briefing took place just six months before Khrushchev's "secret speech" to the Twentieth Party Congress. Eisenhower never revealed what Zhukov told him in July, 1955, nor did he ever provide details about the correspondence they exchanged before the summit conference. As for the summit conference itself, it was neither a success nor a failure. The Soviets displayed eagerness to discuss questions relating to Europe, but the formulas were too general and vague.

Some progress was being made between East and West, however. On May 15, 1955, the Austrian State Treaty was signed in Vienna. The Allies and the Soviets agreed to withdraw their troops from an Austria pledged to neutrality. On Sunday, July 31, the Soviet Union ordered its forty-four thousand occupation troops withdrawn from Austria by October 1 and announced that its armed forces would be reduced by that number. According to Russian claims, Defense Minister Zhukov's Order of the Day implemented a Soviet proposal made at the Geneva meeting: the troops of the four occupying powers were to be demobilized as they were withdrawn from Austria. Zhukov's order came just four days after the treaty restoring Austrian independence went into effect.

On July 14, 1955, the Soviet Communist Party Central Committee announced that the Twentieth Party Congress would be called into session on February 14, 1956.[19] The regime had decided to revamp the committee because of changing conditions and obtain a new mandate for its authority. Although technically the regime was still operating under the mandate issued to Stalin in late 1952, a new one appeared necessary because, under the pressure of modifying Stalin's policies, the regime was progressively undercutting the very factors upon which it based its claim to speak for the Soviet state.[20]

The Twentieth Party Congress is best known for Khrushchev's secret speech denouncing Stalin. Khrushchev not only attacked the myth of Stalin's military genius but heaped praise upon the military commanders. Khrushchev particularly presented himself as Zhukov's loyal friend and defender against Stalin's accusations that the marshal was not really a great army leader. Then Khrushchev embarked on an attack on Stalin's "cult of the personality" and his "lack of personal modesty," which was demonstrated when he "did not cut off the glorification and praises addressed to him, but even supported and encouraged them in every way." Stalin was even accused of editing and glorifying his own biography. The delegates to the congress were told that the wartime marshals, not Stalin, should be given credit for the victory.

Zhukov was one of the few speakers at the congress who did not praise Nikita Khrushchev or his report. "His speech," Wolfe commented soon afterward, "made it clear that one of his functions is to cover with the mantle of his popularity the new demands upon the masses involved in the stepping up of the Stalinist line of the 'primacy of heavy industry.' "[21]

Zhukov did, however, open his speech with a report on disarmament, saying that since August, 1955, the Soviet armed forces had been reduced by 640,000 men. The government would cut military expenditures in 1956 by ten billion rubles, he promised, and troops would be withdrawn from military bases at Port Arthur and the Porkkala Peninsula and the bases would be disbanded. In addition, the Eastern European countries planned to reduce their forces by 180,000 men.[22]

Zhukov lashed out against American bases on foreign territory. Anyone versed in military affairs, he said, must realize that military bases at such a distance from the homeland could not serve defensive purposes. The nations which were permitting American bases on their territory were playing with fire, and retaliatory blows might be dealt the bases, regardless of where they were situated. Zhukov reported that the United States was creating a powerful strategic air force and carriers for atomic weapons, while assigning its partners in the North Atlantic Treaty Organization (NATO) the task of providing ground forces. American military and political figures were concerned with employing atomic weapons on European territory first of all, as far as possible from America's industrial centers.

With the debate between Malenkov and Khrushchev still fresh in his mind, Zhukov spoke for the development of heavy industry, saying that it was the increased capabilities of the Soviet economy and the achievements of heavy industry that had made it possible to rearm the services with first-class military equipment.

After the Twentieth Party Congress the army continued its efforts to rewrite military history, simultaneously demolishing the myth of Stalin's genius. Less than two months after the meeting Stalin was being given the blame for the unpreparedness of Soviet forces in 1941. "The attack by Fascist Germany," according to one military magazine, "caught the Soviet Armed Forces by surprise, although it could by no means have been considered a surprise to the country's top leadership, which at this time was completely in the hands of J. V. Stalin."[23] Attacks in the same article on the mistakes at Stalingrad and elsewhere, for which Stalin was not blamed, must have caused uneasiness in many individuals.

Meanwhile, events were taking place in Eastern Europe which would soon involve Zhukov and the Defense Ministry. In Poland complaints from workers in a Poznań locomotive and heavy-machinery factory had been disregarded by the minister of heavy industry, Juliusz Tokarski, and on June 28 and 29, 1956, the workers struck and staged demonstrations. Street fighting broke out during an international fair which had attracted many foreign visitors to Poznań and, according to official figures, left fifty-three persons dead and more than three hundred wounded. Immediately dispatching a delegation led by Prime Minister Jozef Cyrankiewicz to Poznań, the government termed the uprising the result of a well-prepared provocation by "imperialist agents and the reactionary underground." The reaction in the Soviet Union was identical; the disturbances were attributed to "hostile agents."

Soon, however, the Polish regime admitted that mistakes had been made "by the callousness and bureaucratism of the authorities both central and local." Acknowledging that the complaints of the workers were largely justified, the government dismissed Tokarski on July 8 and a few days later fired Eugene Szyr, chairman of the State Economic Planning Commission.[24] Soviet and Eastern European newspapers continued to blame "provocateurs and diversionists paid by foreign sources," however, and the East German press even announced that the "imperialist agents" responsible had been caught.

The Polish Communist Party believed that the unrest in Poznań was a matter for the Poles themselves to solve, and Soviet interference only served to sharpen the hostility of those Polish Communists who felt that "the calamity of Poznań, in the long run, could be traced to past arbitrary orders from Moscow." The Kremlin's view, it now became obvious, would not easily prevail at the Seventh Plenum of the Polish Party's Central Committee, to be held in Warsaw from July 18 to 28. Prime Minister Bulganin and Marshal Zhukov were sent to the meeting, as Flora Lewis says, "to set matters straight":

. . . it is said that Zhukov, who later provided Khrushchev with major support in his victory over Molotov, did not take the same attitude toward the Poles as Bulganin. . . . With whatever assurances or courage or play on Moscow politics that may have been required, the Polish Politburo steadfastly refused to admit Bulganin to the Plenum. He was politely but firmly sent packing. During the ten days that discussions lasted, an extraordinarily long time and a record for the Polish Party, Bulganin was trotted about the Polish countryside to visit factories, speak to miners, beam at babies, and make what impression he could *outside* the councils of decision.[25]

On July 21, the eve of the Polish National Day celebrations, Bulganin spoke in a manner which could be, and was, interpreted as intervention in Poland's internal affairs. Insisting that the Poznań riots had been caused by hostile agents, he said that the incident showed the need for "a high level of political vigilance, a persevering struggle against shortcomings, a consistent improvement in the work of the State apparatus, . . . and a decisive strengthening of the organs of the dictatorship of the proletariat." Bulganin also lashed out at the "hostile and opportunist elements" that were exploiting the struggle against the cult of the individual by publishing "wrong interpretations in the columns of certain periodicals in socialist countries, including Poland." He warned, "We cannot close our eyes to the attempts at weakening the international bonds of the socialist camp under the label of so-called 'national peculiarity,' or to the attempts at undermining the power of people's democratic countries under the label of an alleged 'broadening of democracy.' "[26]

Bulganin's speech sounded like a directive, and it was clear that he spoke a different language from that of Cyrankiewicz and Edward Ochab, the former first secretary of the Party. The resolutions of the Seventh Plenum ignored the marshal and charted a course toward further liberalization, although no actual progress was made in that direction for some months to come.[27]

When an angry Khrushchev left for Warsaw on October 19, 1956, to do what he could to influence the Eighth Plenum, he took with him "a procession of some of the mightiest men in the world. Never before had so many Soviet Presidium members descended on a foreign capital at once. Behind them came a dazzling military parade."[28] Zhukov was conspicuous by his absence. Although most correspondents reported that he was in the city, he had in fact flown to Legnica, the headquarters of the Soviet Northern Group of Forces, where he was planning a possible move against Warsaw by Red Army units. Simultaneously, the Soviets dispatched a naval squadron across the Gulf of Danzig toward Danzig.

The Russians' arrival at the Warsaw airport produced a bitter confrontation. Khrushchev, Molotov, Mikoyan, and Kaganovich filed out of the plane, followed by Marshal Konev, commander of the Warsaw Pact forces; General Alexei Antonov, first deputy chief of the General Staff and Warsaw Pact chief of staff; and about ten other general officers. With fire in his eyes Khrushchev quickly surveyed the silent group who had come to receive him. Peevishly he took the salute of a group of Russian officers in Polish uniforms and then, turning to their commander, shouted for the benefit of the Poles near by: "We shed our blood for this country and now they're trying to sell it out to the Americans and Zionists. But it won't work!" A voice answered him: "We shed more blood than you and we're not selling out to anyone."

Khrushchev: "Kto ty takoi?" ("Who are you?" He used the contemptuous familiar form of address.)

"I am Gomulka, whom you put in prison."

Khrushchev: "What is he doing here?"

Ochab: "He is here because we decided to elect him first secretary." Khrushchev had not seen Wladyslaw Gomulka since 1945, when Gomulka had been very ill. After eleven years he may not have recognized the Polish leader. At any event, he glared and ignored the retort, finally walking over to Cyrankiewicz.

"Why did you come?" Cyrankiewicz demanded. "We told you that we would talk to you when our meeting was finished."

Khrushchev shouted: "There has been an act of betrayal! We had to come. It is not only a question of Polish-Soviet relations. You're endangering our position in Germany. You're menacing the whole socialist camp."

The argument continued as the visitors sped toward Warsaw. Cyrankiewicz rode with Khrushchev and received the full brunt of the Russian's ire. Offended by the foul language of the Soviet leader, he snapped: "This is not Kercelak [a tough section of Warsaw]."

Although the Russians wanted to go directly to the Council of State Building, where the Central Committee was to convene at 10:00 A.M., the Poles took them instead to Belvedere Palace for discussions. Khrushchev demanded that the Russians be allowed to attend the Central Committee meeting, but the Poles refused. While Khrushchev was engaging in a long harangue about past generosities the Soviets had bestowed on the Poles, a Polish messenger brought word that troops were marching on Warsaw. Springing to his feet, Ochab asked Khrushchev if it was true. Khrushchev feigned amazement and turning to Marshal Konev and General Antonov, led them to an anteroom to confer with the Russian generals waiting there. After some time Khrushchev returned and announced, "Yes, it is true."

Said Ochab: "If you think you can keep us in here and start an armed *putsch* outside, you are mistaken. We are prepared."

Gomulka added: "Unless the troops are called off at once, we will walk out of here and there will be no negotiations. We will not talk while cannons are pointing at Warsaw."

When Khrushchev started to argue, Gomulka promised him that he would "talk to the people. I will say what is on my mind over the radio." Word was sent to Warsaw Radio, alerting the staff to stand by for a possible broadcast by Gomulka. Finally Khrushchev said, "We will order all troop movements halted."[29]

The Soviet troops in Poland (the Northern Group of Forces) had probably begun their move toward Warsaw on October 17, two days before Khrushchev's arrival in the Polish capital. Forces from East Germany and western Russia also rushed toward the Polish frontiers. As minister of defense Zhukov personally directed the troop movements. Undoubtedly the Southern Group of Forces, stationed in Hungary, also went on the alert at this time.

General Waclaw Komar's Polish security troops, loyal to Gomulka, halted a Russian column sixty miles from Warsaw with a barricade of tanks across the road. Both sides waited anxiously.[30] The Soviet leaders realized that to start a fight with General Komar's units during demonstrations of support by Polish workers and students would be extremely dangerous. By evening Khrushchev had learned from Rokossovsky, whom the Soviets had installed as Poland's defense minister and commander in chief of the Polish army, that the army could not be trusted to carry out his orders—that they would, in the event of a showdown, fight the Soviets. To Khrushchev and his associates the only way to impose Soviet will on the Poles was to throw Soviet units against them, and that the Soviet leaders were not really prepared to do.* They decided to yield for the moment and try other tactics. Garthoff notes that units from the U.S.S.R. which had moved to Siedlice halted there and withdrew the next day.[31]

Also on the following day, after the Poles agreed to send a delegation to Moscow "in the nearest future" to discuss the problems of "further strengthening the political and economic cooperation" between the two countries, the uninvited Russian guests departed for Moscow.[32] Gomulka later flew to Moscow for talks. There Zhukov reportedly warned him: "I am still confused [about] what you want to do in Poland. I'll tell you one thing not to do—don't ever even suggest that you will leave the Warsaw Pact."[33]

Still, the Poles had won a partial victory. On November 13, Rokossovsky was replaced by General Marian Spychalski as Poland's defense minister and commander in chief of the Polish army. He returned to the Soviet Union to become deputy defense minister under Zhukov, a tacit admission that the Russians had imposed one of their nationals on Poland in the guise of a Pole (one-third of the "Polish" officers at this time were actually Soviet citizens.)

On November 18, 1956, the two countries signed a treaty concerning the "temporary stay of Soviet troops in Poland," providing, among other things, that the strength of Soviet units in Poland and their location would be determined by special agreements between the two nations. Further, the movement of Soviet troops outside the Polish bases would be determined "on the basis either of plans agreed on with the Polish authorities or with the consent of the [Polish] government." Soviet Minister of Foreign Affairs D. T. Shepilov and Defense Minister Zhukov signed the treaty for the U.S.S.R., and their counterparts, Adam Rapacki and Spychalski, signed for the Polish government.[34]

Philippe Ben, reporting for *Le Monde*, asked several important individuals in Warsaw why, in the end, the Russians decided not to do in Warsaw what they did in Budapest a few days later. Almost invariably

---

* They threatened to do so, however. Miss Lewis reports that during heated discussions Mikoyan told Cyrankiewicz: "The Soviet Union cannot afford any trouble in Poland. If you start trouble, we will crush it by force if necessary." Flora Lewis, *A Case History of Hope: The Story of Poland's Peaceful Revolutions*, 217.

he received the same answer: the Soviets realized that the Polish Central Committee had decided not to yield to pressure. Instead, they would elect a Politburo from which Rokossovsky and pro-Soviet Poles would be excluded. The Soviets had been told that Rokossovsky's army would not march on Warsaw but, on the contrary, would oppose the Soviet divisions and that under such conditions a military *putsch* which had been in preparation for a long time by Russian generals serving in the Polish army and by General Kazimierz Witaszewski would erupt into a Polish-Soviet war. On October 19 the Soviet leaders were not yet ready to unleash such a war.[35] Polish determination to resist was demonstrated when Poles fired on a Soviet regiment entering Poland from East Germany near Szczecin. The force withdrew, and at about the same time another Soviet unit which had arrived at Łódź decided to halt there.[36]

Khrushchev's departure did not put an end to tensions in Warsaw. Soviet divisions from Legnica and East Germany were still dispersed in the forests around Łódź and Poznań, and another division was camped near Warsaw. Rokossovsky's Polish troops, who had surrounded the large Zeran Automobile Works, the center of the revolutionary movement in Warsaw during that critical Friday to Saturday night in October, were still stationed in the suburbs. Soviet units suddenly became more numerous and more active in the Wola suburb of Warsaw. Finally, Soviet warships entered the Gulf of Danzig without invitation. For several days Polish leaders wondered whether the smile Khrushchev flashed as he left Warsaw was not a ruse and whether Mikoyan's bad humor had not betrayed Moscow's true intentions. Although Khrushchev made a telephone call to reassure Gomulka, the Poles' uneasiness deepened when they discovered that the Soviet divisions from East Germany, plus a division from the U.S.S.R., had settled at Legnica, joining the three divisions already stationed there.[37] Eventually, however, those units were withdrawn.

In the meantime, Zhukov had rushed back to Moscow to cope with a new crisis. Events in Poland had had a pronounced effect in Hungary, manifested by the solemn march of Budapest students on October 23 to the statue of Józef Bem, the Polish general who had fought for Hungarian freedom in the bloody uprisings of the mid-nineteenth century. The students had drafted a sixteen-point resolution which demanded immediate evacuation of Soviet troops, a new government under the premiership of Imre Nagy, punishment of the leaders of the Stalin-

Rákósi era, free multiparty elections, the right to strike and a minimum-wage law for workers, freedom of speech and the press, reorganization of the economy, repatriation of persons who had been deported to the Soviet Union, and reappraisal of Hungary's relations with the U.S.S.R. and Yugoslavia. The students also expressed their solidarity with the Polish workers and youth.

The Hungarian minister of the interior first prohibited and then permitted the student demonstration. Soon a crowd of more than two hundred thousand persons had gathered in Parliament Square, and shortly thereafter the political police fired on some demonstrators in front of the Radio Building. Many were students trying to broadcast their resolution. The bloodshed turned the demonstration into a revolution. People in the workers' districts seized arms and began guerrilla warfare.[38]

Zhukov almost certainly issued the orders which sent Soviet tanks into the streets of Budapest in the early hours of October 24. After the traumatic experience in Warsaw, the Russians reacted quickly—and violently. Sir William Hayter, British ambassador to the U.S.S.R. from 1953 to 1957, has written:

> In personal contacts [Zhukov] created a sense of force and vigor, but he had his brutal side; during Khrushchev's set-to with Gomulka he said to a Western Ambassador, "We could have crushed them [the Poles] like flies." As he said this he clenched his huge fist in an illustrative manner, and one could see he would have enjoyed the process. He was clearly a supporter of strong action to put down the Hungarian Revolution in 1956, and he got his way over this.[39]

On October 25, Soviet tanks escorted Mikoyan and Mikhail A. Suslov to the headquarters of the Hungarian Communist Party. Nagy had been appointed prime minister by the Central Committee in a stormy session the evening before. Mikoyan and Suslov figured in the removal of the hated Ernoe Gerö, who was replaced as party secretary by Janos Kadar.

The Stalinist majority still retained some important positions in the government. On October 27, Nagy moved to reduce that power, forming a new government which included both Communists and non-Communists. The Hungarian Central Committee announced that the regime would start negotiations for the immediate withdrawal of Soviet troops, and gradually the fighting came to a halt. On October 30 the Soviet government announced that because the further presence of Soviet military units in Hungary would only serve to aggravate the situation the military command had been ordered to withdraw them from Hungary. At the same time the Soviets said that they were prepared to enter into negotiations on the presence of Red Army troops in Hungary.

The day before, October 29, United States Secretary of State Dulles had cabled Ambassador Bohlen in Moscow, instructing him to convey to Khrushchev and his associates, including Zhukov, assurances that

> the United States has no ulterior purpose in desiring the independence of the satellite countries. We do not look upon these nations as potential military allies. We see them as friends and as part of a new and friendly and no longer divided Europe. We are confident that their independence, if promptly accorded, will contribute immensely to stabilize peace throughout all of Europe, West and East.[40]

On the same evening Marshal Zhukov, replying to questions from journalists during a reception at the Turkish Embassy in Moscow, said: "In Hungary, the situation has improved. A government has been formed in which we have confidence."[41] Nevertheless, he was not happy with developments. Writes Hayter:

> The first phase ended with the withdrawal of Soviet troops from Budapest on October 30th. When Zhukov, then Minister of Defense, told the American Ambassador [Bohlen] that this withdrawal had been ordered he looked very ill-tempered and said "let them [the Hungarians] get on with it as best they can," making as he said this the famous Russian dismissive gesture of the hand. Mikoyan and Suslov were then in, or just back from, Budapest. Mikoyan probably wanted Nagy to be built up as a Gomulka. Suslov probably wanted firm action, and the Army would have supported this. It looked from what Zhukov had said to Bohlen on October 30th as if the strongarm party had been overruled, and the declaration of "Dominion Status" for the satellites issued that day carried the same suggestion. This declaration might have been intended as a deception to lull the Hungarians till reinforcements arrived, but I thought this unlikely; Zhukov had said that there were enough Soviet troops in Hungary to finish the job, and it would surely have been easier to carry on than to announce withdrawal, thus cancelling the invitation received from the Hungarian Government. It thus looked to me as if a real decision to withdraw from Budapest was taken on October 29th or 30th.[42]

The Soviet army withdrew almost entirely from Budapest, and Nagy set about reconstituting his government, forming a broad coalition based on the parties which had existed in 1945. But Nagy failed to do what Mikoyan expected of him. In a move which had disastrous consequences, he not only asked for the withdrawal of all Soviet troops from Hungary but also proclaimed Hungary's neutrality and announced its withdrawal from the Warsaw Pact.[43] This sudden repudiation of the pact gave the Soviets a quasi-legal excuse to intervene, since a member nation was expected to give long-term notice of such action. As Zbigniew Brzezinski and Samuel P. Huntington point out:

> In the eyes of the Soviet leaders, accustomed to Marxist-Leninist black-and-white thinking, Nagy's action was one of betrayal. "Who is not with us is against us" is an old Leninist-Stalinist maxim. . . . Nonintervention would have been contrary to all the precepts of Marxist-Leninist strategy. Or, as Khrushchev put it more pungently, "We would have been called fools, and history would not have forgiven us this stupidity."[44]

A second event which proved catastrophic for the Nagy government was the French and British military action in the Suez after Egyptian President Gamal Abdel Nasser nationalized the canal. The United States and the Soviet Union joined in verbal attacks against the French and British. The division of the West at that critical hour undoubtedly encouraged Soviet action and prevented the formation of a convincing political and military front against Soviet aggression in Hungary.

Khrushchev, taking advantage of the Western dispute, ordered Soviet tanks back into Hungary. Nagy forcefully protested to the Soviet ambassador on November 1 and 2 that new Soviet armored divisions were arriving on Hungarian territory. When the Soviet ambassador professed ignorance of the troop movements, Nagy announced Hungary's withdrawal from the Warsaw Pact, declared Hungary's neutrality with the unanimous approval of the Council of Ministers, and asked the United Nations to consider Hungary's plight.

On November 2, Soviet tanks, arriving by way of Rumania, surrounded airfields, railroad stations, and other strategic sites in eastern Hungary. That evening a reception was held in Moscow to honor President Shukri el-Kuwatly of Syria. Khrushchev was not present, and Marshal Zhukov and Foreign Minister Shepilov made only brief appearances.

On November 3 the Soviet High Command invited Minister of Defense Pal Maleter and other representatives of the Hungarian army to Soviet Army headquarters to discuss the settlement of remaining details of the withdrawal of Red Army troops from Hungary. The Hungarians were feted at a banquet by the Soviet High Command, and Maleter even telephoned Nagy to report progress on the talks. The Hungarians never returned. They were arrested after dinner, reportedly by General Ivan Serov, chief of the Soviet Security Police (KGB).

Soviet tank divisions then began encircling Budapest, attacking the Hungarian capital in the early hours of Sunday, November 4. Fighting continued in the city for three days. Nagy, later to be executed, took asylum in the Yugoslav embassy, while Kadar, who had gone to the Soviet Union for help, arrived in Hungary in the wake of the victorious Soviet tanks.[45]

After Zhukov's dismissal in 1957, he was accused of "adventurism in foreign policy." Some believed that his handling of the Hungarian problem had incurred Khrushchev's displeasure, but Khrushchev sought to dispel such thoughts when he was interviewed by American journalist Robert Considine in Moscow on November 22, 1957:

> Considine: In the U.S.A. people are puzzled by the expression "adventurism in foreign policy" which was applied to Zhukov. I should like to ask what exactly "adventurism in foreign policy" means?
>
> Khrushchev: The pursuance of an unrealistic foreign and home policy—this is adventurism. It should be read as it is written.
>
> Considine: Were any definite countries meant, or any definite crises, as for instance, in Syria or Hungary?
>
> Khrushchev: Syria and Hungary bear no relation to the given case. That was not the policy of one man, that was the policy of the Soviet Government, including Comrade Zhukov, who stood on the same position.[46]

The Soviet leaders analyzed the events in Hungary and concluded that there was no luxury of choices. Although Zhukov was from the first a hard liner, his stand soon became the government's position. Events in Poland and Hungary proved that the Soviets were prepared to use force to maintain Russian hegemony in Eastern Europe. Other Warsaw Pact nations were forcefully reminded of the consequences of openly refusing allegiance to the Soviet camp.

Zhukov was serving Khrushchev well, and the Soviet leader was willing to reward his defense minister for his support. On Zhukov's sixtieth birthday every leading Soviet paper published a large photograph of the marshal on the front page, with praise from the Party Central Committee:

> The Communist Party and the Soviet people highly value your services in the building of the armed forces, in the defense of the Socialistic Fatherland. In the grim years of the Great Patriotic War you skillfully and courageously led the Soviet forces in decisive engagements for the freedom and independence of our fatherland. In the years of peaceful work you unceasingly gave all your strength and knowledge to further building of the Soviet government, to the matter of strengthening of the defensive capacity of the country.

Immediately following the birthday greeting was an announcement by the Presidium of the Supreme Soviet that Zhukov had been awarded the Order of Lenin and his fourth Gold Star medal.[47] Zhukov, the most decorated hero in Soviet history, now became the only holder of four Gold Stars.

The government of India invited Zhukov to visit in January, 1957. He accepted, and his trip was described as "more significant than all recent Soviet foreign policy moves elsewhere."[48] Although it received scant notice in the West, Soviet newspapers gave the visit extensive daily coverage. Soon after Zhukov's return the Soviets released a color documentary film entitled *The Friendship Visit of Marshal of the Soviet Union G. K. Zhukov to India and Burma.*[49]

A detailed study of Zhukov's itinerary and his speeches in India indicates that the trip was more significant than observers in the West realized at the time. In the summer of 1955, Jawaharlal Nehru had commented that "none of the countries of the globe is at present as politically stable and economically well balanced as the Soviet Union." Several days after making this statement, Nehru had led a delegation to Moscow for an official "visit of friendship." Later the Soviet government offered him arms on easy terms, including sixty to one hundred jet fighters at a low price. No doubt this opportunity to become independent of the British arms industry—and save money—was attractive to many Indian military men, but Nehru rejected the offer at that time.[50] While Zhukov was in India, he probably renewed the offer, for soon afterward India turned to the Soviet Union for arms.

Zhukov's visit served other purposes. One was an eighteen-day detailed inspection of India's armed forces. One observer wrote that "few governments have been as ready to show their military establishments to their closest ally as India did to Marshal Zhukov."[51] Accompanied by military experts from all branches of the Soviet armed forces, Zhukov toured military training centers and establishments, naval and air bases, and India's main armaments complexes. He observed field and staff exercises and held conferences and read reports at military schools. His method of inspection, his reports, and his discussions with high-ranking Indian officers indicated that he had been given the task of doing what he could to improve the Indian armed forces. Certain passages in Soviet specialist-press reports tend to confirm this theory.[52]

At the various installations Zhukov, beaming for the cameras, stopped to chat with Indian soldiers. He appeared to be enjoying himself immensely. While touring a recruit camp, he noticed a soldier in bayonet training handling his weapon improperly. The burly marshal took the Indian's rifle and delivered a blow against an imaginary enemy, saying, "This they taught me more than forty-two years ago, when I was the same kind of soldier as you." A photograph taken at the scene found its way into newspapers around the world.

On another occasion Zhukov demonstrated Soviet drill to Indian cadets, and in Bombay he asked to plant a sapling for memory's sake. As he did so, he remarked, "Let it grow well, so by my next trip I can rest with my comrades in its shade."

Along the roads of India, Zhukov found time to stop his vehicle, alight, and greet villagers. And in Burma the politician-in-uniform presented badges to members of track teams.

More important were Zhukov's speeches before military circles. On January 24 he touched upon the development of engineering units and the role of armored units in modern warfare. A few days later at the staff college in Wellington he described war of the future—thermonuclear weapons, the role of ground forces, and combat operations. He also criticized various training methods employed by the Indian army, suggesting improvements in engineer units in defense, infantry in close combat, training procedures, and supply in mountainous regions, as well as simplification of staff studies and an improved daily diet for the troops.

Not all of Zhukov's time was taken up with military affairs. At a dinner given by Defense Minister K. N. Katju, Zhukov reiterated the cur-

rent Soviet line about peaceful coexistence and then attacked the United
States for "trying to seize in the Middle East and Near East the positions
lost by England and France."[53] Zhukov not only spoke of peace, coexistence, and friendship in such talks but also reminded his listeners of
the centuries-old capitalist exploitation of India's people. He sharply
criticized President Eisenhower's Near East policy and then added a
comment about their friendship. "Whether Eisenhower has remained
the person whom I knew as a soldier—I do not know," he said.

Zhukov frequently referred to the "famed qualities of the Indian
soldier, . . . the best in the whole British army." He accused the British
and Americans of supplying the Indian army with obsolete weapons and
equipment. The Soviet government, he said, was willing to continue to
support the struggles of the peoples of the Near and Far East to eman-
cipate themselves. He expressed gratitude to the Indian people for their
support in that struggle.[54]

Zhukov's trip was an important step in the expansion of Soviet influence among the neutral Asian countries. The visit of Bulganin and
Khrushchev in November, 1955, has been described as a Soviet breakthrough in southern Asia. Zhukov's trip can be regarded as a consolidation and extension of that breakthrough.

In addition to their long-range goal of communizing India, the
Soviets had a more pressing immediate task: by promoting a strong
Indian army they could create a powerful counterweight against Pak-
istan, a vital part of the non-Communist world's defensive system. The
Soviets therefore continued to exploit the political, religious, and national
conflicts between the two large states of the Indian subcontinent.[55] Zhukov's journey was another step in that direction.

In March the soldier-politician attended the first postwar Soviet
Armed Forces Conference in Moscow, where he delivered the keynote
address. His speech was true to form: it praised the Party, attacked
Western aggression, and touched on all the world's sensitive spots. Zhukov attacked the Eisenhower Doctrine, described in glowing terms his
recent welcome to India, and urged better results in military and
political training. He criticized those who "grow fat and slow down
before they should." On the subject of future warfare Zhukov said he
had heard the argument that if nuclear weapons were used both sides
would be destroyed and that, therefore, such weapons would not be
employed in any future struggle, just as poison gas had not been used

in World War II. But, he said, such arguments were incorrect, since nuclear weapons were replacing conventional weapons and would inevitably be used in the future. The Soviet Union, he asserted, must prepare to defend itself against these weapons and inflict counterblows on any nation which attacked it.

Throughout his career Zhukov never changed his position that the nation's civil authorities should trust the military commanders to handle their units without constant interference and meddling by political commissars. Now, with Zhukov serving as minister of defense, it was only natural that the professional military establishment should seek for itself greater freedom to practice its profession unencumbered by excessive political controls. Kolkowicz writes:

> Under the firm and self-assured rule of Marshal Zhukov, the military establishment entered a new era in the Soviet state: old ideological-political shackles were found wanting and abandoned; military officers raised issues that had been taboo in the past; the traditional deference to the Party gave way to professional pride and greater independence; and military leaders became public figures for the first time since the early 1930's.
>
> Having gained in institutional stature, confidence and strength, the military began to address itself to some sensitive problems, hoping to reverse the patronizing attitude toward the military characteristic of the Stalin period, and to emancipate itself from the destructive embrace of the Party. These objectives were far removed from any conscious attempt to secure a direct political role in the state. But from the Party's point of view, though they fell short of outright Bonapartism, they tended in that direction, and the military leaders' aspiration to greater professionalism and institutional independence, notwithstanding their unswerving loyalty to the Party, was viewed by the Party *apparat* as a mounting challenge to the Party's hegemony.[56]

Under Zhukov's leadership old Stalinist ideas were swept aside and Soviet strategic doctrine made room for the technology of the nuclear age. Nevertheless, his most remarkable achievement was the curbing of interference by Party hacks in military matters. The position of political officer at the company level was abolished in 1955, and, even earlier, officers had been granted permission to pursue ideological studies on a voluntary basis.[57] In an address to a Party conference of the Moscow Military District in January, 1956, Zhukov vigorously upheld the prerogatives of army commanders: "In the District, certain efforts have been made to subject the official activity of commanders to criticism at [Party] meetings. Such efforts are reprehensible. Our task is the comprehensive strengthening of the authority of the commanders, giving support to exacting officers and generals."[58] A few months later, speaking before a meeting of political workers, Zhukov urged them to be soldiers first and ideologists afterward:

> The task of propaganda consists not only in explaining the theory of Marxism-Leninism but also in contributing to its practical implementation. The theoretical side of propaganda work must give more space to the problems . . . connected with practical tasks of the troops. . . . A political officer who does not know his military duty cannot cope with the tasks which are set him.[59]

Merle Fainsod notes:

> The line which was being pursued by Marshal Zhukov with its obvious implications of a curtailment of the influence of the Party functionaries in the armed forces could not help but arouse Khrushchev's concern, since his own authority ultimately rested on the power and discipline of the Party apparatus. However, as long as the final outcome of the succession struggle remained uncertain and the support of Zhukov appeared useful, Khrushchev was prepared to tolerate the potential challenge. In the meantime he made skillful use of his patronage powers to strengthen his own position in the army command and to exploit leadership rivalries within it. Marshals Konev, Moskalenko, Grechko, and others, who had been closely associated with Khrushchev during the war or in the Ukraine, were singled out for favored treatment. Zhukov himself was treated with the greatest respect and brought into the Presidium circle. During the spring of 1957, when the opposition to Khrushchev was gathering its forces for the final confrontation, Khrushchev went out of his way to conciliate Zhukov and to find common ground with him on the Party role in the armed forces.[60]

In April, 1957, the Party Central Committee published a decree entitled "Instructions to Party Organizations in the Soviet Army and Navy." Although the proclamation reiterated the paramount role of the Party and the independent status of the Main Political Administration (MPA) as a department of the Central Committee, it nevertheless bore every mark of a compromise. According to the instructions the military commander was responsible for both military and political training, and "criticism of the orders and edicts of commanders will not be permitted at Party meetings."[61] As Fainsod points out, "This last provision represented a concession to professionalism which Marshal Zhukov could only welcome."[62]

In the wake of these events political work in the army became mere formality or ceased altogether. Officers began to concentrate on military specialties, to the neglect of political studies. It would be erroneous, however, to consider this process primarily a result of Zhukov's policy. It was caused mainly by demands made on the army in a rapidly unfolding technological era, including the mastery of new and complicated military techniques, the revision of combat training methods to meet the demands of nuclear warfare, and the quest for new insights into the art of war.[63]

During the Twentieth Party Congress, General F. F. Kuznetsov, head of the Political Directorate of the Red Army, was reduced from candidate member of the Central Committee to membership on the Revision Commission, a move in line with Zhukov's policy of downgrading the army's political machine. Another political officer and candidate member of the Central Committee, Admiral S. E. Zakharov, head of the navy's Political Directorate, was not even elected to the Revision Commission.[64] In fact, while the Nineteenth Party Congress listed ten representatives from the Main Political Administration and security agencies as members or candidates, the Twentieth Party Congress drastically reduced their representation to three (Ivan Serov of the KGB and N. P. Dudorov and K. F. Lunev of the MVD).[65]

The wartime fighting marshals fared well. R. Y. Malinovsky and K. S. Moskalenko were promoted to full membership, and Marshals S. S. Biryuzov and A. I. Yeremenko and Admiral S. G. Gorshkov were selected as candidate members. The new appointments did not notably strengthen Zhukov's position, but the total removal of representation by the army's Political Directorate did. At the plenum following the Twentieth Party Congress, Zhukov became the senior candidate member of the Presidium, an unprecedented move.[66]

General A. S. Zheltov, who took over as chief of the Main Political Administration in the spring of 1953, remained in the relatively low rank of colonel general and was not co-opted to the Central Committee. Zheltov resented Zhukov's whittling away at the MPA's authority by restricting its operations to political-educational problems. The radical reduction of its scope of activity to morale building and troop indoctrination was a major victory for Zhukov. To weaken the MPA still more, he added a control link between it and its operational organs in the armed forces: the individual Political Directorate for each branch of service.[67] To Zheltov, this erosion of the MPA was galling. In time he would get his revenge. He would be Zhukov's initial accuser at the November, 1957, plenum.[68]

Zhukov continued to apply pressure to obtain for the military broader authority to pursue its profession without interference from political agents. Eventually the Party would counterattack and recoup some of its losses. In the meantime, however, Khrushchev continued to heap honors on his defense minister, whose help he would soon need in a brewing political crisis.

Zhukov, Montgomery, and Rokossovsky (second row, center) inspect British troops in Berlin, July 12, 1945.

Marshal Joseph Stalin, Admiral William D. Leahy, President Harry S. Truman, Prime Minister Winston Churchill, and their interpreters before the opening of the Big Three meeting in Potsdam, Germany, July 17, 1945.

Officials of the Allied Control Council watch the raising of the colors before their new headquarters in Berlin, August 22, 1945. First row, left to right: General V. D. Sokolovsky, U.S.S.R.; Ambassador Robert D. Murphy, American political adviser for Germany; Montgomery, Zhukov, Eisenhower, French General Joseph Marie Pierre Koenig; and Russian Political Ambassador V. S. Semenov.

General George S. Patton, Jr., and Zhukov review Allied troops of four nations in Berlin, on September 7, 1945, in celebration of the Allied victory over Japan.

An official portrait of Zhukov as Soviet member of the Allied Control Council, Berlin, 1945. From Sovfoto.

Zhukov and a friend of many years, Marshal Vasilevsky, photographed about 1955, perhaps at a meeting of the Central Committee.

Zhukov absorbed in work at his desk in the wood-paneled offices of the Ministry of Defense, Moscow, 1956.

Zhukov as minister of defense (above) chatting with soldiers and (below) inspecting training, about 1956.

After an eight-year absence from public view Zhukov appears
on the viewing stand on Lenin's tomb at a Moscow parade
held on May 9, 1965, the twentieth anniversary of the surrender of the Germans in World War II.

Recent photographs of Zhukov. Above: at work on his memoirs in his dacha near Moscow. Below: with his daughters (left to right) Masha (Mashenka), Ella, and Era, April, 1969. Ella and Era are daughters by his first marriage; Masha, by his second.

The Old Warrior, 1969.

XV. "BLACK SHEEP IN A SMALL FLOCK": THE ANTI-PARTY GROUP

Thus far no strictly military men, or one who could be identified as an advocate of military interests as such, has achieved membership in either the Politburo or its successor, the Presidium. . . . If a military man on the order of a Zhukov, or another whose rise came about solely through the armed forces, should reach the Party Presidium, it would be a very clear indication that the Party must compromise with the demands and requirements of its military instrument far more than was the case under Stalin.

Barrington Moore, Jr., Terror and Progress USSR, 1954

ON July 4, 1957, Soviet newspapers announced that Malenkov, Kaganovich, and Molotov had been dismissed from the Presidium of the Communist Party Central Committee and from the Central Committee itself and that Shepilov had been released from the post of secretary of the Central Committee and expelled from committee membership. In their place new members had been elected to the Presidium, among them Georgi Zhukov. For the first time—and still today the only time—in Communist Party history, a marshal with authentic military credentials had become a member of the Party's supreme political body.

Soviet citizens were not aware of the events which had led to this surprising announcement, but the situation had been developing for some time. By April, 1957, Khrushchev had seemed to his political rivals to be gaining too much power. He had begun attacking what authority they still possessed. Molotov, Kaganovich, and Malenkov had decided that they must act. Although fearful of openly opposing Khrushchev, Bulganin allowed the plotters to meet in his office, agreeing to sanction a new government if they succeeded in overturning Khrushchev. Voroshilov seemed willing to join, as did M. G. Pervukhin and Maxim Saburov, two economic-planning experts who were, along with Mikoyan, first deputy premiers. The group felt that they had at least as many supporters on the eleven-man Presidium as did Khrushchev.

A Presidium meeting was called for June 18 to discuss a rather trivial matter. As the session progressed, a majority began voting against Khrushchev on issue after issue, making attacks on all phases of his policies and accusing him of starting his own personality cult. Finally, Khrushchev's resignation as Party first secretary was demanded. The vote was seven to four, but Khrushchev would not accept the decision.

Bulganin reportedly told him: "Well, we are seven, and you are four."

Khrushchev retorted: "In mathematics, two and two are indeed four, but that does not apply to politics. There, things are different."

Under formal Party rules, one-fourth of the Presidium could demand a full session of the Central Committee. Khrushchev called for a full session, insisting that only a full session could make such an important decision as deposing the first secretary. It was a canny move. Khrushchev knew that he could command his strongest support in a full session.[1] At this point Zhukov demanded and won an adjournment of the Presidium meeting. He then ordered the defense establishment to use military aircraft to rush members of the Central Committee to Moscow. By that evening a number of them had arrived.[2]

On the morning of June 19 more than three hundred persons, including members and candidate members of the Central Committee and members of the Revision Commission, gathered for the historic confrontation. Malenkov, Molotov, and Kaganovich restated their accusations against Khrushchev, but they received little support, even losing two of their Presidium majority, Pervukhin and Saburov.[3] Zhukov delivered a ringing speech in support of Khrushchev. According to Polish sources, he compared the group's tactics to those of Beria, saying that the army understood the true situation, just as it had in Beria's case.[4] He also is reported to have told the plenum that the Red Army would not "permit anyone to bid for power."[5] When the vote came, Khrushchev retained his job.

Khrushchev now decided to rid himself of his enemies, lumping them all together (despite sharp variations on particular policies) as the "anti-Party group." He accused them of a number of crimes. Molotov, Malenkov, and Kaganovich were ousted from the Presidium and the Central Committee. Saburov was fired from the Presidium, while Pervukhin was reduced to a candidate member. Just as swiftly the victorious Khrushchev moved his own supporters, including Georgi Zhukov, into the vacancies. And he succeeded in adding four new seats to the Presidium, which he filled with his own men. A few days earlier Khrushchev had had seven enemies among the eleven members; now he had fifteen members and had chosen nine of them himself.[6]

As soon as the public announcements about the changes were made, Zhukov began to criticize the plotters. His attacks on Kaganovich, Molotov, and Malenkov were extremely severe. The military had a special score to settle with the anti-Party group, for these men had participated in the bloody purge of Red Army command personnel in the late 1930's.

On July 2, two days before the plenum's announcement, a meeting of Party members from the Defense Ministry and the Moscow Garrison was convened. Present at the *aktiv* were nine hundred Communists, among whom were officials from the Defense Ministry and military academies, commanders and political workers of the various garrisons, and secretaries of major Party organizations. Zhukov presented a report in which he attacked the anti-Party group, emphasizing that the decision to oust the old-time Communists was a unanimous one: "In the plenum there could not be found one member of the Central Committee, one candidate for membership to the Central Committee or member of the

Revision Commission of the CPSU who would have supported with one word this anti-Party group."[7]

Zhukov then spoke out against the trio who had not followed the "Lenin course of our Party," had not corrected existing deficiencies, had helped develop the personality cult, did not believe in the fast rise of agriculture, did not recognize the necessity of strengthening the collective farms, and had been guilty of "cutting themselves off from the people, not understanding the people's aspirations, failing to see all the newness that comes into being in the process of life," and "underestimating the creative initiative of the masses."

Moreover, Zhukov declared, the group had continued a struggle against the creation of *Sovnarkhozy* (Soviet People's Economic Units) and against the reorganization of management. The three were against such Party-developed measures as expanding the rights of the union republics in economic and cultural organizations, and they were against the oft-repeated Soviet motto: "In the next few years to overtake the U.S.A. in meat, milk and butter production for the good of the people."

And, reported Zhukov, this group, especially Molotov, did not go along with the Party idea of easing international tension—of peaceful coexistence with other social systems.

Zhukov then praised the Party for its accomplishments, especially since the Twentieth Congress, and promised that the army stood "always prepared for the first call of our mother Party and government to fight bravely in defense of our government's interests."

During the next few weeks Zhukov kept himself busy censuring the anti-Party group. In the middle of July he visited Leningrad for Navy Day celebrations. Speaking before the workers of the Bolshevik Plant, he first extolled the virtues of the city and described the role he had played in its defense during World War II. He then proceeded to tongue-lash the anti-Party group. He noted that "it is a small flock that has no black sheep," and in this case such black sheep appeared even in the Presidium of the Party Central Committee. "I have in mind," he said, "Malenkov, Kaganovich, Molotov, and Shepilov."[8]

Zhukov expounded on a long list of their faults in language similar to that used before the *aktiv* on July 2: they had resisted measures for improving agriculture and had opposed expanding the political, economic, and legislative powers of the union republics, "being reluctant to give up the powers [they] had held for nearly 30 years." Even more damning was his charge that they had stubbornly resisted the Party's attempts to eliminate the cult of the individual leader, particularly the disclosure and calling to account of those mainly responsible for past violations of legality. Now that their own activities had been exposed, it had become clear why they were against exposing the illegal acts committed in the past.[9]

Zhukov's Leningrad speech boomeranged. In his study of Khrushchev, Carl A. Linden observes:

> . . . It is reasonable to infer that one of the factors contributing to Zhukov's sudden downfall at the end of October lay in the fact that he, wittingly or not, threatened to upset the consensus of the leadership on the Stalin and anti-Party issues. Speaking to enthusiastic crowds in Leningrad on July 5, Zhukov began none too subtly urging that the whole question of Stalin and the role in the repressions played by the leaders he purged be brought into the open. *Pravda* edited the speech and excised an obviously sensitive passage where Zhukov spoke of documents proving the guilt of the purged leaders. Zhukov was playing with political dynamite. Although he may have been thinking principally in terms of righting the wrongs perpetrated against himself and the professional military under Stalin in the 1930's and World War II, the Party leaders as a body must have regarded Zhukov's speech as a possible first step in a bid for power. Khrushchev himself must have viewed it as an effort to take the Stalin issue out of his hands; he was not about to be deprived of his prime political weapon.[10]

Although *Pravda* indeed edited Zhukov's speech, it nevertheless noted that "Comrade Zhukov cited instances of the violation of legality by the members of the anti-Party group."[11]

Zhukov's threat to make public documents concerning the activities of Malenkov, Molotov, and Kaganovich was probably extremely effective and surely contributed to Khrushchev's victory. But it was also a two-edged sword which could be used at any time against other Party leaders, including Khrushchev himself. Although the Soviet leader had not played a part comparable to that of Malenkov or Molotov during the purges, nevertheless he could have been seriously discredited by such revelations.[12]

Zhukov may also have alarmed some of the Party chiefs when he declared that the Red Army and Navy "are standing confidently and firmly on guard over the interests of our country and are always ready to carry out the will of the people."[13] One normally would have expected some reference to the Communist Party at this point.[14] Further, the marshal appears to have gone too far in describing his personal role in the Leningrad campaign:

> I was in command of the troops of the Leningrad *Front* in the autumn of 1941, at the most difficult, critical moment—when the Germans had broken through to Pulkovo Heights, and individual German tanks were fighting their way to the meat combine. I saw the Leningraders defend their native city unsparingly. . . . Later on, coordinating the actions of the Leningrad and Volkhov *Fronts* to breach the blockade, I once again admired the heroism of the Leningraders.[15]

When added to earlier utterances of his role in wartime victories, this public assertion of his part in the Leningrad victory could be seen as an effort to establish a new cult of personality and to deny the Communist Party its "proper" credit.[16]

Zhukov was also using his new political status to win concessions for the military. Even before the June plenum, he had persuaded Khrushchev to modify his plan to abolish economic ministries and decentralize industrial administration. Writes Garthoff, "As a conspicuous exception *not* originally included in Khrushchev's proposal, the military industries were in May even further centralized in the powerful Ministry of Defense Industry, and the Ministry of Aviation Industry was preserved." Garthoff notes that after the June plenum Zhukov apparently sought three more concessions: that the Main Political Administration in the armed services cease reporting directly to the Central Committee and report instead to Zhukov; that the military be represented in the secret-police leadership, probably to include assuming responsibility for the internal troops of the MVD and the border guards of the KGB; and that Stalin's purges, especially of high-ranking military officers, be formally denounced.[17]

In the weeks following the June plenum signs of great political activity in the Red Army appeared. There began the slow but perceptible posthumous rehabilitation of high-level officers who had been shot during the purges, among them Marshals M. N. Tukhachevsky and V. K. Blyukher. Since Khrushchev had mentioned neither of these marshals in his secret speech, it was all the more noticeable when, on August 10, *Krasnaya Zvezda* published a biography of Blyukher and thereby rehabilitated him as a hero of the civil war. Three days later the same newspaper criticized Party propaganda and called for more lectures on military topics and the history of World War II. More military experts should be employed for this purpose, the paper declared, because their lectures would "guarantee closer contact with life and be characterized by a wealth of factual material."[18] Eventually a number of articles and books were published, all serving to rehabilitate military leaders purged in 1937. A book-length biography of Tukhachevsky appeared in 1963, one of I. P. Uborevich was published in 1964, and there were articles on Danilo F. Serdich, Aleksandr I. Yegorov, Avgust I. Kork, and others in 1966.

The officer corps backed Zhukov in his rehabilitation efforts, for they not only removed a blot from the army's past but also served to ensure that such a costly purge would not hit its ranks again. Furthermore, the rehabilitations would help remove any implied doubts about the military's loyalty to the Communist cause, thereby reducing the need for strict political controls.[19]

Much of Zhukov's strength was intangible and below the surface, and Khrushchev must have been aware of it. Millions of Soviet citizens who had defended the homeland against the German invaders could identify with Zhukov, the symbol of victory. Most trusted the army more than they did the Party or the police, and the armed forces commanded the people's secret loyalties. Raymond A. Bauer, Alex Inkeles, and Clyde Kluckhohn observe that "a totalitarian society by its very nature impels its citizens consciously or unconsciously to develop *sub rosa* loyalties as a way of getting some psychological independence and to use and, to some extent, create independent concentrations of power as a defense against the excessive demands of the regime." In Soviet Russia alternate loyalties and independent concentrations of power constituted a threat to the regime's desire for total control. The Party was especially anxious to exercise tight control over the army:

> As with all professions, there is in the military a centripetal force of common interest, a common set of values, combined with the need for some autonomy in the conduct of exclusively military matters, that produce a certain drift toward independence of control. Because of this drift toward independence, and since the army is mobile and possesses its own internal communication system, the regime inevitably has a primary concern for control over the military.

The concern was well founded:

> . . . problems of control probably reach their peak in the military because of the high degree of professionalization of Soviet military leaders, the degree of organizational loyalty required by an effective military organization, the isolation of military life, and the commitment of military leaders to the defense of the nation. The relevance of control over the military, additionally, is important for the leadership because of its command over the weapons both of organization and of violence, and because, *more than any other instrument of the regime, it has won the confidence and affection of the Soviet people.*[20]

One way to control Zhukov and the Red Army was to establish a military "collective leadership," following Stalin's practice of divide and rule by appointment to top army posts of individuals who felt a personal animosity toward one another. After Stalin's death, for example, a political marshal, Bulganin, became defense minister, and Zhukov, who disliked Bulganin intensely, was made his first deputy. When Zhukov was appointed defense minister, his long-term opponent Marshal Konev became commander in chief of the Warsaw Pact forces. Konev became a close associate of Khrushchev and served as a restraining influence on Zhukov. He reportedly tried to thwart Zhukov's attempts to rehabilitate Tukhachevsky and other Red Army leaders. Konev is also credited with delaying the reexamination of the case of Shtern, who had been his chief in the Far East in 1939. And Konev would play a major role in Zhukov's downfall in the autumn of 1957.[21]

Someone was waiting to step forward if Zhukov should fall. Marshal R. Y. Malinovsky, who, like Konev, had served with Khrushchev in the Ukraine, had cast his lot with Khrushchev and had been rewarded accordingly. He now became the docile servant of the regime, joining with others in praising the Party's decisive and superior role in the military establishment and becoming a member of the so-called Stalingrad Group, which dominated all historical writing and sought to apotheosize itself and Khrushchev by creating a legend about the Battle of Stalingrad.[22]

These were portents of the future, however. For the moment Zhukov was prominent in the government. He played host to foreign delegations, took part in discussions with ministers of other nations, and kept his name in the Soviet press. Pictures of him appeared in Soviet newspapers several times weekly. On August 6 he was photographed as he witnessed the signing of a joint communiqué issued by the U.S.S.R. and Syria. He was shown with Khrushchev bidding farewell to an East German delegation on August 7, and he and Bulganin were pictured greeting Khrushchev and Mikoyan upon their return from East Germany on August 14.

Zhukov thus had no reason to complain about his news coverage in the summer of 1957. The front page of one edition of *Krasnaya Zvezda* (*Red Star*) made seven references to him.[23] A film about his Indian trip was distributed, and another, entitled *Soldiers of the Motherland*, was released in August. In it Zhukov glorified the role of the Red Army. Many newspaper accounts described his correspondence with Chinese, Rumanian, and Indian military officials; messages of congratulation to tankers, sailors, and workers; and orders issued to the Defense Ministry.

All this attention could scarcely have failed to produce in Zhukov an illusion of personal power. It was an illusion that was soon to be rudely dispelled.

XVI. *YEDINONACHALIE* AND BONAPARTISM: THE DISMISSAL OF ZHUKOV

Every hero becomes a bore at last.

Ralph Waldo Emerson

IN the first week of October, 1957, Zhukov sailed to Yugoslavia aboard the cruiser *Kuybyshev*. A good-will tour, the trip was somewhat reminiscent of his journey to India. He was in high spirits. He appeared to be at the top of the Soviet military ladder and was being given increasingly important political responsibilities. Further, his government was announcing a series of impressive scientific achievements which would help close the gap between East and West.

Zhukov found time to make speeches during the voyage, and it was only natural that he concentrate on Sputnik I, which had just been launched into space. In a short talk to the *Kuybyshev*'s crew he remarked: "On the day of our voyage's beginning, the fourth of October, Soviet scientists accomplished the world's first launching of an artificial earth satellite, which is a great attainment of our Soviet science and technology." He dutifully credited the Communist Party with having provided proper guidance in the scientific efforts which accomplished this feat.[1]

When the ship arrived at Zadar, Zhukov was met by Chief of the General Staff Colonel General Ljubo Vuckovic and other Yugoslav generals and admirals. He then flew to Belgrade, where he was greeted by the defense minister, Ivan Gošnjak. Western correspondents discerned some unusual aspects in the Yugoslavs' greeting: Tito did not interrupt his vacation in Slovenia to meet the Soviet hero, crowds were thin, and applause was scant.[2]

During the next few days Zhukov engaged in those activities typical of high-level visits to foreign countries. On October 8 he placed a wreath at the tomb of the unknown soldier near Belgrade, and the next day in Snomen-Grobla Cemetery he laid wreaths on the graves of Soviet and Yugoslav soldiers killed in the battle for Belgrade.[3] At last, on October 13, Tito received Zhukov at his home near Kranj. The two went hunting in the Slovenian wilds, and that evening Tito gave a dinner in the visitor's honor.

But something was in the wind. Zhukov's publicity in Soviet newspapers was slight compared with that of his Indian trip. He received less and less space—and in obscure sections of the papers. In the United States *Newsweek* offered an explanation for Tito's coolness. In August, the magazine reported, Khrushchev and Tito had met in Rumania and made a secret deal: Khrushchev was to ease controls over Eastern Europe; Tito was to quit flouting the U.S.S.R. Tito heard from Khrushchev—and later from Poland's Gomulka—that Zhukov was gaining too much power, was putting the army before the Party, and was threatening new Hungarys. Tito evidently preferred a "liberal" Khrushchev to a "Napoleonic" Zhukov.

Newsweek described Zhukov as being in an angry mood when he talked with Tito, recklessly complaining that Khrushchev and his politicians were interfering with the army. He reportedly told Tito that he would never permit the Communist Party to regain control of the secret police, "even if Khrushchev wants to." Tito, so the story goes, relayed Zhukov's comment to Khrushchev. Two days later Khrushchev telephoned Tito, asking him to persuade Zhukov not to return directly to Moscow but instead go to Albania to "patch up Yugoslav-Albanian relations."[4]

Zhukov's visit drew to a close. In a Ljubljana metal factory he made a swords-into-plowshares speech: "We must try at all costs to establish a lasting peace, so that you can melt in these furnaces all machine guns and cannons—and they are made of good steel."[5] During the last few days in Yugoslavia he visited several military units and was honored at more dinners. His speeches contained nothing startling; there were no attacks on the United States, which seemed unusual, and the general tone of his remarks appeared watered down.

On October 17, Zhukov left Belgrade for Tiranë, the capital of Albania, where he spent the next week making visits and speeches. At a dinner given by Albanian Defense Minister Colonel General Beqir Balluku, Zhukov discussed the tense Middle East situation. The U.S.S.R. would support Syria in her struggle for independence, he asserted. He attacked Dulles for deepening world tension and claimed that the West was persisting in forming political blocs and clinging to the idea of power politics.[6]

New York Times correspondent Harry Schwartz found some significance in the Soviet treatment of Zhukov's last major speech, which was delivered on October 24, 1957, before a mass meeting in Tiranë. The address touched on several world issues, but *Pravda* and *Izvestia* printed only excerpts of a report on the speech. Zhukov's warm statement about Yugoslavia was printed by *Izvestia*, omitted by *Pravda*. On the Middle East, Zhukov took a hard line, declaring that the Soviet Union was ready to strike at "any military venture organized by the United States near our southern borders," adding: "Regarding this, we resolutely inform the Turkish government." None of these comments were reported in either *Pravda* or *Izvestia*,[7] though they were broadcast by the Tiranë radio station.

At the end of his Albanian visit Zhukov planned a leisurely return trip to Moscow, expecting to review Soviet forces in the Crimea en route. But Khrushchev's secretary called to say that Khrushchev wanted the marshal to fly directly to Moscow: there was much work to be done on the huge military show scheduled for November 7, the fortieth anniversary of the Bolshevik Revolution.[8] On October 26, Zhukov obligingly boarded a plane and flew to Moscow's Vnukovo Airport. Marshal Malinovsky and other armed-forces officials were on hand to meet him—but no high-ranking Communists.

On the day before, Khrushchev had held a meeting with the higher commanders of the Moscow Military District, probably to discuss Zhukov's fate. Khrushchev, fearing the defense minister's strength and popularity, at first planned to promote him to some other post, such as deputy premier, a job which would deprive him of control of the army but avoid a public showdown.

Zhukov went straight from the airport to a meeting of the Presidium. He refused the proffered "promotion," and the showdown was under way. The debate was so lengthy that Khrushchev and others who had accepted invitations to a reception at the Iranian embassy were twice obliged to postpone the hour of their arrival.[9]

Six hours after Zhukov's arrival in Moscow, Tass issued a bulletin on the proceedings, and less than an hour later Radio Moscow broadcast the report as the fifteenth item on its evening news program.[10] The brief announcement, which appeared the next morning in an obscure corner on the back page of *Pravda*, nevertheless made headlines around the globe:

> The Presidium of the Supreme Soviet of the U.S.S.R. appointed Marshal of the Soviet Union Rodion Yakovlevich Malinovsky Defense Minister of the U.S.S.R.
>
> The Presidium of the Supreme Soviet of the U.S.S.R. relieved Marshal of the Soviet Union Georgi Konstantinovich Zhukov from the post of Defense Minister of the U.S.S.R.[11]

In the week that followed, Western observers tried to analyze the move. Some claimed that Zhukov was to be promoted, others predicted that he was to be liquidated, and still others saw in the move an attempt by the marshal to overthrow the regime. Moscow kept quiet, and an effective news blackout frustrated the world press.

Midway through the week of silence reporters had a chance to question Khrushchev while he was attending a reception at the Turkish embassy. Khrushchev told them that Zhukov was alive and well and would be given another job. "We have not decided on a new job for him yet," said Khrushchev, "but he will have one according to his experience and qualifications." He added: "I saw Marshal Zhukov today. I spoke to him. He was in good health."[12]

All of this told the correspondents very little. The top Kremlin leaders declined to discuss Zhukov's dismissal or the possibility that it was being debated that week in the Soviet Union's highest councils. Khrushchev's statement that the marshal would be given a job appropriate to his qualifications was identical to the language used in reference to the anti-Party group dismissed during the summer.

One comment Khrushchev made to reporters that evening did suggest that Zhukov was in trouble: "In life," said Khrushchev stoically, "one cell must die and another take its place. Life goes on."[13] Yet when a reporter asked him about stories abroad that the Soviet Union's Central Committee was in session, he retorted, "You are making these reports yourselves."[14]

Other Soviet leaders said that Zhukov's removal was "an internal matter" and indicated that an explanation would be forthcoming—but not immediately. Several Soviets at the reception countered questions about Zhukov by saying that the recent resignation of United States Secretary of Defense Charles E. Wilson was no different from Zhukov's.[15] Later President Eisenhower expressed the hope that Zhukov's resignation was as completely voluntary as Wilson's, a remark which touched off laughter from reporters.[16]

Today it seems clear that during the week of the news blackout Zhukov and Khrushchev were locked in a struggle for power before the Central Committee. Articles in the Soviet military press, now under the control of the new defense minister, Malinovsky, indicated that a struggle between army and Party was raging within the Kremlin. *Krasnaya Zvezda* told how "one high-ranking military man" had been so carried away by his own successful military career that he committed "serious blunders for which he received strict Party punishment." In a similar attack on "swaggering military leaders," the naval journal *Sovetsky Flot* (*Soviet Fleet*) declared: "Decisive condemnation should be made of efforts to minimize the role of political organs in the life of the armed forces." Somewhat pointedly the publication asserted that, "no matter what a Communist's rank, he not only can but must be subjected at Party meetings to criticism for dereliction in his work."[17]

The main attacks on Zhukov stemmed from his efforts to lessen the influence of Party workers in armed forces and his vocal insistence upon the rehabilitation of those Red Army leaders purged by Stalin. Zhukov felt no personal responsibility in this tragic chapter of Soviet history, but other top Party people, including Khrushchev, obviously did.[18] Moreover, Zhukov probably possessed secret papers which implicated the anti-Party group in the purges, and Khrushchev feared that those documents might also damage him. Soviet citizens might be asking themselves, "What was Khrushchev doing when Stalin was wiping out Party cadres?"

During this period of watchful waiting, Harry Schwartz produced an outstanding piece of journalism. Dated October 29, his report, which originally appeared in the *New York Times*, provided background on Zhukov's troubles:

> An editorial in *Pravda* yesterday stressing the primacy of the Communist Party over the armed forces appears to repeat a theme that has been re-iterated in Soviet service newspapers in the last two weeks. The editorial said it was the Communist Party that must receive credit for World War II victories, implying that no such claim could be made for any individual, including Marshal Georgi Zhukov. . . .
>
> Perhaps the most serious piece of evidence . . . against the Marshal derives from the instructions adopted last spring governing the work of Party units in the Soviet Army and Navy. Such units have been used to assure Party control of the armed forces. The Soviet Navy newspaper *Sovetsky Flot* said on May 12 that the instructions prohibited any criticism of orders of army and navy commanders at Party unit meetings. This is in marked contrast with the situation in Soviet factories, where Party units are encouraged to criticize the orders of factory directors. The armed-services instructions appeared to represent victory for the military commanders over the political officers.
>
> There would seem to be material for charges against Marshal Zhukov, too, in a speech he made in March before a meeting of "crack fighting men of the army and navy" held in Moscow. No such meeting had ever been held before in the postwar period. Those invited to attend apparently included both members and non-members of the Communist Party. Marshal Zhukov's speech before the meeting, reported in *Pravda* on March 20, is notable for the way it plays down the Communist Party by simply omitting mention of it where one normally might expect to find it mentioned. Thus, Marshal Zhukov gave the Soviet people, not the Party, credit for giving Soviet troops the latest weapons. Curious, too, were the Mar-

shal's words that "the political awareness and patriotism of our fighters are shown first of all in high discipline, in strict observance of the requirements of the military oath and statutes, in unquestioning obedience to their commanders." At another point, the Marshal defined a "true patriot" first as "one who is selflessly devoted to the Soviet people," and only second as one who is devoted "to the cause of the Communist Party."[19]

Schwartz then recalled Zhukov's July speech in Leningrad, in which he had declared that the Soviet armed forces are "standing confidently and firmly on guard over the interests of our country and are always ready to carry out the will of the people whom they have been serving faithfully for almost forty years." Here again, Schwartz reminded his readers, one would normally have expected a reference to the Communist Party. Finally, he pointed out that Zhukov "has gone far beyond any other living Soviet figure in claiming specific credit for himself in connection with World War II victories." That could only upset the Soviet leaders, who insisted that the Party was responsible for wartime successes.[20]

On November 3, 1957, the waiting ended with a series of Kremlin announcements. In the "Resolution of Plenary Session of Party Central Committee on Improving Party Political Work in the Soviet Army and Navy," it was made clear that the Party was to triumph over the army command. "The chief source of the might of our army lies in the fact that the Communist Party, the guiding and directing force of the Soviet society, is their organizer, leader and instructor," read the resolution. The policy of the military departments, it continued, is pursued in strict accordance with the Party's directives. Then, turning to Zhukov himself, the resolution sharply attacked the marshal for "violating Leninist Party principles" by attempting to curtail the work of Party organizations in the armed forces and trying to eliminate the leadership and control of the Party over the army.

Zhukov was accused of implanting the cult of personality in the Red Army. "With the help of sycophants and flatterers" the marshal had begun to be "praised to the skies in lectures, reports, articles, films and pamphlets." His role in the war was "excessively glorified." To please Zhukov, the history of the world conflict was distorted, and the contributions of the Soviet people, the commanders and political workers, and the leading role of the Communist Party of the Soviet Union were belittled.

The plenary session of the Central Committee complained that, while

·the Party and government had highly valued Zhukov's services and had bestowed upon him many honors, including high posts in the Party, Zhukov had lost "the Party modesty taught us by V. I. Lenin." He thought that he was "the sole hero of all the victories scored by our people and their armed forces under the Communist Party's leadership." Thus, the Party's Central Committee session claimed, Zhukov failed to justify the confidence placed in him by the Communist Party. "He proved to be a politically unsound person, inclining toward adventurism both in his understanding of the primary objective of the Soviet Union's foreign policy and in his leadership of the Ministry of Defense."

At the end of the resolution Zhukov's punishment was announced, a devastating blow to the marshal's pride and patriotism: he was removed from membership in the Presidium and the Central Committee and was to be given "other work."[21] Zhukov evidently had to vote to remove himself from the Presidium, since it was announced that the vote was unanimous among members present. Thus Zhukov lost his job as defense minister and was stripped of his Party posts, managing only to retain his Party membership and finally to retire with a pension.

In separate articles both *Pravda* and *Izvestia* reiterated the decision of the plenary session in the same edition in which it printed the resolution. Now Zhukov's associates—Malinovsky, Konev, Rokossovsky, Sokolovsky, Yeremenko, Timoshenko, Biryuzov, Gorshkov, Batov, Zakharov, Kazakov, and others—joined in pointing out his "serious shortcomings," sharply criticizing "the mistakes and distortions he had permitted" and unanimously condemning his "incorrect, non-Party behavior in the post of U.S.S.R. Minister of Defense."[22] It was obvious that in his campaign against the marshal Khrushchev had had little difficulty exploiting the rivalries and ambitions of high-ranking members of the armed services. Of course, some of those close to Zhukov probably fell in line to save their own careers.*

At the meeting Zhukov was allowed to "confess" his mistakes. He acknowledged that the criticism of him at the plenary session had "*in*

* One of whom was doubtless Rokossovsky. It is interesting to note that Rokossovsky, who had been temporarily assigned the post of commander in chief of the Transcaucasus Military District (*Pravda*, October 25, 1957, p. 6), did not join in the initial attack on Zhukov. Rokossovsky had incurred Khrushchev's wrath during the Polish October, when things began falling apart for the Soviets, and the Party boss turned on him, shouting: "You're not a marshal. You're a horse's ass!" Seymour Freidin, *The Forgotten People*, 256.

the main been correct." However, he also took the opportunity to protest his earlier ouster from the Central Committee in 1946. In proposing a penalty, some individuals at the present session had pointed out that Zhukov had already been removed once from the Central Committee and that he had failed to see any need to correct those earlier "mistakes." "At that time," Zhukov replied, in an obvious effort to salvage his pride, "I could not and did not admit that my ouster . . . was correct; I did not admit that the accusations made against me were correct." Now it was a different matter, Zhukov said. "I recognize my mistakes . . . and give my word that I will completely eliminate my shortcomings."[23]

The most damning censure came from Marshal Konev. During Stalin's reign and, later, Khrushchev's, he had served by design as a counterbalance to Zhukov's power and popularity. Now Konev bitterly avenged himself on his former superior in an attempt to condemn him once and for all in the eyes of the people. He repeated the accusations about Zhukov's attempts to curtail the work of Party organizations in the army and went on to attack the man himself, saying that Zhukov failed to understand the nature of the Soviet social system, that he had become conceited, and that he had underestimated the leading role of the Party. He had tried to decide by himself all questions of leadership of the armed services without regard to the opinions of others.

Zhukov's mistakes were made worse, Konev said, by certain statements he had made about Soviet military science and the development of the armed forces: Zhukov had stated that Soviet military regulations played a negative role in the education of commanders and did not help them develop creative initiative. At this point Konev reiterated the Party charge that Zhukov was "politically unsound" and "inclined to adventurism" in his understanding of the major objectives of Soviet foreign policy.

Having attacked Zhukov's "political" mistakes, Konev proceeded to heap blame on him for "gross mistakes and blunders" on the eve of World War II. He reminded his audience that Zhukov was chief of the General Staff just before the war and must share responsibility for the Red Army's unpreparedness for combat. Zhukov had indisputable information about the real threat of attack by Germany, Konev charged, but failed to take prompt measures to prepare Soviet troops. He also attacked Zhukov for creating large numbers of mechanized units without providing them with equipment and training cadres. "This had an adverse effect on the course of the fighting at the beginning of the war."[24]

Konev's remarks reflected the Party line on the reasons for the Soviet armed forces' unpreparedness in 1941. Placing on Zhukov the blame for the development of large mechanized formations which could not be equipped before war broke out is an example of the half-truths quickly dredged up by Party historians. It was well known that Zhukov and Shaposhnikov had protested the disbanding of mechanized units in 1939. Stalin, Voroshilov, and Pavlov had decided that they were too vulnerable from the air to play a decisive role on the modern battlefield. But not until 1964 was the full story revealed in an article appearing in *Voyenno-Istorichesky Zhurnal* in March of that year:

> Toward the end of 1939, as a result of incorrect conclusions arrived at . . . in Spain and in our liberation campaigns in the western regions of Belorussia and the Ukraine, these [mechanized] corps were disbanded. The combat experience in the beginning of the Second World War revealed the error of this decision. Therefore, beginning in July 1940, and especially in the spring of 1941, we hurriedly began re-forming the mechanized corps. But this led to another extreme: the realistic capabilities of equipping on a timely basis and the training of command cadres for a large number of expanding tank and mechanized formations were not taken into account.[25]

Thus the decision to re-create the mechanized formations was made in the summer of 1940—six months before Zhukov became chief of the General Staff. Konev's haste in preparing his attack on Zhukov resulted in some glaring errors which his military audience could readily discern.*

Eventually Zhukov would receive less and less blame for the nation's

---

* Other Soviet authors have stated simply that after the experience in Spain, certain "incorrect conclusions" were drawn about armor on the modern battlefield. An October, 1966, article in *Soviet Military Review* provides more information: "After the war in Spain (1936–1939) the erroneous conclusion was drawn that large tank and motorized formations would not be used because they were vulnerable from the air. The existing tank and motorized corps were disbanded. But after Germany attacked Poland and France these corps had to be restored. This miscalculation adversely affected the operations of the Soviet Army at the early stages of the Great Patriotic War." P. Derevianko, "Soviet Military Science," *Soviet Military Review*, October, 1966, 4–5. Certainly Zhukov may have influenced the July, 1940, decision to re-form the mechanized corps, and, as the article points out, the entire process was accelerated in the spring of 1941, when Zhukov was chief of the General Staff. But Konev's attack is both unfair and overstated.

lack of preparedness in June, 1941. He would be depicted as unable to convince Stalin that the armed forces must be brought to greater combat readiness. For himself, he would state simply: "Possibly, I did not have enough influence with [Stalin] for this."[26]

Konev next sought to demolish Zhukov's role in the Stalingrad campaign. He declared that the marshal's lack of modesty became especially apparent when he stressed his special role in directing operations on the various *fronts*. "For example," Konev said, "Zhukov undeservedly ascribes to himself a special role in drafting the plan of strategic offensive operations . . . at Stalingrad." Konev declared that the concept and all the basic points of the plan originated with the commanders of the *fronts* and their staffs.[27] Again he erred or, worse, intentionally distorted the facts. Many Soviet historians and memoirists have testified that Zhukov was one of the chief architects of victory at Stalingrad. Vasilevsky, Rokossovsky, Vorobyev, Malinovsky, and others have agreed that Zhukov, not the *front* commanders, planned the successful counteroffensive against the Germans entrenched along the Volga. Oddly enough, when Konev asserted that all the basic points of the plan originated with the *front* commanders and their staffs, he himself failed to give the Party "proper" credit for the victory.

Konev berated Zhukov for specific errors in the war. Although Zhukov tried to claim that he alone among Soviet military leaders suffered no defeats during the war, Konev says, the marshal was chief of the General Staff and later deputy supreme commander when the Red Army was suffering serious defeats and retreating into the interior. After the victory at Stalingrad in the winter of 1942–43 an opportunity came to surround enemy forces at Demyansk, southeast of Lake Ilmen, and Zhukov was detailed to direct operations on the Northwestern *Front*. The operation was poorly organized, Konev said, with resulting heavy Soviet losses and the escape of the enemy. He declared that at the end of March, 1944, when Soviet troops had surrounded large German forces north of Kamenets-Podolsk, Zhukov, as commander of the First Ukrainian *Front*, did not take the necessary steps to reinforce the First Guards and Fourth Tank armies. As a result, the Germans were able to break out of encirclement and withdraw to the west, where they managed to set up a new defensive line along the approaches to Lvov.

Konev turned next to the Berlin operation, the memory of which was especially painful to him. From later testimony it is known that he was convinced Zhukov's First Belorussian *Front* had received undue credit for the capture of Berlin. Moreover, he felt cheated that the symbol of final victory, the capture of the Reichstag, had been snatched from his First Ukrainian *Front* and handed to Zhukov. While Konev had the floor, he took the opportunity to emphasize the part played by his own *front* and to show that he had helped save the day for Zhukov. He accused Zhukov of underestimating available information on the intentional withdrawal of the Germans to the Seelow Heights and allowing the Soviets to storm the enemy positions without sufficient preparation. Thus the breakthrough was executed too slowly.[28] Of all Konev's charges, this one came closest to the truth. As has been pointed out earlier, Zhukov was indeed slowed down temporarily and was aided to some degree by Konev's troops. Zhukov himself later commented only that Stalin, fearing a delay of the offensive, "ordered the commander of the First Ukrainian *Front* to strike with part of his forces from the south of Berlin."[29]

Konev concluded his attack on a note of intemperate bitterness. He described Zhukov as "an exceptionally vain person" who had tried to implant the cult of personality among the armed services at a time when the Party was conducting a campaign against it. Zhukov had allowed a halo of glory and infallibility to be created around him. He had ordered a painting of himself on a rearing white steed, "just like St. George the Dragon Slayer on an old icon," to be displayed in the Soviet Army Museum. He had had a hand in the script of the film *The Battle of Stalingrad* and had occupied a completely undeserved role in it. Finally, Konev said, Zhukov had repeatedly attacked the Stalin cult, doing so, however, only to extol himself.[30]

In a letter to me Hanson W. Baldwin wrote:

> I met both Zhukov and Konev in Moscow several times in 1956 when I was there with Nate Twining covering Soviet Air Force Day. Of course I spoke to them only through interpreters but it was easy to see the rivalry between the two men. Both give the appearance of tough, no-nonsense—indeed, ruthless—generals, but Zhukov, to my mind, had somewhat the more appealing personality. When I asked Zhukov a question about (I think) the Berlin campaign Konev broke in and said: "Ah, but you should study *my* Kiev campaign." I agree with you that Zhukov was one of the great ones—as far as we can tell from our knowledge of Soviet operations —the best. The vanity that seems to attend most great military leaders undoubtedly had something to do with the Konev-Zhukov rivalry. There

may also have been some past personal clash between the two men about which I know nothing. But, in addition to these factors there were very major political, as well as military reasons, for discord. Zhukov had always espoused the military side of the case; he had opposed—though carefully—the dominance of the political commissars in the Red Army, even before World War II. He won unprecedented popularity during the war; he was the type of leader who—though ruthless—could inspire his men. Bonapartism has always been the dread of the Communist party, and for a time Zhukov appeared to have greater control over the Red Army than the party did after World War II. This is a debatable point, of course, but it has been said that if any one man could "control" the Red Army, it was Zhukov. The party and Khrushchev saw this; so did Stalin; hence their attempts to cut him down to size. Konev, on the other hand, was primarily a party man—though a damn good general; he was not only obviously jealous of Zhukov, his reputation and his hold on the Army, but as a party man he resented it. He acted as the hatchet man in Zhukov's fall.

There are those who believe that Konev was forced to speak against his former commander. I do not agree, largely because of the nature of his attack. He did not confine his criticism to "mistakes" already cited by other government leaders, but went on to name others, and in a tone which revealed his personal animosity toward the marshal. If Konev had merely been dutifully carrying out Khrushchev's request to add another blast against the marshal, he would not have prolonged his attack. Konev not only did his duty—he overfulfilled it. One can speculate that he was sorely disappointed because he had not been appointed defense minister in Zhukov's place, a frustration that may provide a key to the intensity of his onslaught. But Khrushchev was now far too wise to allow the post to be filled by another ambitious marshal, filling it instead with Malinovsky, a docile, almost colorless individual.

Malinovsky also had a few words to say about his predecessor. He scorned Zhukov's "ambition and desire for glory." Zhukov had to his credit services to the Soviet people and Party, and they had been duly recognized. But, he said, the people and the Party would not permit anyone to place himself above everyone else and to lay claim to some special status.[31]

At last the tirades ended. Now the Party launched a campaign to destroy the remnants of Zhukov's influence. The campaign took the form of a major shakeup in the Main Political Administration (where

Colonel General F. I. Golikov replaced Zheltov as chief) and an intensification of Party control and political indoctrination in the armed forces. A new directive for officers set aside a minimum of fifty hours of Marxist-Leninist instruction, and attendance was mandatory. Senior officers were sternly enjoined to schedule their work days to provide "the proper conditions" for such studies.[32]

Steps were also taken to raise the prestige and increase the prerogatives of political officers. A new policy provided for interchanging military and political personnel in command and political assignments, and officers were warned that promotions would depend on political as well as military knowledge. Measures were initiated to strengthen the role of Party and Komsomol organizations in the armed forces, and a special drive was launched to enroll more enlisted men in the Party. With the increase in membership, primary Party organizations were moved down from the regimental to the battalion level, and Party groups were established in more than half the companies and sometimes even at platoon level. By 1961, Communists and Komsomol members made up 82 per cent of the personnel of the Soviet armed forces, and most commanders were Party members.[33]

Zhukov's dictum that commanders were not to be criticized at Party meetings was expressly repudiated. Officers were told that they must welcome Party criticism, even from their subordinates. Party workers sought to impose a new image of the commander as a man who relies on the collective and works through his unit's Communist and Komsomol groups.[34] *Yedinonachalie* took on a different meaning. Fainsod writes:

> Military personnel could no longer limit their activities to issuing operational commands to their subordinates through the traditional military hierarchy; they were not only required to accept responsibilities in the political field but to cooperate with Party and political workers in discharging their military duties. The principle of unified command was reiterated, but with a difference. As interpreted by the Main Political Administration in 1959, it was to be exercised "in strict conformity with the laws of the Soviet state and the decisions of the Communist Party." Commanders were reminded that there were specific instructions from the Central Committee to utilize Party organizations in carrying out their assignments and in enforcing discipline. Thus, the balance was tilted toward Party control, and the Party remained the ultimate master.[35]

With Zhukov's departure from the scene Soviet historians received new guidelines. They were to depict the Party as the "organizer of the national struggle with the enemy" and to describe "its many-sided activities in directing the front, the partisan warfare behind the enemy lines, and the economic and political life of the country."[36]

During Khrushchev's rule, *Istoriya Velikoy Otechestvennoy Voiny Sovetskogo Soyuza* was published by the Department of History of the Great Patriotic War of the Institute of Marxism-Leninism of the Central Committee of the CPSU. In the history the Party, of course, emerged as the organizer of victory, and outstanding leaders such as Zhukov were often relegated to footnotes or to a name in a long list of campaign participants. Khrushchev allowed and even encouraged the so-called historians to portray him as a brilliant wartime leader who played a significant role in planning the counterattack at Stalingrad and influenced events elsewhere.

Zhukov officially retired in March, 1958, reportedly with a pension of 5,500 old rubles (about $1,375) a month. One can only speculate why five months elapsed between his ouster and his retirement. Possibly he was allowed to remain in the Kremlin to brief his successor.

Party leaders were not content to allow Zhukov to slip into oblivion, however. Their campaign to discredit him continued. As late as the Twenty-second Party Congress in 1961, anti-Zhukov tirades were still being delivered. Khrushchev told the gathering that in October, 1957, the Party had "firmly rebuffed attempts by the former minister of defense, Zhukov, to take an adventurist path and to pursue a policy of separating the armed services from the Party."[37] Delivering the report of the Party Central Inspection Commission, A. F. Gorkin attacked Zhukov in similar terms, adding that the former defense minister had lost his sense of modesty and considered himself the sole hero of all the victories won by the armed forces under the leadership of the Communist Party.[38]

Malinovsky's speech before the congress reiterated the reasons for Zhukov's dismissal, but his attack was limited to three terse sentences. Marshal Golikov, chief of the Main Political Administration, was more longwinded. During Zhukov's tenure, he said, military councils, political organs, and Party organizations were "subverted and emasculated." Party criticism of commanding officers at any level was forbidden, and "arrogance, rudeness, arbitrariness, and terror spread in relations with subordinates." Further, "a wedge was driven between commanding officers and political officers." Even worse, as far as Golikov was concerned,

> the Main Political Administration was treated indifferently and humiliated. Parade-ground manners were introduced into military-scientific work. Various attempts were made to avoid the control of the Central Committee, undermine the Party's influence, and wrest the army and navy loose from the Party and people. Zhukov's personality cult was being instituted. Tendencies toward unlimited power in the army and country were growing.

Zhukov, Golikov continued, considered the Soviet armed forces his private domain and sought to eliminate the Central Committee in the settlement of major issues bearing on the life of the services.[39]

It is characteristic of the Soviet scheme of things that the Party was still berating Zhukov four years after his dismissal, when he obviously no longer represented a threat to Khrushchev. The attacks continued interminably, and the Party Congress was not the only forum for them. On October 8, 1961, *Izvestia* reported that Zhukov had sought to curtail the nation's submarine program, thinking missiles were useless and the bayonet the only weapon.[40] The charge was nonsense, of course. It is well known that Zhukov never denied the value of the missile, although he continually reminded the defense establishment that nuclear weapons, while important, were not decisive. The *Izvestia* article appears to be an apologia for the Soviet Union's late start in building nuclear submarines.[41]

Khrushchev visited the United States in September, 1959. President Eisenhower recorded that, during talks with him at Camp David, Maryland, "Khrushchev mentioned my former counterpart in Berlin. Here, for the only time in the conversation, Khrushchev developed a twinkle in his eye. He merely remarked rather parenthetically, 'Your old friend Zhukov is all right. Don't worry about him. He's down in the Ukraine fishing*—and like all generals he is probably writing his memoirs.' "[42] Khrushchev also discussed his own role in the war and described to Eisenhower the Soviet offensive of 1943:

> In this instance the military recommended against a certain large-scale

---

* Actually, Zhukov was probably at his *dacha* on the Publevskoye highway near Moscow. He reportedly maintained an apartment at House No. 3 on Granovsky Street, but spent most of his time at his *dacha*.

attack in the Kharkov area. Khrushchev agreed and, as in the previous year, he called the Kremlin by phone direct. This time, according to his tale (as he waggled that index finger), he talked to Marshal Zhukov, Stalin's military chief at that time, and presented his arguments. Zhukov alleged that Stalin was unavailable to talk, although Khrushchev was certain, from his intimate knowledge of the room in which the call was being handled, that Stalin's desk was only some twenty feet away. Zhukov heard Khrushchev's story, but insisted that the attack go on as planned. . . . The attack jumped off, and as Khrushchev had predicted the Soviets lost some three hundred thousand men.*

During his account of this episode Eisenhower reported that "Khrushchev expressed some grudging admiration for Zhukov. He said Zhukov was blunt, bold, direct and non-diplomatic—as a soldier should be."[43]

In late summer, 1961, at the height of the Berlin crisis, Khrushchev asked Zhukov to return to active service, an obvious propaganda gesture —and a rather ineffective one, since the attacks on Zhukov were continuing in Russia. Zhukov rather understandably refused, although his health was good and he was still relatively young—younger than Khrushchev, at least.

In the winter of 1962–63, Malinovsky reportedly marshaled enough support in the Presidium for a substantial increase in the military budget, jeopardizing Khrushchev's allocations for agriculture and consumer-goods industries. Khrushchev again turned to Zhukov for support, but again the marshal refused to become involved. Apparently Khrushchev was even willing to rehabilitate Zhukov in return for his aid. In May, 1963,[44] the Soviet Foreign Office asked the American Embassy to invite Zhukov to its armed forces party. However, Zhukov did not make an appearance.

In the years since his ouster Zhukov had virtually disappeared from

* Eisenhower wrote: "This particular story has a sequel. Five years after the battle, Khrushchev went on, a group of the Politbureau was sitting at a meal. Mikoyan, having become a little 'tipsy,' began to twit Stalin on the wisdom of his Kharkov decision. 'You see, Comrade Stalin,' he was quoted as saying, 'Comrade Khrushchev was right! The Kharkov attack should never have been made.' In his exuberance, Mikoyan had failed to see Stalin rising in anger from his chair. Hard put to save the situation, Khrushchev barely placated Stalin with hurried assurance: 'Don't worry, Comrade Stalin, we would have lost those three hundred thousand men had we defended or attacked.'" Dwight D. Eisenhower, *Waging Peace*, 442–43.

wartime histories, relegated for the second time in his career to the status of unperson. He suffered, of course, but ultimately Soviet historiography was the greater victim. There were many who mourned this development, including K. P. S. Menon, India's ambassador to the Soviet Union from 1952 to 1961. Menon recorded in his diary on November 5, 1957:

> No star shone in the Russian firmament after Stalin's death with greater lustre than Zhukov's. The attempts that are now being made to blot it out can only be called pitiful. The Party may succeed in keeping Zhukov's figure out of the public eye, but it will not succeed in keeping his memory out of the hearts of men. It might as well hope to cause an eclipse of the moon by means of a sputnik! If Konev's malicious estimate of Zhukov becomes the final official appraisal, attempts may even be made to rewrite the history of the war so as to belittle Zhukov's part in it. But ultimately truth will triumph, and Clio will place Zhukov by the side of such favourites as Aleksandr Suvorov, Mikhail Kutuzov and Alexander Nevsky. Quoting the words of Alexander Nevsky, uttered seven centuries ago, Zhukov in 1941 called upon the Russian people to face the enemy. "He who comes with the sword," declared Zhukov, "shall perish by the sword. Such has always been the law of the Russian land and such it always shall be." And the grateful Russian land will always hold his memory in esteem and affection.[45]

Living outside Moscow in his *dacha*, Zhukov was passing his days hunting, fishing, and writing his memoirs. Occasionally he appeared on the streets of Moscow and was greeted by well-wishers. No doubt he longed for the day when he would be restored to his rightful niche in Soviet history. He was out of favor for the moment, temporarily *hors de combat*, but the door to his rehabilitation had been left open. Khrushchev told Robert Considine:

> Marshal Zhukov was never expelled from the Party and remains a member of our Communist Party. He is a great military specialist, and we are sure that he will devote his strength and knowledge to the cause of the people. The Party has punished him, but has punished him to the extent of his political strength which he himself admitted.[46]

On another occasion, Khrushchev remarked: "Zhukov actually proved himself a splendid soldier and commander."[47]

Nevertheless, Zhukov probably realized that his chances of rehabilitation would be enhanced with Khrushchev's removal from the scene. And that event was not long in coming.

XVII. THE RESURRECTION OF AN UNPERSON

One day there is certain to be another order of the Soviet Union. It will be the Order of Zhukov, and that order will be prized by every man who admires courage, vision, fortitude, and determination in a soldier.

Dwight D. Eisenhower, 1945

ON October 18, 1964, Soviet newspapers announced that the Plenum of the Communist Party Central Committee had "complied with the request of Comrade N. S. Khrushchev to relieve him from his duties as First Secretary of the Central Committee of the CPSU, member of the Presidium of the Central Committee of the CPSU and Chairman of the Council of Ministers of the USSR" for reasons of "advanced age and deterioration in the state of his health." L. I. Brezhnev became Party first secretary, and A. N. Kosygin was named chairman of the Council of Ministers.[1] Soon the attacks on Khrushchev began, and even his closest associates appeared to turn against him.

Khrushchev had weathered many storms: the Cuban missile crisis, the harvest debacle of 1963, the steady deterioration of Soviet authority in Communist satellites, and the decline in Russia's economic-growth rate. But, writes Carl Linden, Khrushchev "had been forced into retreat too often and the aura of success around his leadership had faded. This was a serious vulnerability."[2]

While Khrushchev was away on vacation on the Georgian coast of the Black Sea, his colleagues decided to dethrone him. Observes Edward Crankshaw:

All those who had ever opposed the old master on anything drew together to bring him down. They did not, most of them, oppose the main line of his policy (their subsequent actions proved this), but they were against his rudeness and his precipitance; they were against the hostages he was preparing to give to fortune; they were against the muddle he was making of the economy, the endless "hare-brained" schemes, which led nowhere, which had no systematic direction; above all they were against his final assumption of absolute authority.[3]

On October 13, Khrushchev was summoned from his villa to attend an urgent Presidium meeting in Moscow. He walked into a neat trap. The secret police appear to have been completely under the plotters' control and had probably taken precautions to see that Khrushchev would be isolated from any outside help.[4] Writes Linden:

Also, unlike 1957, he did not have a Zhukov in the military establishment ready to come to his aid. Evidently the anti-Khrushchev coalition was reasonably confident that the Soviet military would at the very least remain neutral during the confrontation in the Presidium. Brezhnev's special toast to the Soviet military at the Kremlin reception on the October Revolution anniversary a few weeks after Khrushchev's fall may have been an oblique gesture of the new leader's gratitude on this score.[5]

Khrushchev discovered that the Presidium meeting was in fact his trial. The prosecution was led by the Party's ideological expert, Mikhail Suslov, and Dmitri Polyansky, one of Khrushchev's protégés.[6] One by one Khrushchev's opponents—some owing all they were to him—stood up to attack him: for economic failure, for agricultural failure, for opportunism and lack of consistency, for endless boasting. They lashed out at him for pushing the Chinese quarrel to such a point that even an appearance of amity was impossible.[7] Crankshaw writes:

> Above all, they attacked him for alienating so many good soldiers, so many able officials, and for promoting sycophants and yes-men to high office. They attacked him for encouraging a personality cult of his own, in breach of solemn promise, for encouraging the glorification of his person and trying to make policy with too little reference to his colleagues and through his own personal network of favorites.[8]

Remembering how he had defeated Molotov's and Malenkov's attempts to unseat him in 1957, Khrushchev demanded that the case be put before the Central Committee. His opponents had anticipated such a move and had already summoned—and prepared—the committee.[9] The vote went against Khrushchev, and a colorful figure bowed out of Soviet politics.

With Khrushchev's departure the possibility of Zhukov's rehabilitation became a probability. On February 10, 1965, for the first time since his fall from grace in 1957, his name appeared in the obituary of a former associate, Major General Ivan Matveevich Karmanov.[10] In April, as the Soviets prepared to celebrate the twentieth anniversary of their victory over Germany, rumors began to circulate that Zhukov would participate in the festivities.[11] On April 28, Tass broadcast some remarks by Konev on Zhukov's wartime role:

> Marshal Zhukov, as is common knowledge, held prominent appointments. His services were highly appreciated by the Soviet government. Zhukov was a great military leader, although he had some shortcomings which have already been mentioned in our press. Marshal Zhukov is now on a pension. He lives in Moscow and evidently, like all Soviet people, will take part in the celebration of the twentieth anniversary of the victory over Fascist Germany.[12]

Thenceforward Zhukov's name appeared with greater frequency in Soviet publications. His role in the final battles of World War II was discussed in articles by Sokolovsky on April 16[13] and Rokossovsky on April 30.[14] Some military writers, however, Konev among them, were still too timid to cite Zhukov by name, referring to him only as the "commander of the First Belorussian *Front*."[15] A few days before the Moscow celebrations the Soviet news agency Novosti released a portrait of Georgi Zhukov, resplendent with battle decorations, and by now it was obvious that the old hero was being resurrected for the occasion.[16]

On May 8, Leonid Brezhnev delivered a two-hour keynote address before an audience of six thousand in the Kremlin's Palace of Congresses. As he began a lengthy account of the German attack on the Soviet Union, he said: "In that crucial situation, the Party and the Soviet people made great, truly heroic efforts to strengthen the army and reorganize the economy along military lines, to turn the country into a solidly united military camp." Then, referring to Stalin, he said: "A State Defense Committee was formed under the direction of the general secretary of the Central Committee of the All Union Communist Party." At that point applause welled up and grew louder as Brezhnev tried to continue reading his speech. Apparently ruffled, he stumbled a bit over his text and then backtracked to pick up: ". . . to direct the activities in organizing the resistance against the enemy." The unplanned applause was the first spontaneous public demonstration in the Kremlin for Stalin since Khrushchev's denunciation of the dictator in 1956. A burst of applause also greeted Zhukov's name, included in Brezhnev's recital of a list of military commanders prominent in the war.[17]

On the following day the Soviets held a massive military parade which, in addition to a one-thousand-piece band, featured new Russian missiles and rockets. Atop Lenin's tomb stood Marshals Budenny, Voroshilov, Zhukov, and Timoshenko and other Soviet heroes.[18] Zhukov's return to public life was welcomed joyously. Former attachés to the Soviet Union have told me that when he appeared on the street in uniform on the anniversary of V-E Day, women street cleaners broke out in tears. At a reception later that day fellow officers greeted him with genuine warmth.

Upon learning that Zhukov had reappeared publicly, former President Eisenhower expressed gratification, saying: "I think it's time he was rehabilitated. He was a very good soldier and he tried his best to make things work in Berlin."[19]

According to one writer, Zhukov's successor, Marshal Malinovsky, may not have been pleased with Zhukov's presence at the mausoleum. He was reportedly cool toward his civilian bosses during V-E Day activities. Speculation centered on whether his displeasure had some connection with Zhukov's reemergence. "It is now known," writes Edmund Stevens, "that Zhukov only received his invitation to attend the

V-E anniversary meeting on May 8 and the military parade on May 9, two days ahead of time."*

Also on May 9, an awards ceremony was held in the Great Kremlin Palace, where Anastas Mikoyan, chairman of the Presidium of the Supreme Soviet, presented jubilee medals to a number of wartime leaders. Inscribed "the 20th Anniversary of the Victory in the Great Patriotic War, 1941–1945," they were awarded to Zhukov, Malinovsky, Bagramyan, Budenny, Voroshilov, Golikov, Rokossovsky, Sokolovsky, Timoshenko, and others. Brezhnev presented inscribed gold watches to those who bore the title Hero of the Soviet Union, and, of course, Zhukov was among them.[20]

In June, 1965, the first installment of Zhukov's memoirs appeared in *Voyenno-Istorichesky Zhurnal*. Entitled "In the Berlin Direction," it caused some excitement because Zhukov accused Chuikov of something very near lying. Other installments followed: three articles on the Battle of Moscow in *Voyenno-Istorichesky Zhurnal* (August, September, October, 1965) and two articles on the Kursk campaign (August and September, 1967) in the same publication. In addition, Zhukov's memoirs of the defense of Moscow were serialized in the English-language publication *Moscow News* between October 22 and December 24, 1966. He also wrote a chapter for two books dealing with the Battle of Moscow, *Bitva za Moskvu* (*Battle for Moscow*) and *Proval Gitlerovskogo Nastupleniya na Moskvu* (*Defeat of the Hitlerite Offensive Against Moscow*). Later he published articles in *Pravda Ukrainy* (*Pravda of the Ukraine*), *Komosomolskaya Pravda* (*Komsomol Pravda*), *Literaturnaya Gazeta, Narodna Armia* (*People's Army-Sofia*), and other periodicals.

* Edmund Stevens, "Malinovsky Cool to Bosses," *Evening Star* (Washington), May 31, 1965, A-5. Stevens also wrote: "Since his retirement, Zhukov has lived mostly in the roomy suburban government dacha assigned to him when he was Defense Minister and which he was permitted to retain. Last year [1964] he obtained a divorce and married a woman named Galina [Aleksandrovna], 25 years his junior, whom he had met on a trip to Sverdlovsk. His former wife has retained his town flat in the apartment house for government officials on Granovsky Street, two blocks from the Kremlin. . . . He is finishing his wartime memoirs, on which he has been working for several years. Because he insists on writing without fear or favor, publication may be delayed for quite a while. He works in a small study, the walls of which are covered with autographed photos, including those of Eisenhower, De Gaulle, Churchill, Montgomery, as well as leading Soviet wartime figures. Stalin is not among them." *Ibid.* Later his second wife bore him a daughter, Masha (Mashenka).

The December, 1966, celebrations of the twenty-fifth anniversary of the victory at Moscow provided another occasion for Zhukov's further rehabilitation. Sokolovsky's article on the great battle described the marshal's decisive role in the campaign,[21] and Moscow Gorkom (City Party Organization) First Secretary Nikita Yegorychev praised the military leaders who helped save Moscow, heading the list with Zhukov.[22] Said Yegorychev: "And we pay tribute to the military deeds of our glorious generals and military commanders—Zhukov, Konev, Budenny . . . ." The audience, which included many decorated war veterans, burst into applause at the mention of Zhukov's name, and Yegorychev had to pause to wait for silence.[23]

In the same month the Presidium of the Supreme Soviet awarded Zhukov the nation's highest award, the Order of Lenin, "for services to the armed forces and in connection with his seventieth birthday."*

Zhukov was honored in still other ways. He sat for a bust by sculptor Victor Dumanian, and he was the subject of a biography by Colonel N. Svetlishin which appeared in *Voyenno-Istorichesky Zhurnal*. Svetlishin based his article on personal interviews with Zhukov, on the marshal's private papers, and on archives of the Ministry of Defense. It is the most nearly complete biography of Zhukov produced by the Soviets to date.[24] Moreover, it is objective, fair, and factual. It is interesting to note that neither this article nor any other published since Zhukov's rehabilitation has denied the charge made in 1957 that he sought to reduce political influences on the armed forces. Svetlishin passes over the episode, merely stating that Zhukov made "serious mistakes, which were noted by the October, 1957, plenum of the Central Committee of the CPSU in its resolution 'Concerning the Strengthening of Party-Political Work in the Soviet Army and Navy.' "[25]

In 1965 an excellent history of the war, *Velikaya Otechestvennaya Voina Sovetskogo Soyuza, 1941–1945, Kratkaya Istoriya (The Great*

---

* "Ukaz Presidiuma Verkhovnogo Soveta SSSR," *Krasnaya Zvezda*, December 3, 1966, 1. On December 13, 1966, Zhukov wrote to the editor of *Krasnaya Zvezda*: "Being unable to answer the multitudinous congratulations concerning the awarding to me of the Order of Lenin and on my seventieth birthday, allow me through the newspaper *Krasnaya Zvezda* to express my deep, heartfelt thanks to the collectives, organizations, troops of the Soviet Army and Navy, officers, generals in the reserve, and all the citizens for their warm congratulations and at the same time to wish them good health and success in their work for the good of our Motherland." *Krasnaya Zvezda*, December 13, 1966, 4.

Patriotic War of the Soviet Union, 1941–1945, Concise History), a one-volume compendium of the six-volume *Istoriya*, was published. The flattering photographs and exaggerated accounts of Khrushchev were gone, and Zhukov reappeared as one of the Russians' outstanding wartime commanders.

Zhukov's rehabilitation was given impetus by memoirs written by his associates. As I have pointed out, Generals Antipenko and Telegin came to Zhukov's rescue in his debate with Chuikov over the Battle of Berlin. Their courage can be appreciated even more when one realizes that they defended Zhukov's actions before his rehabilitation. Marshal Ivan K. Bagramyan also treated Zhukov kindly. In one installment of his memoirs he wrote that "of all the outstanding military commanders who rose with lightning speed in the prewar years, [Zhukov] was, without a doubt, the most brilliant and gifted personality."

By 1965 even the Albanians had good words for Zhukov. An article in *Zeri i Popullit* (*Voice of the People*) described him as a "remarkable Soviet military leader and one of the most eminent Soviet Army officers during the Great Patriotic War, whose name was respected and honored throughout the world." Zhukov "was accused in a cowardly manner by the Khrushchevite group of 'Bonapartism, insubordination toward Party directives,' and other evil deeeds." If Zhukov was guilty of these sins, the Albanian paper asked, then why did the Soviets send him on an official visit to a socialist country? "Did he become 'Bonapartist' during the nine days he stayed there?"*

Zhukov participated in a number of public functions honoring the military. He took part in ceremonies honoring the unknown soldier in December, 1966, and May, 1967, and in festivities on the occasion of the

---

* *Zeri i Popullit* (Tiranë), May 22, 1965. The Albanians had short memories. Less than ten years before, on October 24, 1957, they had warmly greeted Zhukov: "We feel very happy to have among us Comrade Georgi Zhukov, one of the most eminent sons of the motherly Communist Party of the Soviet Union, hero of the legendary Soviet Army." A little more than a week later, on November 2, Radio Tiranë broadcast the news of Zhukov's dismissal "because he committed great mistakes by trampling on the great and decisive principle that the main source of the strength of the renowned Soviet Army is based on the leadership of the Party and Central Committee. Such a measure, which finds unanimous approval, aims at further strengthening the glorious and liberating Army of the Soviet Union." Radio Tiranë, October 24, November 2, 1957; cited in "Before and After," *East Europe*, Vol. VI, No. 2 (December, 1957), 50.

forty-ninth and fiftieth anniversaries of the Soviet armed forces. He signed obituaries and took part in the funeral services of Marshals Malinovsky and Sokolovsky. On August 4, 1968, it was his sad duty to sign the obituary of his old friend Rokossovsky, who died on August 3 after a long illness.

In 1968 an excellent one-volume history of the Soviet armed forces appeared in Russia. Entitled *50 Let Vooruzhennykh Sil SSSR, (50 Years of the Armed Forces of the U.S.S.R.*), it was produced by a commission headed by Marshal M. V. Zakharov. Contributors included a number of wartime commanders, among them Georgi Zhukov. The book contained many references to Zhukov, and he was finally given his place in history as one of the chief architects of victory over the Germans.[26]

When Dwight D. Eisenhower died on March 28, 1969, there were rumors that Zhukov would represent the Soviet Union at the funeral. Not too long before, however, the marshal had suffered a stroke. Although he was recovering, he was not well enough to make the trip.

Honors continued to make their way to Zhukov. On August 14, 1969, on the occasion of the thirtieth anniversary of the defeat of the Japanese at Khalkhin-Gol, First Secretary of the Mongolian People's Revolutionary Party and Chairman of the Council of Ministers Yumzhgyn Tsedenbal presented Zhukov the Gold Star of the Hero of the Mongolian People's Republic.

In 1970, Khrushchev, himself ailing, paid a tribute to Zhukov:

> I still have great respect for him as a commander, despite our subsequent parting of the ways. He didn't correctly understand his role as Minister of Defense, and we were compelled to take action against him in order to prevent him from going through with certain schemes which he had concocted. But even then I valued him highly as a soldier, and I don't retreat one step today from my high evaluation of him.[27]

A year earlier, in 1969, Zhukov's memoirs of the battles of Moscow, Stalingrad, Kursk, and Berlin had been translated into English and published in the United States under the title *Marshal Zhukov's Greatest Battles*.[28] At about the same time it was announced that his memoirs were being published in Moscow. The long-awaited memoirs, which had a monumental first printing of 600,000 copies, first appeared in Russian bookstores in the United States early in 1970. Regrettably, they end with Zhukov's departure from Germany in 1946, and the world is denied the old warrior's account of his greatest personal battles. Zhukov's long-term associate, Marshal Budenny, now in his eighties, lavishly praised the memoirs:

> Many errors were made by our own historians and writers, especially in describing the prewar years and the early period of the war. The contribution which Georgi Konstantinovich Zhukov has made is that he, in his work as an authoritative witness and participant in these events, has shattered all attempts to distort historical facts and has restored the truth.[29]

Zhukov has thus emerged in his twilight years to take his proper place in Soviet history. The resurrection of this great soldier, first a patriot and only then a Party member, can be viewed as an attempt by Brezhnev and his fellow leaders to give credit where credit is due and to make Soviet history a more factual record of events. Zhukov still commands the loyalty of many Russians in all walks of life, especially the veterans of World War II.[30] Zhukov is an enduring symbol of victory on the battlefield.

APPENDICES

APPENDICES

A. Chronology of Significant Events in Zhukov's Career

AUGUST 7, 1915	Mobilized in the Tsarist army as a private.
SEPTEMBER, 1915	Sent to the Ukraine to the Fifth Reserve Cavalry Division.
AUGUST, 1916	Completes NCO training and sent to the front. Joins Tenth Cavalry Division. As member of Tenth Regiment of Novogorod Dragoons receives two Saint George crosses.
OCTOBER, 1916	Wounded; upon recovery, ordered to a training command.
MARCH, 1917	Votes with unit to support Bolsheviks.
MAY, 1917	Issued discharge by Bolshevik Soldiers' Committee.
AUGUST, 1918	Volunteers for service in the Red Army. Joins Fourth Cavalry Regiment of the First Moscow Cavalry Division.
MARCH 1, 1919	Joins Communist Party.
SEPTEMBER, 1919	Wounded at Tsaritsyn (Stalingrad).
JANUARY, 1920	Enrolls in cavalry course for Red commanders in Ryazan.
JULY, 1920	Sent to Moscow for further training.
AUGUST, 1920	Participates in operations against Wrangel. Assigned to First Cavalry Regiment as platoon commander. Assigned as commander of Second Squadron, First Cavalry Regiment.
DECEMBER, 1920	His Fourteenth Separate Cavalry Brigade transferred to Voronezh Province to put down a kulak uprising.
APRIL, 1921	Participates in operations against Antonov's Social Revolutionary bands.
SUMMER, 1921	Participates in operations against small bands in Tambov Region.
JUNE, 1922–MARCH, 1923	Squadron commander in the Thirty-eighth Cavalry Regiment and then assistant commander of the Fortieth Cavalry Regiment, Seventh Samara Cavalry Division.
APRIL, 1923	Appointed commander of Thirty-ninth Buzuluksk Cavalry Regiment.

1924–25	Attends cavalry course for command personnel in Leningrad. Upon graduation returns to Thirty-ninth Regiment.
1929–SPRING, 1930	Attends advanced course for senior officers at Frunze Academy, Moscow.
MAY, 1930	Appointed commander of Second Cavalry Brigade, Seventh Samara Cavalry Division under Rokossovsky. (Zhukov's brigade consisted of two cavalry regiments, the Thirty-ninth and the Fortieth.)
FEBRUARY, 1931	Named assistant to the inspector of cavalry of the Red Army.
MARCH, 1933	Assigned command of Fourth Cavalry Division, part of the Belorussian Military District.
AUTUMN, 1936–SUMMER, 1937	One of the principal Soviet military advisers in Spain (?).
FALL, 1937	Appointed commander of Third Cavalry Corps. Appointed commander of Sixth Kazach Corps.
SUMMER, 1938	Serves in China as military adviser.
WINTER, 1938	Deputy commander of Belorussian Special Military District.
JUNE, 1939	Commander of all Soviet-Mongolian troops along Khalkhin-Gol River.
AUGUST 20, 1939	Institutes massive offensive against Japanese.
AUGUST 31, 1939	Clears Japanese forces from Mongolian People's Republic.
AUTUMN, 1939	Deputy commander of Ukrainian Military District.
WINTER, 1939–40	Serves briefly as chief of the General Staff, temporarily relieving the ailing Shaposhnikov.
JUNE, 1940	Promoted ahead of time to general of the army; assigned to command Kiev Special Military District.
JUNE 28, 1940	Leads forces into Bessarabia and northern Bucovina.
DECEMBER, 1940–JANUARY, 1941	Participates in High Command war games in Moscow; commands Kiev Special Military District.
JANUARY 13, 1941	Appointed chief of the General Staff.
FEBRUARY, 1941	Elected alternate member of the Party Central Committee.
MARCH, 1941	Named deputy defense commissar; heads Directorates of Communications, Fuel Supply, and Air Defense.
JUNE 23, 1941	Appointed to newly created Stavka.

Chronology of Significant Events in Zhukov's Career

JULY 30, 1941	Leaves General Staff to take command of Reserve *Front*. Occasionally visited Southwestern *Front* to assist *Front* commander in planning of operations.
SEPTEMBER 12–OCTOBER 7, 1941	Commander of Leningrad *Front*.
OCTOBER 9, 1941	Appointed commander of Western *Front*, fighting on Moscow's approaches.
FEBRUARY 1, 1942	Appointed commander in chief of Western Direction, retaining command of Western *Front*.
AUGUST 26, 1942	Named deputy supreme commander in chief.
AUGUST, 1942	Sent to Stalingrad to organize defenses and plan counteroffensive.
NOVEMBER 17, 1942	Summoned from Stalingrad to begin planning the counteroffensive on the Kalinin and Western *fronts*.
JANUARY 18, 1943	Made marshal of the Soviet Union.
EARLY 1943	Sent to Leningrad to help breach blockade.
APRIL, 1943	Assigned to Voronezh *Front*.
MAY–AUGUST, 1943	Coordinates actions of Central, Bryansk, and Western *fronts* in Battle of Kursk.
NOVEMBER 21, 1943	With Khrushchev makes triumphant entry into Kiev.
EARLY 1944	Sent to Ukraine to coordinate actions of Vatutin's First Ukrainian *Front* and Konev's Second Ukrainian *Front*.
MARCH 1–MAY, 1944	Replaces Vatutin as commander of First Ukrainian *Front*.
MAY–JULY, 1944	Coordinates actions of First and Second Belorussian *fronts*.
JULY 29, 1944	Appointed to conduct operations of First Ukrainian and First and Second Belorussian *fronts*.
MID-SEPTEMBER, 1944	Assumes command of First Polish Army; helps Poles plan crossing of Vistula.
NOVEMBER 19, 1944	Given command of First Belorussian *Front* (one of two to advance on Berlin).
MAY 9, 1945	Represents U.S.S.R. in surrender negotiations with Germany.
END OF MAY, 1945	Appointed Soviet member of Allied Control Council.
APRIL 10, 1946	Leaves Berlin to become commander of all Soviet ground forces.
JULY, 1946	Ordered to Odessa Military District.

1948–49	Transferred to Ural Military District.
SUMMER, 1952	Returns to Moscow to assume posts of deputy defense minister and inspector general.
MARCH 6, 1953	Named first deputy minister of defense.
JUNE, 1953	Participates in the arrest of Beria.
FEBRUARY, 1955	Minister of defense.
JULY, 1955	Delegate to Geneva Conference.
OCTOBER, 1956	Directs Soviet military movements in Poland; orders Soviet forces into Hungary.
JANUARY–FEBRUARY, 1957	Inspects armed forces of India.
JUNE, 1957	Supports Khrushchev in struggle with "anti-Party group."
OCTOBER 27, 1957	Relieved as defense minister.
MARCH, 1958	Retired.
MAY 9, 1965	Appears in public for V-E Day celebrations. Long "rehabilitation" process begins.
DECEMBER 1, 1966	Awarded the Soviet Union's highest award, the Order of Lenin, for "services to the Armed Forces."
1969	*Memoirs and Reflections* published. In August received Hero of the Mongolian People's Republic award.

B. Soviet Army Military Ranks and United States Army Equivalents (Officers)

SOVIET UNION	UNITED STATES
Marshal of the Soviet Union	General of the army (wartime only)
Chief marshal of an arm	(None)
Marshal of an arm	(None)
General of the army	General
Colonel general	Lieutenant general
Lieutenant general	Major general
Major general	Brigadier general
Colonel	Colonel
Lieutenant colonel	Lieutenant colonel
Major	Major
Captain	Captain
Senior lieutenant	First lieutenant
Lieutenant	Second lieutenant
Junior lieutenant	(None)

C. Organization of the Direction of the Soviet Armed Forces, 1939

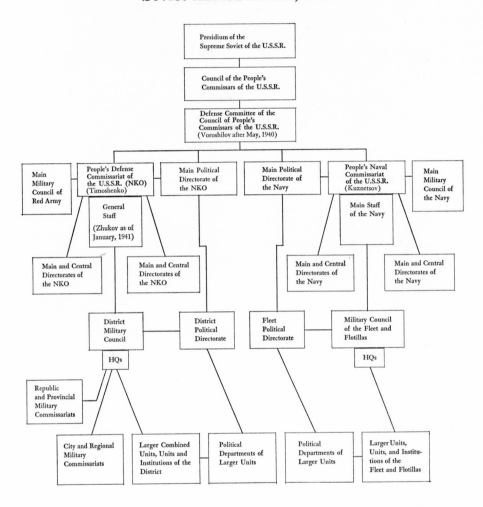

Presidium of the Supreme Soviet of the U.S.S.R.

Council of the People's Commissars of the U.S.S.R.

Defense Committee of the Council of People's Commissars of the U.S.S.R. (Voroshilov after May, 1940)

Main Military Council of Red Army

People's Defense Commissariat of the U.S.S.R. (NKO) (Timoshenko)

General Staff (Zhukov as of January, 1941)

Main Political Directorate of the NKO

Main Political Directorate of the Navy

People's Naval Commissariat of the U.S.S.R. (Kuznetsov)

Main Staff of the Navy

Main Military Council of the Navy

Main and Central Directorates of the NKO

Main and Central Directorates of the NKO

Main and Central Directorates of the Navy

Main and Central Directorates of the Navy

District Military Council

District Political Directorate

Fleet Political Directorate

Military Council of the Fleet and Flotillas

HQs

HQs

Republic and Provincial Military Commissariats

City and Regional Military Commissariats

Larger Combined Units, Units and Institutions of the District

Political Departments of Larger Units

Political Departments of Larger Units

Larger Units, Units, and Institutions of the Fleet and Flotillas

D. Actual Soviet Chain of Command in World War II

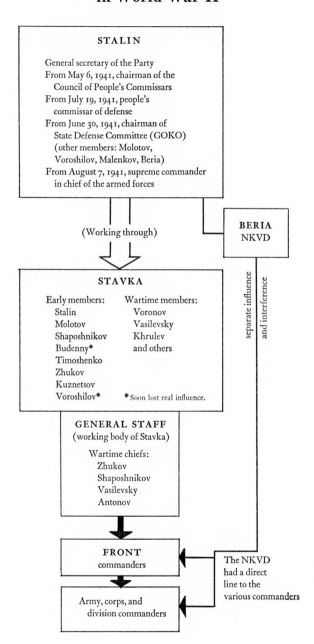

STALIN

General secretary of the Party
From May 6, 1941, chairman of the
Council of People's Commissars
From July 19, 1941, people's
commissar of defense
From June 30, 1941, chairman of
State Defense Committee (GOKO)
(other members: Molotov,
Voroshilov, Malenkov, Beria)
From August 7, 1941, supreme commander
in chief of the armed forces

(Working through)

BERIA
NKVD

separate influence
and interference

STAVKA

Early members: Wartime members:
Stalin   Voronov
Molotov   Vasilevsky
Shaposhnikov   Khrulev
Budenny*   and others
Timoshenko
Zhukov
Kuznetsov
Voroshilov*   * Soon lost real influence.

GENERAL STAFF
(working body of Stavka)

Wartime chiefs:
Zhukov
Shaposhnikov
Vasilevsky
Antonov

FRONT
commanders

The NKVD
had a direct
line to the
various commanders

Army, corps, and
division commanders

441

NOTES

Chapter I

1. Georgi K. Zhukov, *Vospominaniya i Razmyshleniya*, 7–8. Unless otherwise indicated, all translations are mine.
2. *Ibid.*, 8–9.
3. *Ibid.*, 9–10.
4. *Ibid.*, 38.
5. *Ibid.*, 41.
6. John Erickson, *The Soviet High Command: A Military-Political History, 1918–1941*, 70.
7. J. Malcolm Mackintosh, *Juggernaut: A History of the Soviet Armed Forces*, 25–26.
8. *Ibid.*, 28.
9. Zhukov, *op. cit.*, 52.
10. *Ibid.*, 53.
11. Erickson, *op. cit.*, 97–102.
12. *Ibid.*, 102–107. See also G. Gorelov, "The Defeat of Wrangel," *Soviet Military Review*, October, 1970, 42–45.
13. Zhukov, *op. cit.*, 63–64.
14. *Ibid.*, 64.
15. Erickson, *op. cit.*, 114.
16. P. Ruslanov, "Marshal Zhukov," *Russian Review*, Vol. XV (April, 1956), 124.
17. I. Vakurov, "Frunze Academy Graduates," *Soviet Military Review*, December, 1968, 38.
18. Edward Hallett Carr, *German-Soviet Relations Between the Two World Wars, 1919–1939*, 13.
19. Gustav Hilger and Alfred G. Meyer, *The Incompatible Allies: A Memoir History of German-Soviet Relations, 1918–1941*, 192–99.
20. J. Malcolm Mackintosh, "The Red Army, 1920–1926," in B. H. Liddell Hart (ed.), *The Soviet Army*, 59.
21. Major General F. W. von Mellenthin, *Panzer Battles: A Study of the Employment of Armor in the Second World War*, 192.

Chapter II

1. N. Svetlishin, "Ot Soldata do Marshala, k 70-letiyu G. K. Zhukova," *Voyenno-Istorichesky Zhurnal*, November, 1966, 32.
2. *Ibid.* Svetlishin cites Zhukov's personal files as the source of this efficiency report.
3. "Yedinonachalie v Vooruzhennykh Silakh SSSR," *Bolshaya Sovetskaya Entsiklopediya*, 2d ed., XV, 476. See also N. Galay, "Principles of Command in the Soviet Armed Forces," *Bulletin of the Institute for the Study of the History and Culture of the USSR*, Vol. II (June, 1955), 11.
4. Galay, "Principles of Command," *loc. cit.*, 12–13.
5. Ruslanov, "Marshal Zhukov," *loc. cit.*, 125. This article and the one that appeared in the July, 1956, issue of *Russian Review* are translations from the Russian, in abridged form, of articles which appeared in the Russian-language magazine *Sotsialistichesky Vestnik* (New York), Nos. 2–4 (February–April, 1955).

6. *Ibid.*, 125–27.

7. *Ibid.*, 128.

8. *Ibid.*, 129.

9. *Ibid.*, July, 1956, 186.

10. *Ibid.*, 187–89.

11. Svetlishin, "Ot Soldata do Marshala," *loc. cit.*, 32.

12. *Ibid.*

13. "Dragoon's Day," *Time*, May 9, 1955, 27.

14. Erickson, *op. cit.*, 537.

15. *Ibid.*

16. Svetlishin, "Ot Soldata do Marshala," *loc. cit.*, 32.

17. *Ibid.*

18. *Ibid.*

19. George F. Kennan, *Soviet Foreign Policy, 1917–1941*, 86–87.

20. *Ibid.*, 87.

21. Robert L. Plumb, "Soviet Participation in the Spanish Civil War" (Ph.D. dissertation, Georgetown University, 1956), 89. Plumb was most kind in helping me find materials dealing with Zhukov's stay in Spain.

22. "V Avangarde Sukhoputnykh Voysk," *Kommunist Vooruzhennykh Sil*, No. 15 (August, 1966), 39.

23. Richard E. Lauterbach, *These Are the Russians*, 124.

24. Plumb, *op. cit.*, 308.

25. *Ibid.*, 318–19. Pavlov's activities were observed by Robert Gladnick, who described them in a letter to Plumb in March, 1955.

26. *Ibid.*, 319–20.

27. Letter to Plumb from Robert Gladnick, April 5, 1955, *ibid.*, 332.

28. Alexander Orlov, "The Sensational Secret Behind the Damnation of Stalin," *Life*, Vol. XL (April 23, 1956), 44. Orlov, a former NKVD officer, accompanied his article with a photograph of Zhukov, which was probably taken in Spain.

29. According to Tukhachevsky's sister-in-law. Cited in Michel Garder, *A History of the Soviet Army*, 94.

30. Plumb, *op. cit.*, 291.

31. Jane Degras (ed.), *Soviet Documents on Foreign Policy, 1933–1941*, III, 228.

32. Plumb, *op. cit.*, 291–95.

33. Letter to Plumb from Robert Gladnick, March 21, 1955, *ibid.*, 299–300.

34. *Ibid.*, 300–306, 354–55.

35. Kennan, *op. cit.*, 88–89.

Chapter III

1. Alexander N. Shelepin's speech before the Twenty-second Party Congress, October 26, 1961, *Pravda*, October 27, 1961.

2. From the concluding remarks of N. S. Khrushchev at the Twenty-second Party Congress, *ibid.*, October 29, 1961.

3. G. I. Antonov, "Zhukov—Ministr Oborony SSSR" (unpublished eight-page article), 1–2. Antonov is a former Red Army colonel who took up residence in Munich.

4. The source for these figures is Raymond L. Garthoff, *How Russia Makes War* (*Soviet Military Doctrine*), 220.

5. Plumb, *op. cit.*, 569, 571, 575, 578–800. See also W. G. Krivitsky, *In Stalin's Secret Service*, 103–14. Krivitsky was chief of Soviet intelligence in Western Europe.

6. Plumb, *op. cit.*, 579–80. Letter to Plumb from Robert Gladnick, April 5, 1955.

7. *Pravda*, October 29, 1961. This translation is from *Problems of Communism* (Washington), No. 1 (January–February, 1962), 27.

8. Antonov, *op. cit.*, 1–2.

9. Erickson, *op. cit.*, 462–63.

10. Yu. I. Korablev and M. I. Loginov (eds.), *KPSS i Stroitelstvo Vooruzhennykh Sil SSSR (1918–Iyun 1941)*, 431.

11. Leonard Schapiro, "The Great Purge," in Hart (ed.), *op. cit.*, 71.

12. Erickson, *op. cit.*, 502.

13. *Ibid.*, 502–503.

14. Isaac Deutscher, *Stalin: A Political Biography*, 425.

15. Winston S. Churchill, *The Gathering Storm*, 289.

16. F. F. Liu, *A Military History of Modern China, 1924–1929*, 6, 20, 167. See also Erickson, *op. cit.*, 847; O. Edmund Clubb, *Twentieth Century China*, 220, 228.

17. Chiang Kai-shek. *Soviet Russia in China: A Summing-Up at Seventy*, 71.

18. *Ibid.*, 86.

19. Boris Aleksandrovich Borodin, *Pomoshch SSSR Kitaiskomu Narodu v Antiyaponskoy Voine, 1937–1941*, 159–60.

20. Liu, *op. cit.*, 169–70.

21. *Ibid.*, 170.

22. Borodin, *op. cit.*, 171–72.

23. Clubb, *op. cit.*, 220. See also Borodin, *op. cit.*, 173.

24. Vasily Ivanovich Chuikov, *The Battle for Stalingrad*, 13–14.

25. Clubb, *op. cit.*, 228.

Chapter IV

1. *Istoriya Velikoy Otechestvennoy Voiny Sovetskogo Soyuza, 1941–1945*, I, 230. Hereafter cited as *IVOVSS*.

2. *Ibid.*

3. G. H. Sevostyanov, "Voyennoe i Diplomaticheskoe Porazhenie Yaponii v Period Sobytiy u Reki Khalkhin-Gol," *Voprosy Istorii*, August, 1957, 63–64.

4. Michel Berchin and Eliahu Ben-Horin, *The Red Army*, 173.

5. *Ibid.*

6. *Ibid.*, 174–75.

7. *IVOVSS*, I, 236.

8. *Ibid.*

9. Sevostyanov, "Voyennoe i Diplomaticheskoe Porazhenie Yaponii," *loc. cit.*, 64–65.

10. *IVOVSS*, I, 236–38.

11. *Ibid.*, 238. See also Sevostyanov, "Voyennoe i Diplomaticheskoe Porazhenie Yaponii," *loc. cit.*, 66.

12. *IVOVSS*, I, 238.

13. Erickson, *op. cit.*, 521–22.

14. *Ibid.*, 522.

15. The military rank of Komkor was awarded to Zhukov by decree of the People's Defense Commissariat on July 31, 1939. See Svetlishin, "Ot Soldata do Marshala," *loc. cit.*, 33.

16. Ruslanov, "Marshal Zhukov," *loc. cit.*, July, 1956, 189.

17. *IVOVSS*, I, 240–41.

18. Erickson, *op. cit.*, 533–34.

19. Ruslanov, "Marshal Zhukov," *loc. cit.*, July, 1956, 190.

20. Lauterbach, *op. cit.*, 122.

21. *Ibid.*, 125.

22. *IVOVSS*, I, 241–44.

23. Sevostyanov, "Voyennoe i Diplomaticheskoe Porazhenie Yaponii," *loc. cit.*, 81.

24. Saburo Hayashi, *Kogun: The Japanese Army in the Pacific War*, 15.

25. *Ibid.*

26. *Ibid.*, 16.

27. Svetlishin, "Ot Soldata do Marshala," *loc. cit.*, 33.

28. Erickson, *op. cit.*, 537. See also N. Galay, "The Armoured Forces: Recent Trends," in Hart (ed.), *op. cit.*, 316.

29. Erickson, *op. cit.*, 559–67.

Chapter V

1. Churchill, *The Gathering Storm*, 262–63.

2. *Ibid.*, 170.

3. *Ibid.*, 270–71.

4. *Ibid.*, 320–21, 343–45.

5. Quoted in Alexander Werth, *Russia at War, 1941–1945*, 4.

6. Joachim von Ribbentrop, *Zwischen London und Moskau*, 180.

7. *Pravda*, August 24, 1939.

8. Raymond James Sontag and James Stuart Beddie (eds.), *Nazi-Soviet Relations, 1939–1941: Documents from the Archives of the German Foreign Office*, 76–78.

9. Vaino Tanner, *The Winter War: Finland Against Russia, 1939–1940*, 66–67.

10. Erickson, *op. cit.*, 543–44, 547–48.

11. *Ibid.*, 847. See also Albert Parry, *Russian Cavalcade: A Military Record*, 200.

12. Nikita S. Khrushchev, *Khrushchev Remembers* (intro., commentary, and notes by Edward Crankshaw; trans. and ed. by Strobe Talbott), 160–64.

13. Lauterbach, *op. cit.*, 126.

14. *Ibid.*, 126–27.

15. A. I. Yeremenko, *V Nachale Voiny*, 34–35.

16. *Ibid.*, 45.

17. M. I. Kazakov, *Nad Kartoy Bylykh Srazhenii*, 60–61. The quotations which follow are also taken from Kazakov.

18. *Ibid.*, 62–66.

19. Lauterbach, *op. cit.*, 127–29.

20. *Ibid.* See also Werth, *op. cit.*, 115–16.

21. See George F. Kennan, *Russia and the West Under Lenin and Stalin*, 339–43.

22. Valentin Berezhkov, "Molotov in Berlin," *Atlas*, Vol. X, No. 6 (December, 1965), 352–55.

23. Hilger and Meyer, *op. cit.*, 324.

24. Ribbentrop, *op. cit.*, 240.

25. Franz Halder, "The Private War Journal of Generaloberst Franz Halder, Chief of the General Staff of the Supreme Command of the German Army (OKH), 14 August

1939 to 24 September 1942" (mimeographed). Halder's journal, comprising nine volumes and covering the period of his tenure as chief of staff, contains shorthand notes of conferences, staff talks, memoranda, lectures, and reports.

26. *Ibid.*, October 18, 1939.

27. *Ibid.*, July 22, 1940.

28. *Ibid.*, July 31, 1940; italics in the original.

29. *IVOVSS*, II, 10.

30. *Ibid.*

31. Kennan, *Russia and the West*, 336.

32. *Ibid.*, 344.

33. Hilger and Meyer, *op. cit.*, 327.

34. *Pravda* and *Izvestia*, June 14, 1941.

35. Svetlishin, "Ot Soldata do Marshala," *loc. cit.*, 33–34.

36. Ivan Khristoforovich Bagramyan, "Zapiski Nachalnika Operativnogo Otdela," *Voyenno-Istorichesky Zhurnal*, January, 1967, 55–56.

37. *Ibid.*, 50–51, 56.

38. Erickson, *op. cit.*, 568–69.

39. *Ibid.*, 570–72.

40. Winston S. Churchill, *Their Finest Hour*, 579.

41. N. G. Kuznetsov, "Before the War," *International Affairs* (Moscow), January, 1967, 99–100.

42. *Ibid.*, 100–101.

43. *Ibid.*, 101.

44. *Ibid.*

45. *Ibid.*, 104.

46. *Ibid.*, 103.

47. Kazakov, *op. cit.*, 67–71.

48. Ivan I. Fedyuninsky, *Podnyate po Trevoge*, 10–14.

49. Kazakov, *op. cit.*, 72–73.

Chapter VI

1. Heinz Guderian, *Panzer Leader*, 153.

2. Alan Clark, "25 Years After the Day Hitler Attacked Russia," *New York Times Magazine*, June 19, 1966, 13, 68.

3. *IVOVSS*, II, 11.

4. *Ibid.*

5. Guderian, *op. cit.*, 145–50.

6. Hilger and Meyer, *op. cit.*, 336.

7. Gunther Blumentritt, "Moscow," in Seymour Freidin and William Richardson (eds.), *The Fatal Decisions*, 59.

8. Erich von Manstein, *Lost Victories* (trans. by Anthony G. Powell), 182–86.

9. Halder, *op. cit.*, June 22, 1941.

10. "V Avangarde Sukhoputnykh Voysk," *Kommunist Vooruzhennykh Sil*, No. 15 (August, 1966), 39.

11. Winston S. Churchill, *The Grand Alliance*, 472.

12. *Ibid.*, 472–73.

13. Guderian, *op. cit.*, 143.

14. *IVOVSS*, I, 439.

15. N. Galay, "Tank Forces in the Soviet Army," *Bulletin of the Institute for the Study of the History and Culture of the USSR*, Vol. I (October, 1954), 7–8.

16. See Werth, *op. cit.*, 168.

17. *Ibid.*, 169.

18. Orlov, "The Sensational Secret Behind the Damnation of Stalin," *loc. cit.*, 44.

19. Blumentritt, "Moscow," in Freidin and Richardson (eds.), *op. cit.*, 60.

20. Guderian, *op. cit.*, 180–85, 189–90.

21. *Ibid.*, 190.

22. *Ibid.*, 198.

23. V. Ivanov and K. Cheremukhin, "O Knige 'V Nachale Voiny,' " *Voyenno-Istorichesky Zhurnal*, June, 1965, 74–75.

24. Guderian, *op. cit.*, 195.

25. *Ibid.*, 212.

26. Werth, *op. cit.*, 172–73.

27. B. H. Liddell Hart, *The German Generals Talk*, 179.

28. *Ibid.*, 180.

29. Ivan Krylov, *Soviet Staff Officer*, 126–30.

30. Hart, *op. cit.*, 181.

Chapter VII

1. Halder, *op. cit.*, July 8, 1941. See also Trumbull Higgins, *Hitler and Russia: The Third Reich in a Two-Front War, 1937–1943*, 139.

2. Halder, *op. cit.*, July 8, 1941.

3. Leon Goure, *The Siege of Leningrad*, 3.

4. I. P. Barbashin et al., *Bitva za Leningrad* (ed. by S. P. Platonov), 591.

5. Quoted in Goure, *op. cit.*, 90.

6. Dmitri V. Pavlov, *Leningrad, 1941: The Blockade*, 14–18.

7. Werth, *op. cit.*, 201–307.

8. Goure, *op. cit.*, 135.

9. Barbashin et al., *op. cit.*, 592. In the editor's comment to Zhukov's article "V Bitve za Stolitsu," *Voyenno-Istorichesky Zhurnal*, August, 1966, 53, the verb used to describe Voroshilov's transfer, *ubyl*, can imply being kicked upstairs, i.e., reduced in rank, power, or authority.

10. Alan Clark, *Barbarossa: The Russian-German Conflict, 1941–1945*, 119.

11. Fedyuninsky, *op. cit.*, 41.

12. Zhukov, "V Bitve za Stolitsu," *loc. cit.*, August, 1966, 56.

13. Alexander Werth, *Leningrad*, 165.

14. Werth, *Russia at War*, 306–307. Werth claims that Zhukov took command of the Leningrad *Front* on September 11, 1941, while other sources give September 13. Zhukov received his assignment on September 11 and arrived in Leningrad on September 13. See also Dmitri V. Pavlov, *Leningrad v Vlokade*, 34.

15. "Rech Marshala Sovetskogo Soyuza G. K. Zhukova," *Pravda*, July 16, 1957, 3.

16. Boris Vladimirovich Bychevsky, *Gorod-Front*, 92.

17. *Ibid.*

18. *Ibid.*, 92–93.

19. *Ibid.*, 93–94.

20. *Ibid.*, 94.

21. *Ibid.*, 94–95.

22. Quoted by Goure, *op. cit.*, 92, who used a German document, Gen. Kdo. XXVIII Army Korps, Abt. Ic, "Befehl an die Truppen der Nordwest Front No. 1," August 20, 1941, 18233 13.

23. *Ibid.*, 92–93.

24. Bychevsky, *op. cit.*, 98–100.

25. Goure, *op. cit.*, 87.

26. Halder, *op. cit.*, September 18, 1941.

27. Fedyuninsky, *op. cit.*, 57–58.

28. Zhukov, "V Bitve za Stolitsu," *loc. cit.*, August, 1966, 53.

29. Pavlov, *op. cit.*, 166–67.

30. Guderian, *op. cit.*, 233–34.

31. *Ibid.*, 235.

32. Zhukov, "V Bitve za Stolitsu," *loc. cit.*, August, 1966, 56.

33. Halder, *op. cit.*, October 5, 1941.

34. Zhukov, "V Bitve za Stolitsu," *loc. cit.*, August, 1966, 56.

35. Fedyuninsky, *op. cit.*, 60.

36. Barbashin et al., *Bitva za Leningrad*, 97–98.

Chapter VIII

1. Zhukov, "V Bitve za Stolitsu," *loc. cit.*, August, 1966, 56. See also Georgi K. Zhukov, "Pervoe Strategicheskoe Porazhenie Vermakhta," in *Proval Gitlerovskogo Nastupleniya na Moskvu*, 15–57.

2. Werth, *Leningrad*, 168–69.

3. Erickson, *op. cit.*, 681.

4. K. K. Rokossovsky, "Na Volokolamskom Napravlenii," *Voyenno-Istorichesky Zhurnal*, November, 1966, 47.

5. Zhukov, "V Bitve za Stolitsu," *loc. cit.*, September, 166, 55.

6. Guderian, *op. cit.*, 236.

7. *Ibid.*, 237.

8. *Ibid.*, 239.

9. Zhukov, "V Bitve za Stolitsu," *loc. cit.*, September, 1966; August, 1966, 63.

10. *Ibid.*

11. Werth, *Russia at War*, 234–37; A. M. Samsonov, *Velikaya Bitva pod Moskvoy*, 70–72.

12. Henry C. Cassidy, *Moscow Dateline, 1941–1943*, 148–50.

13. *Ibid.*, 150.

14. A. M. Samsonov, *Die Grosse Schlacht vor Moskau, 1941–1942*, 70.

15. Zhukov, "V Bitve za Stolitsu," *loc. cit.*, September, 1966, 55–56.

16. *Ibid.*, 59. Zhukov quotes K. Tippelskirch, *Istoriya Vtoroy Mirovoy Voiny*, 200–201.

17. Zhukov, "V Bitve za Stolitsu," *loc. cit.*, September, 1966.

18. Pavel Alekseevich Belov, *Za Nami Moskva*, 42–43.

19. *Ibid.*, 43.

20. Georgi K. Zhukov, "The First Strategic Defeat of the Wehrmacht," *Moscow News*, November 19, 1966, 12. See also Zhukov, "V Bitve za Stolitsu," *loc. cit.*, September, 1966, 62.

21. K. K. Rokossovsky, "Na Severnykh Podstupakh k Stolitse," *Voyenno-Istorichesky Zhurnal*, December, 1966, 52–53.

22. *Ibid.*, 53.

23. *Ibid.*

24. *Ibid.*

25. *Ibid.*

26. *Ibid.*, editor's footnote.

27. *Ibid.*, 53–54.

28. Guderian, *op. cit.*, 249–50.

29. *Ibid.*, 252.

30. Werth, *Russia at War*, 254–55.

31. Guderian, *op. cit.*, 260.

32. Halder, *op. cit.*, November 30, 1941.

33. Quoted in Werth, *Russia at War*, 256–57. Werth has translated a portion of Ivan V. Boldin's history of the 1941 campaigns, *Stranitsy Zhizni*, 184–85.

34. Guderian, *op. cit.*, 245–49.

35. Zhukov, "V Bitve za Stolitsu," *loc. cit.,* September, 1966, 64–65.

36. Georgi K. Zhukov, "Kontrnastuplenie pod Moskvoy," *Voyenno-Istorichesky Zhurnal*, October, 1966, 68.

37. *Ibid.*, 68–70.

38. *Ibid.*, 70.

39. *Ibid.*, 71–72.

40. Kyrill Dmitrievich Kalinov, *Sowjetmarschälle Haben das Wort*, 159.

41. *Ibid.*, 159–60.

42. Halder, *op. cit.*, December 12, 1941.

43. Zhukov, "Kontrnastuplenie pod Moskvoy," *loc. cit.*, 73.

44. *Ibid.*, 75–76.

45. *Ibid.*, 77.

46. *Ibid.*

47. Halder, *op. cit.*, December 16, 1941.

48. Guderian, *op. cit.*, 263–67.

49. Zhukov, "Kontrnastuplenie pod Moskvoy," *loc. cit.*, 79–80.

50. *Ibid.*, 81.

51. *Ibid.*, 82–83.

52. *Ibid.*, 84.

53. *Ibid.*, 84–85.

54. *Ibid.*, 85.

55. *Ibid.*

56. Blumentritt, "Moscow," in Freidin and Richardson (eds.), *op. cit.*, 35, 38, 64, 71–72.

57. Kalinov, *op. cit.*, 150.

Chapter IX

1. Ilya Ehrenburg, *The War: 1941–1945*, Vol. V of *Men, Years—Life*, 44.

2. Kurt Assmann, "The Battle for Moscow, Turning Point of the War," *Foreign Affairs*, January, 1950, 325.

3. Winston S. Churchill, *The Hinge of Fate*, 342–43.

4. *Ibid.*, 583.

5. Manstein, *op. cit.*, 225.

6. *Velikaya Otechestvennaya Voina Sovetskogo Soyuza* (hereafter cited as *VOVSS*), 163.

7. Halder, *op. cit.*, July 18, 1942.

8. A. Vasilevsky, "Nezabyvaemiye Dni," *Voyenno-Istorichesky Zhurnal*, October, 1965, 15.

9. Garthoff, *op. cit.*, 193.

10. *Ibid.*, 193–95.

11. *Ibid.*, 195.

12. Werth, *Russia at War*, 773–960.

13. Garthoff, *op. cit.*, 196.

14. Vasilevsky, "Nezabyvaemiye Dni," *loc. cit.*, 16–17.

15. Halder, *op. cit.*, August 30, 1942.

16. *Ibid.*, September 24, 1942.

17. G. K. Zhukov, "Razgrom Nemetskikh Voysk v. Rayone Dona, Volgi i Stalingrada," in *Stalingradskaya Epopeya* (ed. by A. M. Samsonov), 17–72. Zhukov's account provides the basis for much of the remainder of this chapter.

18. Hans Doerr, *Der Feldzug nach Stalingrad*, 56.

19. Vasilevsky, "Nezabyvaemiye Dni," *loc. cit.*, 21–22.

20. *IVOVSS*, III, 18.

21. Manstein, *op. cit.*, 311–12.

22. *Ibid.*, 329–30, 335, 345.

23. Mellenthin, *op. cit.*, 180, 191–93.

24. Werth, *Russia at War*, 502–503.

25. *Ibid.*, 504–505, 535.

26. F. Vorobyev, "Ob Oberatsii 'Koltso,'" *Voyenno-Istorichesky Zhurnal*, November, 1962, 52–54.

27. *Ibid.*, 54–55.

28. *Ibid.*, 55–58.

29. Werth, *Russia at War*, 496.

30. Hanson W. Baldwin, *Battles Lost and Won: Great Campaigns of World War II*, 170.

31. *Ibid.*, 435–36.

32. *Ibid.*, 436.

33. Roman Kolkowicz, *The Soviet Army and the Communist Party*, 192.

34. *Ibid.*, 192–93, citing *Voprosy Istorii*, November, 1957, 22.

35. *Pravda*, February 2, 1963. See also Thomas W. Wolfe, *Soviet Strategy at the Crossroads*, 125.

36. Thomas W. Wolfe, *op. cit.*, 125–26. See also Otto Preston Chaney, Jr., "The Resurrection of an Unperson," *Army*, Vol. XVI (March, 1966), 53.

37. *Izvestia*, July 10, 1965, 3.

38. See, for example, A. A. Strokov (ed.), *Istoriya Voyennogo Iskusstva*, 409–11.

39. Viktor Platonovich Nekrasov, *V Okopakh Stalingrada*, 145–48. This work, originally published in 1946, won the Stalin Prize. See also the outstanding work by Matthew P. Gallagher, *The Soviet History of World War II: Myths, Memories and Realities*, 171–74.

40. Werth, *Russia at War*, 426–28.

41. Walter Goerlitz, "The Battle for Stalingrad, 1942–43," in H. A. Jacobsen and J. Rohwer (eds.), *Decisive Battles of World War II: The German View* (trans. by Edward Fitzgerald), 250.

42. Quoted in "Stalingrad," in Desmond Flower and James Reeves (eds.), *The Taste of Courage: The War, 1939–1945*, 487.

43. *Ibid.*

44. Werth, *Russia at War*, 539–41, 543.

45. Kurt Zeitzler, "Stalingrad," in Freidin and Richardson (eds.), *op. cit.*, 188–89.

46. Lauterbach, *op. cit.*, 132.

47. Alexander Werth, *The Year of Stalingrad: A Historical Record and a Study of Russian Mentality, Methods, and Policies*, 378. See also *Izvestia*, January 19, 1943, 1.

48. *Ibid.*, 448.

Chapter X

1. Manstein, *op. cit.*, 443.

2. *Ibid.*

3. *Ibid.*, 445–47.

4. Georgi K. Zhukov, "Na Kurskoy Duge," *Voyenno-Istorichesky Zhurnal*, August, 1967, 70–71.

5. Manstein, *op. cit.*, 447.

6. Mellenthin, *op. cit.*, 220.

7. *Ibid.*, 228–29.

8. Manstein, *op. cit.*, 448.

9. Mellenthin, *op. cit.*, 229.

10. Manstein, *op. cit.*, 450.

11. Werth, *Russia at War*, 685.

12. Nikolai Kirillovich Popel, *Tanki Povernuli na Zapad*, 164.

13. *Ibid.*, 165.

14. *Ibid.*

15. Mellenthin, *op. cit.*, 274.

16. The *Izvestia* article is cited in *Soviet War News*, April 5, 1944, 1.

17. "Zhukov's Twenty-eight Days," *Soviet War News*, April 5, 1944, 2.

18. *IVOVSS*, IV, 79.

19. Svetlishin, "Ot Soldata do Marshala," *loc. cit.*, 39.

20. M. Shtemenko, "Pered Udarom v Belorussii," *Voyenno-Istorichesky Zhurnal*, September, 1965, 44.

21. *Ibid.*

22. Tadeusz Bor-Komorowski, *The Secret Army*, 199–396.

23. Chester Wilmot, *The Struggle for Europe*, 630–31.

24. Winston S. Churchill, *Triumph and Tragedy*, 129.

25. Guderian, *op. cit.*, 358–59.

26. Churchill, *Triumph and Tragedy*, 134, 136.

27. *Ibid.*, 133.

28. *Ibid.*, 134.

29. *Ibid.*, 135–36.

30. *IVOVSS*, IV, 198.

31. Churchill, *Triumph and Tragedy*, 144.

32. *Ibid.*, 145.

33. Kolkowicz, *op. cit.*, 236.

Chapter XI

1. N. A. Antipenko, "Tyl Fronta," *Novy Mir*, August, 1965, 138.

2. N. A. Antipenko, "Ot Visly do Odera," *Voyenno-Istorichesky Zhurnal*, March, 1965, 71.

3. *Ibid.*, 71–72.

4. Lauterbach, *op. cit.*, 140–41.

5. *IVOVSS*, V, 58–61.

6. *Ibid.*

7. Svetlishin, "Ot Soldata do Marshala," *loc. cit.*, 39, citing the manuscript of K. F. Telegin's memoirs.

8. *Ibid.*, 37, citing *Voyenno-Istorichesky Zhurnal*, January, 1965, 75.

9. Georgi K. Zhukov, "Na Berlinskom Napravlenii," *Voyenno-Istorichesky Zhurnal*, June, 1965, 12–13.

10. *Ibid.*, 14.

11. *Ibid.*

12. *Ibid.*, 14–15. See also A. S. Zavyalov and T. E. Kalyadin, *Vostochno-Pomeranskaya Operatsiya Sovetskikh Voysk, Fevral–Mart 1945 g.*, 7–10.

13. Kolkowicz, *op. cit.*, 214, citing *Oktyabr*, Nos. 3–5 (1964); and *Novaya i Noveishaya Istoriya*, No. 2 (March–April, 1965), 6.

14. *Ibid.*, 218–19, citing *Voyenno-Istorichesky Zhurnal*, March, April, and June, 1965, 69–79, 63, and 15, respectively.

15. Zhukov, "Na Berlinskom Napravlenii," *loc. cit.*, 15, citing articles in *Novaya i Noveishaya Istoriya*, No. 2 (1965), 6–7, and *Voyenno-Istorichesky Zhurnal*, No. 3 (1965), 74–76, 80–81; No. 4 (1965), 62–64.

16. Kolkowicz, *op. cit.*, 236–37.

17. Zhukov, "Na Berlinskom Napravlenii," *loc. cit.*, 17–18, citing Chuikov's article in *Oktyabr*, No. 4 (1964), 128–29.

18. Guderian, *op. cit.*, 411–15.

19. Zavyalov and Kalyadin, *op. cit.*, 9.

20. *IVOVSS*, V, 84, 86.

21. Several accounts of this conversation are available. See, for example, I. Konev, "Sorok Pyatyy God," *Novy Mir*, May, 1965, 38; I. Konev, "The Year 1945," *Soviet Military Review*, May, 1966, 6–7; Cornelius Ryan, *The Last Battle*, 248–50.

22. Boris I. Nicolaevsky, *Power and the Soviet Elite: The Letter of an Old Bolshevik and Other Essays* (ed. by Janet D. Zagoria), 247.

23. Ryan, *op. cit.*, 256.

24. Zhukov, "Na Berlinskom Napravlenii," *loc. cit.*, 19.

25. *Ibid.*

26. Ryan, *op. cit.*, 70–71, 73–74.

27. *Ibid.*, 299–300, 332–35, 342, 345–48.

28. John Toland, *The Last 100 Days*, 402.

29. Ryan, *op. cit.*, 360.

30. *Ibid.*, 361–63.

31. Zhukov, "Na Berlinskom Napravlenii," *loc. cit.*, 19.

32. Ryan, *op. cit.*, 360, 393–94. Ryan interviewed Troyanosky in Moscow.

33. Quoted in Zhukov, "Na Berlinskom Napravlenii," *loc. cit.*

34. Ryan, *op. cit.*, 449.

35. Wilhelm Willemer, "The German Defense of Berlin" (manuscript), 58–59.

36. Churchill, *Triumph and Tragedy*, 533.

37. Vasily Ivanovich Chuikov, "Konets Tretogo Reikha," *Sovetsky Voin*, May, 1964, 5.

38. Charles B. MacDonald, *The Mighty Endeavor: American Armed Forces in the European Theater in World War II*, 496–97.

39. I. S. Konev, *Sorok Pyati*, 220–28.

Chapter XII

1. Kay Summersby, *Eisenhower Was My Boss*, 244.

2. John R. Deane, *The Strange Alliance: The Story of Our Efforts at Wartime Coopera-tion with Russia*, 168–70.

3. *Ibid.*, 174.

4. *Ibid.*, 175. See also Harry C. Butcher, *My Three Years with Eisenhower*, 836–38.

5. Arthur W. Tedder, *With Prejudice*, 684–85.

6. See, for example, Robert Murphy, *Diplomat Among Warriors*, 258.

7. Dwight D. Eisenhower, *At Ease: Stories I Tell to Friends*, 310.

8. Deane, *op. cit.*, 177–78.

9. Konstantin Simonov, "Every Day the Longest," *Soviet Life*, May, 1965, 26–27.

10. *Ibid.*, 27.

11. Butcher, *op. cit.*, 843.

12. Simonov, "Every Day the Longest," *loc. cit.*, 27.

13. *Ibid.*

14. *Ibid.*

15. Deane, *op. cit.*, 179.

16. Butcher, *op. cit.*, 845.

17. Deane, *op. cit.*, 180–81.

18. Dwight D. Eisenhower, *Crusade in Europe*, 435.

19. Butcher, *op. cit.*, 85.

20. Murphy, *op. cit.*, 257.

21. Eisenhower, *Crusade in Europe*, 435.

22. Murphy, *op. cit.*, 257–58.

23. *Ibid.*, 258–95.

24. *Ibid.*, 259.

25. *Ibid.*, 259–60.

26. Eisenhower, *Crusade in Europe*, 436–37.

27. Deane, *op. cit.*, 214.

28. Butcher, *op. cit.*, 860–61.

29. *Ibid.*, 861–62.

30. Eisenhower, *Crusade in Europe*, 438.

31. Murphy, *op. cit.*, 260.

32. *Ibid.*, 260–61.

33. *Ibid.*, 261.

34. *Ibid.*

35. *Ibid.*, 262–63.

36. S. V. Donnison, *Civil Affairs and Military Government: North-West Europe, 1944–1946*, 268–69.

37. Frank Howley, *Berlin Command*, 26, 47–56.

38. Donnison, *op. cit.*, 270.

39. Howley, *op. cit.*, 57–60.

40. Donnison, *op. cit.*, 270.

41. *Ibid.*, 274.

42. Eisenhower, *Crusade in Europe*, 438.

43. Walter Bedell Smith, *My Three Years in Moscow*, 22–23.

44. Zhukov, *Vospominaniya i Razmyshleniya*, 705–706.

45. Harry S. Truman, *Year of Decisions*, Vol. I of *Memoirs by Harry S. Truman*, 343–44.

46. Donald W. Treadgold, *Twentieth Century Russia*, 399–400. See also Herbert Feis, *Between War and Peace: The Potsdam Conference.*

47. Zhukov, *Vospominaniya i Razmyshleniya*, 714.

48. Eisenhower, *Crusade in Europe*, 459–60.

49. Deane, *op. cit.*, 215.

50. Eisenhower, *Crusade in Europe*, 460–62.

51. *Ibid.*, 462–63.

52. *Ibid.*, 463.

53. Deane, *op. cit.*, 217.

54. *Ibid.*, 217–19.

55. *Ibid.*, 219.

56. Eisenhower, *Crusade in Europe*, 464–67.

57. *Ibid.*, 467.

58. *Ibid.*, 467–69.

59. *Ibid.*, 470–72.

60. *Ibid.*, 471–72.

61. Walter Kerr, *The Russian Army: Its Leaders and Its Battles*, 19–20.

62. Eisenhower, *Crusade in Europe*, 472.

63. *Ibid.*, 472–73.

Chapter XIII

1. *Krasnaya Zvezda*, January 1–4, 1946.

2. *Ibid.*, January 5, 1946, 3.

3. *Ibid.*

4. *Ibid.*, January 8, 25, 1946, 1.

5. *Ibid.*, January 8–10, 1946.

6. N. Dontsov and M. Karpovich, "Marshal of the Soviet Union Georgi Konstantinovich Zhukov," *Krasnaya Zvezda*, January 24, 1946, 2.

7. "The Meeting of Marshal of the Soviet Union G. K. Zhukov with the Voters," *Krasnaya Zvezda*, January 29, 1946, 2.

8. *Krasnaya Zvezda*, February 10, 14, 1946.

9. *Ibid.*, March 19, 1946, 3.

10. United Press dispatch, Berlin, April 10, 1946.

11. *Krasnaya Zvezda*, May 4, 1946, 1.

12. *Ibid.*, May 26, 1946, 1.

13. Cited by Benson Lee Grayson, "What About Zhukov?" *Army (Combat Forces) Journal*, Vol. V (April, 1955), 26.

14. *Pravda*, November 3, 1957; italics added.

15. Eisenhower, *Crusade in Europe*, 472.

16. Yuri A. Rastvorov, "How Red Titans Fought for Supreme Power," *Life*, Vol. XXXVII (November 29, 1954), 146–48.

17. "One Myth for Another: From Military Genius to Military Idiot," *Army Magazine*, Vol. VI (July, 1956), 55, quoting from the text of Khrushchev's secret speech to the Twentieth Communist Party Congress. The text of the speech was released by the U.S. Department of State on June 4, 1956.

18. Khrushchev, *op. cit.*, 162.

19. Antonov, *op. cit.*, 5–7.

20. Malcolm Mackintosh, *Juggernaut: A History of the Soviet Armed Forces*, 176.

21. Belov, Dmitriev, and Tuschim, "Political Education of the Soviet Troops," in Zbigniew Brzezinski (ed.), *Political Controls in the Soviet Army*, 46 & n.

22. *Krasnaya Zvezda*, December 31, 1948.

23. Kalinov, *op. cit.*, 5–7.

24. Mackintosh, *Juggernaut*, 279.

25. Eisenhower, *Crusade in Europe*, 473.

26. Reuters, Taipei, November 13, 1950; Tokyo, PANA (in English Morse), November 14, 1950, 11:40 GMT.

27. Raymond L. Garthoff, *Soviet Military Policy: A Historical Analysis*, 44.

28. Grayson, "What About Zhukov?" *loc. cit.*, 26–27. See also *Pravda*, July 22, 1951, 2.

29. Mackintosh, *Juggernaut*, 284.

30. *Ibid.*

31. "Sokolovsky, Vasily Danilovich," *Bolshaya Sovetskaya Entsiklopediya*, 10.

32. M. V. Zakharov (ed.), *50 Let Vooruzhennykh Sil SSSR*, 478, 518.

33. *Evening Star* (Washington), August 10, 1952.

34. See Raymond L. Garthoff's excellent study, *The Role of the Military in Recent Soviet Politics*.

35. Mackintosh, *Juggernaut*, 284.

36. *Ibid.*, 285.

37. Garthoff, *Soviet Military Policy*, 45.

38. Svetlana Alliluyeva, *Twenty Letters to a Friend* (trans. by Priscilla Johnson McMillan), 207.

39. Khrushchev, *op. cit.*, 333–38.

40. Raymond L. Garthoff, "The Role of the Military in Recent Soviet Politics," *Russian Review*, Vol. XVI, No. 2 (April, 1957), 15–16, 21.

41. Mackintosh, *Juggernaut*, 287.

42. Garthoff, *Soviet Military Policy*, 48.

43. *Izvestia*, December 28, 1954, 2-4.

44. Garthoff, "The Role of the Military," *loc. cit.*

45. Mackintosh, *Strategy and Tactics*, 52n.

46. Marshal Zhukov's interview with Hearst, Smith, and Conniff, Moscow, February 7, 1955, *Manchester Guardian*, February 12, 1955, cited by Mackintosh, *Strategy and Tactics*, 96.

47. Raymond L. Garthoff, *Soviet Strategy in the Nuclear Age*, 23.

48. *Ibid.*, citing Bulganin's speech, which appeared in *Pravda*, February 10, 1955.

49. G. D. Embree, *The Soviet Union Between the 19th and 20th Party Congresses, 1952–1956*, 192–93.

50. Raymond L. Garthoff, *The Soviet Image of Future War*, 9–10.

51. Lincoln P. Bloomfield, Walter C. Clemens, Jr., and Franklyn Griffiths. *Khrushchev and the Arms Race: Soviet Interests in Arms Control and Disarmament, 1954–1964*, 35–36. See also Arnold L. Horelick and Myron Rush, *Strategic Power and Soviet Foreign Policy*, 27–31.

52. Dwight D. Eisenhower, *Mandate for Change, 1953–1956*, 132–33.

53. Sir Phillip Joubert, "Long Range Air Attack," in Asher Lee (ed.), *The Soviet Air and Rocket Forces*, 109.

54. Cited in Garthoff, *The Soviet Image*, 16–17, 19.

55. The *Voyennaya Mysl* editorial is cited in Garthoff, *Soviet Strategy*, 67–68.

56. *Ibid.*, 70.

57. Cited in Garthoff, *The Soviet Image*, 43.

58. Embree, *op. cit.*, 194.

Chapter XIV

1. Bertram D. Wolfe, *Khrushchev and Stalin's Ghost*, 39–40.

2. *New York Times*, April 28, 1955, 1, 12.

3. *Ibid.*

4. David J. Dallin, *Soviet Foreign Policy After Stalin*, 247, 274–77.

5. Eisenhower, *Mandate for Change*, 505.

6. *Ibid.*, 506.

7. *Ibid.*

8. Khrushchev, *op. cit.*, 398–99.

9. *New York Times*, July 15, 1955, 1–2.

10. *Ibid.*

11. *Ibid.*, July 16, 1955, 1–2.

12. *Ibid.*, July 20, 1955, 1, 4, 8.

13. Eisenhower, *Mandate for Change*, 517–18; italics added.

14. *Ibid.*, 518.

15. *Ibid.*

16. *Ibid.*, 524.

17. *Ibid.*, 524–25.

18. Harrison E. Salisbury, "Kremlin Facts Given President by Zhukov," *New York Times*, July 28, 1955, 1, 10.

19. *Pravda* and *Izvestia*, July 14, 1955, 1.

20. Embree, *op. cit.*, 261.

21. Bertram D. Wolfe, *op. cit.*, 40.

22. *Pravda*, February 20, 1956, 4.

23. *Voyenny Vestnik*, April, 1956, 2–9.

24. Oscar Haleki, "Poland," in Stephen D. Kertesz (ed.), *East Central Europe and the World: Developments in the Post-Stalin Era*, 51–52.

25. Flora Lewis, *A Case History of Hope: The Story of Poland's Peaceful Revolutions*, 165–66.

26. Konrad Syrop, *Spring in October: The Story of the Polish Revolution, 1956*, 61–64.

27. *Ibid.*

28. Lewis, *op. cit.*, 210.

29. The incidents at the airport and at Belvedere Palace are reported by Lewis, *op. cit.*, 209–17; and by Philippe Ben, "La Pologne de Gomulka," *Le Monde*, November 22, 1956.

30. Lewis, *op. cit.*, 217.

31. Syrop, *op. cit.*, 96–97; Garthoff, *Soviet Military Policy*, 152.

32. Haleki, "Poland," in Kertesz (ed)., *op. cit.*, 53.

33. Quoted in Seymour Freidin, *The Forgotten People*, 256.

34. *Pravda*, December 18, 1956, 1, 3.

35. Ben, "La Pologne de Gomulka," *loc. cit.*

36. Garthoff, *Soviet Military Policy*, 158.

37. *Ibid.*

38. Stephen D. Kertesz, "Hungary," in Kertesz (ed.), *op. cit.*, 125–26.

39. Sir William Hayter, *The Kremlin and the Embassy*, 112.

40. Dwight D. Eisenhower, *Waging Peace, 1956–1961*, 67.

41. Tibor Meray, *Thirteen Days That Shook the Kremlin*, 150.

42. Hayter, *op. cit.*, 152–53.

43. *Ibid.*, 153.

44. Zbigniew Brzezinski and Samuel P. Huntington, *Political Power: USA/USSR*, 377–78.

45. Kertesz (ed.), *op. cit.*, 129–31.

46. N. S. Khrushchev, *Speeches and Interviews on World Problems, 1957*, 319.

47. *Krasnaya Zvezda*, December 2, 1956, 1.

48. N. Galay, "Zhukov in India," *Bulletin of the Institute for the Study of the USSR*, Vol. IV, No. 4 (April, 1957), 3.

49. *Krasnaya Zvezda*, June 30, 1957, 4; July 2, 1957, 3.

50. Dallin, *op. cit.*, 305.

51. Galay, "Zhukov in India," *loc. cit.*, 4.

52. *Ibid.*, 4, 6.

53. *Krasnaya Zvezda*, January 26, 1957, 1, 2.

54. Galay, "Zhukov in India," *loc. cit.*, 7.

55. *Ibid.*, 9.

56. Kolkowicz, *op. cit.*, 115–16.

57. Merle Fainsod, *How Russia Is Ruled*, 483.

58. *Ibid.*, 483–84, citing *Krasnaya Zvezda*, January 25, 1956.

59. *Ibid.*, 484, citing *Krasnaya Zvezda*, April 26, 1956.

60. *Ibid.*

61. *Ibid.*, citing *Krasnaya Zvezda*, May 12, 1957.

62. *Ibid.*

63. N. Galay, "Revisionism, Dogmatism, and the Soviet Armed Forces," *Bulletin of the Institute for the Study of the USSR*, Vol. V, No. 11 (November, 1958), 5.

64. Robert Conquest, *Power and Policy in the USSR: The Study of Soviet Dynastics*, 336–37.

65. Kolkowicz, *op. cit.*, 124n.

66. Conquest, *op. cit.*, 337.

67. Kolkowicz, *op. cit.*, 123–24.

68. *Ibid.*, 124n., 358–59.

Chapter XV

1. This summary of events is provided by William J. Miller, Henry L. Roberts, and Marshall D. Shulman in *The Meaning of Communism*, 123–25.

2. D. Floyd in the *Daily Telegraph* (London), September 11, 1957; cited in Roger Pethybridge, *A Key to Soviet Politics: The Crisis of the Anti-Party Group*, 105.

3. Miller, Roberts, and Shulman, *op. cit.*, 123–25.

4. Pethybridge, *op. cit.*, 103n.

5. Garthoff, *Soviet Strategy*, 30.

6. Miller, Roberts, and Shulman, *op. cit.*, 125.

7. *Krasnaya Zvezda*, July 5, 1957, 1.

8. *Pravda*, July 15, 1957, 3.

9. *Ibid.*, 3–4.

10. Carl A. Linden, *Khrushchev and the Soviet Leadership, 1957–1964*, 48.

11. *Pravda*, July 15, 1957, 3.

12. Wolfgang Leonhard, *The Kremlin Since Stalin*, 256.

13. *Pravda*, July 15, 1957, 3.

14. "The Background for Charges Against Zhukov," in Harry Schwartz, *The Red Phoenix: Russia Since World War II*, 94–96.

15. *Pravda*, July 15, 1957, 3.

16. Schwartz, *op. cit.*, 96.

17. Garthoff, *Soviet Strategy*, 30–31.

18. Leonhard, *op. cit.*

19. Brzezinski and Huntington, *op. cit.*, 348.

20. Raymond A. Bauer, Alex Inkeles, and Clyde Kluckhohn, *How the Soviet System Works*, 60–61, 174; italics added.

21. Nicolaevsky, *op. cit.*, 250.

22. Kolkowicz, *op. cit.*, 192.

23. *Krasnaya Zvezda*, July 26, 1957, 1.

Chapter XVI

1. *Krasnaya Zvezda*, October 9, 1957, 1.

2. "Yugoslavia: The Bait on the Hook," *Newsweek*, Vol. L (October 21, 1957).

3. *Krasnaya Zvezda*, October 10, 1957, 1.

4. "K vs. Z: How the Rug Was Pulled," *Newsweek*, Vol. L (November 11, 1957), 18.

5. *Krasnaya Zvezda*, October 15, 1957, 3.

6. *Ibid.*, October 20, 1957, 3.

7. Harry Schwartz, "Zhukov's Speech Studied for Clue," *New York Times* (International Edition), October 31, 1957, 4.

8. "K vs. Z," *loc. cit.*

9. "How the Deed Was Done," *Time*, November 11, 1957, 18.

10. "Convulsion in the Kremlin," *Time* (Atlantic Edition), Vol. LXX (November 4, 1957), 23.

11. *Pravda*, October 17, 1957, 6.

12. "Khrushchev to Give Zhukov 'New Job,' " *Stars and Stripes* (European Edition), October 13, 1957, 1.

13. *Ibid.*

14. *Ibid.*, 24.

15. *Ibid.*

16. "Apology Made by President in Zhukov Case," *Stars and Stripes* (European Edition), November 1, 1957, 1.

17. "How the Deed Was Done," *loc. cit.*, 18, 19.

18. "Khrushchev to Give Zhukov 'New Job,' " *loc. cit.*, 24.

19. Reprinted in Schwartz, *The Red Phoenix*, 94–95.

20. *Ibid.*, 95–96.

21. *Pravda*, November 3, 1957, 1.

22. *Pravda* and *Izvestia*, November 3, 1957, 2.

23. *Ibid.* Italics added.

24. *Ibid.*

25. M. Dorofeev, "O Nekotorykh Prichinakh Neudachnykh Deistvii Mekhanizirovannykh Korpusov v Nachalnom Periode Velikoy Otechestvennoy Voiny," *Voyenno-Istorichesky Zhurnal*, March, 1964, 33.

26. Svetlishin, "Ot Soldata do Marshala," *loc. cit.*, 33–34.

27. *Pravda*, November 3, 1957, 3–4.

28. *Ibid.*
29. Zhukov, "Na Berlinskom Napravlenii," *loc. cit.*, 20.
30. *Pravda*, November 3, 1957, 3–4.
31. *Ibid.*, 2.
32. Fainsod, *op. cit.*, 486.
33. *Ibid.*
34. *Ibid.*, 486–87.
35. *Ibid.*, 487.
36. Kolkowicz, *op. cit.*, 192, citing *Voprosy Istorii*, November, 1957, 22.
37. *Pravda* and *Izvestia*, October 18, 1961, 2–11.
38. *Ibid.*, 11–12.
39. Harry Schwartz, *Russia Enters the 1960's*, 59–60, 135–37.
40. *Izvestia*, October 8, 1961, 6.
41. Seymour Topping, "Zhukov Is Blamed in Submarine Lag," *New York Times*, October 10, 1961, 13.
42. Eisenhower, *Waging Peace*, 442–43.
43. *Ibid.*, 443.
44. "Shifting Sands," *Newsweek*, Vol. LXI, No. 21 (May 27, 1963), 46.
45. K. P. S. Menon, *The Flying Troika*, 196.
46. Khrushchev, *Speeches and Interviews*, 324.
47. *Ibid.*, 281.

Chapter XVII

1. See *Sovetsky Patriot*, October 18, 1964, 1; *Pravda*, October 16, 1964, 1.
2. Linden, *op. cit.*, 206.
3. Edward Crankshaw, *Khrushchev: A Career*, 286.
4. Mark Frankland, *Khrushchev*, 205.
5. Linden, *op. cit.*, 205.
6. Frankland, *op. cit.*, 205.
7. Crankshaw, *op. cit.*, 286.
8. *Ibid.*, 286–87.
9. Frankland, *op. cit.*, 205–206.
10. *Krasnaya Zvezda*, February 10, 1965, 4.
11. "The Periscope," *Newsweek*, Vol. XV, No. 16 (April 19, 1965), 19.
12. Moscow Tass International Service in English, April 28, 1965, 9:27 GMT.
13. See *Pravda*, April 16, 1965.
14. *Izvestia*, April 30, 1965.
15. See, for example, Konev's articles in *Sovetskaya Rossiya*, April 16, 1965, and *Pravda*, April 21, 1965.
16. *Evening Star* (Washington), May 7, 1965, A-4.
17. See "Stalin, Mao Applauded by Kremlin Audience," *Sunday Star* (Washington), May 9, 1965, A-12; Theodore Shabad, "Soviet Rally Hails Stalin; Zhukov Emerges in Honor," *New York Times*, May 9, 1965, 1, 3.
18. Moscow Tass International Service in English, May 9, 1965, 6:59 GMT.
19. "Eisenhower Welcomes Zhukov Re-emergence," *New York Times*, May 10, 1965, 2.
20. Moscow Domestic Service in Russian, May 9, 1965, 12:00 GMT.
21. See *Pravda*, December 1, 1966.
22. Moscow Domestic Service in Russian, December 6, 1966, 12:55 GMT.

23. Raymond H. Anderson, "Stalin and Zhukov Hailed in Kremlin for War Role," *New York Times*, December 7, 1966, 12.

24. Svetlishin, "Ot Soldata do Marshala," *loc. cit.*, 31–40. The official biography in the *Bolshaya Sovetskaya Entsiklopediya* contains only thirty-five lines.

25. Svetlishin, "Ot Soldata do Marshala," *loc. cit.*, 32.

26. Zakharov, *op. cit.*

27. Khrushchev, *Khrushchev Remembers*, 162.

28. Ed. by Harrison E. Salisbury, trans. by Theodore Shabad, 1969.

29. S. M. Budenny, "Proydenny Put," *Don*, August, 1970.

30. See Chaney, "The Resurrection of an Unperson," *loc. cit.*, 51–53.

SELECTED BIBLIOGRAPHY

I. SOVIET SOURCES

A. Marshal Zhukov's Reminiscences

In the preparation of this book primary reliance was placed on Georgi K. Zhukov's memoirs in various Soviet publications, beginning in 1965. The most important of them appeared in *Voyenno-Istorichesky Zhurnal* (*Military-Historical Journal*), in several volumes dealing with the Battle of Moscow, and finally in his *Vospominaniya i Razmyshleniya* (*Memoirs and Reflections*), which made its appearance in 1969. Unfortunately, this work ends with Zhukov's departure from Germany in April, 1946. Thus many of the most fascinating episodes of his colorful career—his ouster, his reappearance in 1953, his term as defense minister, his dismissal and eventual rehabilitation —are not covered.

In 1969, Harper and Row published *Marshal Zhukov's Greatest Battles*, edited with an introduction and commentary by Harrison E. Salisbury and translated by Theodore Shabad. The accounts of the battles of Moscow, Kursk, and Berlin were from Zhukov's *Voyenno-Istorichesky Zhurnal* articles which appeared between June, 1965, and September, 1967. The Stalingrad campaign was described by Zhukov in A. M. Samsonov's collection entitled *Stalingradskaya Epopeya*, published in Moscow in 1968. Mr. Salisbury's excellent editorial comments and explanatory footnotes enchance Zhukov's account of the four critical campaigns he helped plan and conduct.

In January, 1970, an article appeared in *Kommunist* under Georgi Zhukov's name (pp. 85–86, 92–93). Entitled "The Grandeur of the Soviet Victory and the Impotence of the Falsifiers of History," it was reprinted in abridged form in the *Soviet Military Review* in May and June, 1970. The author—whoever he may be—is probably not Zhukov, who has been ailing for the past several years owing to a disabling stroke. The author of the article attacks the Harper and Row book, saying that "the excerpts do not give the reader an idea of the war as a whole, since they omit much that is essential. Second and more important is that . . . Mr. Salisbury, as editor of this collection, has supplied it with an introduction and notes whose military competence and scientific improbity are in direct contradiction with my ideas, as well as with the text and the principles underlying my articles." On and on it goes, but the author fails to convince the reader. Salisbury has largely relied on Soviet sources for his comments and footnotes.

Critic "Zhukov" writes that "more and more frequently we come across attempts to personalize Soviet military prowess. Thus, Mr. Salisbury writes of a 'Zhukov strategy,' a special 'Zhukov style' of conducting operations, and the like. To link up Soviet military strategy with the name of one man, and to speak of a 'Zhukov' or any other kind of personal strategy, means taking up false positions, showing a complete misconception and absolute ignorance of the very essence of our art of war."

Again, the author is unconvincing. In Zhukov's serialized memoirs and in his book he tries over and over again to reassert his place in the planning of Soviet campaigns. As Earl F. Ziemke wrote in his review of *Marshal Zhukov's Greatest Battles* (*Military Affairs*, Vol. XXXIV, No. 2 [April, 1970], 9): "In the six years since his partial rehabilitation Zhukov has been working on his memoirs. His purpose has been twofold: To restore his name as the true architect of the Soviet Union's greatest World War II victories, and to settle scores with his former rivals and present detractors in the upper reaches of the Soviet Army. Zhukov is less concerned with the battles than with reasserting his place in them."

As has been shown throughout this biography, Zhukov—when provided an opportunity—described his role in Stavka planning, frequently using the personal pronoun "I" to emphasize his point. I for one would not criticize him for this. He deserves the long-overdue recognition.

"The First Strategic Defeat of the Wehrmacht," *Moscow News*, October 22–December 24, 1966, 12–13 [in each weekly issue].

"Kontrnastuplenie pod Moskvoy," *Voyenno-Istorichesky Zhurnal*, October, 1966, 68–85.

"Na Berlinskom Napravlenii," *Voyenno-Istorichesky Zhurnal*, June, 1965, 12–22.

"Na Kurskoy Duge," *Voyenno-Istorichesky Zhurnal*, August, 1965, 69–83; September, 1967, 81–97.

"Razgrom Nemetskikh Voysk v Rayone Dona, Volgi i Stalingrada," in A. M. Samsonov, ed. *Stalingradskaya Epopeya*. Moscow, Nauka Press, 1968, 17–72.

"V Bitve za Stolitsu," *Voyenno-Istorichesky Zhurnal*, August, 1966, 53–63; September, 1966, 55–65.

Vospominaniya i Razmyshleniya. Moscow, Novosti Press Agency, 1969. Zhukov's long-awaited memoirs.

B. Books

1. General Military Histories

Probably the most important Soviet history of World War II and events leading up to it is the massive six-volume *Istoriya Velikoy Otechestvennoy Voiny Sovetskogo Soyuza, 1941–45* (*History of the Great Patriotic War of the Soviet Union, 1941–1945*), Moscow, Military Press of the Ministry of Defense of the U.S.S.R. Published between 1960 and 1965, this history represents the collective efforts of many Soviet scholars and experts, who relied mainly on archival material, including Foreign Policy Archives, Archives of the Ministry of Defense, the war archives of the Institute of Marxism-Leninism, the Central Party Archives, and many others. The history was sponsored by the Department of History of the Great Patriotic War of the Institute of Marxism-Leninism attached to the Central Committee of the Communist Party of the Soviet Union. The work contains a number of the shortcomings generally found in Soviet histories, such as the omission of names of individuals currently out of favor, the glorification of Khrushchev, the exaggeration of the Party's role in individual campaigns, and other compromises with fact.

In 1965 an excellent one-volume history based on the larger *Istoriya*, entitled *Velikaya Otechestvennaya Voina Sovetskogo Soyuza, 1941–1945: Kratkaya Istoriya*, was published by the same commission. The flattering photographs and magnified accounts of Khrushchev are gone, and Stalin's role in the planning and execution of Red Army operations has reappeared, though without the former heroics. On page 573 one reads: "The Supreme Commander-in-Chief was I. V. Stalin. Displaying great resoluteness, he directed military actions, on the whole, correctly, and he performed no small service in this area."

Another rich source of information is the second edition of *Bolshaya Sovetskaya Entsiklopediya*, published between 1949 and 1958, and its annual *yezhegodniki* (yearbooks). These volumes, issued over a critical time span, have been subject to rewrites, some of them unashamedly offered to subscribers to the encyclopedia. I have in my possession a note to subscribers, asking them to remove pages 21 to 24 of Volume V with "scissors or razor blade" and affix in their place new pages from the State Scientific Press. Thus the article on Beria is replaced by one on the Bering Sea. Needless to say, such attitudes and practices have had their effect on Soviet historiography.

Alakhverdov, G. G., et al. *Kratkaya Istoriya Grazhdanskoy Voiny v. SSSR.* Moscow, State Press of Political Literature, 1960.

Andronikov, N. G., et al. *Bronetankovyye i Mekhanizirovannyye Voiska Sovetskoy Armii.* Moscow, Military Press of the Ministry of Defense of the U.S.S.R., 1958.

Anisimov, I. V., and G. B. Kuzmin. *Velikaya Otechestvennaya Voina Sovetskogo Soyuza, 1941–1945.* Moscow, Military Press of the Ministry of Defense of the U.S.S.R., 1952.

Barbashin, I. P., and A. D. Kharitonov. *Boyevyye Deistviya Sovetskoy Armii pod Tikhvinom v. 1941 godu*. Moscow, Military Press of the Ministry of Defense of the U.S.S.R., 1958.

————, A. I. Kuznetsov, V. P. Morosov, A. D. Kharitonov, and B. N. Yakovlev. *Bitva za Leningrad*. Ed. by S. P. Platonov. Moscow, Military Press of the Ministry of Defense of the U.S.S.R., 1964.

Biryuzov, S. S. *Surovye Gody*. Moscow, Nauka Press, 1966.

Bitva za Moskvu. Moscow, Moskovskiy Rabochiy, 1966.

Bitva za Tula. Tula, Tula Book Press, 1957.

Boevye Podvigi Chastei Krasnoy Armii (1918–1922 gg). Moscow, Military Press of the Ministry of Defense of the U.S.S.R., 1957.

Ehrenburg, Ilya. *Russia at War*. London, Hamish Hamilton, 1943.

————. *The War: 1941–1945*. Vol. V of *Men, Years—Life*. New York, World Publishing Company, 1964.

Fadeyev, Aleksandr Aleksandrovich. *Leningrad in the Days of the Blockade*. London, Hutchinson and Company, Ltd., 1945.

Govorov, Leonid Aleksandrovich. *V Boyakh za Gorod Lenina*. Leningrad, Military Press of the People's Defense Commissariat, 1945.

Grossman, Vassili Semenovich. *The Years of War (1941–1945)*. Moscow, Foreign Languages Publishing House, 1946.

Institut Marksizma-Leninizma pri TsK KPSS. *Istoriya Velikoy Otechestvennoy Voiny Sovetskogo Soyuza, 1941–1945*. 6 vols. Moscow, Military Press of the Ministry of Defense of the U.S.S.R., 1960–65.

————. *Velikaya Otechestvennaya Voina Sovetskogo Soyuza, 1941–1945: Kratkaya Istoriya*. Moscow, Military Press of the Ministry of Defense of the U.S.S.R., 1965.

Institute of History of the Academy of Sciences of the U.S.S.R. *SSSR v Velikoy Otechestvennoy Voine, 1941–1945 gg*. Moscow, Military Press of the Ministry of Defense of the U.S.S.R., 1964.

Kadishev, A. B., et al., eds. *Voprosy Strategii i Operativnogo Iskusstva v Sovetskikh Voyennykh Trudakh (1917–1940)*. Moscow, Military Press of the Ministry of Defense of the U.S.S.R., 1965.

Karasev, A. V. *Leningradtsy v Gody Blokady, 1941–1943*. Moscow, Press of the Academy of Sciences of the U.S.S.R., 1959.

Kiryaev, N. M., Yu. I Korablev, and E. F. Nikitin. *KPSS i Stroitelstvo Sovetskikh Vooruzhennykh Sil, 1917–1964*. Moscow, Military Press of the Ministry of Defense of the U.S.S.R., 1965.

Korablev, Yu. I., and M. I. Loginov, eds. *KPSS i Stroitelstvo Vooruzhennykh Sil SSSR (1918–Iyun 1941)*. Moscow, Military Press of the Ministry of Defense of the U.S.S.R., 1959.

BIBLIOGRAPHY

Korotskov, I. S., ed. *Ocherki Istorii Velikoy Otechestvennoy Voiny, 1941–1945.* Moscow, Press of the Academy of Sciences of the U.S.S.R., 1955.

———. *Protiv Falsifikatsii Istorii Vtoroy Mirovoy Voiny.* Moscow, Nauka Press, 1964.

———. *Velikaya Bitva pod Moskvoy.* Moscow, Military Press of the Ministry of Defense of the U.S.S.R., 1961.

Kozlov, S. N., et al. *O Sovetskoy Voyennoy Nauke.* Moscow, Military Press of the Ministry of Defense of the U.S.S.R., 1964.

Kuzmin, Nikolai Fedorovich. *Na Strazhe Mirnogo Truda (1921–1940 gg.).* Moscow, Military Press of the Ministry of Defense of the U.S.S.R., 1959.

Loboda, V. F. *Komandnyye Kadry i Zakonodatelstvo o Kadrakh v Razvitii Vooruzhennykh Sil SSSR.* Moscow, Military Press of the Ministry of Defense of the U.S.S.R., 1960.

Lyzhniki na Fronte (Vospominaniya Uchastnikov Boyev s Belofinnami v 1939–1940 godakh). Moscow, Military Press of the People's Commissariat of Defense, 1942.

Malanin, K. A., ed. *Polki Idut na Zapad.* Moscow, Military Press of the Ministry of Defense of the U.S.S.R., 1964.

———. *Razgrom Vraga v Belorussii.* Moscow, Military Press of the Ministry of Defense of the U.S.S.R., 1961.

Markin, Ilya Ivanovich. *Kurskaya Bitva.* Moscow, Military Press of the Ministry of Defense of the U.S.S.R., 1958.

Matsulenko, V. A. *Razgrom Nemetsko-Fashistskikh Voisk na Balkanskom Napravlenii, Avgust–Sentyabr 1944 goda.* Moscow, Military Press of the Ministry of Defense of the U.S.S.R., 1957.

Minz, I. *The Red Army.* New York, International Publishers, 1947.

Moskovskiy, V. P. *Rodnaya Armiya.* Moscow, Military Press of the Ministry of Defense of the U.S.S.R., 1961.

One Year of Soviet Struggle Against German Invasion. Washington, Embassy of the U.S.S.R., 1942.

Oskin, G. I. *Sovetskaya Armiya-Detishche Sovetskogo Naroda.* Moscow, Military Press of the Ministry of Defense of the U.S.S.R., 1963.

Pavlov, Dmitri V. *Leningrad 1941: The Blockade.* Chicago, University of Chicago Press, 1965.

———. *Leningrad v Blokade.* Moscow, Soviet Russia Press, 1969.

Plamya nad Nevoy. Leningrad, Leningrad Press, 1964.

Popel, Nikolai Kirillovich. *Tani Povernuli na Zapod.* Moscow, Military Press of the Ministry of Defense of the U.S.S.R., 1960.

Poplavskiy, Stanislav Gilyarovich. *Tovarishchi v Borbe.* Moscow, Military Press of the Ministry of Defense of the U.S.S.R., 1963. The author is a Polish general.

———, ed. *Boyevyye Deistviya Narodnogo Voiska Polskogo*. Moscow, Military Press of the Ministry of Defense of the U.S.S.R., 1961. Polish title: *Wybrane Operacje I Walki Ludowego Wojska Polskiego*.

Posledniy Shturm. Moscow, Press of Political Literature, 1965.

Proval Gitlerovskogo Nastupleniya na Moskvu. Moscow, Nauka Press, 1966.

Rokossovsky, K. K., ed. *Velikaya Pobeda na Volge*. Moscow, Military Press of the Ministry of Defense of the U.S.S.R., 1965.

Rotmistrov, P. A., ed. *Istoriya Voyennogo Iskusstva*. 2 vols. Moscow, Military Press of the Ministry of Defense of the U.S.S.R., 1963.

Samsonov, A. M. *Ot Volgi do Baltiki*. Moscow, Press of the Academy of Sciences of the U.S.S.R., 1963.

———. *Velikaya Bitva pod Moskvoy, 1941–1942*. Moscow, Press of the Academy of Sciences, 1958. Also, *Die Grosse Schlacht vor Moskau, 1941–1942*. Berlin, Publishing House of the Ministry of National Defense, 1959.

———, ed. *Stalingradskaya Epopeya*. Moscow, Military Press of the Ministry of Defense of the U.S.S.R., 1968.

Shatagin, N. I., and I. P. Prusanov. *Sovetskaya Armiya: Armiya Novogo Tipa*. Moscow, Military Press of the Ministry of Defense of the U.S.S.R., 1957.

Shtemenko, S. M. *The Soviet General Staff at War, 1941–1945*. Moscow, Progress Publishers, 1970.

Strokov, A. A., ed. *Istoriya Voyennogo Iskusstva*. Moscow, Military Press of the Ministry of Defense of the U.S.S.R., 1966.

Vysotskiy, F. I., et al. *Gvardeiskaya Tankovaya*. Moscow, Military Press of the Ministry of Defense of the U.S.S.R., 1963.

Za Moskvu, za Rodinu! Moscow, Moscow Worker, 1964.

Zakhavov, M. V., ed. *50 Let Vooruzhennykh Sil SSSR*. Moscow, Military Press of the Ministry of Defense of the U.S.S.R., 1968.

Zamyatin, N. M., et al. *Desyat Sokrushitelnykh Udarov (Kratskiy Obzor Operatsii Krasnoy Armii v 1944 g.)*. Moscow, Military Press of the People's Commissariat of Defense, 1945.

Zavyalov, A. S., and T. E. Kalyadin. *Vostochno-Pomeranskaya Operatsiya Sovetskikh Voisk, Fevral-Mart, 1945 g*. Moscow, Military Press of the Ministry of Defense of the U.S.S.R., 1960.

Zhdanov, N. N. *Ognevoy Schchit Leningrada*. Moscow, Military Press of the Ministry of Defense of the U.S.S.R., 1965.

Zhilin, Pavel Andreivich, ed. *Vazheishiye Operatsii Velikoy Otechestvennoy Voiny, 1941–1945 gg*. Moscow, Military Press of the Ministry of Defense of the U.S.S.R., 1956.

Zubakov, V. E., ed. *Boyevoy Put Sovetskikh Vooruzhennikh Sil*. Moscow, Military Press of the Ministry of Defense of the U.S.S.R., 1960.

BIBLIOGRAPHY

2. *Memoirs of Wartime Commanders*

Batov, P. I. *Operatsiya "Oder."* Moscow, Military Press of the Ministry of Defense of the U.S.S.R., 1965.

———. *V Pokhodakh i Boyakh*. Moscow, Military Press of the Ministry of Defense of the U.S.S.R., 1962.

Belov, P. A. *Za Nami Moskva*. Moscow, Military Press of the Ministry of Defense of the U.S.S.R., 1963.

Biryuzov, S. S. *Kogda Gremeli Pushki*. Moscow, Military Press of the Ministry of Defense of the U.S.S.R., 1962.

Boldin, Ivan Vasilevich. *Stranitsy Zhizni*. Moscow, Military Press of the Ministry of Defense of the U.S.S.R., 1961.

Budenny, Semyen Mikhailovich. *Proidennyy Put*. 2 vols. Moscow, Military Press of the Ministry of Defense of the U.S.S.R., 1958, 1965.

Bychevskiy, Boris Vladimirovich. *Gorod-Front*. Moscow, Military Press of the Ministry of Defense of the U.S.S.R., 1963.

Chuikov, Vasili Ivanovich. *The Battle for Stalingrad*. New York, Holt, Rinehart and Winston, 1964.

———. *The Fall of Berlin*. New York, Holt, Rinehart and Winston, 1967.

Fedyuninsky, Ivan I. *Podnyatye po Trevoge*. Moscow, Military Press of the Ministry of Defense of the U.S.S.R., 1964.

Gorbatov, Aleksandr Vassilevich. *Years Off My Life*. New York, W. W. Norton and Company, 1964.

Gulyaev, V. G. *Chelovek v Brone*. Moscow, Military Press of the Ministry of Defense of the U.S.S.R., 1964.

Kazakov, I. I. *Na Perelome*. Moscow, Military Press of the Ministry of Defense of the U.S.S.R., 1962.

Kazakov, M. I. *Nad Kartoy Bylykh Srazhenii*. Moscow, Military Press of the Ministry of Defense of the U.S.S.R., 1965.

Kuznetsov, Pavel Grigorevich. *Dni Boevyye*. Moscow, Military Press of the Ministry of Defense of the U.S.S.R., 1964.

Shatilov, Vasiliy Mitrofanovich. *Znamya nad Reikhstagom*. Moscow, Military Press of the Ministry of Defense of the U.S.S.R., 1966.

Tyl Sovetskoy Armii. Moscow, Military Press of the Ministry of Defense of the U.S.S.R., 1968.

Voronov, N. N. *Na Sluzhbe Voyennoy*. Moscow, Military Press of the Ministry of Defense of the U.S.S.R., 1970.

Voronov, N. N. *Na Sluzhbe Voyennoy*. Moscow, Military Press of the Ministry of Defense of the U.S.S.R., 1963.

Yeremenko, A. I. *Na Zapadnom Napravlenii*. Moscow, Military Press of the Ministry of Defense of the U.S.S.R., 1959.

———. *V Nachale Voiny*. Moscow, Nauka Press, 1965.

3. Other Recollections

Khrushchev, Nikita S. *Khrushchev Remembers*. Intro., commentary, and notes by Edward Crankshaw, trans. and ed. by Strobe Talbott. Boston, Little, Brown and Company, 1970.

4. Biographies

Aleksandrov, G. F., et al. *Iosif Vissarionovich Stalin: Kratkaya Biografiya*. Moscow, Publishing House of Political Literature, 1948.

Dushenkin, V. *Ot Soldata do Marshala*. Moscow, Press of Political Literature, 1964.

Komandarm Uborevich (Vospominaniya Druzei i Soratnikov). Moscow, Military Press of the Ministry of Defense of the U.S.S.R., 1964.

Nikulin, Lev. *Tukhachevskiy: Biograficheskiy Ocherk*. Moscow, Military Press of the Ministry of Defense of the U.S.S.R., 1963.

Semichev, D. A. *General Armii N. F. Vatutin*. Moscow, Military Press of the Ministry of Defense, 1956.

5. General Studies

Avtoritet Komandira. Moscow, Military Press of the Ministry of Defense of the U.S.S.R., 1963.

Berkhin, I. B. *Voyennaya Reforma v SSSR (1924–1925)*. Moscow, Military Press of the Ministry of Defense of the U.S.S.R., 1959.

Borodin, Boris Aleksandrovich. *Pomoshch SSSR Kitaiskomu Narodu v Antiyaponskoy Voine, 1937–1941*. Moscow, Mysl Press, 1965.

Isachenko, S. M. *Pochemu v Armii Neobkhodimo Yedinonachalie*. Moscow, Military Press of the Ministry of Defense of the U.S.S.R., 1965.

Larkov, A. M. and N. T. Filippov. *Yedinonachalie v Sovetskikh Vooruzhennykh Silakh*. Moscow, Military Press of the Ministry of Defense of the U.S.S.R., 1960.

Molotov, V. M. *Soviet Foreign Policy: The Meaning of the War with Finland*. New York, Workers Library Publishers, Inc., 1940.

Nekotorie Voprosy Partiino-Organizatsionnoy Raboty v Sovetskikh Vooruzhennykh Silakh. Moscow, Military Press of the Ministry of Defense of the U.S.S.R., 1963.

Sokolovsky, V. D., ed. *Voyennaya Strategiya*. Moscow, Military Press of the Ministry of Defense of the U.S.S.R., 1962.

6. Collections of Speeches and Articles

Blyukher, V. K. *Stati i Rechi*. Moscow, Military Press of the Ministry of Defense of the U.S.S.R., 1963.

Khrushchev, N. S. *Speeches and Interviews on World Problems, 1957.* Moscow, Foreign Languages Publishing House, 1958.

Stalin, Joseph V. *The Great Patriotic War of the Soviet Union.* New York, International Publishers, 1945.

———. *On the Great Patriotic War of the Soviet Union.* London, Hutchinson and Company, Ltd., n.d. (probably 1944).

———. *O Velikoy Otechestvennoy Voine Sovetskogo Soyuza.* Moscow, Publishing House of Political Literature, 1947.

———. *Works.* 13 vols. Moscow, Foreign Languages Publishing House, 1952–55.

Voroshilov, K., et al. *The Red Army Today (Speeches Delivered at the Eighteenth Congress of the C.P.S.U. (B.), March 10–21, 1939).* Moscow, Foreign Languages Publishing House, 1939.

C. Periodicals

Antipenko, N. A. "Ot Visly do Odera," *Voyenno-Istoricheskiy Zhurnal,* March, 1965, 69–81.

———. "Tyl Fronta," *Novy Mir.* August, 1965, 116–35.

Baskakov, V. "Frunze Military Academy," *Soviet Military Review,* September, 1966, 7–9.

Batov, P., and P. Troyanovskiy. "Chelovek, Bolshevik, Polkovodets," *Voyenno-Istoricheskiy Zhurnal,* December, 1966, 32–43.

Begishev, A. "Primeneniye Tankov Neposredstvennoy Podderzhki v Nastupatelnykh Operatsiyakh Velikoy Otechestvennoy Voiny," *Voyenno-Istoricheskiy Zhurnal,* June, 1962, 19–31.

Berezhkov, Valentin. "Molotov in Berlin," "On the Eve of Hitler's Invasion," and "The Beleaguered Embassy" (trans. from *Novy Mir*), *Atlas,* December, 1965, 352–55; January, 1966, 10–15; February, 1966, 74–79.

Boltin, E. A. "Pobeda Sovetskoy Armii pod Moskvoy v 1941 godu," *Voprosy Istorii,* January, 1957, 20–32.

Cheremukhin, K. "Na Smolensko-Moskovskom Strategicheskom Napravlenii Letom 1941 goda," *Voyenno-Istoricheskiy Zhurnal,* October, 1966, 3–18.

———. "Velikaya Pobeda pod Moskvoy," *Voyenno-Istoricheskiy Zhurnal,* November, 1966, 3–9.

Chuikov, V. I. "Kapitulyatsiya Gitlerovskoy Germanii," *Novaya i Noveishaya Istoriya,* February, 1965, 3–25.

———. "Konets Tretego Reikha," *Oktyabr,* March, 1965, 101–49; April, 1965, 123–69; May, 1965, 125–62.

———. "Konets Tretego Reikha," *Sovetskiy Voin,* May, 1964, 4–7.

Dorofyeev, M. "O Nekotorykh Prichinakh Neudachnykh Deistvii Mekhanizirovannykh Korpusov v Nachalnom Periode Velikoy Otechestvennoy Voiny," *Voyenno-Istorichesky Zhurnal*, March, 1964, 32–44.

Getman, A. "Za Nami Byla Stolitsa," *Voennye Znaniya*, December, 1966, 2–5.

Golikov, F. "Reservnaya Armiya Vstupaet v Srazhenie Yuzhnee Moskvy," *Voyenno-Istorichesky Zhurnal*, November, 1966, 56–68.

Gorelov, G. "The Defeat of Wrangel," *Soviet Military Review*, October, 1970, 42–45.

"Gorod-Geroi," *Starshina-Serzhant*, November, 1966, 4–6.

Grechko, A. "25 Let Tomu Nazad," *Voyenno-Istorichesky Zhurnal*, June, 1966, 3–15.

Ivanov, V., and K. Cheremukhin. "O Knige 'V Nachale Voiny,'" *Voyenno-Istorichesky Zhurnal*, June, 1965, 72–80.

Kiselev, A. "Odin iz Talantliveishikh . . .," *Voyenno-Istorichesky Zhurnal*, June, 1966, 36–49.

Konev, I. "Nachalo Moskovskoy Bitvy," *Voyenno-Istorichesky Zhurnal*, October, 1966, 56–67.

———. "Nineteen Forty Five," *International Affairs* (Moscow), August, 1965–April, 1966; also published in *Novy Mir* under the title "Sorok Pyatyy God," May, 1965, 3–60; June, 1965, 3–59; July, 1965, 100–42.

Korkodinov, P. "Fakty i Mysli o Nachalnom Periode Velikoy Otechestvennoy Voiny," *Voyenno-Istorichesky Zhurnal*, October, 1965, 26–34.

Kornyushin, P. "Dayesh Volokolamsk!" *Starshina-Serzhant*, November, 1966, 7.

Korochkin, P. "Geroicheskiy Podvig Nashikh Vooruzhennykh Sil," *Kommunist*, May, 1965, 15–27.

Krasilnikov, S. "O Strategicheskom Rukovodstve v Velikoy Otechestvennoy Voine," *Voyenno-Istorichesky Zhurnal*, June, 1960, 3–13.

Krupchevnko, I. "Tankovyye Armii v Berlinskoy Operatsii," *Voyenno-Istorichesky Zhurnal*, July, 1960, 14–34.

Kuznetsov, N. "Before the War," *International Affairs*, January, 1967, 99–104.

Kuznetsov, V. "Operatsiya Zavershivshaya Razgrom Fashistkoy Germanii," *Voyenno-Istorichesky Zhurnal*, May, 1960, 26–41.

Loboda, V. "Orden Pobedy," *Voyenno-Istorichesky Zhurnal*, May, 1965, 124–25.

Luchinskiy, A. "Na Berlin!" *Voyenno-Istorichesky Zhurnal*, May, 1965, 81–91.

"Marshal Zhukov," *USSR Illustrated Monthly* (Washington), September, 1956, 1–5. This magazine is published by reciprocal agreement between the governments of the United States and the Soviet Union. The agreement provides for the publication and circulation of the magazine *USSR* in the United States and the distribution of *Amerika* in the Soviet Union.

The name of the Russian magazine has since been changed to *Soviet Life*.

Neustroev, S. "Shturm Reikhstaga," *Voyenno-Istorichesky Zhurnal*, May, 1960, 42–51.

Novaya i Noveishaya Istoriya, 1965–66 (bimonthly journal of the Academy of Sciences of the U.S.S.R.).

Ochak, N. "Komkor D. F. Serdich," *Voyenno-Istorichesky Zhurnal*, August, 1966, 127–28.

Oktyabr, 1965–66. Monthly journal of the Union of Writers of the Russian Soviet Federated Socialist Republic.

Oskin, G. "Eto Bylo v Kontse Voiny," *Voyenno-Istorichesky Zhurnal*, May, 1965, 126–28.

Pavlenko, N. "Kharakternyye Cherty Strategicheskogo Nastupleniya Sovet-skikh Vooruzhennykh Sil v Velikoy Otechestvennoy Voine," *Voyenno-Istorichesky Zhurnal*, March, 1966, 9–23.

Poznyak, N. "Zavershayushchie Udary po Vragu," *Voyenno-Istorichesky Zhurnal*, May, 1965, 26–35.

Rokossovsky, K. "Na Severnykh Podstupakh k Stolitse," *Voyenno-Istorichesky Zhurnal*, December, 1966, 50–62.

———. "Na Volokolamskom Napravlenii," *Voyenno-Istorichesky Zhurnal*, November, 1966, 46–55.

———. "Severnee Berlina," *Voyenno-Istorichesky Zhurnal*, May, 1965, 36–41.

Rotmistrov, P. "O Sovetskom Voyennom Iskusstve v Bitve na Volge," *Voyenno-Istorichesky Zhurnal*, December, 1962, 3–14.

"Rozhdenie Sovetskoy Gvardii," *Vestnik Protivovozdushnoy Oborony*, September, 1966, 89–90.

Sevostyanov, G. H. "Voyennoe i Diplomaticheskoe Porazhenie Yaponii v Periode Sobytiy u Reki Khalkhin-Gol," *Voprosy Istorii*, August, 1957, 63–84.

Shtemenko, S. "Kak Planirovalas Poslednaya Kampaniya po Razgromu Gitlerovskoy Germanii," *Voyenno-Istorichesky Zhurnal*, May, 1965, 56–72.

———. "Na Puti k Pobede," *Znamya*, June, 1970, 135–40.

———. "Pered Udarom v Belorussii," *Voyenno-Istorichesky Zhurnal*, September, 1965, 44–59.

Sidelnikov, I. "Politicheskoe Soderzhanie i Vozrosshaya Rol Yedinonacha-liya," *Voyennyy Vestnik*, May, 1966, 63–69.

Simonov, Konstantin. "Every Day the Longest," *Soviet Life*, May, 1965, 22–27.

Svetlishin, N. "Ot Soldata do Marshala, k 70-letiyu G. K. Zhukova," *Voyenno-Istorichesky Zhurnal*, November, 1966, 31–40.

Tamonov, F., and V. Tsyganov "Nekotorye Problemy Istorii Moskovskoy Bitvy," *Kommunist Vooruzhennykh Sil*, January, 1967, 90–94.

Telegin, K. "Moskovskaya Zona Oborony," *Voyenno-Istorichesky Zhurnal*, January, 1962, 35–46.

Vasilevsky, A. M. "The Battle of Stalingrad," *Soviet Military Review*, February, 1966, 8–12.

———. "Hezabyvaemyye Dni," *Voyenno-Istorichesky Zhurnal*, October, 1965, 13–25.

"V Avangarde Sukhoputnykh Voysk," *Kommunist Vooruzhennykh Sil*, August, 1966, 38–42.

"Visla-Oderskaya Operatsiya v Tsifrakh," *Voyenno-Istorichesky Zhurnal*, January, 1965, 71–81.

Vorobyev, F. "Ob Operatsii 'Koltso'," *Voyenno-Istorichesky Zhurnal*, November, 1962, 52–53.

Voronov, N. N. "Podvig Sovetskogo Naroda," *Istoriya SSSR*, May–June, 1965, 3–29; July–August, 1965, 13–27.

———. "Vospominaniya-Operatsiya 'Koltso,'" *Voyenno-Istorichesky Zhurnal*, May, 1962, 71–84; June, 1962, 67–76.

Voyenno-Istorichesky Zhurnal, 1959–67. Monthly historical journal of the Ministry of Defense of the U.S.S.R. An extremely valuable source of information on the Red Army from its beginnings through World War II.

D. Newspapers

Izvestia, 1953–67.

Krasnaya Zvezda, 1946–67.

Moscow News, October–December, 1966 (English-language weekly).

Pravda, 1941–67.

Soviet War News, July 11, 1941–May 19, 1945. Published by the Press Department of the Soviet Embassy, London.

E. Fiction

Nekrasov, Viktor Platonovich. *V Okopakh Stalingrada*. Moscow, Military Press of the Ministry of Defense of the U.S.S.R., 1955.

II. WORKS BY FORMER SOVIET CITIZENS

A. Books

Alliluyeva, Svetlana. *Twenty Letters to a Friend*. Trans. by Priscilla Johnson McMillan. New York, Harper and Row, 1967.

BIBLIOGRAPHY

Avtorkhanov, Abdurakhman. *The Communist Party Apparatus*. Chicago, Henry Regnery Company, 1966.

———. *Stalin and the Soviet Communist Party*. New York, Frederick A. Praeger, 1959. Avtorkhanov also wrote, under the pseudonym Alexander Uralov, *The Reign of Stalin*. London, Bodley Head, 1953.

Kalinov, Kyrill Dmitrievich. *Sowjetmarschälle Haben das Wort*. Hamburg, Hansa Verlag Josef Toth, 1950.

Krivitsky, W. G. *In Stalin's Secret Service*. New York, Harper and Brothers, 1939.

Krylov, Ivan. *Soviet Staff Officer*. London, Falcon Press, 1951.

Tokaev, Grigori Aleksandrovich. *Stalin Means War*. London, George Weidenfeld and Nicolson, Ltd., 1951.

B. Periodicals

Artemiev, Vyacheslav P. "The Communist Party and the Soviet Armed Forces," *Military Review*, Vol. XLIV (February, 1964), 29–37.

Baritz, J. "Kreml i Armiya: Vzlet i Padenie Marshala Zhukova," *Svoboda* (Munich), November, 1957, 5–7.

———. "Sovetskie Marshaly," *Svoboda*, March, 1958, 31–34.

Markhoff, Alexei. "How Russia Almost Lost the War," *Saturday Evening Post*, Vol. CCXXII (May 13, 1950), 31, 175–78.

Orlov, Alexander. "The Sensational Secret Behind the Damnation of Stalin," *Life*, Vol. XL (April 23, 1956), 44.

Rastvorov, Yuri A. "How Red Titans Fought for Supreme Power," *Life*, Vol. XXXVII (November 29, 1954), 18–21, 146, 148, 153, 155–56.

Ruslanov, P. "Marshal Zhukov," *Russian Review*, Vol. XV (April, 1956), 122–29; Vol. XV (July, 1956), 186–95.

C. Unpublished Materials

Antonov, G. I. "Zhukov: Ministr Oborony SSSR." Eight-page paper prepared for a lecture to students of the U.S. Army Institute for Advanced Russian and East European Studies, Oberammergau, Germany, 1957.

The U.S. Army Institute for Advanced Russian and East European Studies, whose faculty is composed of former Soviet officers, professors, and scholars, prepares its own mimeographed texts, many of which have been consulted in the preparation of this book. Two of these works were particularly helpful: G. S. Burlutsky's "Vtoraya Mirovaya Voina na Vostochnom Fronte" (1956) and Abdurakhman Avtorkhanov's "Kommunisticheskaya Partiya Sovetskogo Soyuza" (1956).

D. Conversations and Interviews

In the course of writing this book, I consulted a number of individuals directly or indirectly involved in the events of the period:

Colonel Georg Antonov, who participated in the move into Poland, the Finnish campaign, and World War II.

V. P. Artemiev, a former field-grade officer in the Red Army.

Abdurakhman Avtorkhanov, who in 1937 was assigned to the Propaganda and Agitation Department of the Communist Party Central Committee, only to be arrested later the same year as an "enemy of the people."

Joseph Baritz, a former Soviet citizen, now a member of the faculty of the United States Army Institute for Advanced Russian and East European Studies. An authority on the Soviet military, he is a frequent contributor to the *Bulletin for the Study of the U.S.S.R.*, (Munich).

G. S. Burlutsky, a former field-grade officer in the Red Army.

III. EAST EUROPEAN NEWSPAPERS

Trybuna Ludu (Warsaw), 1956. The Polish Communist Party newspaper.
Zeri i Popullit (Tiranë), May 22, 1956. The Albanian Communist Party newspaper.

IV. GERMAN SOURCES

A. Books

Aaken, Wolf van. *Hexenkessel Ostfront: Von Smolensk nach Breslau.* Rastatt, Erich Pabel Verlag, 1964.

Carell, Paul. *Hitler Moves East, 1941–1943.* Trans. by Ewald Osers. Boston and Toronto, Little, Brown and Company, 1964.

———. *Scorched Earth: The Russian-German War, 1943–1944.* Trans. by Ewald Osers. Boston and Toronto, Little, Brown and Company, 1970.

Doerr, Hans. *Der Feldzug nach Stalingrad.* Darmstadt, E. S. Mittler und Sohn CmbH, 1955. Also, *Pokhod na Stalingrad.* Moscow, Military Press of the Ministry of Defense of the U.S.S.R., 1957.

Goerlitz, Walter. *Paulus and Stalingrad.* Trans. by R. H. Stevens. New York, Citadel Press, 1963.

Guderian, Heinz. *Panzer Leader.* Trans. by Constantine Fitzgibbon. New York, E. P. Dutton and Company, 1952.

Roth, Herman. *Panzer-Operationen.* Heidelberg, Kurt Vowinckel Verlag, 1956.

BIBLIOGRAPHY

Jacobsen, H. A., and J. Rohwer, eds. *Decisive Battles of World War II: The German View*. Trans. by Edward Fitzgerald. New York, G. P. Putnam's Sons, 1965. German title: *Entscheidungsschlachten des Zweiten Weltkrieges*.

Keitel, Wilhelm. *The Memoirs of Field-Marshal Keitel*. Trans. by David Irving. Ed. by Walter Goerlitz. New York, Stein and Day, 1966.

Manstein, Erich von. *Lost Victories*. Trans. by Anthony G. Powell. Chicago, Henry Regnery Company, 1958.

Mellenthin, Major General F. W. von. *Panzer Battles: A Study of the Employment of Armor in the Second World War*. Trans. by H. Betzler. Norman, University of Oklahoma Press, 1956.

Ribbentrop, Joachim von. *Zwischen London und Moskau*. Leoni am Starnberger see, Druffel-Verlag, 1961.

Schroter, Heinz. *Stalingrad*. Trans. by Constantine Fitzgibbon. New York, Ballantine Books, 1958.

Thorwald, Juergen. *Defeat in the East*. Trans. by Fred Wieck. New York, Ballantine Books, 1959.

Tippelskirch, Kurt von. *Geschichte des Zweiten Weltkriegs*. Bonn, Athenaum Verlag, 1951.

Warlimont, Walter. *Inside Hitler's Headquarters, 1939–1945*. Trans. by R. H. Barry. New York, Frederick A. Praeger, 1964.

B. Unpublished Materials

Halder, Franz. "The Private War Journal of Generaloberst Franz Halder, Chief of the General Staff of the Supreme Command of the German Army (OKH), 14 August 1939 to 24 September 1942." Mimeographed 9 vols. Washington, U.S. Department of the Army, n.d. Other editions have been issued.

Willemer, Wilhelm. "The German Defense of Berlin." Manuscript, No. P-136. Heidelberg, Historical Division, Headquarters, U.S. Army, Europe, 1953.

V. OTHER WESTERN SOURCES

A. Books

Two outstanding volumes deserve special mention. The best study of the Soviet armed forces in the period before World War II is John Erickson's *The Soviet High Command: A Military-Political History, 1918–1941*, London, St. Martin's Press, 1962. This massive history, although heavily detailed, provides stimulating reading and an accurate, uncluttered account of those important years. Erickson, educated at St. John's College, Cambridge, has lectured in government at Manchester University and is now a member of the faculty of the University of Edinburgh. *The Soviet High Command* ends with the Battle of Moscow in 1941.

An excellent history of the war years, and thus a natural sequel to Erickson's book, is Alexander Werth's *Russia at War, 1941–1945*, New York, E. P. Dutton and Company, Inc., 1964. William L. Shirer described this work as "the best book we probably shall ever have in English on Russia at war."

Alexander Werth was born in St. Petersburg in 1901 and emigrated to England after the Revolution of 1917. Upon the outbreak of war in 1941, he flew to the Soviet Union, where he remained until 1948 as correspondent for the *London Sunday Times* and commentator for the BBC. Much of this book is based on his wartime books: *Moscow '41*, *Leningrad*, and *The Year of Stalingrad*. In addition, he consulted many of the memoirs of Red Army commanders and the six-volume *Istoriya Velikoy Otechestvennoy Voiny Sovetskogo Soyuza*. What makes his book especially valuable and original is his knowledge of the Russian people. He moved among them, sometimes even in combat zones. He spent a week in 1941 at the Smolensk Front, where he was almost killed. He made journeys to the Rzhev combat sector, to Sevastopol, to Stalingrad, and to other places where history was being made. He talked with peasant women, Red Army privates and NCO's, generals and marshals, teachers, kolkhozniks, captured Germans, orphans and widows. Speaking their language, he was able to draw the Russians out and encourage them to share their personal stories with him.

Alexandrov, Victor. *Khrushchev of the Ukraine*. London, Victor Gollancz, Ltd., 1957.
———. *The Tukhachevsky Affair*. Englewood Cliffs, N.J., Prentice-Hall, Inc., 1963.
Anders, Wladyslaw. *Hitler's Defeat in Russia*. Chicago, Henry Regnery Company, 1953.
Armstrong, John A. *The Politics of Totalitarianism: The Communist Party of the Soviet Union from 1934 to the Present*. New York, Random House, 1961.
Baldwin, Hanson W. *Battles Lost and Won: Great Campaigns of World War II*. New York, Harper and Row, 1966.
Bauer, Raymond A., Alex Inkeles, and Clyde Kluckhohn. *How the Soviet System Works*. New York, Vintage Books, 1960.
Beloff, Max. *The Foreign Policy of Soviet Russia, 1929–1941*. 2 vols. London, Oxford University Press, 1947–49.

Berchin, Michel, and Eliahu Ben-Horin. *The Red Army*. New York, W. W. Norton and Company, Inc., 1942.

Berman, Harold J., and Miroslav Kerner. *Soviet Military and Administration*. Cambridge, Mass., Harvard University Press, 1955.

Bialer, Seweryn. *Stalin and His Generals*. New York, Pegasus, 1969.

Bloomfield, Lincoln P., Walter C. Clemens Jr., and Franklyn Griffiths. *Khrushchev and the Arms Race: Soviet Interests in Arms Control and Disarmament, 1954–1964*. Cambridge, Mass., M.I.T. Press, 1966.

Bor-Komorowski, Tadeusz. *The Secret Army*. London, Victor Gollancz, 1951.

Brett-Smith, Richard. *Berlin '45: The Grey City*. New York, St. Martin's Press, 1967.

Brumberg, Abraham, ed. *Russia Under Khrushchev*. New York, Frederick A. Praeger, 1962.

Brzezinski, Zbigniew, ed. *Political Controls in the Soviet Army*. New York, Research Program on the U.S.S.R., 1954.

——, and Samuel P. Huntington. *Political Power: USA/USSR*. New York, Viking Press, 1963, 1964.

Butcher Harry C. *My Three Years with Eisenhower*. New York, Simon and Schuster, 1946.

Carr, Edward Hallett. *German-Soviet Relations Between the Two World Wars, 1919–1939*. Baltimore, Johns Hopkins Press, 1951.

Cassidy, Henry C. *Moscow Dateline, 1941–1943*. Boston, Houghton Mifflin Company, 1943.

Chamberlain, William Henry. *The Russian Revolution*. 2 vols. New York, Macmillan and Company, 1935.

Chiang Kai-Shek. *Soviet Russia in China: A Summing-Up at Seventy*. New York, Farrar, Straus and Cudahy, Inc., 1957.

Churchill, Winston S. *The Second World War*. 6 vols.: *The Gathering Storm, Their Finest Hour, The Grand Alliance, The Hinge of Fate, Closing the Ring, Triumph and Tragedy*. Boston, Houghton Mifflin Company, 1948–53.

Ciano, Conte Galeazzo. *Ciano's Diary, 1939–1943*. Ed. by Hugh Gibson. London, William Heinemann, Ltd., 1947.

Clark, Alan. *Barbarossa: The Russian-German Conflict, 1941–45*. New York, William Morrow and Company, 1965.

Clay, Lucius D. *Decision in Germany*. Garden City, N.Y., Doubleday and Company, 1950.

Clubb, O. Edmund. *Twentieth Century China*. New York, Columbia University Press, 1964.

Conquest, Robert. *Power and Policy in the USSR: The Study of Soviet Dynastics*. New York, St. Martin's Press, 1961.

————. *Russia After Khrushchev*. New York, Frederick A. Praeger, 1965.

Crankshaw, Edward. *Khrushchev: A Career*. New York, Viking Press, 1966.

Dallin, David J. *Soviet Foreign Policy After Stalin*. Philadelphia, J. B. Lippincott Company, 1961.

————. *Soviet Russia's Foreign Policy, 1939–1942*. New Haven, Yale University Press, 1942.

Davidson, Eugene. *The Death and Life of Germany: An Account of the American Occupation*. New York, Alfred A. Knopf, 1959.

Deane, John R. *The Strange Alliance: The Story of Our Efforts at Wartime Cooperation with Russia*. New York, Viking Press, 1947.

Degras, Jane, ed. *Soviet Documents on Foreign Policy, 1933–1941*. 3 vols. London, Oxford University Press, 1953.

Deutscher, Isaac. *Russia: What Next?* New York, Oxford University Press, 1953.

————. *Stalin: A Political Biography*. New York, Vintage Books, 1960.

Doenitz, Karl. *Memoirs: Ten Years and Twenty Days*. Trans. by R. H. Stevens. New York, World Publishing Company, 1959.

Donnison, F. S. V. *Civil Affairs and Military Government: North-West Europe, 1944–1946*. London, H.M. Stationery Office, 1961.

Ebon, Martin. *Malenkov: Stalin's Successor*. New York, McGraw-Hill Book Company, Inc., 1953.

Eden, Anthony. *Memoirs*. 3 vols. Boston, Houghton Mifflin Company, 1960, 1962, 1965.

Eisenhower, Dwight D. *At Ease: Stories I Tell to Friends*. Garden City, N.Y., Doubleday and Company, 1967.

————. *Crusade in Europe*. Garden City, N.Y., Doubleday and Company, 1952.

————. *Mandate for Change, 1953–1956*. Garden City, N.Y., Doubleday and Company, 1963.

————. *Waging Peace, 1956–1961*. Garden City, N.Y., Doubleday and Company, 1965.

Ely, Louis B. *The Red Army Today*. Harrisburg, Military Service Publishing Company, 1953.

Embree, G. D. *The Soviet Union Between the 19th and 20th Congresses, 1952–1956*. The Hague, Martinus Nijhoff, 1959.

Erickson, John. *The Soviet High Command: A Military-Political History, 1918–1941*. London, St. Martin's Press, 1962.

Fainsod, Merle. *How Russia Is Ruled*. Cambridge, Mass., Harvard University Press, 1963.

Feis, Herbert. *Between War and Peace: The Potsdam Conference*. Princeton, Princeton University Press, 1960.

Fisher, George. *Soviet Opposition to Stalin*. Cambridge, Mass., Harvard University Press, 1952.

Flower, Desmond, and James Reeves, eds. *The Taste of Courage: The War, 1939–1945*. New York, Harper and Row, 1960.

Frankland, Mark. *Khrushchev*. New York, Stein and Day, 1967.

Freidin, Seymour. *The Forgotten People*. New York, Charles Scribner's Sons, 1962.

———, and William Richardson, eds. *The Fatal Decisions*. New York, William Sloane Associates, 1956.

Gallagher, Matthew P. *The Soviet History of World War II: Myths, Memories and Realities*. New York, Frederick A. Praeger, 1963.

Garder, Michel. *A History of the Soviet Army*. New York, Frederick A. Praeger, 1966.

Garthoff, Raymond L. *How Russia Makes War (Soviet Military Doctrine)*. London, George Allen and Unwin, Ltd., 1954.

———. *The Role of the Military in Recent Soviet Politics*. Santa Monica, Calif., Rand Corporation, 1956.

———. *The Soviet Image of Future War*. Washington, Public Affairs Press, 1959.

———. *Soviet Military Policy: A Historical Analysis*. New York, Frederick A. Praeger, 1966.

———. *Soviet Strategy in the Nuclear Age*. New York, Frederick A. Praeger, 1958.

———, ed. *Sino-Soviet Military Relations*. New York, Frederick A. Praeger, 1966.

Goerlitz, Walter. *History of the German General Staff*. New York, Frederick A. Praeger, 1953.

Goure, Leon. *The Siege of Leningrad*. Stanford, Stanford University Press, 1962.

———, and Herbert Dinerstein. *Moscow in Crisis*. Glencoe, Ill., Free Press, 1955.

Guillaume, Augustin. *Soviet Arms and Soviet Power: The Secrets of Russia's Might*. Washington, Infantry Journal Press, 1949.

Hart, B. H. Liddell. *Defense of the West*. New York, William Morrow and Company, 1950.

———. *The German Generals Talk*. New York, William Morrow and Company, 1948.

———., ed. *The Soviet Army*. London, Weidenfeld and Nicolson, 1956.

Hayashi, Saburo. *Kogun: The Japanese Army in the Pacific War*. Quantico, Va., Marine Corps Association, 1959.

Sir William Hayter. *The Kremlin and the Embassy*. New York, Macmillan Company, 1966.

Higgins, Trumbull. *Hitler and Russia: The Third Reich in a Two-Front War, 1937–1943*. New York, Macmillan Company, 1966.

Hilger, Gustav, and Alfred G. Meyer. *The Incompatible Allies: A Memoir-History of German Soviet Relations, 1918–1941*. New York, Macmillan Company, 1953.

Hittle, J. B. *The Military Staff, Its History and Development*. Harrisburg, Pa., Stackpole Company, 1961.

Holborn, Hajo. *American Military Government: Its Organization and Policies*. Washington, Infantry Journal Press, 1947.

Horelick, Arnold L., and Myron Rush. *Strategic Power and Soviet Foreign Policy*. Chicago, University of Chicago Press, 1965, 1966.

Howard, Michael, ed. *Soldiers and Government: Nine Studies in Civil-Military Relations*. London, Eyre & Spottiswoode, 1957.

Howley, Frank. *Berlin Command*. New York, G. P. Putnam's Sons, 1950.

Hyland, William, and Richard W. Shryock. *The Fall of Khrushchev*. New York, Funk and Wagnalls, 1968.

Jones, Robert Huhn. *The Roads to Russia: United States Lend-Lease to the Soviet Union*. Norman, University of Oklahoma Press, 1969.

Kahle, Hans. *Under Stalin's Command*. London, Caledonian Press, 1943.

Kennan, George F. *Russia and the West Under Lenin and Stalin*. Boston, Little, Brown and Company, 1961.

———. *Soviet Foreign Policy, 1917–1941*. Princeton, D. Van Nostrand Company, Inc., 1960.

Kerr, Walter. *The Russian Army: Its Men, Its Leaders and Its Battles*. New York, Alfred A. Knopf, 1956.

Kertesz, Stephen D., ed. *East Central Europe and the World: Developments in the Post-Stalin Era*. Notre Dame, Ind., University of Notre Dame Press, 1962.

Kolkowicz, Roman. *The Impact of Modern Technology on the Soviet Officer Corps*. Santa Monica, Calif., Rand Corporation, 1966.

———. *Political Controls in the Red Army: Professional Autonomy Versus Political Integration*. Santa Monica, Calif., Rand Corporation, 1966.

———. *The Soviet Army and the Communist Party*. Princeton, Princeton University Press, 1967.

———. *Soviet Party–Military Relations: Contained Conflict*. Santa Monica, Calif., Rand Corporation, 1966.

Laquer, Walter. *Russia and Germany: A Century of Conflict*. Boston, Little, Brown and Company, 1965.

BIBLIOGRAPHY

Lauterbach, Richard E. *These Are the Russians*. New York, Harper and Brothers, 1944, 1945.

Lee, Asher, ed. *The Soviet Air and Rocket Forces*. New York, Frederick A. Praeger, 1959.

Leonhard, Wolfgang. *The Kremlin Since Stalin*. Trans. by Elizabeth Wiskemann and Marian Jackson. New York, Frederick A. Praeger, 1962.

Lewis, Flora. *A Case History of Hope: The Story of Poland's Peaceful Revolutions*. Garden City, N.Y., Doubleday and Company, 1958.

Linden, Carl A. *Khrushchev and the Soviet Leadership, 1957–1964*. Baltimore, Johns Hopkins Press, 1966.

Liu, F. F. *A Military History of Modern China, 1924–1929*. Princeton, Princeton University Press, 1956.

MacDonald, Charles B. *The Mighty Endeavor: American Armed Forces in the European Theater in World War II*. New York, Oxford University Press, 1969.

Mackintosh, J. Malcolm. *Juggernaut: A History of the Soviet Armed Forces*. New York, Macmillan Company, 1967.

———. *Strategy and Tactics of Soviet Foreign Policy*. London, Oxford University Press, 1962.

Menon, K. P. S. *The Flying Troika*. London, Oxford University Press, 1963.

Meray, Tibor. *Thirteen Days That Shook the Kremlin*. New York, Frederick A. Praeger, 1959.

Miller, William J., Henry L. Roberts, and Marshall D. Shulman. *The Meaning of Communism*. Morristown, N.J., Silver Burdett Company, 1963.

Moore, Barrington, Jr. *Terror and Progress USSR: Some Sources of Change and Stability in the Soviet Dictatorship*. Cambridge, Mass., Harvard University Press, 1954.

Murphy, Robert. *Diplomat Among Warriors*. Garden City, N.Y., Doubleday and Company, Inc., 1964.

Nicolaevsky Boris I. *Power and the Soviet Elite*. Ed. by Janet D. Zagoria. New York, Frederick A. Praeger, 1965.

O'Ballance, Edgar. *The Red Army*. New York, Frederick A. Praeger, 1964.

Parry, Albert. *Russian Cavalcade: A Military Record*. New York, Ives Washburn, Inc., 1944.

Payne, Robert. *The Rise and Fall of Stalin*. New York, Simon and Schuster, 1965.

Pethybridge, Roger. *A Key to Soviet Politics: The Crisis of the Anti-Party Group*. New York, Frederick A. Praeger, 1962.

Petrov, Vladimir. *June 22, 1941: Soviet Historians and the German Invasion*. Columbia, University of South Carolina Press, 1968.

Rauch, Georg von. *A History of Soviet Russia.* Trans. by Peter and Annette Jacobsohn. New York, Frederick A. Praeger, 1957.

Ripka, Hubert. *Eastern Europe in the Postwar World.* New York, Frederick A. Praeger, 1957, 1961.

Rundstedt, Karl Rudolf Gert, et al. *Weltkrieg, 1939–1945.* Stuttgart, 1957. Also, *Mirovaya Voina, 1939–1945 gody.* Moscow, Foreign Literature Press, 1957.

Rush, Myron. *Political Succession in the USSR.* New York, Columbia University Press, 1965.

Ryan, Cornelius. *The Last Battle.* New York, Simon and Schuster, 1966.

Salisbury, Harrison E. *American in Russia.* New York, Harper and Brothers, 1955.

————, ed. *Marshal Zhukov's Greatest Battles.* Trans. by Theodore Shabad. New York, Harper and Row, 1969.

————. *The 900 Days: The Siege of Leningrad.* New York, Harper and Row, 1969.

Saunders, M. G., ed. *The Soviet Navy.* New York, Frederick A. Praeger, 1958.

Schuman, Frederick L. *Soviet Politics at Home and Abroad.* New York, Alfred A. Knopf, 1947.

Schwartz, Harry. *The Red Phoenix: Russia Since World War II.* New York, Frederick A. Praeger, 1961.

————, ed. *Russia Enters the 1960's.* Philadelphia, J. B. Lippincott Company, 1962.

Sharp, Samuel L. *Poland: White Eagle on a Red Field.* Cambridge, Mass., Harvard University Press, 1953.

Sherwood, Robert E. *Roosevelt and Hopkins: An Intimate History.* New York, Harper and Brothers, 1948, 1950.

Shirer, William L. *The Rise and Fall of the Third Reich.* New York, Simon and Schuster, 1960.

Shulman, Marshall D. *Stalin's Foreign Policy Reappraised.* Cambridge, Mass., Harvard University Press, 1963

Skomorovsky, Boris, and E. G. Morris. *The Siege of Leningrad.* New York, Books, Inc., 1944.

Smith, Jean Edward. *The Defense of Berlin.* Baltimore, Johns Hopkins Press, 1963.

Smith, Walter Bedell. *My Three Years in Moscow.* Philadelphia and New York, J. B. Lippincott Company, 1950.

Sontag, Raymond James, and James Stuart Beddie, eds. *Nazi-Soviet Relations 1939–1941: Documents from the Archives of the German Foreign Office.* Washington, U.S. Department of State, 1948.

Spahr, William J. *De-Stalinization and the Soviet Army*. Washington, National War College, 1964.

Stalingrad. An Eyewitness Account by Soviet Correspondents and Red Army Commanders. London, Hutchinson and Company, n.d. (probably 1943).

Stehle, Hansjakob. *The Independent Satellite: Society and Politics in Poland Since 1945*. New York, Frederick A. Praeger, 1965.

Stipp, John L. *Soviet Russia Today: Patterns and Prospects*. New York, Harper and Brothers, 1956.

Studnitz, Hans-Georg von. *While Berlin Burns, 1943–1945*. Englewood Cliffs, N.J., Prentice-Hall, Inc., 1964.

Stypulkowski, Zbigniew. *Invitation to Moscow*. New York, Walker and Company, 1962.

Sulzberger, C. L. *The American Heritage Picture History of World War II*. 2 vols. New York, American Heritage Publishing Company, 1966.

Summersby, Kay. *Eisenhower Was My Boss*. New York, Prentice-Hall Inc., 1948.

Syrop, Konrad. *Spring in October: The Story of the Polish Revolution, 1956*. New York, Frederick A. Praeger, 1957.

Tanner, Vaino. *The Winter War: Finland Against Russia, 1939–1940*. Stanford, Stanford University Press, 1957. Tanner was formerly foreign minister of Finland.

Taylor, A. J. P. *The Origins of the Second World War*. New York, Harper and Brothers, 1961.

Tedder, Arthur. *With Prejudice*. Boston, Little, Brown and Company, 1966.

Thomas, Hugh. *The Spanish Civil War*. New York, Harper and Brothers, 1961.

Toland, John. *The Last 100 Days*. New York, Random House, 1966.

Treadgold, Donald W. *Twentieth Century Russia*. Chicago, Rand McNally and Company, 1959.

Truman, Harry S. *Year of Decisions*. Vol. I of *Memoirs of Harry S. Truman*. Garden City, N.Y., Doubleday and Company, Inc., 1955.

Tully, Andrew. *Berlin: Story of a Battle, April–May, 1945*. New York, Simon and Schuster, 1963.

U.S. Department of the Army. *The German Campaign in Russia: Planning and Operations (1940–1942)*. Washington, 1955.

———. *German Defense Tactics Against Russian Breakthroughs*. Washington, 1951.

———. *Russian Combat Methods in World War II*. Washington, 1950.

———. *Small Unit Actions During the German Campaign in Russia*. Washington, 1953.

Vali, Ferenc A. *Rift and Revolt in Hungary.* Cambridge, Mass., Harvard University Press, 1961.

Weinburg, Gerhard L. *Germany and the Soviet Union, 1939–1941.* Leiden, E. J. Brill, 1954.

Werth, Alexander. *Leningrad.* New York, Alfred A. Knopf, 1944.

———. *Moscow '41.* London, Hamish Hamilton, 1942. Also, in *Moscow War Diary.* New York, Alfred A. Knopf, 1942.

———. *Russia at War, 1941–1945.* New York, E. P. Dutton and Company, 1964.

———. *Russia Under Khrushchev.* New York, Crest Books, 1962.

———. *The Year of Stalingrad: A Historical Record and a Study of Russian Mentality, Methods and Policies.* New York, Alfred A. Knopf, 1947.

White, D. Fedotoff. *The Growth of the Red Army.* Princeton, Princeton University Press, 1944.

Whiting, Kenneth R. *The Soviet Union Today.* New York, Frederick A. Praeger, 1962.

Wilmot, Chester. *The Struggle for Europe.* New York, Harper and Brothers, 1952.

Wolfe, Bertram D. *Khrushchev and Stalin's Ghost.* New York, Frederick A. Praeger, 1957.

Wolfe, Thomas W. *Soviet Strategy at the Crossroads.* Santa Monica, Calif., Rand Corporation, 1964.

Young, Gordon. *Stalin's Heirs.* London, Derek Verschoyle, 1953.

Zacharias, Ellis M., with Ladislaw Farago. *Behind Closed Doors.* New York, G. P. Putnam's Sons, 1950.

C. Unpublished Materials

Plumb, Robert L. "Soviet Participation in the Spanish Civil War." Ph.D. dissertation, Georgetown University, Washington.

D. Periodicals

"Along Embassy Row," *Newsweek,* Vol. LXV (January 4, 1965), 6.

"April Session of the Supreme Soviet of the USSR," *Bulletin of the Institute for the Study of the History and Culture of the USSR,* Vol. I (May, 1954), 29–31.

"The Army and the Supreme Soviet," *Bulletin of the Institute for the Study of the History and Culture of the USSR,* Vol. I (April, 1954), 23–26.

Assmann, Kurt. "The Battle for Moscow, Turning Point of the War," *Foreign Affairs,* Vol. XXVIII (January, 1950), 309–26.

———. "Stalin and Hitler," *United States Naval Institute Proceedings*, Vol. LXXV (June, 1949), 638–51; Vol. LXXV (July, 1949), 758–73.

"The Bait on the Hook," *Newsweek*, Vol. L (October 21, 1957), 32.

Bess, Demaree. "Strange Alliance in the Kremlin," *The Saturday Evening Post*, Vol. CCXXX (September 28, 1957), 171.

"The Blowup—Whys and Whats," *Newsweek*, Vol. XLVIII (November 19, 1956), 17.

"Brezhnev's V-E Day Speech," *Radio Free Europe*, May 10, 1965. Research Department paper.

Chaney, Otto Preston, Jr. "The Agony of Soviet Military Historians," *Military Review*, Vol. XLVIII (June, 1968), 24–28.

———. "The Resurrection of an Unperson," *Army*, Vol. XVI (March, 1966), 51–53.

———. "Was It Surprise?" *Military Review*, Vol. XLIX (April, 1969), 56–67.

Clark, Alan. "Twenty Five Years After the Day Hitler Attacked Russia," *New York Times Magazine*, June 19, 1966, 12–13, 68–70, 72.

"Convulsion in the Kremlin," *Time* (Atlantic Edition), Vol. LXX (November 4, 1957), 23.

Crankshaw, Edward. "An Old Bolshevik Regression to Rule of Jungle," *Life*, Vol. XXXVIII (February 21, 1955), 36–39.

Current Digest of the Soviet Press, June 8, 1955–December 4, 1957.

"Decentralization of Leadership," *Bulletin of the Institute for the Study of the History and Culture of the USSR*, Vol. I (May, 1954), 27–29.

"Demobilization of Soviet Troops," *Bulletin of the Institute for the Study of the History and Culture of the USSR*, Vol. I (November, 1954), 22–25.

"Dragoon's Day," *Time*, Vol. LXV (May 9, 1955), 26–30.

East Europe (New York), July–December, 1957.

Eitner, Hans-Jurgen. "Soviet Marshals and the Khrushchev Regime," *Military Review*, Vol. XL (April, 1960), 101–108.

Eliot, George Fielding. "The Red Army and Soviet Policy," *American Mercury*, Vol. LXXXI (October, 1955), 93–99.

Erickson, John. "The Military Factor in Soviet Policy," *International Affairs*, Vol. XXXIX (April, 1963), 214–26.

———. "The Soviet Union at War (1941–1945): An Essay on Sources and Studies," *Soviet Studies*, Vol. XIV (January, 1963), 249–74.

"Family Portrait," *Time*, Vol. LXVI (September 12, 1955), 19.

Fischer, Louis. "The Fatal Mistake of Marshal Zhukov, *Reader's Digest*, Vol. LXXII (March, 1958), 96–99.

Frank, Victor S. "The Unsolved Crisis," *Bulletin of the Institute for the*

Study of the History and Culture of the USSR, Vol. II (February, 1955), 3–9.

Galay, N. "Guided Missiles and Soviet Military Doctrine," *Bulletin of the Institute for the Study of the USSR*, Vol. IV (October, 1957), 14–21.

———. "The New Marshals," *Bulletin of the Institute for the Study of the History and Culture of the USSR*, Vol. II (March, 1955), 7–12.

——— "Principles of Command in the Soviet Armed Forces," *Bulletin of the Institute for the Study of the History and Culture of the USSR*, Vol. II (June, 1955), 11–15.

———. "Revisionism, Dogmatism, and the Soviet Armed Forces," *Bulletin of the Institute for the Study of the USSR*, Vol. V, (November, 1958), 5.

———. "The Role of the Soviet Army in the Crisis of Collective Leadership," *Bulletin of the Institute for the Study of the USSR*, Vol. IV (August, 1957), 13–20.

———. "Tank Forces in the Soviet Army," *Bulletin of the Institute for the Study of the History and Culture of the USSR*, Vol. I (October, 1954), 7–8.

———. "Zhukov in India," *Bulletin of the Institute for the Study of the USSR*, Vol. IV (April, 1957), 3–9.

Gallagher, Matthew P. "Military Manpower: A Case Study," *Problems of Communism* (Washington), Vol. XIII (May–June, 1965), 53–62.

Garthoff, Raymond L. "The Role of the Military in Recent Soviet Politics," *Russian Review*, Vol. XVI (April, 1957), 15–24.

Grayson, Benson Lee. "What About Zhukov?" *Army (Combat Forces) Journal*, Vol. V (April, 1955), 25–27.

Gunther, John. "Inside Russia," *Look*, Vol. XXI (April 2, 1957), 33–52.

Kintner, William R. "The Military as an Element of Soviet State Power," *United States Naval Institute Proceedings*, Vol. LXXXI (July, 1955), 770–83.

"K vs. Z: How the Rug Was Pulled," *Newsweek*, Vol. L (November 11, 1957), 18, 20–21.

Lauterbach, Richard E. "Zhukov," *Life*, Vol. XVIII (February 12, 1945), 94–106.

Lindley, Ernest K. "No One Can Be Sure," *Newsweek*, Vol. L (July 15, 1957), 21.

Liszczynskyj, G. "Malenkov's Resignation," *Bulletin of the Institute for the Study of the History and Culture of the USSR*, Vol. II (February, 1955), 15–18.

Mackintosh, Malcolm. "Soldiers of the Party," *Military Review*, Vol. XLIII (May, 1963), 27–31.

BIBLIOGRAPHY

Newsweek, October–December, 1956; May, 1963; January–May, 1965.

"One Myth for Another: From Military Genius to Military Idiot," *Army*, Vol. VI (July, 1956), 55. Khrushchev's Secret Speech to the Twentieth Communist Party Congress, 24–25 February, 1956.

"The Periscope: Moscow," *Newsweek*, Vol. LXV (April 19, 1965), 19.

"Polishing the Escutcheons," *Time*, Vol. LXXXV (June 19, 1965), 31A.

"The Politics of the Red Army," *Fortune*, Vol. XLVII (May, 1953), 91, 94, 96, 98.

Problems of Communism (Washington), 1961–65.

"The Quiet Man," *Time*, Vol. LXXXV (May 14, 1965), 34–35.

Raudakoff, Paul P. "Ike and Zhukov—Minutes of Their Last Meeting," *Colliers*, Vol. CXXXVI (July 22, 1955), 82–84.

"The Red Army High Command," *Bulletin of the Institute for the Study of the History and Culture of the USSR*, Vol. I (May, 1954), 25–27.

Salisbury, Harrison E. "Mystery Man of the Red Army," *Colliers*, Vol. CXXXVI (September 2, 1955), 78–81.

"Selective Objectivity," *Newsweek*, Vol. LXV (May 24, 1965), 54–55.

"Shifting Sands," *Newsweek*, Vol. LXI (May 27, 1963), 45–56.

Shub, Boris. "Krasnaya Armiya," *Osvobozhdeniye* (Munich), August 2, 1957, 219–31.

"Soviet Armed Forces Day," *Bulletin of the Institute for the Study of the History and Culture of the USSR*, Vol. II (March, 1955), 40–45.

"Soviet Troop Agreement," *East Europe*, Vol. VI (July, 1957), 45–46.

"Soviet Troops in Hungary," *East Europe* (New York), Vol. XIII (November, 1964), 2–6.

"The Stubby Peasant," *Time*, Vol. LXX (November 11, 1957), 18.

"Topsy-Turvy in the Kremlin," *Newsweek*, Vol. L (November 4, 1957), 18, 20.

Volkov, Leon. "The 'Hero's' Role," *Newsweek*, Vol. XLVIII (November 19, 1956), 17–18.

———. "Khrushchev's Big Game—Red Party vs. Red Army," *Newsweek*, Vol. L (November 11, 1957), 21.

———. "Malenkov and the Red Army," *Newsweek*, Vol. XLIV (May 25, 1953), 43.

———. "Nikita Khrushchev's Pinnacle," *Newsweek*, Vol. L (July 15, 1957), 25.

Wolfe, Bertram D. "The Struggle for Soviet Succession," *Foreign Affairs*, Vol. XXXI (July, 1953), 556–65.

Wolfe, Thomas W. "Political Primacy vs. Professional Elan," *Problems of Communism* (Washington), Vol. XIII (May–June, 1964), 45–52.

"Battle of Moscow," *Washington Post*, December 2, 1966, A-29.

E. Newspapers

"Birthday Pose," *Washington Post*, December 3, 1966, A-7.

"Eisenhower Welcomes Zhukov Re-emergence," *New York Times*, May 10, 1965, 2.

"Embattled Soviet Hero—Georgi Konstantinovich Zhukov," *New York Times*, June 28, 1965, 2.

Evening Star (Washington), 1956–67.

"Former Soviet Defense Minister Marshal Georgi K. Zhukov . . .," *Philadelphia Inquirer*, December 4, 1966, 1.

Johnson, Priscilla. "Many Demoted Reds Living in Disgrace," *Evening Star* (Washington), August 9, 1960, 12-A.

Jorden, William J. "Zhukov Humbled," *New York Times*, November 3, 1957, 1.

Kent, Arthur. "When Red Army Genius Was Given a Free Hand," *Philadelphia Inquirer*, February 18, 1945.

"Marshal Zhukov, 70, Gets Order of Lenin," *New York Times*, December 2, 1966, 21.

New York Times, 1955–67.

"Reds Pay Timoshenko New Honor," *Washington Post*, February 20, 1965, A-9.

"Role of Stalin," *Washington Post*, January 5, 1967, A-18.

Schwartz, Harry. "Zhukov's Speech Studied for Clue," *New York Times* (International Edition), October 31, 1957, 4.

Shabad, Theodore. "Russians Adopting a 'Rational' Approach to History," *New York Times*, May 10, 1965, 2.

———. "Soviet Rally Hails Stalin; Zhukov Emerges in Honor," *New York Times*, May 9, 1965, 1, 3.

———. "Stalin Gets Credit in Soviet on Plans for Berlin Capture," *New York Times*, April 17, 1965, 4.

Shapiro, Henry. "Found Hitler's Body, Russians Say," *Washington Post*, May 6, 1963, 1.

———. "Zhukov Begins Story, Gives Credit to Stalin," *Washington Post*, September 3, 1966, A-10.

SOURCES OF ILLUSTRATIONS

Page 41: Zhukov, *Vospominaniya i Razmyshleniya*.

Page 42: *50 Let Sovetskikh Vooruzhennikh Sil, Fotodokumenty*, Moscow, Military Press of the Ministry of Defense, 1967.

Page 43: Zhukov, *Vospominaniya i Razmyshleniya*.

Page 44: Above, Zhukov, *Vospominaniya i Razmyshleniya*. Below, *50 Let Sovetskikh Vooruzhennikh Sil*.

Page 45: *50 Let Sovetskikh Vooruzhennikh Sil*.

Page 46: Zhukov, *Vospominaniya i Razmyshleniya*.

Page 47: *50 Let Sovetskikh Vooruzhennikh Sil*.

Page 48: *Vospominaniya i Razmyshleniya*.

Page 113: U.S. Army photographs, from Joachim von Ribbentrop's albums captured after World War II.

Page 114: World War II Collection of Seized Enemy Records, National Archives, Washington, D.C.

Page 115: World War II Collection of Seized Enemy Records, National Archives, Washington, D.C.

Page 116: World War II Collection of Seized Enemy Records, National Archives, Washington, D.C.

Page 117: World War II Collection of Seized Enemy Records, National Archives, Washington, D.C.

Page 118: World War II Collection of Seized Enemy Records, National Archives, Washington, D.C.

Page 119: Courtesy of Ullstein Photographic Service, West Berlin.

Page 120: Above, *Velikiy Podvig*, Moscow, Political Literature Press, 1966. Below, *Pravda*, July 3, 1941.

Page 121: *Velikiy Podvig*.

Page 122: Above, *Velikiy Podvig*. Below, *USSR Illustrated Monthly*, September, 1956.

Page 123: *50 Let Sovetskikh Vooruzhennikh Sil*.

Page 124: Above, A. N. Kiselev (ed.), *Polkovodtsy i Voyenachalniki Velikay Otechestvennoy*. Below, Zhukov, *Vospominaniya i Razmyshleniya*.

Page 125: Süddeutscher Verlag, Munich, photographer Hoffmann.

Page 126: Zhukov, *Vospominaniya i Razmyshleniya*.

Page 127: Zhukov, *Vospominaniya i Razmyshleniya*.

Page 128: *Soviet Life*.

Page 277: *50 Let Sovetskikh Vooruzhennikh Sil*.

Page 278: Above, *USSR Illustrated Monthly*, September, 1956. Below, *50 Let Sovetskikh Vooruzhennikh Sil*.

Page 279: Zhukov, *Vospominaniya i Razmyshleniya*.

Page 280: *50 Let Sovetskikh Vooruzhennikh Sil*.

Page 281: U.S. Army photograph.

Page 282: U.S. Army photograph.

Page 283: U.S. Army photographs.

Page 284: U.S. Army photograph.

Page 285: U.S. Army photograph.

Page 286: U.S. Army photograph.

Page 287: U.S. Army photograph.

Page 288: Above, *USSR Illustrated Monthly*, September, 1956. Below, U.S. Army photograph.

Page 289: U.S. Army photographs.

Page 290: Above, U.S. Army photograph. Inset, *Soviet Life*, May, 1970.

Page 291: U.S. Army photograph.

Page 292: U.S. Army photographs.

Page 389: U.S. Army photographs.

Page 390: U.S. Army photographs.

Page 391: Sovfoto.

Page 392: Above, Zhukov, *Vospominaniya i Razmyshleniya*. Below, *USSR Illustrated Monthly*, September, 1956.

Page 393: Above, *USSR Illustrated Monthly*, September, 1956. Below, Zhukov, *Vospominaniya i Razmyshleniya*.

Page 394: Author's collection.

Page 395: Zhukov, *Vospominaniya i Razmyshleniya*.

Page 396: Zhukov, *Vospominaniya i Razmyshleniya*.

INDEX

INDEX

INDEX

INDEX

The paper on which this book is printed bears the watermark of the University of Oklahoma Press and has an effective life of at least three hundred years.

UNIVERSITY OF OKLAHOMA PRESS

NORMAN